THE ROAD TO MIDDLE-EARTH

BOOKS BY TOM SHIPPEY

J.R.R. Tolkien: Author of the Century

The Road to Middle-earth:
Revised and Expanded Edition

THE ROAD TO MIDDLE-EARTH

Revised and Expanded Edition

TOM SHIPPEY

HOUGHTON MIFFLIN COMPANY

Boston   New York

For information about permission to reproduce selections from this book, write to Permissions, Houghton Mifflin Company, 215 Park Avenue South, New York, New York 10003.

Visit our Web site: www.houghtonmifflinbooks.com.

Library of Congress Cataloging-in Publication Data
Shippey, T. A.
The road to Middle-earth / Tom Shippey.—Rev. and expanded ed.
p. cm.
Includes bibliographical references and index.
ISBN 0-618-25760-8
1. Tolkien, J.R.R. (John Ronald Reuel), 1892–1973—Criticism and interpretation. 2. Tolkien, J.R.R. (John Ronald Reuel), 1892–1973—Knowledge and learning. 3. Fantasy literature, English—History and criticism. 4. Middle Earth (Imaginary place) 5. Myth in literature. I. Title.

PR6039.O32Z824 2003   823′.912—dc21
2003042349

Diagram from Theodore M. Andersson, *The Legend of Brynhild,* copyright © 1980 by Cornell University Press, used by permission of the publisher, Cornell University Press, and Theodore M. Andersson.

Some of the material in this book first appeared in different form in the following publications: *J.R.R. Tolkien, Scholar and Story-Teller: Essays in Memoriam,* Mary B. Salu and Robert T. Farrell, eds. (Cornell University Press, 1979); *Scholarship and Fantasy: The Tolkien Phenomenon,* Keith J. Battarbee, ed. (Turku University Press, 1993); *J.R.R. Tolkien and His Literary Resonances: Views of Middle-earth,* George Clark and Dan Timmons, eds. (Greenwood Press, 2000); and "Allegory Versus Bounce: Tolkien's *Smith of Wootton Major,*" *Journal of the Fantastic in the Arts* 12, no. 2 (2001).

Book design by Melissa Lotfy

Printed in the United States of America

QUM 10 9 8 7 6 5 4 3

DEDICATED TO THE MEMORY OF

John Ernest Kjelgaard
lost at sea, H.M.S. *Beverley*
11 April 1943

CONTENTS

ACKNOWLEDGEMENTS AND
ABBREVIATIONS

I have incurred many debts in the writing of the three editions of this book, firstly and most importantly from Professor Tolkien himself, for a prompt and salutary correction, as mentioned in the 'Preface' below. I hope that over the years I have come to realise and to express some part of what he meant.

This book could further not have been written without the immense assistance of Humphrey Carpenter's three works, *J.R.R. Tolkien: A Biography, The Inklings* and the *Letters of J.R.R. Tolkien*, edited by Mr Carpenter with the assistance of Christopher Tolkien. They have provided a frame for my inquiries, and I have referred to them continually. Both Mr Carpenter and Mr Tolkien furthermore read many hundreds of pages of typescript for the first edition, and corrected many errors, both factual and of interpretation, thoughtfully and magnanimously. Those that remain are my responsibility alone, as is the general trend of this book's argument, which no adviser, perhaps, could satisfactorily modify. I am much indebted also to the late and much-regretted Rayner Unwin for encouragement without pressure over too long a period; and to Mrs Pam Armitage for typing repeated drafts of the first edition (written before word-processors came into general use) with exemplary care.

Friends and colleagues past and present have provided me with much additional information, in particular, for the first edition, John Bourne, Lesley Burnett, Janet and Malcolm Godden, Tony Green, Constance Hieatt, David Masson and Rory McTurk; while Tolkienists both within and without the Tolkien Society have put me straight on details. I must thank especially Rhona Beare and Jessica Yates for many long letters and contributions, as also Charles Noad and Gary Kuris. For this third edition, I have had yet more assistance, gratefully acknowledged, from Douglas Anderson, David Bratman, Patrick Curry, Charles Noad (again), Carl Hostetter, John Rateliff and Dan Timmons. Some of these debts are acknowledged more fully in text and notes.

Cornell University Press has kindly permitted me to reproduce in successive editions the substance of my chapter 'Creation from Philology in *The Lord of the Rings*', from *J.R.R. Tolkien, Scholar and Story-Teller: Essays in Memoriam*, edited by Mary Salu and Robert T. Farrell; and also, in this and the second edition, the stemma from Theodore Andersson's *The Legend of Brynhild*, both copyright © 1979 by Cornell University, for which I also have to thank Dr Andersson. The University of Turku, Finland, has given the same permission for my conference paper 'Tolkien as a Post-War Writer,' in *Scholarship and Fantasy: The Tolkien Phenomenon*, ed. Keith J. Battarbee, University of Turku, Finland, 1993, 217–36, as has Greenwood Press for my article 'Orcs, Wraiths, Wights: Tolkien's Images of Evil,' in *J.R.R. Tolkien and his Literary Resonances: Views of Middle-earth*, ed. George Clark and Dan Timmons, Greenwood Press, 2000, 183–98.

I have also to thank Tolkien's literary executors for permission to translate the four poems in Appendix B. They and Houghton Mifflin have further allowed me to quote freely from all Tolkien's published works. Thanks are due to the Oxford University Press for permission to quote from the *Oxford English Dictionary*, and indeed the most courteous deed of all is that of Mr Robert Burchfield, formerly the Dictionary's General Editor, who gave such permission in spite of all the shafts which Tolkien and I have levelled at the work of his predecessors. It should not need me to say that, whatever additions one can make to it, the *OED* remains the most useful work any English critic can possess.

When it comes to citation of ancient texts (as in this book it often does), I have not given full references in academic style. Partly this is because they would be useless to the general reader. More forcefully, one can say that there is no subject for which 'standard editions' are less relevant than the works of Tolkien. He knew *Beowulf*, and the *Anglo-Saxon Poetic Re-*

cords, and the *Elder Edda*, and *Pearl* and *Sir Gawain* and Saxo Grammaticus, a good deal better than most of their editors, even when, as happened occasionally, his earlier self *was* the editor. It may be taken, then, that 'standard editions' have been referred to, and some are cited in Appendix A to this work, but quotations rest on the authority of the original manuscripts, and have sometimes been emended to what I think are the most 'Tolkienian' forms. With Old English and Old Norse I have used marks of vowel-length similar to those in *The Lord of the Rings*, though I have not introduced them to *The Hobbit* nor to much-mentioned Old English names such as Beowulf (Béowulf). All translations, unless separately acknowledged, are my own.

Abbreviations used in the text and notes are as follows (all works mentioned being by Tolkien himself, unless otherwise stated). Dates of first publication are given as well as editions actually used.

Artist. Wayne G. Hammond and Christina Scull, *J.R.R. Tolkien, Artist and Illustrator* (Boston: Houghton Mifflin, 1995).

Author. Tom Shippey, *J.R.R. Tolkien: Author of the Century* (2000; Boston: Houghton Mifflin, 2001).

'AW'. *'Ancrene Wisse* and *Hali Meiðhad'*, *Essays and Studies*, vol. 14 (1929), pp. 104–26.

Bibliography. Wayne G. Hammond, with Douglas A. Anderson, *J.R.R. Tolkien: A Descriptive Bibliography* (St Paul's Bibliographies: Winchester, 1993; Oak Knoll Books: New Castle, Del., 1993).

Biography. *J.R.R. Tolkien: A Biography*, by Humphrey Carpenter (1977; Boston: Houghton Mifflin, 2000, the latter containing an updated list of Tolkien's published works).

BLT1. *The Book of Lost Tales, Part One*, edited by Christopher Tolkien (1983; Boston: Houghton Mifflin, 1984).

BLT2. *The Book Of Lost Tales, Part Two*, edited by Christopher Tolkien (Boston: Houghton Mifflin, 1984).

Essays. *The Monsters and the Critics and Other Essays*, edited by Christopher Tolkien (London: George Allen & Unwin, 1983).

'EW'. 'English and Welsh', in *Angles and Britons: O'Donnell Lectures* (Cardiff: University of Wales Press, 1963), pp. 1–41. Reprinted in *Essays*.

Exodus. *The Old English Exodus: Text, Translation and Commentary*, edited by Joan Turville-Petre (Oxford: Clarendon, 1981).

Finn. *Finn and Hengest: The Fragment and the Episode*, edited by Alan Bliss (London: George Allen & Unwin, 1982).

Giles. *Farmer Giles of Ham* (London: George Allen & Unwin, 1949). Reprinted in and here cited from *Reader*.

'Guide'. 'Guide to the Names in *The Lord of The Rings*', in *A Tolkien Compass*, edited by Jared Lobdell (La Salle, Ill.: Open Court, 1975), pp. 153–201.

Hobbit. *The Hobbit: or, There and Back Again* (1937; cited here from the corrected edition, with 'Note on the Text' by Douglas A. Anderson, Boston: Houghton Mifflin, 2001).

'Homecoming'. 'The Homecoming of Beorhtnoth Beorhthelm's Son', *Essays and Studies*, N.S. vol.6 (1953), pp. 1–18. Reprinted in and here cited from *Reader*.

Inklings. *The Inklings: C. S. Lewis, J.R.R. Tolkien, Charles Williams and Their Friends*, by Humphrey Carpenter (London: George Allen & Unwin, 1978).

Jewels. *The War of the Jewels: The Later Silmarillion, Part Two, The Legends of Beleriand*, edited by Christopher Tolkien (Boston: Houghton Mifflin, 1994).

Lays. *The Lays of Beleriand*, edited by Christopher Tolkien (Boston: Houghton Mifflin, 1985).

'Leaf'. 'Leaf by Niggle', first printed in *Dublin Review*, January 1945, pp. 46–61. Reprinted in *Reader* as the second part of 'Tree and Leaf', and here cited from there.

Legendarium. *Tolkien's* Legendarium: *Essays on The History of Middle-earth*, edited by Verlyn Flieger and Carl F. Hostetter (Westport, Conn.: Greenwood, 2000).

Letters. *The Letters of J.R.R. Tolkien*, edited by Humphrey Carpenter with the assistance of Christopher Tolkien (1981; Boston: Houghton Mifflin, 1999).

Lost Road. *The Lost Road and Other Writings: Language and Legend before The Lord of the Rings*, edited by Christopher Tolkien (Boston: Houghton Mifflin, 1987).

LOTR. *The Lord of the Rings* (first printed in three vols., 1954–1955, 2nd ed., 1966; cited here from the corrected one-volume edition, with 'Note on the Text' by Douglas A. Anderson, Boston: Houghton Mifflin, 2001, by page, or by book and chapter).

Memoriam Essays. *J.R.R. Tolkien, Scholar and Story-Teller: Essays in Memoriam,* edited by Mary Salu and Robert T. Farrell (Ithaca and London: Cornell University Press, 1979).

'Monsters'. 'Beowulf: the Monsters and the Critics', *Proceedings of the British Academy,* vol. 22 (1936), pp. 245–95. Reprinted in *Essays.*

MR. *Morgoth's Ring: The Later Silmarillion, Part One, The Legends of Aman,* edited by Christopher Tolkien (Boston: Houghton Mifflin, 1993).

OED. *The Oxford English Dictionary* (13 vols., Oxford: Clarendon Press, 1933 and Supplement in 4 vols., 1972–1986). Note that the 13 volumes of 1933 are a reprint of *The New English Dictionary on Historical Principles,* issued in 10 volumes, 1884–1928.

'OES'. 'The Oxford English School', *The Oxford Magazine,* vol. 48, no. 21, 29 May 1930, pp. 778–82.

'OFS'. 'On Fairy-Stories', first printed in *Essays Presented to Charles Williams* (London: Oxford University Press, 1947), pp. 38–89. Reprinted in *Essays* and, as the first part of 'Tree and Leaf', in *Reader,* and here cited from the latter.

Peoples. *The Peoples of Middle-earth,* edited by Christopher Tolkien (Boston: Houghton Mifflin, 1996).

Pictures. *Pictures by J.R.R. Tolkien* (London: George Allen & Unwin, 1979; Boston: Houghton Mifflin, 1991).

'Preface'. 'Prefatory Remarks' to *Beowulf and the Finnesburg Fragment: A Translation into Modern English* by J R Clark Hall, revised by C. L. Wrenn (London: George Allen & Unwin, 1940), pp. ix-xliii. Reprinted in *Essays* as 'On Translating Beowulf'.

Reader. *The Tolkien Reader* (New York: Ballantine, 1966). Contains *Giles,* 'Homecoming', 'Leaf' and 'OFS' together as 'Tree and Leaf', and *TB.*

Road. *The Road Goes Ever On: A Song Cycle,* poems by J.R.R. Tolkien set to music by Donald Swann (London: George Allen & Unwin, 1968).

S. *The Silmarillion,* edited by Christopher Tolkien (1977; Boston: Houghton Mifflin, 2001).

SD. *Sauron Defeated: The End of the Third Age (The History of the Lord of the Rings, Part Four),* edited by Christopher Tolkien (Boston: Houghton Mifflin, 1991).

SGGK. *Sir Gawain and the Green Knight,* edited by J.R.R. Tolkien and E. V. Gordon (Oxford: Clarendon Press, 1925).

SGPO. *Sir Gawain and the Green Knight, Pearl and Sir Orfeo,* translated and with introduction by J.R.R. Tolkien, edited by Christopher Tolkien (London: George Allen & Unwin, 1975).

Shadow. *The Return of the Shadow: The History of The Lord of the Rings, Part One,* edited by Christopher Tolkien (Boston: Houghton Mifflin, 1988).

Shaping. *The Shaping of Middle-earth: The Quenta, the Ambarkanta and the Annals,* edited by Christopher Tolkien (Boston: Houghton Mifflin, 1986).

Smith. *Smith of Wootton Major* (London: George Allen & Unwin, 1967).

Songs. *Songs for the Philologists,* by J.R.R. Tolkien, E. V. Gordon and others (privately printed at the Dept. of English, University College, London, 1936).

TB. *The Adventures of Tom Bombadil and Other Verses from the Red Book* (London: George Allen & Unwin, 1962). Reprinted in and cited from *Reader.*

Treason. *The Treason of Isengard: The History of The Lord of the Rings, Part Two,* edited by Christopher Tolkien (Boston: Houghton Mifflin, 1989).

UT. *Unfinished Tales of Númenor and Middle-earth,* edited by Christopher Tolkien (1981; Boston: Houghton Mifflin, 2001).

War. *The War of the Ring: The History of The Lord of the Rings, Part Three,* edited by Christopher Tolkien (Boston: Houghton Mifflin, 1990).

YWES. Chapters on 'Philology, General Works' in *The Year's Work in English Studies,* vols. 4–6 for 1923–1925. Cited by volume number and page.

For fuller bibliographical details, especially of Tolkien's many separately-printed poems and learned articles, one should consult the updated list of his published writings in *Biography* (2000), pp. 266–75, or in further detail in *Bibliography.*

PREFACE TO THE REVISED EDITION

My involvement with Tolkien's fiction now goes back almost fifty years, to a first reading of *The Hobbit* some time in the mid-1950s. My first attempt to comment publicly on Tolkien did not come, however, till late 1969 or early 1970, when I was recruited, as a very junior lecturer at the University of Birmingham, to speak on 'Tolkien as philologist' at a Tolkien day organised by some now-forgotten association. It was my good fortune that Tolkien's secretary, Joy Hill, was in the audience, and asked me for a copy of my script to show the Professor. It was my further good fortune that he read it, perhaps out of good will to Birmingham and to King Edward's School, Birmingham, which we both attended, he (with a gap) from 1900 to 1911, and I from 1954 to 1960. Tolkien furthermore replied to it, with his habitual courtesy, in a letter dated 13 April 1970, though it took me a very long time to understand what he meant, as I discuss below.

It was not till 1972 that I met Tolkien in person, by which time I had been promoted from Birmingham to a Fellowship at St. John's College, Oxford, to teach Old and Middle English along the lines which Tolkien had laid down many years before. Just after I arrived in Oxford, Tolkien's successor in the Merton Chair of English Language, Norman Davis, invited me to dine at Merton and meet Tolkien, who was then living in college lodgings following the death of his wife. The meeting left me with a strong sense of obligation and even professional piety, in the old sense of that word, i.e. 'affectionate loyalty and respect, esp. to parents', or in this case predecessors. After Tolkien's death I felt increasingly that he would not have been happy with many of the things people said about his writings, and that someone with a similar background to his own ought to try to provide — as Tolkien and E. V. Gordon wrote in the

'Preface' to their 1925 edition of *Sir Gawain and the Green Knight* — 'a sufficient apparatus for reading [these remarkable works] with an appreciation as far as possible of the sort which its author may be supposed to have desired'.

In 1975, accordingly, I contributed an article on 'Creation from Philology in *The Lord of the Rings*' to the volume of *Essays in Memoriam* edited by Mary Salu and R. T. Farrell, essentially an expansion of my 1970 script. In 1979, however, I followed Tolkien's track yet again, this time going to the Chair of English Language and Medieval English Literature at the University of Leeds, which Tolkien had held more than fifty years before. This only increased the sense of professional piety mentioned above, and the result was the first edition of the present work, which appeared in 1982. I assumed at the time that that would be my last word on the subject. But since then, of course, the whole 'History of Middle-earth' has appeared, twelve volumes of Tolkien's unpublished drafts and stories edited by his son Christopher, as well as a volume of academic essays including some new material, and the 'reconstructed' editions of the Old English *Exodus* and *Finnsburg* poems: each separate publication a valuable source of information, but also of some trepidation to the writer who has committed himself to explaining 'how Tolkien worked' or 'what Tolkien must have been thinking'. A second edition of *The Road to Middle-earth*, in 1992, accordingly tried to take some of this material into account.

A further thought, however, had slowly been growing upon me, first expressed in the article on 'Tolkien as a Post-War Writer', delivered as a lecture at the 'Tolkien Phenomenon' conference at the University of Turku, Finland, in 1992, and printed in the proceedings of that conference, *Scholarship and Fantasy*, edited by Keith J. Battarbee. This thought was that I had from 1970 always thought of Tolkien as a philologist, a professional ancestor, one of a line of historical linguists descended essentially from Jacob Grimm, of 'Grimm's Law' and 'Grimms' Fairy Tales'. I had in other words habitually seen him, to use the linguists' term, 'diachronically'. But language can and should also be viewed 'synchronically', and so could Tolkien. What happened if one considered him in the literary context of his time, the early to mid-twentieth century? My unconsidered assumption had been that he had no literary context, that he was a 'one-off' — certainly the impression one would get from reading any literary histories of the period which happened to mention him. But if one reflected on Orwell and William Golding, Vonnegut and T. H. White, C. S. Lewis and even Ursula Le Guin, several of them close to him in age or experience or date of publication, a different picture emerged: one of a group of (as I have called them) 'traumatised authors', writing fantasy, but voicing in that fantasy the most pressing and most immediately relevant issues of the whole monstrous twentieth century — questions of industrialised warfare, the origin of evil, the nature of humanity. This 'synchronic' view of Tolkien took shape in my book *J.R.R. Tolkien: Author of the Century* (2000). (Grammarians will note the absence of an article before the first word of the sub-title.) I hope that my two books now complement each other through their different approaches, though they present essentially the same explanations of the central works.

The present, third edition of *The Road to Middle-earth* naturally allows and obliges some reconsiderations, especially as a result of the new information contained in 'The History of Middle-earth'. On the whole I feel my first edition got off relatively lightly, confirmed as often as disproved. The rolling years and volumes have allowed me some clear hits: 'angel' as Tolkien speech for messenger (see note 11 to chapter 5 below, and c.p. *Treason of Isengard,* p. 422), or the importance of Old Mercian (see below p. 123 and c.p. *Sauron Defeated,* p. 257). Of course when it comes to philology, a real discipline, one ought to get things right. I was pleased when Anders Stenström, staying with me in Leeds in 1984, found in a Leeds journal for 1922 an anonymous poem in Middle English which we concluded was by Tolkien; but almost as pleased when the emendations I proposed to the text as (mis)printed were confirmed by Christopher Tolkien from his father's manuscript (see the journal of the Swedish Tolkien Society, *Arda,* vols. 4 [for 1984] and 6 [for 1986], for the poem and Stenström's account of his search).

Meanwhile, some unmistakable wides have also been called: in my allegorisation of 'Leaf by Niggle', on p. 44 below, I should not have written 'his "Tree" = *The Lord of the Rings*', but have put down something much more extensive; despite p. 76, Sauron was not part of Tolkien's 'subsequent inspiration' but there already; while on p. 271, writing 'There is, in a way, no more of "middle-earth" to consider' was just tempting Providence. Even more significantly, my 1982 discussion of 'depth' in Tolkien, pp. 308–17 below, was extensively answered by Christopher Tolkien a year later in his 'Foreword' to *The Book of Lost Tales, Part 1*, pp. 1–5, with a further note in *Part 2*, p. 57. It is clear that all my discussions of Tolkien were affected by reading his works (as almost everyone does) in order of publication, not order of composition. It is a temptation to try to remedy this retrospectively, but I have not done so. Studying Tolkien's fiction as it developed in his own mind, possible now as it was not in 1982, would be a different book. In general, then, I am happy to stand by what I published in 1982, and again in 1992, remembering the data I had, and expanding or updating wherever necessary.

Yet I do turn back to the letter Professor Tolkien wrote to me on 13 April 1970, charmingly courteous and even flattering as it was from one at the top of his profession to one then at the bottom ('I don't like to fob people off with a formal thanks . . . one of the nearest to my heart, or the nearest, of the many I have received . . . I am honoured to have received your attention'). And yet, and yet . . . What I should have realised — perhaps did half-realise, for I speak the dialect myself — was that this letter was written in the specialised politeness-language of Old Western Man, in which doubt and correction are in direct proportion to the obliquity of expression. The Professor's letter had invisible italics in it, which I now supply. 'I am in agreement with *nearly* all that you say, and I only regret that I have not the time to talk more about your paper: especially about design as it appears *or may be found* in a large *finished* work, and the *actual* events or experiences as seen or felt by the waking mind *in the course of actual composition*'. It has taken me thirty years (and the perusal of fifteen volumes unpublished in 1970) to see the point of the italics. Tolkien, however, closed his letter to me with the proverb: 'Need brooks no delay, yet late is better than never?' I can only repeat his saying, question-mark and all.

CHAPTER 1

'LIT. AND LANG.'

Old Antipathies

'This is not a work that many adults will read right through more than once.' With these words the anonymous reviewer for the *Times Literary Supplement* (25 November 1955) summed up his judgement of J.R.R. Tolkien's *The Lord of the Rings*.[1] It must have seemed a pretty safe prophecy at the time, for of course very few adults (or children) read anything right through more than once, still less anything as long as *The Lord of the Rings*. However, it could not have been more wrong. This did not stop critics continuing to say the same thing. Six years later, after the three separate volumes had gone through eight or nine hardback impressions each, Philip Toynbee in the *Observer* (6 August 1961) voiced delight at the way sales, he thought, were dropping. Most of Professor Tolkien's more ardent supporters, he declared, were beginning to 'sell out their shares' in him, so that 'today these books have passed into a merciful oblivion'. Five years afterwards the authorised American paperback edition of *The Lord of the Rings* was moving rapidly past its first million copies, starting a wave which never receded even to the more-than-respectable levels of 1961, and which has been revived in the twenty-first century to levels Toynbee could not have dreamed of.

The point is not that reviewers make mistakes (something which happens too often to deserve comment). It is that they should insist so perversely in making statements not about literary merit, where their opinions could rest undisprovable, but about popular appeal, where they can be shown up beyond all possibility of doubt. Matters are not much better with those critics who have been able to bring themselves to recognise the fact that some people do like Tolkien. Why was this 'balderdash' so popular, Edmund Wilson asked himself, in *The Nation* (14 April 1956). Well, he concluded, it was because 'certain people — especially, perhaps, in Britain have a life-long appetite for juvenile trash'. Some twenty-five years before, the same critic had delivered a little homily on the subject of intolerant responses to new fictions, in his book *Axel's Castle* —:

> it is well to remember the mysteriousness of the states with which we respond to the stimulus of works of literature and the primarily suggestive character of the language in which these works are written, on any occasion when we may be tempted to characterise as 'nonsense', 'balderdash' or 'gibberish' some new and outlandish-looking piece of writing to which we do not happen to respond. If other persons say they do respond, and derive from doing so pleasure or profit, we must take them at their word.[2]

A good rule, one must admit! But Mr Wilson had evidently forgotten it by the time he came to read *The Lord of the Rings:* or perhaps every time he said 'we' in the passage just quoted, he really meant 'you'.

Very similar play is made with pronouns in C. N. Manlove's *Modern Fantasy* (1975), a book dedicated to the thesis that no work of modern fantasy has remained 'true to its original vision', but one which like Edmund Wilson's review does at least confront the problem of Tolkienian popularity — of course much more evident in 1975 than 1956. Dr Manlove also thinks that the whole thing might be mere national aberration, though he prefers to blame the United States and 'the perennial American longing for roots'. Or could it all be due to mere length?

> Doubtless there is such a thing as the sheer number of pages the reader has had to turn that can add poignancy to the story — one almost feels this is the case as we come to the great close of Malory's epic. But not with Tolkien's book, for we have never been very much involved anyway.[3]

Who are 'we'? Readers of *Modern Fantasy*? Readers of *The Lord of the Rings*? There is no sensible answer to the question. For all the display of scholarly reflection this is, just like the bits from Messrs Toynbee and Wilson and the *TLS* reviewer, once more the criticism of blank denial. *Some* people may like reading Tolkien—after fifty years and scores of millions of readers, the point is nowadays usually grudgingly conceded— but they are wrong to do so, and whoever they are, they are not 'us'! Tolkien's 'mission as a literary preservationist', declared Judith Shulevitz in the *New York Times Book Review* (22 April 2001, p. 35), has turned out to be 'death to literature itself'.

In an exasperated kind of way Tolkien would, I think, have been particularly delighted to read Dr Manlove's essay, and probably (see pp. 6–7 below) Ms Shulevitz's review as well. He had run into criticism like Manlove's before; indeed it is a major theme of his tauntingly titled British Academy lecture of 1936, '*Beowulf:* the Monsters and the Critics'. The critics he had in mind were critics of *Beowulf,* but they were saying pretty much the same thing as Manlove on Tolkien: *Beowulf* didn't work, just like *The Lord of the Rings,* it was intrinsically silly, and 'we' weren't involved with it. 'Correct and sober taste', Tolkien wrote, 'may refuse to admit that there can be an interest for *us*—the proud we that includes all intelligent living people—in ogres and dragons; we then perceive its puzzlement in face of the odd fact that it has derived great pleasure from a poem that is actually about these unfashionable creatures' ('Monsters', p. 257). Tolkien had not, in 1936, realised how quickly 'correct and sober taste' could stamp 'puzzlement' out, and 'pleasure' along with it. However, for the rest he might just as well have been writing about responses to his own fiction. No doubt he would have felt honoured, in a way, to find himself as well as the *Beowulf*-poet driving critics to take refuge in threadbare and hopeless 'we's'.

The similarities between responses to *Beowulf* (as analysed by Tolkien) and to *The Lord of the Rings* do not end there. If one looks at Tolkien's remarks about the *Beowulf* critics, one can see that the thing he found worst about them was their monoglottery: they seemed able to read only one language, and even if they knew a bit of French or some other modern tongue, they were quite incapable of reading ancient texts, ancient English texts, with anything like the degree of detailed verbal insight that was required. They relied on translations and summaries; they did not pay close attention to particular words. 'This is an age of potted criticism and predigested literary opinion', Tolkien wrote in 1940 in apologetic preface to a translation of *Beowulf* which he hoped would only be used as a crib; 'in the making of these cheap substitutes for food translations unfortunately are too often used' (p. x). Now this could hardly be said about *The Lord of the Rings,* which is after all mostly in modern English. Or could it? Were people really paying close attention to words, Tolkien must have wondered as he read through the reviews? Or were they just skipping through for the plot again?

His irritation surfaced in the 1966 Foreword to the second edition of *The Lord of the Rings,* where he wrote, rather cattily:

> Some who have read the book, or at any rate have reviewed it, have found it boring, absurd, or contemptible; and I have no cause to complain, since I have similar opinions of their works, or of the kinds of writing that they evidently prefer. (*LOTR*, p. xvi)

Probably this was, strictly speaking, unfair. All the reviewers I have come across do seem to have read the book right through with no more than a normal run of first-reading miscomprehensions. However, it is a surprising fact that Edmund Wilson, who declared that he had not only read the book but had read the whole thousand pages out loud to his seven-year-old daughter, nevertheless managed consistently to spell the name of a central character wrong: 'Gandalph', for 'Gandalf'. Edwin Muir in the *Observer* preferred 'Gandolf'. This may seem purely trivial; but Tolkien would not have looked at it that way. He knew that 'ph' for 'f' was a learned spelling, introduced sporadically into English from Latin from about the fourteenth century, mostly in words of Greek origin like 'physics' or 'philosophy'. It is not used for native words like 'foot' or 'fire'. Now in the rather similar linguistic correspondences of Middle-earth (they are laid out in Appendices E and F of *The Lord of the Rings,* for those who haven't already noticed) it is clear

4

that 'Gandalf' belongs to the latter set rather than the former. 'Gandalph' would accordingly have seemed to Tolkien as intrinsically ludicrous as 'phat' or 'phool', or come to that 'elph' or 'dwarph'. He could hardly have conceived of the state of mind that would regard such variations as meaningless, or beneath notice. As for 'Gandolf', that is an Italian miscomprehension, familiar from Browning's poem 'The Bishop Orders His Tomb', but wildly inappropriate to a work which does its best to avoid Latinisms.

No compromise is possible between what one might call 'the Gandalph mentality' and Tolkien's. Perhaps this is why *The Lord of the Rings* (and to a lesser extent Tolkien's other writings as well) makes so many literary critics avert their eyes, get names wrong, write about things that aren't there and miss the most obvious points of success.[4] Tolkien thought this instinctive antipathy was an ancient one: people who couldn't stand his books hadn't been able to bear *Beowulf*, or *Pearl*, or Chaucer, or *Sir Gawain*, or *Sir Orfeo* either. For millennia they had been trying to impose their views on a recalcitrant succession of authors, who had fortunately taken no notice. In the rather steely 'Preface' to their edition of *Sir Gawain and the Green Knight* (in which the word 'criticism' is conspicuously shunned), Tolkien and his colleague E. V. Gordon declared that they wanted to help people read the poem 'with an appreciation as far as possible of the sort which its author may be supposed to have desired' (p. v). Doing the same job for Tolkien ought to be easier, since he is so much more our contemporary than the *Gawain*-poet; on the other hand Tolkien's mind was one of unmatchable subtlety, not without a streak of deliberate guile. However, nothing is to be gained by applying to it the criteria of 'correct and sober taste', of the great but one-sided traditions of later English literature, of those 'higher literary aspirations' so haughtily opposed by Anthony Burgess to 'allegories with animals or fairies' *(Observer,* 26 November 1978). These lead only to the conclusion that there is nothing to be said and no phenomenon to consider. Still, something made Tolkien different, gave him the power so markedly to provoke these twin reactions of popular appeal and critical rage.

The Nature of Philology

Whatever it was, it almost self-evidently had something to do with his job. For most of his active life Tolkien taught Old English, Middle English, the history of the English language; in doing so he was competing with teachers of English literature for time, funds and students, on the whole a thankless task since for all that Tolkien could do, the current was setting firmly away from him and from his subjects. Tolkien was by all accounts as capable of keeping up a grudge as the next man, and his minor writings often show it. The anthology of *Songs for the Philologists* which he and E. V. Gordon compiled, later to be privately printed in 1936, contains at least two poems by Tolkien attacking teachers of 'lit.'; one of them, titled variously 'Two Little Schemes' and 'Lit. and Lang.', the worst he ever wrote, so bad indeed that it makes me think (or hope) that something must have gone wrong with it en route between poet and printer. Meanwhile he was from the start of his learned career barely able to use the word 'literature' at all without putting inverted commas round it to show he couldn't take it seriously, which suggests that Ms Shulevitz's 'death to literature' remark would not have disturbed him. Thus his famous article on *'Ancrene Wisse* and *Hali Meiðhad'*,† published in 1929, opens with the remark that: 'The *Ancrene Wisse* has already developed a "literature", and it is very possible that nothing I can say about it will be either new or illuminating to the industrious or leisured that have kept up with it. I have not' ('AW', p. 104). There are variants on the same innuendo at the start of the *Beowulf* lecture of 1936 and in the *Sir Gawain* 'Preface' of 1925. Of course there is a reason (of characteristic deviousness) for this repeated Tolkienian joke, and one which can easily be extracted from the pages of the *Oxford English Dictionary,* on which Tolkien had himself worked in youth. There

---

† The letter 'ð' here is used in several Old English, Middle English and Old Norse quotations throughout this book. Like the other (runic) letter retained almost into the modern era, 'þ', it stands for 'th'. Thus Meiðhad = Meith-had = Maid(en)hood. The work mentioned is a treatise on 'Holy Virginity'.

6

one can find that the meaning which Tolkien foisted on to 'literature' is indeed recognised, under heading 3b: 'The body of books and writings that treat of a particular subject'. But why should Tolkien insist on using *that* one when heading 3a is less narrow and much more generally pertinent: 'Literature' meaning 'literary productions as a whole . . . Now also, in a more restricted sense, applied to writing which has claim to consideration on the ground of beauty of form or emotional effect'? The sting for Tolkien lay in the illustrative quotations which form the backbone of the definition, of which the sixth reads 'The full glory of the new literature broke in England with Edmund Spenser', i.e. in 1579. The true mordancy of that opinion may not appear till later. It is enough to note that if you took the *OED* seriously you could argue (a) that the valueless accumulation of books about *Beowulf* and the *Ancrene Wisse* and *Sir Gawain* were all 'literature', under heading 3b, but (b) the original and creative works themselves, all very much pre-1579, were not, under 3a. Naturally no one would be stupid enough to put forward such a proposition seriously and in so many words. Still, Tolkien did not think these semantic tangles entirely fortuitous; the *OED* might not mirror truth but it did represent orthodox learned opinion. It was typical of him to note the confusion and the slur it implied, to use the one to avenge the other — 'literature' was 'books about books', the dead Latin 'letter' opposed to the ancient English spirit.

Yet what this obsessive playing with words shows, better than anything, is that beneath the fog and fury of academic politics, Tolkien realised that all discussions of 'language' and 'literature' were irretrievably poisoned by the very terms they were bound to use. When he was not simply playing for his side, he accepted that 'lang.' was just as foolish a rallying-cry as 'lit.'. In his manifesto of 1930, 'The Oxford English School', he even suggested that both terms should be scrapped in favour of 'A' and 'B' — thus attempting, with something very close to *lèse majesté,* to introduce the curriculum of a 'redbrick' university, Leeds, to the ivory towers of Oxford, with sad if entirely predictable lack of success.[5] The same article makes it clear that he thought both 'linguistic' and 'literary' approaches too narrow for a full response to works of art, especially early works of art, and that furthermore what was needed was not some tame compromise between them (which is all most Schools of English usually manage to provide), but something as it were at right angles to both. This third dimension was the 'philological' one: it was from this that he trained himself to see things, from this too that he wrote his works of fiction. 'Philology' is indeed the only proper guide to a view of Middle-earth 'of the sort which its author may be supposed to have desired'. It is not Tolkien's fault that over the last hundred years 'philology', as a term and as a discipline, has been getting itself into even worse tangles than 'English literature'.

Dictionary definitions are, symptomatically, unhelpful. The *OED*, though conceived and created by philologists and borne along by the subject's nineteenth-century prestige, has almost nothing useful to offer. 'Philology', it suggests, is: '1. Love of learning and literature; the study of literature in a wide sense, including grammar, literary criticism and interpretation . . . polite learning. Now *rare* in *general* sense.' Under 2 it offers 'love of talk, speech or argument' (this is an offensive sense in which philology is mere logic-chopping, the opposite of true philosophy); while 3 recovers any ground abandoned in 1 by saying it is 'the study of the structure and development of language; the science of language; linguistics. (Really one branch of sense 1.)' So 'philology' is 'lang.' and 'lit.' too, all very charitable but too vague to be any use. The *Deutsches Wörterbuch* set in motion by Jacob Grimm (himself perhaps the greatest of all philologists and responsible in true philological style for both 'Grimm's Law of Consonants' and *Grimms' Fairy Tales*) could do little better, defining *philologie* with similar inclusiveness as 'the learned study of the (especially Classical) languages and literatures'. The illustrative quotation from Grimm's own work is more interesting in its declaration that 'none among all the sciences is prouder, nobler, more disputatious than philology, or less merciful to error'; this at least indicates the expectations the study had aroused. Still, if you didn't know what 'philology' was already, the Grimm definition would not enlighten you.

The matter is not cleared up by Holger Pedersen's assertion of 1924 that philology is 'a study whose task is the interpretation of the literary monuments in which the spiritual life of a given period has found expression'[6] (for this leaves you wondering why 'spiritual' has been put in and 'language' for once left out); nor by Leonard Bloomfield's aside a year later, when, proposing the foundation of a Linguistic Society for America, he explicitly rejected the term 'philological' and noted that while British scholars tended to use it to mean 'linguistic', Americans would prefer to keep the latter term and to revere philology rather more from a distance as 'that noblest of sciences . . . the study of national culture . . . something much greater than a misfit combination of language plus literature'.[7] Anyway, some Britons were very far removed from his position. John Churton Collins, nineteenth-century man of letters and candidate for an Oxford Chair, had written in 1891 (it was part of his campaign to keep men like Joseph Wright, Tolkien's tutor, out of any prospective English School at Oxford):

> it [i.e. philology] too often induces or confirms that peculiar woodenness and opacity, that singular coarseness of feeling and purblindness of moral and intellectual vision, which has in all ages been the characteristic of mere philologists . . . [It] too often resembles that rustic who, after listening for several hours to Cicero's most brilliant conversation, noticed nothing and remembered nothing but the wart on the great orator's nose.[8]

Opinions such as this clung on a long time in England. Tolkien wrote in 1924 '"Philology" is in some quarters treated as though it were one of the things that the late war was fought to end' (*YWES* 4, p. 37). When I first read this I took it to be a joke. However, just three years before the British Board of Education had printed a Report on *The Teaching of English in England* which declared, among much else, that philology ought not to be taught to undergraduates, that it was a 'German-made' science and (this comes in a footnote on p. 286) that by contributing to German arrogance it had led in a direct way to the outbreak of World War I.

Philology was 'the noblest of sciences'; it was literary; it was linguistic; it was German; it was Classical; it was different in America; it was about warts on noses; it was 'the special burden of the Northern tongues' (Tolkien speaking, 'OES' p. 780); also 'the special advantage they possess as a discipline' (Tolkien once again, in the same sentence). This begins to sound like the Babel of conflicting voices which Tolkien guyed so fiercely in his lecture on *Beowulf,* except that in this case the final universal chorus of all voices 'it is worth studying!' would clearly be somewhat ragged. If no single answer to the question 'what is philology?' can be found, at least few authorities would dissent from the view that the redefinition of philology—the moment when it stopped being used in the *OED*'s vaguest senses of 'love of talk' or 'love of learning'—came in 1786 when Sir William Jones informed the Bengal Society in Calcutta that Sanskrit resembled Greek and Latin too strongly for this to be the result of chance, but that all three, together with Germanic and Celtic, must have 'sprung from some common source which, perhaps, no longer exists'.[9]

Obviously this thought must have crossed many minds before 1786, for even between English and Latin, say, there are enough similarities—one, two, three, *unus, duo, tres*—to make one think there may be some sort of a connection. But until the turn of the eighteenth century such speculations had foundered immediately on the great reefs of dissimilarity surrounding the occasional identical rocks. After all, the main thing anyone knew about languages was that they were so different they had to be learnt one at a time. The great alteration Jones and his successors brought to the problem was the idea of looking not for chance resemblances—which had already been used to 'prove' relationships all over the map—but for regular change. *Bad* in modern Persian had the same sound and sense as 'bad' in English (remarked A. E. Pott in 1833), but that was just coincidence. On the other hand, *xvāhar* in Persian was originally the same word as *xo* in Ossetic, and both were related to English 'sister'; furthermore, the intermediate stages could be inferred and on occasion recovered.[10] Like many mental revolutions, this linguistic one depended on being counterintuitive. It was also to an intense degree *comparative,* using many languages to explain and corroborate each other; and, since different stages of the same language could be used comparatively, by nature overwhelmingly historical. 'Philology unfolds the genesis of those laws of speech which grammar contemplates as a finished result', says a citation in the *OED,* dated 1852. Its author did not mean 'philology' in any of the senses quoted from the *OED* on p. 8 above; he meant *comparative* philology,

the science inspired by Sir William and carried on through
many inheritors to Professor Tolkien himself. One may remark
that the confidence with which 'genesis' is approached was
characteristic of the time.

By 1852, indeed, 'the new philology' had many triumphs to
look back on, with several yet to come: one might pick out the
prize-winning essay of Rasmus Rask in 1814, on Old Icelandic,
and on the relationship of Scandinavian languages to Slavic,
Celtic, Finnish and Classical ones; the enormous 'Comparative
Grammar' or *Vergleichende Grammatik* of Franz Bopp in 1833–
49, which covered Sanskrit, Zend, Armenian, Greek, Latin,
Lithuanian, Old Slavic, Gothic and German; the *Deutsche
Grammatik* (1819) of Jacob Grimm, and all their many successors.[11] The point which all these works brandished was the intensely *systematic* nature of discovery, expressed as time went
on increasingly by the word 'laws' (see *OED* citation above),
and on the analogy of physics or chemistry by the association
of laws with discoverers: Grimm's Law, Verner's Law, Kuhn's
Law, Thomsen's Law, etc. There was and still is something
insidiously fascinating about the relationships these laws un-
cover, in such detail and such profusion. Latin *pisces* is the
same word as Old English *fisc*, observed Jacob Grimm, or indeed modern English 'fish'; *pes* is the same as 'foot' and *pellis* as
'fell' (the old word for 'skin'). What about *porcus* and 'pig',
though, where the p/f alternation breaks down? Well, there is
an Old English word *fearh* which corresponds properly, noted
Grimm, its modern descendant being 'farrow', again an old or
dialectal word for a 'birth' of piglets. The mill of comparisons
will not work on basic or standard or literary languages alone,
but demands ever-increasing grist from older or localised or
sub-standard forms. The reward it offers is first an increasing
sense that everything can be worked out, given time and material, second an exciting tension between the modern meanings
of words—words everyone has known all their lives—and
what appear as the ancient meanings. 'Daughter' in modern
Hindustani comes out as *beti;* yet there is a connection between the two languages in the word *dudh,* 'milk'. In ancient
days, it seems, a word like Sanskrit *duhitar* meant 'the little
milker'; but the job was so often given to daughters that task
and relationship became fused. It 'opens before our eyes a little

idyll of the poetical and pastoral life of the early Aryans', enthused Max Müller,[12] whose lectures on comparative philology bowled over not only (or not even) the learned world in the 1860s and after, but also London's high society. Comparison was the rage: it didn't tell you only about words, it told you about people.

But somewhere towards the end of the nineteenth century things had begun to go wrong. As is obvious from all that Tolkien ever said about literature and about philology, he felt that he had taken over (perhaps unfairly, but possibly not) a losing position in the academic game from his predecessors. Why — he could hardly have helped wondering — was that? Why had philology so ignominiously belied its promise?

Probably the short answer is that the essence of comparative philology was slog. There is something wistful in Tolkien's astonished praise of the 'dull stodges' of Leeds University (*Biography*, p. 111), in his insistence that at Leeds anyway 'philology is making headway . . . and there is no trace of the press-gang!' (*Letters*, p. 11). For matters were different elsewhere. No science, Jacob Grimm had said of philology, was 'prouder, nobler, more disputatious, *or less merciful to error*' (my italics). All its practitioners accepted, to a degree now incredible, a philosophy of rigid accuracy, total coverage, utter right and utter wrong: in 1919 the old and massively distinguished Eduard Sievers happily put his reputation on the line when he offered to dissect a text provided unseen by Hans Lietzmann, and to show from linguistic evidence how many authors had composed it (he had already done the same thing to the Epistles of Paul). He got Lietzmann's specimen totally wrong. But no one said the idea of the test itself was unfair.[13] Further down the scale, the discoveries of Grimm and his successors as far as Ferdinand de Saussure (now famous for inventing 'structuralism' but before that a student of *Ablaut*) were communicated increasingly to students as facts, systems of facts, systems divorced from the texts they had been found in. We must have philology within English Studies, wrote F. York Powell the Icelandicist in 1887, 'or goodbye to accuracy'.[14] The claim was false — you can be accurate about other things besides sound-shifts — but after seventy years of unbroken progress for the subject it was also damningly unambitious. Looking back many years later, R. W. Chambers (the man who turned down the Chair of Anglo-Saxon which eventually went to Tolkien in 1925) summed up success and failure by observing that in 1828 'the comparative philologist was like Ulysses', but 'scoffers may say that my parallel is all too true — that students of comparative language, like [Dante's] Ulysses, found only the mountain of Purgatory — Grimm's Law, Verner's Law, Grassmann's Law — rising in successive terraces of horror — and then were overwhelmed . . .'[15] Scoffers said exactly that; their viewpoint became dominant; comparative philology seen as 'hypothetical sound-shiftings in the primeval German forests'[16] went into a decline nearly as precipitate as its rise.

This is why 'philology' has first the old vague sense of 'love of learning'; then the new nineteenth-century one of 'study of texts leading to comparative study of language leading to comprehension of its evolution'; and in the twentieth century the specialised meaning, within departments of English Studies, of 'anti-literary science kept up by pedants (like Professor Tolkien) which ought to be stopped as soon as possible'. But these interesting semantic changes leave something out: the 'spiritual life' waved at by Holger Pedersen, the 'national culture' saluted by Leonard Bloomfield — or, to put it another way, the *Grimms' Fairy Tales*.

Lost Romances

For philology, after the Rask-Bopp-Grimm breakthrough, had moved in other directions beside the phonological and morphological. The mill of historical comparison called increasingly for fresh material, and one natural effect, besides the study of language in general, was the study of languages in particular. Scholars became much more interested in unread texts; they also became spectacularly better at reading them, at producing dictionaries of stone-dead languages. As Tolkien noted himself ('Preface', p. xii), the word *hós(e)* in *Beowulf* was never found anywhere else in Old English, so that one would have to guess at its meaning from context, were it not for the fact that philology proved it was the 'same' word as Old High German *hansa,* as in 'Hanseatic League', with the meaning 'retinue', or possibly 'band of people connected by mutual oaths'. The dead languages furnished comparative material; the comparative material illuminated dead languages. Men learnt to read Hittite, recognised as an Indo-European language in the 1920s (with marked effect on Old Testament studies), Tokharian (another Indo-European language once spoken by steppe-nomads but now represented mostly by texts preserved accidentally in an oasis in Turkestan), more recently to decipher 'Linear B' (an exploration of Cretan archaeology which would have been impossible in a pre-Bopp era). Much obscurer discoveries were made. A whole nation was theorised to lie behind the tiny fragments of Kottish, a language spoken when it was investigated by only five people. Holger Pedersen said of their relatives the Yenisei that they seem to be 'the last remnants of a powerful folk who, with the Thibetan empire as their southern neighbour, ruled over a great part of Siberia, but were at length compelled to submit to the Turks'.[17] Yet of their rule no traces remain other than linguistic ones. The romance of these investigations can still be felt. It is a large-scale analogue of Müller's remarks on *duhitar,* of the awareness that some forms even of modern language took you back to the Stone Age (as in English 'hammer', cognate with Old Slavic *kamy,* 'stone'). The romance became stronger, perversely, the closer it got to home.

Thus Old English itself looked very strikingly different after the philologists got hold of it — and it was they who insisted on calling it Old English instead of Anglo-Saxon to mark what they saw as an essential continuity. The story of Gothic, however, was even more dramatic. Some awareness of this language had been around from an early period. People knew that such texts as the Uppsala *Codex Argenteus* were in Gothic, that the Goths were an East Germanic tribe who had overrun parts of the Roman Empire from about A.D. 376, that they had been converted to literacy and Christianity, and become linguistically extinct some time round the eighth century. Philology shattered this picture. For one thing, Gothic became suddenly more than comprehensible, it became vital: it was the earliest Germanic language recorded at any length, Germanic was the area of most philologists' main interest (they were mostly Germans), and Gothic exhibited, in ways that Old English and Old

High German did not, stages in the history of all the Germanic languages inferable from but not recorded in its cousins. So, modern English says 'old' but 'elder', Old English (in its Early West Saxon form) *eald* but *ieldra,* both say (more or less) 'to heal' but 'hale (and hearty)'. For these Gothic offers respectively *altheis, althiza, háiljan, háils.* The common element deduced is that when an *i* or *j* followed *a* or *ái* in *old* Old English (this goes back to the time before Englishmen had learnt to write), speakers began to change the earlier vowel into *e, æ* — with similar changes affecting other vowels. Where there is a succeeding *i* in Gothic there is a change of vowel in Old (and often still in modern) English; not otherwise.

This phenomenon, known as 'i-mutation', became one of the most familiar horrors of university philology, but there is in it something both mysterious and satisfactory: a whole series of things which people said, and still *say,* without in the least knowing why, turn out to have one very old but clear, 100 per cent predictable reason. It is almost like genetics. No wonder that Grimm said Gothic was a 'perfect' language, Tolkien ('EW', p. 38) that it took him by storm. A further stage in the developing romance of 'Gothia' was the thought that the Goths might not be extinct. At some time in the 1560s one Ogier van Busbecq, a Fleming then acting as ambassador in Istanbul, had heard some foreigners whose speech sounded familiar. He recorded a list of words from them and printed it in 1589. They proved to be Gothic, nearly a thousand years out of place. Their interest aroused several centuries later, scholars could for a while entertain the hope that a living Gothic was still somewhere in existence, as a kind of Abominable Snowman of language. Alas, it wasn't. But at least it became clearer how Gothic had survived, in the remote Crimea, and it became possible to piece together once again the history of a vanished people.

It is not too much to say that this language and this people haunted Tolkien all his life. As is noted by Christopher Tolkien (*UT,* p. 311), the names of the leaders of the Rohirrim before the dynasty of Eorl are not Old English, like everything else in the Riders' culture, but Gothic, e.g. Vidugavia, Vidumavi, Marhwini, etc. (see *LOTR,* pp. 1021–22). They function there to suggest language behind language and age behind age, a phenomenon philologists so often detected. On a larger scale the Battle of the Pelennor Fields closely follows the account, in Jordanes's *Gothic History,* of the Battle of the Catalaunian Plains, in which also the civilisation of the West was preserved from the 'Easterlings', and in which the Gothic king Theodorid was trampled by his own victorious cavalry with much the same mixture of grief and glory as Tolkien's Théoden. Perhaps the most revealing remark, however, comes in a letter from Tolkien to his son Christopher after the latter had read a paper on the heroes of northern legend. In this he praised his son's paper for the light it shed on men and on history, but added:

> All the same, I suddenly realized that I am a *pure* philologist. I like history, and am moved by it, but its finest moments for me are those in which it throws light on words and names! Several people (and I agree) spoke to me of the art with which you made the beady-eyed Attila on his couch almost vividly present. Yet oddly, I find the thing that thrills my nerves is the one you mentioned casually: *atta, attila.* Without those syllables the whole great drama both of history and legend loses savour for me. (*Letters,* p. 264)

The point is that Attila, though a Hun, an enemy of the Goths under Theodorid and a byword for bloody ferocity, nevertheless does not appear to bear a barbarian name. 'Attila' is the diminutive form of the Gothic word for 'father', *atta:* it means 'little father', or even 'dad', and it suggests very strongly the presence of many Goths in Attila's conquering armies who found loot and success much more attractive than any questions of saving the West, Rome or civilisation! As with *duhitar,* 'little milker', or *kamy* as a cognate for 'hammer', the word tells the story. Tolkien went on in his letter to say that in his mind that was exactly how *The Lord of the Rings* grew and worked. He had not constructed a design. Instead he had tried 'to create a situation in which a common greeting would be *elen síla lúmenn' omentielmo*'. Literary critics might not believe him, but philologists (if any were left) ought to know better.

Atta, Attila: what's in a name? One answer is, a total revaluation of history. It is instructive to look at older and newer editions of Edward Gibbon's *Decline and Fall of the Roman Em-*

pire (first published 1776–88). Gibbon knew the Goths from many Roman and Greek historians, including Jordanes, but these were his only sources of information and he could not imagine another one. 'The memory of past events', he remarked with classically-educated superciliousness, 'cannot long be preserved, in the frequent and remote emigrations of illiterate Barbarians' (chapter 26). As for the great Gothic king of the fourth century, he said, 'The name of Hermanric is almost buried in oblivion'. It did not stay buried. 'Hermanric' turned up in recognisable form in *Beowulf* (not printed till 1815) as *Eormenric*. The same name and man, with little stories attached, appeared also in the Old English poems *Deor* and *Widsith*. As *Ermenrich* he survived into the Middle High German romances of *Dietrichs Flucht, Alpharts Tod,* and many others. Most powerfully, *Jörmunrekkr* turned out to be a most prominent character in the Old Norse poems of the *Elder Edda,* which had lain unnoticed in an Icelandic farmhouse till the 1640s and not been published in full till Rasmus Rask did the job in 1818. The 'illiterate Barbarians' were not as forgetful as Gibbon thought. They could at least remember names, and even if these had been affected by sound-changes in the same way as other words, no archaic poet produced anything as false as Gibbon's '(H)ermanric'. From the joint evidence of old poems in English, Norse and German one could in fact deduce that the king's name, though never recorded in Gothic, must have been *Aírmanareiks*.

And, as with 'Attila', there is a thrill of old passion lurking in the name, buried though this may be in editors' footnotes and the inferences of scholarly works. The tales of Ermanaric's death vary. He committed suicide (round A.D. 375) for fear of the Huns, says an early Roman source. Jordanes tells a more complicated story of treachery, punishment and revenge. The Old Norse poems, more grisly and more personal, insist that Ermanaric was attacked by his brothers-in-law for murdering their sister, and was left after their death under a hail of Gothic stones — for on them no weapon would bite — to survive as a *heimnár* or 'living corpse', a trunk with both arms and legs cut off. This last tale seems totally unlikely. But it does preserve some agreement over names and incidents with Jordanes: maybe something peculiar and tragic did take place during the collapse of the Gothic Empire in the fourth century. To the philologist who compared these versions there was a further charm in guessing what strange chains of transmission and quirks of national bias had transformed king into villain. Had the defeated Goths cast him as a scapegoat? Had he been made a wife-murderer to gloss over the feelings of those Goths who changed sides and joined the 'Easterlings', calling the Hunnish king their 'little father'? Had Crimean Goths sung lays of Ermanaric to Norsemen of the Varangian Guard in the courts of the Greek emperor? Tolkien followed these inquiries closely, buying for instance the volumes of Hermann Schneider's *Germanische Heldensage* as they came out 1928–1934,[†] and claiming in 1930 ('OES', pp. 779–80) that Gothic was being studied under his direction not only for sound-laws but 'as a main source of the poetic inspiration of ancient England and the North'. As he said in the letter quoted above, the legends of heroes had a fascination in themselves; they were also part of 'a rational and exacting discipline'.

Philology illuminated the Dark Ages. Certainly, when it comes to Gothic chieftains, J. B. Bury's revised edition of Gibbon (in 1896) proceeds with a new caution! But the essential point — it is a point which Tolkien's academic predecessors had signally failed to grasp, with consequent ruin for their subject — lies in the immense stretch of the philological imagination. At one extreme scholars were drawing conclusions from the very *letters* of a language: they had little hesitation in ascribing texts to Gothic or Lombardic authors, to West Saxons or Kentishmen or Northumbrians, on the evidence of sound-changes recorded in spelling. At the other extreme they were prepared to pronounce categorically on the existence or otherwise of nations and empires on the basis of poetic tradition or linguistic spread. They found information, and romance, in songs and fragments everywhere. The *Lex Burgundionum* of King Gundobad opened, as had been known for centuries, with a list of royal ancestors, Gibica, Gundomar, Gislaharius, Gundaharius. It took philology to equate nos. 1, 3 and 4 with

---

[†] His signed copies are in the Taylorian Library at Oxford.

the Gifica, Gíslhere and Gúthhere of Old English poems, nos. 1 and 4 with the Gibeche and Gunther of the Germans' epic, the *Nibelungenlied*. Simultaneously it became apparent that the epic had a kernel of truth: the Huns *had* wiped out a Burgundian king and army in the 430s (as Gibbon had vaguely noted); some of the names were authentic; there had been a continuing tradition of poetry from fifth to twelfth century, even if it had all vanished and never been written down. Sidonius Apollinaris, bishop of Clermont, indeed mentioned the Burgundians' songs with distaste in a sixth-century lyric. 'The learned and eloquent Sidonius', Gibbon calls him. 'How gladly would we now give all his verses for ten lines of the songs in which these "long-haired seven-foot high, onion-eating barbarians" celebrated, it may be, the openhandedness of Gibica, or perhaps told how, in that last terrible battle, their fathers had fallen fighting round Gundahari', wrote R. W. Chambers more sourly.[18] The change of viewpoint marks an enormous if temporary shift of poetic and literary interest from Classical to native. It also shows how philology could seem, to some, the 'noblest of sciences', the key to 'spiritual life', certainly 'something much greater than a misfit combination of language plus literature'.

'Asterisk-Reality'

Nevertheless, Sidonius's poems had survived, and the Burgundian epics hadn't. There was an image forming in many men's minds of the days when an enormous Germanic empire had stretched from the Baltic to the Black Sea, only to go down before the Huns and disperse into settlements everywhere from Sweden to Spain — but the image remained tantalisingly on the edge of sight. 'The ill-grace of fate has saved hardly anything . . . of the poetry possessed by the eighth, seventh and earlier centuries', lamented Jacob Grimm and his brother Wilhelm.[19] 'It grieves me to say it', said Axel Olrik, 'the old *Biarkamál,* the most beloved and most honoured of songs in all the North, is not known to us in the form it had.'[20] 'Alas for the lost lore, the annals and old poets', wrote Tolkien, referring indeed to Virgil but by analogy to the sources of

Beowulf ('Monsters', p. 271). Gudbrand Vigfusson and F. York Powell, editing the *Corpus Poeticum Boreale,* the whole poetry of the North, in the 1880s, might look back on past ages and see the 'field of Northern scholarship' as 'a vast plain, filled with dry bones', up and down which there walked 'a company of men, doing their best to set these bones in order, skull by skull, thigh by thigh, with no hope or thought of the breath that was to shake this plain with the awakening of the immortal dead'.[21] But though philology did come and breathe life into the dry bones of old poems, filling history with the reverberations of forgotten battles and empires, still there was a point beyond which it could not go; old languages could be understood, old stories edited and annotated, but living speakers could not be found. Nor were the poems left usually the poems most ardently desired.

That is why the characteristic activity of the philologist came, in the end, to be 'reconstruction'. This might be no more than verbal. From the circumstance that English and German both change the vowel of 'man' in the plural to 'men' or *Männer,* you could infer that Primitive Germanic, of which not one word has ever been recorded, would have said **manniz,* producing as usual 'i-mutation'. The * is the sign of the reconstructed form, proposed by August Schleicher in the 1860s and used widely ever since. On a higher level you might reconstruct a language. Schleicher indeed wrote a little fable in 'Indo-European', that 'common source' for Sanskrit, Latin and Greek which Sir William Jones had suggested. *Avis, jasmin varna na a ast, dadarka akvams,* it began, 'A sheep, which had no wool on it, saw a horse . . .' Schleicher's colleagues were not much impressed, and indeed the researches of Verner, Brugmann and de Saussure in the 1870s prompted H. Hirt to offer a corrected version of it some years later; no language changed as quickly in the 1870s as Primitive Indo-European, ran the philological joke.[22] But the method itself was not seriously questioned, only the answer reached. In between these two extremes an editor might find himself rewriting a poem. *Eorl sceal on éos boge, worod sceal getrume rídan,* says the Old English poem *Maxims I,* 'Earl shall on horse's back, warband *(worod)* ride in a body'. Most warbands in Old English history marched on their feet; and anyway *worod* fails to keep up the poetic alliteration. *Éored* is the proper word here, say the editors, and it means 'a troop of cavalry', being related to the word *eoh,* 'horse', cp. Latin *equus.* It's true that the word is used by itself only twice elsewhere in Old English, and only once correctly—the word and idea must have become unfamiliar. But that is no deterrent. The post-philological editor can assume he knows more, indeed knows better than the native speaker or scribe, if not the original poet—another reason, be it said, for beliefs like Tolkien's, that he had a cultivated sympathy with the authors of *Beowulf* or *Sir Gawain* or 'The Reeve's Tale' which even the poet's contemporaries had not and which would certainly never be reached by straight 'literary criticism'.

Examples could be multiplied almost indefinitely: it is impossible to avoid mentioning the fact that the very core and kernel of *Beowulf* criticism in the last hundred years has been the story of 'the fall of the house of the Scyldings', which, as it happens, neither the poet nor any other ancient writer ever got round to explaining, but which was 'reconstructed' in great and (to my mind) totally convincing detail by a succession of scholars up to R. W. Chambers. But the vital points to grasp are these:

(1) The thousands of pages of 'dry as dust' theorems about language-change, sound-shifts and ablaut-gradations were, in the minds of most philologists, an essential and natural basis for the far more exciting speculations about the wide plains of 'Gothia' and the hidden, secret trade routes across the primitive forests of the North, *Myrkviðr inn ókunni,* 'the pathless Mirkwood' itself. You could not have, you would never have *got,* the one without the other.

(2) In spite of the subject's apparent schizophrenia and the determination of its practitioners to make nothing easy, philology was, for a time, the cutting edge of all the 'soft' or 'behavioural' sciences, literature, history, sociology and anthropology at once. That is why it attracted such a following and why Jacob Grimm, for instance, could hope to sell his dictionary, the *Wörterbuch der deutschen Sprache,* to a mass-audience as something designed for entertainment.

(3) In this entire process the thing which was perhaps eroded most of all was the philologists' sense of a line be-

tween imagination and reality. The whole of their science conditioned them to the acceptance of what one might call '*-' or 'asterisk-reality', that which no longer existed but could with 100 per cent certainty be inferred.

(4) In a sense, the non-existence of the most desired objects of study created a romance of its own. If we had the lost Gothic 'Ermanaric-lays' we might think little of them, but find them lame, crude or brutal; quite likely, the very first version of the *Nibelungenlied* (composed in the ashes of the Burgundian kingdom) was just an attempt by the poet to cheer himself up. But the fact that these things do not exist, hover forever on the fringe of sight, makes them more tantalising and the references to them more thrilling. There is a book by R. M. Wilson called *The Lost Literature of Medieval England,* which Tolkien must often have read — see note 24 below. *The Lost Literature of Dark-Age Europe,* however, would be a title almost too painful for words. Still, it would cover plenty of material. The best lines about King Arthur are not the long explicit descriptions of the later medieval romances, but those in the almost deliberately uninformative Welsh triads, e.g. from the Black Book of Carmarthen:

> *Bet y March, bet y Guythur,*
> *bet y Gugaun Cledyfrut;*
> *anoeth bid bet y Arthur*

> 'There is a grave for March, a grave for Gwythur,
> a grave for Gwgawn Red-sword;
> the world's wonder a grave for Arthur.'[23]

As for Old English, my guess is that the most stirring lines to Tolkien must have come, not even from *Beowulf,* but from the fragment *Waldere,* where an unknown speaker reminds the hero that his sword was given by Theodoric to Widia 'because Wayland's child let him out of captivity, hurried him out of the hands of the monsters'. Somewhere in the Dark Ages, this seems to suggest, there must have been a legend, a story of how the Gothic king *Thiudoreiks was stolen away to the land of giants, to be rescued after long adventures by his faithful retainers Widia and Hildebrand. Why did the giants take him, where and how did they live, what were their relations with humanity? Once upon a time many people must have known the answers: the story survives in a decadent form in the medieval German romances of *Das Eckenlied, Sigenot, Laurin* and others, while there is an intensely irritating scrap of a Middle English poem on the subject tucked into a dull sermon on humility:

> *Summe sende ylues, and summe sende nadderes:*
> *summe sende nikeres, the bi den watere wunien.*
> *Nister man nenne, bute Ildebrand onne.*

> 'Some sent elves, and some sent serpents,
> some sent sea-monsters, that live by the water.
> No one knew any of them, but Hildebrand alone.'[24]

What must it have been like in Old English — a poem not about monsters erupting on humanity, as in *Beowulf,* but about men going into the heart of the monsterworld, for adventures in the 'Ettenmoors' themselves! But fate had snatched that prospect (almost) into utter oblivion.

The Wilderness of Dragons, the Shrewedness of Apes

Probably the most disheartening conclusion to be drawn from this brief review of intellectual history is that the history of English studies in British and American universities has been forever marred by incomprehension and missed opportunities. Professor D. J. Palmer has shown how the birth of the Oxford English School in particular was accompanied by desperate struggles between language and literature, philologists and critics, ending not in mutual illumination but in a compromise demarcation of interests.[25] Quite possibly the philologists were most to blame in this. Peter Ganz, Professor of German at Oxford, has pointed out that Jacob Grimm's chief intellectual defect was a refusal to generalise.[26] Indeed, as he neared the end of his *Teutonic Mythology* (four volumes in the translation of J. S. Stallybrass, and 1887 pages), Grimm wrote a 'Preface' referring to himself as a gleaner, whose observations he left to 'him who, standing on my shoulders, shall hereafter get into full swing the harvesting of this great field'.[27] But actually there was no field left to harvest; while few would relish the thought of spending a lifetime putting someone else's observations in order, without the fun of first collecting them! So the impetus of philology ran out in a series of Primers and Readers and Grammars, endless academic brickmaking without any sign of an architect. No wonder the early critics got annoyed. On the other hand they showed little magnanimity, or even curiosity, once they got control.

The overt result for the young Tolkien must have been that, when he returned from World War I to Oxford University in 1919, he found himself once again in a battle being fought by two sides from deep entrenchments, and one whose stalemates were as unlikely to be broken as the greater ones of Ypres or the Somme by frontal offensives. Still, both sides kept trying them. Tolkien did his best to make peace. His 1930 'manifesto' led at least to the elimination of some academic 'no man's land'; during the syllabus campaign of 1951 he even emerged from his trench to fraternise with the enemy (till C. S. Lewis stopped him; see *Inklings,* pp. 229–30). But a covert result may have been that he gave up hope, at least from time to time, of penetrating other people's vested interests and making them understand the appeal of the subjects he would have liked to teach. His jokes on the subject get wryer, his gestures of rapprochement — 'the boundary line between linguistic and literary history is as imaginary as the equator — a certain heat is observable, perhaps, as either is approached' (*YWES* 6, p. 59) or 'the "pure philologist who cannot do literature" . . . is as rare as the unicorn' ('OES', p. 782) — these become more perfunctory and finally disappear. What was possibly a natural bent towards reserve became more pronounced; it is hard to escape the feeling that in some of the interviews given after celebrity had arrived Tolkien was still liable to give easy or unnoticedly ambiguous answers to save the trouble of explaining something which he knew had proved incomprehensible many times before. *The Hobbit* and *The Lord of the Rings* had made his point, whether it had been intellectually apprehended or not; and the hostile or even malignant reaction it evoked from so many on the 'lit.' side was only what he might have expected.

Indeed, to go back to the animus *The Lord of the Rings* created: it is striking that next to the books' sheer success the thing that irritated reviewers most was their author's obstinate insistence on talking about language as if it might be a subject of interest. 'The invention of languages is the foundation', Tolkien had said. 'The "stories" were made rather to provide a world for the languages than the reverse' (*Letters*, p. 219). 'Invention' of course comes from Latin *invenire,* 'to find'; its older sense, as Tolkien knew perfectly well, was 'discovery'. If one were to say of nineteenth-century philology that 'the discovery of languages was *its* foundation', one would be stating literal truth; as often, probably, Tolkien was playing with words, juxtaposing the languages he had made up out of his own head with those that others had found or 'reconstructed' all over the world, so aligning himself yet again with his professional inheritance. Meanwhile the second sentence, though no doubt personally true again, might almost have been said of Ermanaric or Theodoric or the nineteenth-century vision of a 'historical' King Arthur. An element of generalisation underlay the particular application to Tolkien's own case.

This remained completely unperceived by his critics. 'He has explained that he began it to amuse himself, as a philological game', translated Edmund Wilson. 'An overgrown fairy story, a philological curiosity — that is, then, what *The Lord of the Rings* really is.' Philology, you note, is peculiar but not serious. Lin Carter (who prepared for his commentary on Tolkien by looking up 'philology' in 'the dictionary', to little profit maybe it was the wrong dictionary) professed the same opinion even more blankly, if kindly, by claiming that Tolkien was really interested in 'the eternal verities of human nature', and that the appendices of *The Lord of the Rings* needed to be seen that way and not just as 'the outgrowth of a don's scholarly hobbies'. The idea could be right, but the notion of 'scholarly hobbies' is singularly naive. Neil D. Isaacs, also writing in Tolkien's defence, took the blunder on by asserting that 'Tolkien's own off-hand remarks about the importance of philology to the creative conception of the trilogy need not be taken too seriously', and R. J. Reilly put the tin lid on the whole discussion by saying, in attempted refutation of Edmund Wilson, that *The Lord of the Rings* can't have been a philological game because it's too serious, and therefore, seemingly, cannot possibly be philology. 'No one ever exposed the nerves and fibres of his be-

ing in order to make up a language; it is not only insane but unnecessary.'[28] Like the reviewers quoted at the start of this chapter, Mr Reilly here makes a factual statement about humanity
which is factually wrong. The aberration he talks about may
not be common, but is not unprecedented. August Schleicher
exposed the nerves and fibres of his being to make up Primitive
Indo-European, and had them shredded for his trouble. Willy
Krogmann, of the University of Hamburg, not only came to
the conclusion that the Old High German *Hildebrandslied* (the
oldest German heroic poem) must originally have been composed in Lombardic, a West Germanic language surviving outside '*-reality' only in a handful of names, but also reconstructed the language and rewrote the poem, publishing his
new edition as late as 1959. No one, as far as I know, went so
far as to reconstruct the Burgundian Nibelung-story, the first
Ostrogothic Ermanaric-lay or the Danish *Ur-Beowulf;* but
such thoughts were in many minds. The only extant Gothic
poem is by Tolkien, 'Bagme Bloma', in *Songs for the Philologists,* reprinted and translated in Appendix B below. Nor was
this his only attempt at poetic reconstruction; see *Letters,*
p. 379. The drives towards creativity do not all emanate from
the little area already mapped by 'literary' criticism. Awareness
of this fact should have aroused a certain humility, or anyway
caution, in Tolkienian commentators.

As it is, some of Tolkien's earliest writings seem to carry a
certain foreboding truth. It has already been remarked that he
tended to open learned articles with attacks on, or ripostes
to, the 'literature' or the 'criticism' of his particular subject,
whether this was Chaucer or the *Ancrene Wisse* or translators
of *Beowulf.* Probably the sharpest and most revealing instance
comes in the British Academy lecture on 'The Monsters and
the Critics', as Tolkien moves on from the melancholy state
of *Beowulf* criticism as a whole to the remarks of W. P. Ker
and then of R. W. Chambers — philologists whom Tolkien respected but who he thought had given too much away to the
other side. 'In this conflict between plighted troth and the duty
of revenge', wrote Chambers, of a subject the *Beowulf*-poet
had neglected for the sake of monsters, 'we have a situation
which the old heroic poets loved, and would not have sold for a
wilderness of dragons.' 'A wilderness of dragons!' exploded

Tolkien, repeating the phrase and grasping instantly its deliberate syntactic ambiguity (between phrases like 'a field of cows' and phrases like 'a pride of lions'):

> There is a sting in this Shylockian plural, the sharper for coming from a critic, who deserves the title of the poet's best friend. It is in the tradition of the Book of St. Albans, from which the poet might retort upon his critics: 'Yea, a desserte of lapwynges, a shrewednes of apes, a raffull of knaues, and a gagle of gees.' ('Monsters', p. 252)

Geese, knaves, apes, lapwings: these formed Tolkien's image of the literary critic, and they are emblematic respectively of silliness, fraud, mindless imitation and (see Horatio in *Hamlet* V ii) immaturity. But there is a multiple barb on the second phrase, the 'shrewednes of apes'. For 'shrewednes', like most words, has changed its meaning, and as with 'literature', Tolkien thought the changes themselves significant. Nowadays it means (*OED* again) 'sagacity or keenness of mental perception or discrimination; sagacity in practical affairs'. Once upon a time it meant 'maliciousness', with particular reference to feminine scolding or nagging. No doubt the transit came via such phrases as 'a shrewd blow', first a blow which was meant to hurt, then one that did hurt, then one that was accurately directed, and so on. In all these senses Tolkien's remark was 'shrewd' itself. It created a vivid if exaggerated picture of the merits and demerits of the literary profession seen *en bloc:* undeniably clever, active, dexterous (so exemplifying 'shrewdness' in the modern sense), but also bitter, negative and far too fond of 'back-seat driving' (see 'shrewed' in the old sense) — overall, too, apish, derivative, cut off from the full range of human interests. It would be a pity for his claim to ring true. But the history of reactions to Tolkien has tended to uphold it. One can sum up by saying that whether the hostile criticism directed at *The Lord of the Rings* was right or wrong — an issue still to be judged — it was demonstrably compulsive, rooted only just beneath the surface in ancient dogma and dispute.

CHAPTER 2

PHILOLOGICAL INQUIRIES

Roads and Butterflies

The Grimms and Tolkien prove that philological approaches to poetry did not have to exclude everything that would now be called 'literary'. Still, their attitudes were sharply distinct from those now normal among literary critics. For one thing, philologists were much more likely than critics to brood on the sense, the form, the other recorded uses (or unrecorded uses) of single words. They were not, on the whole, less likely to respect the original author's intentions, but their training did make them prone to consider not only what a word was doing in its immediate contexts, but also its roots, its analogues in other languages, its descendants in modern languages and all the processes of cultural change that might be hinted at by its history. It might be said that to Tolkien a word was not like a brick, a single delimitable unit, but like the top of a stalactite, interesting in itself but more so as part of something growing. It might also be said that he thought there was in this process something superhuman, certainly super-any-one-particular-human, for no one knew how words would change, even if he knew how they *had*. In one of his last published poems, a tribute in Old English to W. H. Auden, with facing-page modern English translation, Tolkien begins by calling Auden a *wóðbora,* and ends by promising him lasting praise from the *searopancle.*[1] The first noun is translated 'one [who] has poetry in him', the second as 'the word-lovers'. 'Word-lovers' is, however, etymologically parallel with 'philologists', while the first element of *wóð-bora* is also the word recorded in the god-name Woden, or Othinn, and in the archaic adjective 'wood', meaning 'crazy'; it refers to the mystic rage of bard or shaman or (as we now say) berserker. Poets and philologists, Tolkien felt, were the ones to appreciate that.

An associated difference was that philologists were more likely than critics to believe in what one might call 'the reality of history'. One good reason for this was that they tended to work with manuscripts rather than printed books, and the former are much more instructive than the latter. In some cases they have been physically written by the original poet or author; in others they have been corrected by him; in others they all too clearly have not, with incomprehension so thick on the page that one can visualise the author's baffled rage were he ever to guess (as Chaucer did, occasionally) what had happened or was going to. The sense that ghosts cluster in old libraries is very strong. Another reason for the feeling of intimate involvement with history, though, lies in the philologists' awareness of the shaping of present by past — the stalactites of words again, but also the creation of nation-states by language-separation (e.g. Dutch and German), the growth of national myth from forgotten history (as with the Finnish *Kalevala*), but perhaps as much as anything the fastening down of landscape to popular consciousness by the habit of naming places. Less than thirty miles from Tolkien's study stands the prehistoric barrow known as 'Wayland's Smithy'. Its name is more than a thousand years old; perhaps it was in the mind of King Alfred (born at Wantage, seven miles off) when he interjected into his translation of Boethius the outcry: *Hwæt synt nú þæs foreméran ond þæs wisan goldsmiðes bán Wélondes?* 'What now are the bones of Wayland, the goldsmith preeminently wise?' Alfred might also have thought of Wayland as the father of Widia, who in the lost poems released Theodoric from the power of the monsters; maybe Alfred had heard them sung. But though the poems had gone, and the monsters with them, and 'Wayland' no longer meant anything at all to English people, the name survived down the centuries and carried with it a hint of what once had been. Such chains of association littered the landscape for Tolkien; they did not have to be confined to books. When he said that 'History often resembles "Myth"', or when

Wilhelm Grimm refused to segregate 'Myth' from 'Heroic Legend', both had entirely prosaic reasons for doing so.[2] They knew that legend often became a matter of everyday.

Something like these two awarenesses, of continuing history and continuing linguistic change, can be inferred (admittedly with the aid of vast quantities of hindsight) from the first thing Tolkien ever published, bar a few lines in school and college magazines: the poem 'Goblin Feet' in *Oxford Poetry 1915*.[3] This begins:

> I am off down the road
> Where the fairy lanterns glowed
> And the little pretty flittermice are flying:
> A slender band of grey
> It runs creepily away
> And the hedges and the grasses are a-sighing.
> The air is full of wings
> And of blundering beetle-things
> That warn you with their whirring and their humming.
> O! I hear the tiny horns
> Of enchanted leprechauns
> And the padding feet of many gnomes a-coming.

This is, admittedly, not very good. Indeed, one can imagine the response to it of the literary 'side', full of armèd vision, not to mention critical temper. 'Why', it might ask, 'do we have the past tense in line 2 and the present everywhere else? Does this mean the "fairy lanterns" have gone out and the "I-narrator" is pursuing them? Or could it be that the author is stuck for a rhyme to "road"? As for "*a*-sighing" and "*a*-coming", these look like scansion devices, mere padding. But in any case there is nothing in nature to suggest that the hedges and the grasses *were* "sighing" at all, while the "creepiness" of the road is just something the poet has decided to project onto the landscape from himself. That's why we don't *believe* the "I-narrator" when he says he hears "tiny horns"! And what about "enchanted leprechauns"? Does that mean they've *been* enchanted by someone else, or that they're enchant*ing*, or are all leprechauns enchanted, i.e. magic, i.e. not-real? The poet gives himself away. This is an evasive poem, a self-indulgent one. "Off down the road" indeed! Road to nowhere!'

So the critical indictment might run, and it is hard to counter. Readers of *The Lord of the Rings* will have noted further the as yet undiscriminating use of 'fairy', 'gnome' and later 'goblin', not to mention the quite cross-cultural use of 'leprechauns' and the insistence (later to be most strongly abjured) on the little, the tiny, the insect-like. Still, there are hints of hope in the poem after all, and better questions to be asked than those which have been.

What is this 'road', for instance, the 'slender band of grey', the 'crooked fairy lane'? It clearly is not a tarmac one; on another level it is to be a recurring Tolkienian image:

> The Road goes ever on and on
> Down from the door where it began . . .

And oddly, G. B. Smith — Tolkien's school and college friend, killed the following year in Flanders, to have his poems posthumously published with a foreword by Tolkien — had addressed himself to the same theme in a poem four pages earlier in the *Oxford Poetry* collection:

> This is the road the Romans made,
>   This track half lost in the green hills,
> Or fading in a forest glade
>   'Mid violets and daffodils.
>
> The years have fallen like dead leaves
>   Unwept, uncounted and unstayed
> (Such as the autumn tempest thieves)
>   Since first this road the Romans made.[4]

Now this theme of time is intensely Tolkienian (if one may be permitted to put it that way round). The last sight of Lórien in *The Fellowship of the Ring,* published thirty-nine years later, is of Galadriel singing *Ai! laurië lantar lassi súrinen!* 'Ah! like gold fall the leaves in the wind! And numberless as the wings of trees are the years . . .' (*LOTR*, p. 368, and see also Fangorn's song, p. 458). In this case the hope which G. B. Smith expressed in his final letter to Tolkien before death — 'May God bless you, my dear John Ronald, and may you say the things I have tried to say long after I am not there to say them' — appears against all probability to have been fulfilled (*Biography,*

p. 94). However, the clue to follow, for the moment, is 'the road the Romans made'.

It may seem perverse to seek to identify this road, but on the other hand it isn't very hard. There are only two Roman roads near Oxford, and the better preserved is the old highway from Bath to Towcester, still visible as a straight line across the map but dwindled along much of its Oxford stretch to a footpath. It is now called 'Akeman Street', like 'Wayland's Smithy' a name of some fascination for philologists. It implies for one thing an old and massive population change. No town in Roman Britain had a more simply descriptive name than Aquae Sulis, 'the waters of Sul', and so prominent were its mineral springs with the Roman spa around them that even the Anglo-Saxons began to call it *æt baðum,* 'at the baths', and later Bath. One of them wrote a poem about the site, now called *The Ruin.* However, they also called the town *Acemannesceaster,* 'Akeman's chester' or 'Akeman's (fortified) town'. That is why the Bath-Towcester road acquired the name 'Akeman Street'; the people who called it that knew it went to Bath, but had forgotten that Bath was ever Aquae Sulis; they were invaders, of a lower cultural level than the Romans, and soon they ceased to use the road for anything like the traffic it had once carried. Its name and its decline in status from highway to footpath bear witness to the oblivion that can fall on a civilisation. But what was the reaction of these invaders to the historical monuments they could hardly help seeing in their new land — the stone roads, the villas, the great ruins which they (as in *The Ruin*) called vaguely the *eald enta geweorc,* 'the old work of giants'? Place-names again give suggestive clues.

About nine miles north-west of Oxford and half a mile from Akeman Street across the river Evenlode stands a villa, excavated in 1865 and once the property of some Romano-British noble. It is distinguished by the remains of a fourth-century tessellated pavement in different colours. The village nearby is called Fawler. To most people, including its inhabitants, this name now means nothing. But once it was *Fauflor,* a spelling recorded in 1205, and before that, in Old English, *fág flór,* 'the coloured floor, the painted floor'. There can be little doubt that the village was called after the pavement; so the pavement was still visible when the invaders came. Why, then, did they not occupy the villa, but choose to live instead on an undeveloped site a few furlongs off? No one can tell, but perhaps they were afraid. A further twist in the story is that there is another *fág flór* in Anglo-Saxon record, in the great hall of *Beowulf*, haunted by Grendel the maneater:

> on fágne flór   féond treddode,
> éode yrremód;   him of éagum stód
> ligge gelicost   léoht unfæger.

'The fiend stepped on to the painted floor, angrily he paced; from his eyes there stood an ugly light, like fire.'

So wrote the poet, in one of his classic passages of 'Gothic' suggestion. Could *Beowulf* have been sung in Fawler? What would its inhabitants have thought? Tolkien knew *Beowulf*, of course, virtually by heart, and he knew what 'Fawler' meant, for he hailed the etymology with delight in his 1926 review of the *Introduction to the Survey of Place-Names;* such work, he pointed out, is fired by 'love of the land of England', by 'the allurement of the riddle of the past'; it leads to 'the recapturing of fitful and tantalising glimpses in the dark' (*YWES* 5, p. 64). He was interested in the names of roads, too, for he had argued the year before that 'Watling Street' was an old name for the Milky Way, 'an old mythological term that was first applied to the *eald enta geweorc* [i.e. the Roman road from Dover to Chester] after the English invasion' (*YWES* 4, p. 21). Nor did he forget Bath and *The Ruin*. Legolas's 'lament of the stones' on page 276 of *The Fellowship of the Ring* is an adaptation of part of the poem. At some stage of his life Tolkien must certainly have noted all the strange implications and suggestions of 'Akeman Street'.

Did he know them in 1915, and share them with his friend G. B. Smith? Is the quest for Fairyland in 'Goblin Feet' a kind of translation of the quest for the romantic realities of history? Probably the answer to both questions is 'No'. However, disentangling fact from inference as carefully as possible, one can say first that Tolkien and Smith evidently shared a feeling for the ancient roads, the 'old straight tracks' and 'crooked lanes' of

England; second, that Smith even in 1915 appreciated the sadness of the relationship between what these are and what they were; third, that before many years were out it would be certain that Tolkien appreciated the same thing much more fully, with a wealth of reference to history and poetry and present-day reality. Even in 1915, one might say, a road, a real road, could possess a 'creepiness' for him which was based on some factual knowledge, not entirely self-generated. Philology would reinforce this. But already one image in his poem drew on some historical force.

Further, Tolkien was already thinking of words as 'stalactites'. 'Flittermice' in line 3 is not normal English. According to the *OED* it was introduced in the sixteenth century by analogy with German *Fledermaus,* for 'bat'. However, 'bat' is not recorded in Old English, and it is possible that some ancestor of 'flittermouse', e.g. **fleðer-mús,* was natural to English all along, but never got written down. There is an apparently similar puzzle over 'rabbit' (for which see pp. 67–68 below), which Tolkien at least signals awareness of in the second stanza by using the odd term 'coney-rabbits'. Finally 'honey-flies' in line 30 is elsewhere unrecorded. From context one would think he meant 'butterflies'. Perhaps he was aware, though, of the unexpected scatalogical sense of that innocent-looking word in Old English — a language which has had many rudenesses pruned by educated usage. He could have found out by looking up 'butterfly' in the *OED,* and at least it had occurred to him to wonder why butterflies were always and for no apparent reason so called. These verbal creations admittedly do not add much to the overall effect of 'Goblin Feet', but they exemplify an attempt to combine philological insight with poetry. Both roads and words hint at the early complexity of Tolkien's inner life, its unusual combination of emotion with inquiry.

Survivals in the West

Such hints, of course, fizzle out immediately. *The Silmarillion* had begun its sixty-year gestation by 1914,[5] but in 1915 Tolkien went off to the war in which G. B. Smith was to die. On demobilisation he was preoccupied with the problem of earning a living, first in Oxford with the *OED,* then in the English

Department at Leeds University, finally, with secure status and no lure of further advancement, back in Oxford again in 1925. He published nothing (bar the note to Smith's posthumous collection of poems) for five years after 'Goblin Feet', and a good deal of his subsequent work was written for simple motives — money, or to keep his name in front of the people who counted, who made appointments 'with tenure'. Much of his inner life *did* find its way into the twenty or thirty poems contributed to various periodicals or collections between 1920 and 1937; Tolkien's habit of thriftily rewriting them and using them in *The Hobbit* or *The Lord of the Rings* or *The Adventures of Tom Bombadil* shows how important some of them were to him.[6] Still, it is fair to say that these remain by themselves thin, or uncertain. The brew that was to become his fiction needed a good deal of thickening yet; and this could only come from the interaction of poetry with philology.

From this point of view one of Tolkien's most revealing pre-*Hobbit* pieces is his almost unread comment on 'The Name "Nodens"' for the Society of Antiquaries in 1932.[7] This virtually repeats the story of 'Fawler'. In 1928 excavations on a site near Lydney in the west of England had revealed a temple devoted to some kind of mystery cult and still flourishing in the fourth century, i.e. well after the introduction of Christianity to England. The temple was eventually abandoned as a result of the barbarian and also non-Christian English, who, however, had their own cults. As with the villa at Fawler, the Lydney temple fell into disuse — but not completely into oblivion. The iron-mines not far away were remembered: and whether because of them or from a continuing superstitious respect for the site, it was given a new Anglo-Saxon name, persisting to modern times — Dwarf's Hill. The Society of Antiquaries made no comment on all this, but in the story and the place-name one can hear the echo of a hopeless resistance from the Darkest of Dark Ages, pagan to Christian, pagan to pagan, Welsh to English, all ending in forgetfulness with even the memory of the resisters blurred, till recovered by archaeology — and by philology. For Tolkien's job was to comment on the name 'Nodens' found in an inscription on the site, and he did it with immense thoroughness.

His conclusion was that the name meant 'snarer' or

'hunter', from an Indo-European root surviving in English only in the archaic phrase 'good neat's leather'. More interesting was his tracing of the descent of Nodens from god to Irish hero (*Núadu Argat-lam,* 'Silverhand'), then to Welsh hero (*Lludd Llaw Ereint,* also 'Silverhand'), finally to Shakespearean hero — King Lear. Even Cordelia, Tolkien noted, was derived from the semi-divine *Creiddylad,* of whom was told a version of the story of 'the Everlasting Battle', which interested Tolkien in other ways. Shakespeare can naturally have known nothing about 'Nodens', or about *Beowulf* (a poem in which some have seen the first dim stirrings of 'Hamlet the Dane'). That did not mean that the old stories were not in some way working through him, present even in his much-altered version. Like 'Akeman Street' and 'Wayland's Smithy', Tolkien might have concluded, even *King Lear* could bear witness to a sort of English, or British, continuity.

And one could say the same of Old King Cole. Tolkien never actually rewrote his saga in epic verse (though one can now see why he remarked casually of Milton ['Monsters', p. 254] that he 'might have done worse' than recount 'the story of Jack and the Beanstalk in noble verse' — it would have been a monster-poem, like the lost 'Rescue of Theodoric'). Still, he would certainly have recognised the 'merry old soul' as a figure similar in ultimate origin and final 'vulgarisation' to King Arthur or King Lear.[8] This interest in the descent of fables probably explains why Tolkien did try his hand at two 'Man in the Moon' poems, 'The Man in the Moon came down too soon' (which appeared first in 1923 and was collected in *The Adventures of Tom Bombadil* thirty-nine years after), and 'The Cat and the Fiddle: A Nursery Rhyme Undone and its Scandalous Secret Unlocked' (also out first in 1923 but to achieve far wider circulation as sung by Frodo in Book 1, chapter 9 of *The Fellowship of the Ring,* 'At the Sign of the Prancing Pony'). No one would call either of these serious poems. But what they do is to provide a narrative and semi-rational frame for the string of totally irrational non sequiturs which we now call 'nursery rhymes'. How could 'the cow jump over the moon'? Well, it might if the Moon were a kind of vehicle parked on the village green while its driver had a drink. How could the Man in the Moon have 'come by the south And burnt his mouth With eating cold plum porridge'? Well, it doesn't seem very likely, but perhaps it points to an ancient story of earthly disillusionment. If one assumes a long tradition of 'idle children' repeating 'thoughtless tales' in increasing confusion, one might think that poems like Tolkien's were the remote ancestors of the modern rhymes. They are 'asterisk-poems', reconstructed like the attributes of Nodens. They also contain, at least in their early versions, hints of mythological significance — the Man in the Moon who fails to drive his chariot while mortals panic and his white horses champ their silver bits and the Sun comes up to overtake him is not totally unlike the Greek myth of Phaethon, who drove the horses of the Sun too close to Earth and scorched it. Finally, the reason why Tolkien picked 'the Man in the Moon' for treatment rather than 'Old King Cole' or 'Little Bo-Peep' is, no doubt, that he knew of the existence of a similar 'Man in the Moon' poem, in Middle English and from a time and place in which he took particular interest.

This is the lyric from Harley Manuscript no. 2253, now known generally as 'The Man in the Moon'.[9] It is perhaps the best medieval English lyric surviving, and certainly one of the hardest, prompting many learned articles and interpretations. However, three points about it are clear, and all gave it especial charm for Tolkien. In the first place it is extremely bizarre; it is presented as a speech by an English villager *about* the Man in the Moon, asking why he doesn't come down or move. It also has a very sharp and professional eye for English landscape; the villager concludes that the Man in the Moon is so stiff because he has been caught stealing thorns and carrying them home to mend his hedges with (an old image of the Moon's markings is of a man with a lamp, a dog and a thornbush; see Starveling in *A Midsummer Night's Dream* V i). Finally, for all the poem's thick dialect and involvement with peasant life, it is full of self-confidence. 'Never mind if the hayward has caught you pinching thorns', calls the narrator to the Man in the Moon, 'we'll deal with that. We'll ask him home':

> 'Drynke to hym deorly of fol god bous,
> Ant oure dame douse shal sitten hym by.
> When that he is dronke ase a dreynt mous,
> Thenne we schule borewe the wed ate bayly.'

'We'll drink to him like friends in excellent booze,
and our sweet lady will sit right next to him.
When he's as drunk as a drowned mouse,
we'll go to the bailiff and redeem your pledge.'

And without this evidence, clearly, the indictment will be quashed! It all sounds a most plausible way to work, and one which casts an unexpected light on the downtrodden serfs of medieval England — not as downtrodden as all that, obviously. Their good-natured resourcefulness seems to be an element in the make-up of Tolkien's hobbits. More significantly, the poem makes one wonder about the unofficial elements of early literary culture. Were there other 'Man in the Moon' poems? Was there a whole genre of sophisticated play on folk-belief? There *could* have been. Tolkien's 1923 poems attempt to revive it, or invent it, fitting into the gaps between modern doggerel and medieval lyric, creating something that might have existed and would, if it had, account for the jumble and litter of later periods — very like Gothic and 'i-mutation'.

One sees that the thing which attracted Tolkien most was darkness: the blank spaces, much bigger than most people realise, on the literary and historical map, especially those after the Romans left in A.D. 419, or after Harold died at Hastings in 1066. The post-Roman era produced 'King Arthur', to whose cycle King Lear and King Cole and the rest became eventual tributaries. Tolkien knew this tradition well and used it for *Farmer Giles of Ham* (published 1949, but written much earlier), the opening paragraphs of which play jokingly with the first few lines of *Sir Gawain*. However, he also knew that whatever the author of *Sir Gawain* thought, the Arthurian tradition was originally non-English, indeed dedicated to the overthrow of England; its commemoration in English verse was merely a final consequence of the stamping-out of native culture after Hastings, a literary 'defoliation' which had also led to the meaninglessness of English names like 'Fawler' and the near-total loss of all Old English heroic tradition, apart from *Beowulf*. What, then, had happened to England and the English during those 'Norman centuries' when, it might be said, 'language' and 'literature' had first and lastingly separated?

Tolkien had been interested in that question for some time.

Not much was known about Early Middle English, and indeed several of its major texts remain without satisfactory editions today. However, one important work was evidently the *Ancrene Wisse,* a 'guide for anchoresses (or female hermits)', existing in several manuscripts from different times and places, but one of few Middle English works to be translated into French rather than out of it. With this were associated several other texts with a 'feminist' bias, the tract on virginity *Hali Meiðhad,* the saints' lives *Seinte Juliene, Seinte Marherete, Seinte Katherine,* the little allegory *Sawles Warde.* All looked similar in dialect, and in sophistication of phrase; on the other hand their subject-matter meant they were unlikely ever to take the 'literature' side by storm. What *could* be said about them?

Tolkien began with a review of F. J. Furnivall's edition of *Hali Meiðhad,* in 1923; he went on to make 'Some Contributions to Middle English Lexicography' in *Review of English Studies* (1925), most of them drawn from *Ancrene Wisse,* and some of them incidentally interesting, like the remark that *medi wið wicchen* must mean not 'meddle with witches' but 'bribe, purchase the service of witches', apparently a known practice to the author of the 'Rule'. In 'The Devil's Coach-Horses' in the same periodical that year he spent enormous effort on the single word *eaueres* from *Hali Meiðhad,* arguing that it did not mean 'boars' as the *OED* had said, but 'heavy horses, draft horses'. Philologically this was interesting as showing a Germanic root **abra-z,* meaning 'work' and connected with Latin *opus.* Mythologically it was interesting too, as showing an image of the devil galloping away not on fire-breathing steeds, but on 'heavy old dobbins' — a contemptuous barnyard image of evil. All very well, but still, some would have said, distinctly peripheral.

The breakthrough came with Tolkien's article for *Essays and Studies* (1929), *'Ancrene Wisse and Hali Meiðhad',* the most perfect though not the best known of his academic pieces. This rested in classic philological style on an observation of the utmost tininess. In Old English a distinction was regularly made between verbs like *hé híereð, híe híerað,* 'he hears, they hear', and *hé lócað, híe lóciað,* 'he looks, they look'. An *-að* ending could be singular or plural, depending on what sort of a verb it was attached to. This clear but to outsiders utterly unmemorable distinction was, after Hastings, rapidly dropped. Two manuscripts, however, one of *Ancrene Wisse*, the other of its five associated texts, not only preserved the distinction but went on to make another new one, between verbs within the *lócian* class: they distinguished e.g. between *ha þolieð*, 'they endure', O.E. *híe þoliað*, and *ha fondið*, 'they inquire', O.E. *híe fondiað*. The distinction had a sound phonological basis and was not the result of mere whim. Furthermore the two manuscripts could not have been by the same man, for they were in different handwriting. Evidently — I summarise the chain of logic — they were the product of a 'school'; so were the works themselves, composed in the same dialect by another man or men; and this 'school' was one that operated in English, and in an English descended without interruption from Old English, owing words certainly to the Norse and the French but not affected by the confusion their invasions had caused. To put it Tolkien's way:

> There is an English older than Dan Michel's and richer, as regular in spelling as Orm's [these are two other relatively consistent writers of Middle English] but less queer; one that has preserved something of its former cultivation. It is not a language long relegated to the 'uplands' struggling once more for expression in apologetic emulation of its betters or out of compassion for the lewd, but rather one that has never fallen back into 'lewdness', and has contrived in troublous times to maintain the air of a gentleman, if a country gentleman. It has traditions and some acquaintance with the pen, but it is also in close touch with a good living speech — a soil somewhere in England. (*'AW'*, p. 106)

It is in short a language which had defied conquest and the Conqueror.

There are several signs here of Tolkien's underlying preoccupations. One is the power of philology: the regularity and rigour of its observations can resurrect from the dead a society long since vanished of which no other trace remains than the nature of dialect forms in a few old manuscripts. These observations are incontestable. They are also suggestive, permitting us to make informed guesses at, say, the level of independence of western shires in the twelfth century and the nature of their race-relations. They pleased Tolkien further because their implication was so clearly patriotic, that there had been an England beyond England even in the days when anyone who was anyone spoke French. In that way they also corroborated the impression of self-confidence made by the 'Man in the Moon' poem, itself an example of what Tolkien in that article (p. 116) called 'the westerly lyric, whose little world lay between Wirral and the Wye'. As for the *Ancrene Wisse* itself, Tolkien had little doubt that the 'soil somewhere in England' to which it should be ascribed was Herefordshire, a decision confirmed by later research. All in all, the picture these inquiries gave was of a far-West shire, cut off from and undisturbed by foreigners, adhering to the English traditions elsewhere in ruins. If only such a civilisation had endured to be the ancestor of ours! Tolkien, with his family connections in and nostalgic memories of Worcestershire, the next most western county to Hereford and like it a storehouse of Old English tradition, felt the pull of this 'might have been' strongly and personally. In a revealing passage at the end of the article (p. 122), he noted a few exceptions to his general rule and remarked:

> Personally I have no doubt that if we could call the scribes of A and B before us and silently point to these forms, they would thank us, pick up a pen, and immediately substitute the *-in* forms, as certainly as one of the present day would emend a minor aberration from spelling or accidence, if it was pointed to.

The ghosts would be gentlemen, scholars, Englishmen too. Tolkien felt at home with them.

This sentiment may have been misguided: if we really *had* the 'lays' on which *Beowulf* was based, we might not think much of them, and if we had to deal with the scribes of *Ancrene Wisse,* we might find them difficult people. There is a streak of wishful thinking in Tolkien's remark near the end of this article that if his argument was sound, English in the west at that time must have been 'at once more alive, and more traditional and organized as a written form, than anywhere else'. He was used to having 'traditional' literature viewed as dead: it was nice to think of a time when tradition was rated higher than modern fashion. Still, it is hard to say his sentiment was wrong.

It was based on rational argument, and the whole theory integrated (as theories should) many thousands of separate facts which had been needing explanation already. With hindsight one can see that this philological vision of ancient Herefordshire was a strong component of Tolkien's later conception of the hobbits' 'Shire', also cut-off, dimly remembering former empires, but effectively turned in on itself to preserve an idealised 'English' way of life. But 'the Shire' is fiction, and philology fact. The questions which begin to show themselves in Tolkien's work from about this time on are: how far did he distinguish the two states? And how much of his later success was caused by reluctance to admit a distinction?

Connections are exemplified in Tolkien's article '*Sigelwara land*', published in two parts in *Medium Aevum* 1932 and 1934. Typically this considers a single Old English word, *Sigelware,* and typically corrects that briskly to *Sigelhearwan*. What were these? Literate Anglo-Saxons used the word to translate *Æthiops,* 'Ethiopian', but, Tolkien argued, the word must have been older than English knowledge of Latin, let alone Ethiopians, and must have had some other and earlier referent. Pursuing *sigel* and *hearwa* separately through many examples and analogues, he emerged with two thoughts and an image: (1) that *sigel* meant originally both 'sun' and 'jewel', (2) that *hearwa* was related to Latin *carbo,* 'soot', (3) that when an Anglo-Saxon of the pre-literate Dark Age said *sigelhearwan,* what he had in mind was 'rather the sons of Múspell [the Norse fire-giant] than of Ham, the ancestors of the Silhearwan with red-hot eyes that emitted sparks, with faces black as soot'. What was the point of the speculation, admittedly 'guess-work', admittedly 'inconclusive'? It offers some glimpses of a lost mythology, suggested Tolkien with academic caution, something 'which has coloured the verse-treatment of Scripture and determined the diction of poems'.[10] A good deal less boringly, one might say, it had helped to naturalise the 'Balrog' in the traditions of the North, and it had helped to create (or corroborate) the image of the *silmaril,* that fusion of 'sun' and 'jewel' in physical form. Tolkien was already thinking along these lines. His scholarly rigour was not put on, but it was no longer only being directed to academic, uncreative ends.

Allegories, Potatoes, Fantasy and Glamour

One may now see in rather a different light the four minor prose works written by Tolkien in the late 1930s and early 1940s, those years in which *The Hobbit* came to term and *The Lord of the Rings* began to get under way — the years, one may say, when Tolkien turned away from pursuing his trade and began instead to use it. He knew he was doing this, as one can see from the little allegory 'Leaf by Niggle' (published 1945, but written c. 1943). Since Tolkien said in later years that he 'cordially disliked' allegory, it is perhaps worth repeating that 'Leaf by Niggle' quite certainly *is* one.[11] The story's first words are, 'There was once a little man called Niggle, who had a long journey to make', and to any Anglo-Saxonist this is bound to recall the Old Northumbrian poem known as *Bede's Death-Song*, memorable (a) for being in Old Northumbrian, (b) for being so clearly the true, last words of the Venerable Bede, England's greatest churchman, all of whose other works are in Latin. This goes: 'Before that compelled journey *(néidfáerae)* no man is wiser than he needs to be, in considering, before his departure, what will be judged to his soul after his deathday, good or evil.' Obviously someone should have said this to Niggle! But the lines also give a good and ancient reason for carrying out the basic operation of allegory, which is to start making equations.

Thus journey = death. Niggle the painter further = Tolkien the writer. One can see as much from the accusation of being 'just idle', softened later to being 'the sort of painter who can paint leaves better than trees', or to being unable to organise his time; Tolkien was sensitive to accusations of laziness, but it is clear enough that he was a perfectionist, and also easily distracted.[12] Niggle's 'leaf' = *The Hobbit,* his 'Tree' = *The Lord of the Rings,* the 'country' that opens from it = Middle-earth, and the 'other pictures . . . tacked on to the edges of his great picture' = the poems and other works which Tolkien kept on fitting into his own greater one.[13] Meanwhile the garden which Niggle does not keep up looks ominously like Tolkien's professorial duties; the visitors who hinted 'that he might get a visit from an Inspector' remind one of that discourteous colleague of Tolkien's, who even *after The Lord of the Rings* came out snapped ungraciously, 'He ought to have been teaching!'[14] One can go on making these equations, and one is *supposed* to; the essence of an allegory, Tolkien thought, was that it should be 'just', i.e. that all the bits should fit exactly together, compelling assent (and amusement) by their minuteness. If one realises that, there is a certain bite in the place where Niggle does his painting. He keeps his great canvas 'in the tall shed that had been built for it out in his garden (on a plot where once he had grown potatoes)'. Niggle sacrificed potatoes to paint. What did Tolkien sacrifice to *The Lord of the Rings*? The real answer is, articles like those on *Ancrene Wisse* and the *Sigelware;* after 1940 (when he was only forty-eight) Tolkien wrote only five more, and two of these were collaborations and two others not entirely academic in style. Still, Tolkien never went over to despising the advancement of learning. It is Niggle's expressed gratitude for Parish's 'excellent potatoes' which persuades the First Voice to let him out of the Workhouse (= Purgatory). One could say that the whole tale expresses both Tolkien's self-accusation and self-justification, and that its solution in Heaven lies in Niggle and Parish, the creative and the practical aspects of Tolkien himself, learning to work together — though what they work on, you notice, is very definitely Niggle's Tree and Country, not Parish's potatoes at all.

Tolkien was giving up the academic *cursus honorum* in the late 1930s, and he knew it. How did he justify this to himself, and how far could he reconcile the claims of 'potatoes' and 'Trees' (= scholarship and fantasy)? These questions underlie, often unsuspectedly, the three critical works roughly contemporary with 'Leaf by Niggle', i.e. *'Beowulf:* the Monsters and the Critics' (published 1936), 'On Fairy-Stories' (first version 1939), and the 'Preface' to C. L. Wrenn's revision of the Clark Hall translation of *Beowulf* (1940). None of these contains very much philology in the narrow sense of sound-changes or verb-paradigms, and they have accordingly been fallen on gratefully by commentators who never wanted to learn any. However, philology still remains their essential guts; while they lead forward to fantasy, they also look back to and rest always on an intensely rigorous study of 'the word'.

So, to take the last piece first, the 'Clark Hall' introduction has only one main point to make, and that is that words mean more than their dictionary entries. What happens if you look up *Sigelware* in the standard Old English dictionary of J. Bosworth and T. N. Toller? It says 'the Ethiopians', and that's all. What of *éacen,* a word in *Beowulf*? The dictionary says 'increased, great, vast, powerful'. To 'the enquirer into ancient beliefs', wrote Tolkien, only the first was right, for *éacen* meant not 'large' but 'enlarged' and denoted a supernatural addition of power. As for runes, Bosworth-Toller translated the Beowulfian phrase *onband beadurúne* (meaninglessly) as 'unbound the war-secret', while Clark Hall tried 'gave vent to secret thoughts of strife'. 'It means "unbound a battle rune"', declared Tolkien. 'What exactly is implied is not clear. The expression has an antique air, as if it had descended from an older time to our poet: a suggestion lingers of the spells by which men of wizardry could stir up storms in a clear sky' (pp. xiii–xiv). Fanciful, the shades of Bosworth and Toller might have said. If the facts point to fantasy, Tolkien could have retorted, fantasy is what we must have! The 'Preface' is in a wider sense a protest against translating *Beowulf* only into polite modern English, a plea for listening to the vision contained, not in plots, but in words — words like *flæsc-homa, bán-hús, hreðerloca, ellor-síð* ('flesh-raiment', 'bone-house', 'heart-prison', 'elsewhere-journey'). The poet who used these words, Tolkien wrote, did not see the world like us, but:

saw in his thought the brave men of old walking under the vault of heaven upon the island earth *(middangeard)* beleaguered by the Shoreless *Seas (gársecg)* and the outer darkness, enduring with stern courage the brief days of life *(læne líf),* until the hour of fate *(metodsceaft),* when all things should perish, *léoht ond líf samod* [light and life together]. (p. xxvii)

He 'did not say all this fully or explicitly'. Nevertheless, the insistence ran, *it was there.* You didn't need a mythological handbook of Old English if you paid attention to the words; like place-names or Roman roads or Gothic vowels, they carried quite enough information all by themselves.

The same insistence on 'the reality of language' permeates the British Academy lecture of 1936. There, however, it is further intertwined with beliefs about 'the reality of history' — rather curious beliefs which Tolkien does not seem to have wanted to express directly. The general flow of the lecture is in fact extremely sinuous, causing great trouble to the many later Beowulfians who have tried to paraphrase it; it abounds in asides, in hilarious images like the Babel of conflicting critics and the 'jabberwocks of historical and antiquarian research', in wildernesses of dragons and shrewdnesses of apes. However a vital point about it, never directly stated or defended, is Tolkien's conviction that he knew exactly when and under what circumstances the poem was written. *'At a given point'*, he says (his italics, p. 262), there was a fusion, reflected in the poem; at this 'precise point' (p. 269) an imagination was kindled. Since there is no unquestioned evidence at all for the date and place when *Beowulf* was composed (it could be anywhere from Tyne to Severn, from A.D. 650 to 1000), one wonders what Tolkien meant. But the nearest he approaches to an answer is via allegory once more, in his little story of the man and the tower, on pp. 248–49.

This runs as follows:

A man inherited a field in which was an accumulation of old stone, part of an older hall. Of the old stone some had already been used in building the house in which he actually lived, not far from the old house of his fathers. Of the rest he took some and built a tower. But his friends coming perceived at once (without troubling to climb the steps) that these stones had formerly belonged to a more ancient building. So they pushed the tower over, with no little labour, in order to look for hidden carvings . . . They all said 'This tower is most interesting.' But they also said (after pushing it over): 'What a muddle it is in!' And even the man's own descendants, who might have been expected to consider what he had been about, were heard to murmur: 'He is such an odd fellow! Imagine using these old stones just to build a nonsensical tower! Why did not he restore the old hall? He had no sense of proportion.' But from the top of that tower the man had been able to look out upon the sea.

Now, as with 'Leaf by Niggle', everything in this story can be 'equated'. 'The man' = the *Beowulf*-poet. The 'friends' looking for hidden carvings = the *Beowulf*-scholars trying to reconstruct history. The 'tower' with its view on the sea = *Beowulf* itself, with its non-scholarly impulse towards pure poetry. More difficult are 'the accumulation of old stone', the 'older hall' (also 'the old house of his fathers'), and 'the house in which he actually lived'. From this one can deduce that Tolkien thought that there had been older poems than *Beowulf,* pagan ones, in the time of the Christian past already abandoned; they are the 'older hall'. However, debris from them remained available, poetic formulas and indeed stray pagan concepts like the *Sigelware;* that is the 'accumulation of old stone'. Indeed, some of this was used for Biblical poems like *Exodus,* in which the *Sigelware* figure, part of the new civilisation of Christian Northumbria (or Mercia), the new civilization being 'the house' in which the man 'actually lived'. Rejected bits were nevertheless used by the poet to build his poem or 'tower'; and *they* are preeminently the monsters, the dragon, the *eotenas* and *ylfe,* 'elves' and 'giants', words once common but used either not at all or very rarely in the rest of Old English literature.

The gist of this is that no one, friends or descendants or maybe even contemporaries, had understood *Beowulf* except Tolkien. The work had always been something personal, even freakish, and it took someone with the same instincts to explain it. Sympathy furthermore depended on being a descendant, on living in the same country and beneath the same sky, on speaking the same language — being 'native to that tongue and land'. This is not the terminology of strict scholarship, though that does not prove the opinion wrong. What it does prove is that Tolkien felt more than continuity with the *Beowulf*-poet, he felt a virtual identity of motive and of technique.[†] Nowhere

---

[†] The tower looking out over the sea, for instance, is a strong and private image of Tolkien's own for what he desired in literature. The 1920 poem 'The Happy Mariners' begins 'I know a window in a western tower / That opens on celestial seas . . .' In *The Lord of the Rings* (p. 7) the hobbits believe that you can see the sea from the top of the tallest elvish tower on the Tower Hills; but none of them has ever tried to climb it.

was the identity stronger than over 'the monsters and the critics', the latter deeply antipathetic to both of them as Tolkien thought he had proved—the former deeply interesting. But what did the dragon, for instance, mean to the *Beowulf*-poet? For him, Tolkien argued, dragons might have been very close to the edge of reality; certainly the poet's pagan ancestors could have thought of dragons as things they might one day have to face. Equally certainly dragons had to the poet not yet become allegorical, as they would to his descendants — the dragon as Leviathan, the devil, 'that old serpent underground', etc. Yet even to the poet a dragon could not be mere matter-of-fact. He was indeed phenomenally lucky in his freedom to balance exactly between 'dragon-as-simple-beast' and 'dragon-as-just-allegory', between pagan and Christian worlds, on a pinpoint of literary artifice and mythic suggestion. One sees why Tolkien insisted on a 'precise' kindling point of imagination, a 'given point' of 'fusion', a 'pregnant moment of poise'. Knowing exactly when the poem was written was part of knowing its exact literary mode, and that literary mode was the one he himself wanted! But the circumstances of the modern literary world made things much harder for him than for his mighty predecessor and kindred spirit.

'A dragon is no idle fancy', wrote Tolkien. 'Whatever may be his origins, in fact or invention, the dragon in legend is a potent creation of men's imagination, richer in significance than his barrow is in gold. Even to-day (despite the critics) you may find men . . . who have yet been caught by the fascination of the worm' (pp. 257–58). This last sentence is true mainly of Tolkien, whose 1923 poem 'Iumonna Gold Galdre Bewunden' is about a dragon-hoard and self-evidently *Beowulf*-derived.[15] The one before is no doubt true as regards 'significance', but smacks of special pleading; Tolkien didn't want dragons to be symbolic, he wanted them to have a claw still planted on *fact* (as well as 'invention'). What did he mean by 'no idle fancy'? The truth of it is, I think, that Tolkien was very used to scrutinising old texts and drawing from them surprising but rational conclusions about history and language and ancient belief. In the process he developed very strongly a sort of tracker-dog instinct for validity, one which enabled him to say that such and such a word, like *éacen* or *beadurún* or **hearwa* or *éored,* was true, even if unrecorded, meaning by 'true' a genuine fragment of older civilisation consistent with the others. All his instincts told him that dragons were like that — widespread in Northern legend, found in related languages from Italy to Iceland, deeply embedded in ancient story.[16] Could this mean nothing? He was bound to answer 'No', and hardly deterred by the thought that 'intelligent living people' would disagree with him. After all, what did they know about butterflies, let alone dragons! Still, though dragons, and balrogs, and Shires, and silmarils were all taking shape in his mind as fiction, and were all simultaneously related to philological fact, he had not at this stage evolved a theory to connect the two. Possibly he never quite managed to make the link.

He had a determined try in 'On Fairy-Stories' three years later. However, this is Tolkien's least successful, if most discussed, piece of argumentative prose. The main reason for its comparative failure, almost certainly, is its lack of a philological core or kernel; Tolkien was talking to, later writing for, an unspecialised audience, and there is some sign that he tried to talk down to them. Repeatedly he plays the trick of pretending that fairies are real — they tell 'human stories' instead of 'fairy stories', they put on plays for men 'according to abundant records', and so on. This comes perilously close to whimsy, the pretence that something not true *is* true to create an air of comic innocence. However, beneath this, and beneath the very strong sense that Tolkien is 'counterpunching' to a whole string of modern theories which he did not like (fairies were small, only children liked fairies, Thórr was a nature-myth, etc., etc.), it is just about possible to make out the bones of an argument, or rather of a conviction.

The conviction is that fantasy is not entirely made up. Tolkien was not prepared to say this in so many words to other people, to sceptics, maybe not to himself. That is why he continually equivocated with words like 'invention' and 'no idle fancy', and also why a good deal of 'On Fairy-Stories' is a plea for the power of literary art; this is dignified with the form 'Sub-Creation', and to it are ascribed the continuing power of *Grimms' Fairy-Tales,* the (partial) success of *Macbeth,* the very existence of 'fantasy' as an art-form — views Tolkien also expressed through yet another neologism, the word and poem

'Mythopoeia', eventually to be published in later editions of the collection *Tree and Leaf* (Boston: Houghton Mifflin, 1989). Bobbing continually above the surface of these rational and literary opinions, however, are other, more puzzling statements. By 'fantasy', Tolkien declared (with a long haggle over the inadequacies of the *OED* and S. T. Coleridge), he meant first 'the Sub-creative Art in itself', but second 'a quality of strangeness and wonder in the Expression, derived from the Image'. The last phrase is the critical one, for it implies that the 'Image' was there before anyone derived any expression from it at all. The same implication lurks in Tolkien's autobiographical statement, *à propos* of dragons, that 'Fantasy, the making or glimpsing of Otherworlds, was the heart of the desire of Faërie'. Making up dragons is Art; 'glimpsing' them and the worlds they come from is not. Tolkien would not let 'fantasy' mean either the one (rational) or the other (mystic) activity, but kept hinting it was both. He does so particularly, through the whole of the essay, with the idea of 'elves': these, he insists, may be (1) 'creations of Man's mind', which is what nearly everybody thinks, or (2) true, i.e. they 'really exist independently of our tales about them'. But (3) the essence of their activity even as 'creations of Man's mind' is that they are also creators, supreme illusionists, capable of luring mortals away, by their beauty, to the 'elf-hills' from which they will dazedly emerge centuries later, unaware of the passage of time. They form an image, a true image, of the 'elvish craft' of fantasy itself; stories about them are man-made fantasies about independent fantasts.

There is a strong sense of circularity in all these statements, as if Tolkien were hovering around some central point on which he dared not or could not land, and it is easy to dismiss that central point as mere personal delusion. We are back, indeed, with 'creepiness', that quality that 'Goblin Feet', in one view, thrusts subjectively on to something in reality perfectly ordinary; but which, in another view, stems from something still perfectly real and rational but which Tolkien was much better at detecting than most others. It seems to me that this 'real centre' was philological, and that Tolkien could not express it in ordinary literary terms. He came closest to it, in

'On Fairy-Stories', when he brushed past the edges of single words, especially *spell* and *evangelium*. These two words are related historically, for the Old English translation of Greek *evangelion,* 'good news', was *gód spell,* 'the good story', now 'Gospel'. *Spell* continued to mean, however, 'a story, something said in formal style', eventually 'a formula of power', a magic spell. The word embodies much of what Tolkien meant by 'fantasy', i.e. something unnaturally powerful (magic spell), something literary (a story), something in essence true (Gospel). At the very end of his essay he asserts that the Gospels have the 'supremely convincing tone' of Primary Art, of truth — a quality he would also like to assert, but could never hope to prove, of elves and dragons.

There is a better word, though, buried in Tolkien's remarks, which I can only conclude he decided not to discuss as being too complicated for a non-philological piece; he would have done better to focus on it. This is 'glamour'. Actually Tolkien may also have been too revolted by the semantic poisonings of modernity to want to discuss the word, for now in common parlance it means overwhelmingly the aura of female sexual attraction, or to be more exact female sexual attraction *at a distance* — a showbiz word, an advertiser's word, false and meretricious, taking a part in such nasty compounds as 'glamour-girl', 'glamour-puss', and even 'glamour-pants'. The 1972 Supplement to the *OED* concedes the point and adds the coinages 'glamourize', 'glammed-up', and even 'glam' (a word Tolkien would have especially hated as showing that the old word used in dialect and in *Sir Gawain* for 'mirth, merriment', *glam, glaum,* was so dead as to be no competitor). The main G volume, published in 1897, however, tells a story not much happier. 'Glamour', it alleges, is a made-up word, 'introduced into the literary language by Sir Walter Scott'. What it means is 'magic, enchantment, spell; esp. in the phrase *to cast the glamour over one*'; from this sense has evolved the idea of 'a magical or fictitious beauty . . . a delusive or alluring charm', and so, pretty obviously, the cardboard senses of today. Tolkien would have been more interested in the quotation cited from Scott, which says, 'This species of witchcraft is well known in Scotland as the glamour, or *deceptio visus,* and was supposed to be a special attribute of the race of Gipsies'. What he knew, and what the *OED* didn't, was that exactly this phenomenon was at the centre of Snorri Sturluson's *Prose Edda,* which begins with the *Gylfaginning* or 'Delusion of Gilfi', and includes within that the highly prominent and amusing tale of the delusion of Thórr by *sjónhverfing* = 'aversion of the sight' = *deceptio visus* = 'glamour'. 'Glamour' was then well exemplified in Norse tradition and never mind the gypsies.

Further, the word was evidently by origin a corruption of 'grammar', and paralleled in sense by 'gramarye' = 'occult learning, magic, necromancy', says the *OED,* 'revived in literary use by Scott'. Cambridge University had indeed preserved for centuries the office of 'Master of Glomerye', whose job it was to teach the younger undergraduates Latin. Tolkien must have been amused at the thought of a University official combining instruction in language — his own job — with classes in magic and spell-binding — his own desire. He wrote of the parson in *Farmer Giles of Ham* (a figure underrated by critics, but having some of the good as well as the bad points of the professional philologist), 'he was a grammarian, and could doubtless see further into the future than most'. But once again Tolkien knew more than the *OED.* The first citation it gives under 'gramarye' in the 'magic' sense is from the ballad of *King Estmere,* 'My mother was a westerne woman, And learned in gramarye'. How right that a 'western' woman should know grammar, like the sages of Herefordshire! How pleasing if the study should turn out to have a few practical advantages. But besides, the vital facts about *King Estmere,* as Tolkien could have observed from a glance at the introduction to the poem in F. J. Child's famous collection of *English and Scottish Popular Ballads* (1882–1898), were that its closest analogues came from Faroese and Danish (which once again related 'glamour' to the ancient traditions of the North); and that the philologist Sophus Bugge had gone so far as to relate it to the Old Norse *Hervarar saga.* This is possibly the most romantically traditional of all the Norse 'sagas of old times'; it contains fragments with a claim to being the oldest heroic poetry of the North; and it was edited and translated in 1960 by Tolkien's son Christopher, under the title *The Saga of King Heidrek the Wise.*

þess galt hon gedda
fyrir Grafár ósi,
er Heiðrekr var veginn
undir Harvaða fjǫllum.

So writes the forgotten poet: 'The pike has paid / by the pools
of Grafá / for Heidrek's slaying / under Harvad-fells'. But,
Christopher Tolkien comments, 'the view is not challenged . . .
that *Harvaða* is the same name in origin as "Carpathians".
Since this name in its Germanic form is found nowhere else at
all, and must be a relic of extremely ancient tradition, one can
hardly conclude otherwise than that these few lines are a fragment of a lost poem . . . that preserved names at least going
back to poetry sung in the halls of Germanic peoples in central
or south-eastern Europe'. One could hardly have a more romantically suggestive comment, or a more rigorously philological one, for as Christopher Tolkien footnotes, 'The stem
karpat- was regularly transformed into *xarfaþ-* by the operation of the Germanic Consonant Shift (Grimm's Law)'.[17]
'Glamour', 'gramarye', grammar, philology — these were on
several levels much the same thing.

One can see now why Tolkien used the same word for
both the characteristic literary quality of *Beowulf,* a 'glamour
of Poesis' ('Monsters', p. 248), and for the characteristic but
maybe not literary quality of 'fairy-stories', the 'glamour of
Elfland' ('OFS', *Reader,* p. 35). He did not know quite what he
was detecting, but he was in no doubt that he felt something
consistent in many stories and poems which could not all be the
work of the same man. It might after all only be the result of
age and distance, the 'elvish hone of antiquity', or we might
think the distorting glass of philology; it might point to some
great lost truth in the areas of utter historical darkness of
which he was so conscious; it might be a memory, or a prophecy, of Paradise, as in 'Leaf by Niggle'; or, again as in 'Leaf by
Niggle', it might be mankind's one chance to create a vision of
Paradise which would be true in the future if never in the past.
Tolkien's theories on all this never coalesced. Still, we can say
that the quality he evidently valued more than anything in literature was that shimmer of suggestion which never quite be-

comes clear sight but always hints at something deeper further on, a quality shared by *Beowulf, Hervarar saga,* 'Fawler', 'The Man in the Moon', 'Wayland's Smithy', and so much else. This was 'glamour', the opposite, one may say, of 'shrewdness' — for as the one had climbed into favour, the other had been debased, in simultaneous proof of the superiority of ancient over modern world views. If Tolkien took 'glamour' too seriously, translating it into an entirely personal concept of fantasy, he had at any rate precedent and reason. As Jacob Grimm wrote (it is quoted under the definition of *philologie* in the *Deutsches Wörterbuch*):

> You can divide all philologists into these groups, those who study words only for the sake of the things, or those who study things only for the sake of the words.

Grimm had no doubt that the former class was superior, the latter falling away into pedantry and dictionaries. Of that former class Tolkien was the pre-eminent example.

CHAPTER 3

———

THE BOURGEOIS BURGLAR

The Word and the Thing: Elves and Dwarves

Sigelhearwan, Nodens, Fawler, fancy, glamour: stripped of its layers of scholarly guardedness, the essence of Tolkien's belief was that 'the word authenticates the thing'. This was a belief grounded on philology. Tolkien thought, indeed he knew, that he could distinguish many words and word-forms into two classes, one 'old-traditional-genuine', the other 'new-unhistorical-mistaken'. From this he went on to form the opinion, less certain but still highly plausible, that the first group was not only more correct but also more interesting than the second; it had compelled assent over the millennia; it had a definite 'inner consistency', whether or not that was the 'inner consistency of reality' or merely of Secondary Art.

These beliefs go a long way towards explaining Tolkien's sudden displays of scrupulosity. In 1954 he was 'infuriated' to find that the printers of the first edition of *The Lord of the Rings* had gone through it, with the best will in the world and in conformity with standard English practice, changing 'dwarves' to 'dwarfs', 'dwarvish' to 'dwarfish', 'elven' to 'elfin', and so on. Considering the hundreds of changes involved (and the cost of proof correction), many authors might have let the matter ride; but Tolkien had all the original forms restored (see *Biography,* p. 221). In 1961 Puffin Books did much the same thing to a reprint of *The Hobbit,* and Tolkien complained to his publishers (*Letters,* p. 236) at greater length. His point was that even in modern English many old words ending in *f* can still be told

55

from new ones by their plural forms: old words (or at least old words of one particular class in Old English) behave like 'hoof' or 'loaf' and become 'hooves', 'loaves', while new ones (unaffected by sound-changes in the Old English period) simply add *s,* as in 'proofs', 'tiffs', 'rebuffs'. Writing 'dwarfs' was then, to Tolkien's acute and trained sensibility, the equivalent of denying the word its age and its roots. Much the same reasoning had led Jacob Grimm, many years before, to leave the word *Elfen* out of his dictionary altogether, as an English import, replacing it with the native form *Elben* (which no one actually used anymore) — his argument is repeated almost verbatim in the advice to German translators in Tolkien's 'Guide to the Names in *The Lord of the Rings'*, p. 164. Even more than 'dwarfs', Tolkien disliked the word 'elfin', since this was a personal and pseudo-medieval coinage by Edmund Spenser — the poet hailed by the *OED*'s citations as the dawn of modern literature, and also the man whose first poem, *The Shepheardes Calendar* of 1579, was ornamented by the most offensive gloss that Tolkien probably ever encountered. In quick succession this declared that for all its age 'that rancke opinion of Elfes' [*sic*] should be rooted 'oute of mens hearts' as being a mistaken form of the Italian faction the 'Guelfes', and was in any case a Papistical notion spread by 'bald Friers and knauish shauelings'.[1] Tolkien would not have known whether to be offended most as philologist, as patriot, or as Roman Catholic! All round, the gloss no doubt confirmed him in the belief that modern and erroneous spellings went with stupid and self-opinionated people.

Belief was reinforced further by the history of the word 'fairy'. The *OED,* true to form, said that this was the word that should be used: 'In mod. literature, elf is a mere synonym of FAIRY, which has to a great extent superseded it even in dialects.' But whether this particular fact was true or not, Tolkien knew that much else of the *OED*'s information on such points was wrong. Its first citation for 'fairy' in its present sense is from John Gower, 1393, 'And as he were a fairie'; but as Tolkien remarked in 'On Fairy-Stories' (*Reader,* p. 37), what Gower really wrote was 'as he were of faierie', 'as if he had come from (the land of) Faërie'. Just above the *OED* cites the earlier poem of *Sir Orfeo* as evidence for the belief that 'the fairy' could be a collective noun, 'the fairy-folk': 'Awey with the fayré sche was ynome', i.e. presumably 'she was taken away by the fairy-people'. Tolkien made no overt remark on the matter, but his translation of *Sir Orfeo,* published in 1975, has the line correctly translated, 'By magic was she from them caught'. 'Fayré' in that context means 'glamour', the *deceptio visus* of the inhabitants of Fairyland. The gist of these observations for Tolkien must have been that 'fairy' in its modern sense was a newer word than the *OED* realised; that it was furthermore a foreign word derived from French *fée,* and had been throughout its history a source of delusion and error for English people, ending in the compound words 'fairy-tale' and 'fairy-story' which as Tolkien observed in 'On Fairy-Stories' were badly defined, uninformed and associated with literary works (like Drayton's *Nymphidia*) bereft of the slightest trace of sub-creation or any other respectable literary art.

Good writing began with right words. Tolkien accordingly schooled himself to drop forms like 'elfin', 'dwarfish', 'fairy',' gnome' and eventually 'goblin', though he had used all of them in early works up to and including *The Hobbit*.[2] More importantly, he began to work out their replacements, and to ponder what concepts lay behind the words and uses which he recognised as linguistically authentic. This activity of re-creation — creation from philology — lies at the heart of Tolkien's 'invention' (though maybe not of his 'inspiration'); it was an activity which he kept up throughout his life, and one which is relatively easy to trace, or to 'reconstruct'. Thus there can be little doubt what Tolkien thought of the 'elves' of English and Germanic tradition. He knew to begin with that Old English *œlf* was the ancestor of the modern word, was cognate with Old Norse *álfr,* Old High German *alp,* and for that matter, had it survived, Gothic **albs*. It was used in *Beowulf,* where the descendants of Cain include *eotenas ond ylfe ond orcnéas,* 'ettens and elves and demon-corpses', and in *Sir Gawain and the Green Knight,* where the seven-foot green giant with his monstrous axe is described nervously by bystanders as an *aluisch mon* or uncanny creature. The wide distribution of the word in space and time proves that belief in such creatures, whatever they were, was once both normal and immemorially old, going back to the times when the ancestors of Englishmen and Germans and Norwegians still spoke the same tongue. Yet what did the belief involve? Considering concept rather than word, Tolkien must soon have come to the conclusion that all linguistically authentic accounts of the elves, from whichever country they came, agreed on one thing: that the elves were in several ways paradoxical.

For one thing, people did not know where to place them between the polarities of good and evil. They were the descendants of Cain, the primal murderer, said the Beowulf-poet. They weren't as bad as *that*, imply the characters in *Sir Gawain*—actually the green giant plays fair and even lets Sir Gawain off—but they were certainly very frightening. It was wrong to offer sacrifice to them (*álfa-blót*), concurred all post-Christian Icelanders. On the other hand it might have seemed a good idea to propitiate them; if you didn't, Anglo-Saxons perhaps reminded each other, you might get *wæterælfádl*, the 'water-elf disease', maybe dropsy, or *ælfsogoða*, lunacy. There was a widespread belief in 'elf-shot', associated on the one hand with the flint arrows of prehistoric man and on the other with the metaphorical arrows of diabolic temptation. The consensus of these references is fear.

Simultaneous with that, though, is allure. *Ælfscýne* is an approbatory Anglo-Saxon adjective for a woman, 'elf-beautiful'. *Fríð sem álfkona,* said the Icelanders, 'fair as an elf-woman'. The standing and much-repeated story about the elves stresses their mesmeric charm. It may be 'True Thomas' on Huntly bank who sees 'the queen of fair Elfland', or a young woman who hears the elf-horn blowing, but either way the immediate reaction is of desire. True Thomas disregards all warnings to make off with the elf-queen, does not return to earth for seven years, and (in Walter Scott's version) leaves immediately again as soon as he is called. The medieval romance of *Sir Launfal* ends with the same glad desertion. For women to run off with elves was regarded with more suspicion. 'Lady Isabel' in the Scottish ballad saves her maidenhood and her life from the treacherous elf-knight she herself has summoned, and at the start of *The Wife of Bath's Tale* Chaucer makes a series of jokes about elves and friars, the burden of which is that the latter are sexually more rapacious than the former, though the former had a bad reputation with young women as well.

The allure and the danger are mixed. Indeed, a common variant of the 'young man / elf-queen' story ends with him in despair, not at having been seduced but at being deserted. It is the memory of former happiness, the 'disillusionment' of loss of 'glamour', which leaves Keats's character 'alone and palely loitering'.

Now one can see very easily how such an apparent discrepancy of fear and attraction might in sober reality arise. Beauty is itself dangerous: this is what Sam Gamgee tries to explain to Faramir in *The Two Towers,* when interrogated on the nature of Galadriel, the elf-queen herself. 'I don't know about *perilous*', says Sam (pp. 664–65), replying to Faramir's highly accurate remark that she must be 'perilously fair':

> 'It strikes me that folk takes their peril with them into Lórien, and finds it there because they've brought it. But perhaps you could call her perilous, because she's so strong in herself. You, you could dash yourself to pieces on her, like a ship on a rock; or drownd yourself, like a hobbit in a river. But neither rock nor river would be to blame.'

One could say the same of Sir Launfal's lady, or True Thomas's. One can also see how the rejected wives and fiancées, or husbands and fathers, of people under elvish allure would concoct a very different story! Before long they would have the *ylfe* in exactly the same category as Cain—or Moloch. But this would be a second-hand opinion, and a prejudiced one (like those of Boromir, or Éomer and the Riders; *LOTR,* p. 329 or p. 422).

It is in fact the strong point of Tolkien's 're-creations' that they take in all available evidence, trying to explain both good and bad sides of popular story; the sense of inquiry, prejudice, hearsay and conflicting opinion often gives the elves (and other races) depth. In Lothlórien we can see Tolkien exploiting, for instance, variant ideas about the elves and time. Most stories agreed that humans returning from Elf-land were temporally confused. Usually they thought time outside had speeded up: three nights in Elf-land might be three years outside, or a century. But sometimes they thought it had stood still. When the elf-maid sings in the Danish ballad of 'Elverhøj', or 'Elf-hill', time stops:

59

Striden strom den stiltes derved,
som førre var van at rinde;
de liden smaafiske, i floden svam,
de legte med deres finne.

'The swift stream then stood still, that before had been running; the little fish that swam in it played their fins in time.'[3]

Did the discrepancy disprove the stories? Tolkien thought it pointed rather to what C. S. Lewis called the 'unexpectedness' of reality,[4] and paused to explain the phenomenon in *The Fellowship of the Ring*, p. 379. There Sam thinks that their stay in Lothlórien, the 'elf-hill' itself, might have been three nights, but 'never a whole month. Anyone would think that time did not count in there!' Frodo agrees, but Legolas says that from an elvish viewpoint things are more complicated than that:

'For the Elves the world moves, and it moves both very swift and very slow. Swift, because they themselves change little, and all else fleets by: it is a grief to them. Slow, because they do not count the running years, not for themselves. The passing seasons are but ripples ever repeated in the long long stream.'

His remarks harmonise the motifs of 'The Night that Lasted a Year' and 'The Stream that Stood Still'. They are in a way redundant to the mere action, the plot of *The Lord of the Rings*. Yet they, and many other incidental turns, explanations, allusions,† help to keep up a sense of mixed strangeness and familiarity, of reason operating round a mysterious centre. This

---

† There are too many of these to fit into an argument: one might note, though, that the skill of Tolkien's elves in archery goes back to 'elf-shot'; that their association with the sea and their taking of Frodo is very like the passing of Arthur in (and only in) the account of Laȝamon, a twelfth-century Worcestershire poet whom Tolkien regarded as the last preserver of Old English tradition; that the gifts of Galadriel correspond to stories preserved in English and Scandinavian family traditions such as that of 'the Luck of Edenhall' or the one recorded in Sigrid Undset's novel *Kristin Lavransdatter*, part 2, ch. 6; that 'elvishness' is a quality recognized in men several times in *The Lord of the Rings*, but also ascribed to himself by the poet Geoffrey Chaucer. Tolkien makes no use, however, of the very common 'changeling' belief.

feeling Tolkien himself acquired from long pondering on literary and philological cruxes; it explains why he laid such stress on 'consistency' and 'tone'.

To cut matters short, one can remark that Tolkien went through much the same process with the 'dwarves'. This is also an old word, cf. Old English *dweorh,* Old Norse *dvergr,* Old High German *twerg,* Gothic **dvairgs,* etc. It seems to have cohabited with the word for 'elf' over long periods, causing a sequence of confusions over 'light-elves' (= elves), 'black-elves' (= ? dwarves) and 'dark-elves' (= ?), which Tolkien never forgot and eventually brought to prominence in the story of Eöl in *The Silmarillion.* More interesting is some slight sense in various sources that men dealt with dwarves in a way they could not with elves, on an equal basis marred often by hostility. The seven dwarves help Snow-White in the familiar fairy-tale (from the Grimms' collection), but in 'Snow-White and Rose-Red' (also from Grimm) the dwarf combines great wealth with sullen ingratitude. The association with gold and mining is strong, as in the site of 'Dwarf's Hill' (see p. 35 above); so are the stories of broken bargains, as when the Norse god Loki refuses to pay a dwarf the head he has lost, with Portia-like quibbles, or when Loki again strips the dwarf Andvari of all his wealth, even the last little (fatal) ring that Andvari pleads for.[5] *Inter uos nemo loquitur, nisi corde doloso,* says the dwarf in the eleventh-century German poem *Ruodlieb,* with hostile truth: 'Among you (men) no one speaks except with a deceitful heart. That is why you will never come to long life . . .' Both the longevity of dwarves and their tendency to get into disputes over payment are remembered on several occasions in *The Hobbit.* Their 'under-the-mountain' setting there is traditional too. The great Old Norse poem on world's end, the *Völuspá,* links them with stone: *stynia dvergar fyr steindurom,* 'the dwarves groan before their stone-doors'. Snorri Sturluson (a kind of Northern Laȝamon) says that they 'quickened in the earth . . . like maggots', while his Icelandic countrymen long called echoes *dvergmál,* 'dwarf-talk'. The correspondence between such separated works as Snorri's *Prose Edda* (thirteenth-century Icelandic) and the Grimms' *Kindermärchen* (nineteenth-century German) is indeed in this matter surprisingly, even provocatively, strong, and Tolkien was not the first to see it; the

Grimms themselves observed that such things were a proof of some 'original unity', *des ursprünglichen Zusammenhangs.*[6] *Zusammenhang:* a 'hanging together'. That is very much what Tolkien thought of all these tales, and the phenomenon remains no matter what interpretation one puts on it.

However, both with elves and with dwarves there is one further factor to which Tolkien gave great weight; and that is literary art. No matter how many cross-references he could find and use, it looks as if he gave greatest weight and longest consideration to single poems, tales, phrases, images, using these as the centre of his portrayals of whole races or species. Naturally it is a speculative business to identify these, but I would suggest that the 'master-text' for Tolkien's portrayal of the elves is the description of the hunting king in *Sir Orfeo;* and for the dwarves is the account of the *Hjaðningavíg,* the 'Everlasting Battle', in Snorri's *Edda.* These give further the 'master-qualities' of, respectively, evasiveness and revenge.

To take the simpler one first, the story of the 'Everlasting Battle' is as follows: once upon a time there was a king called Högni, whose daughter was Hildr. She, however, was abducted in his absence (some versions say seduced by a master-harper) by a pirate king called Hethinn. Högni pursued them and caught up at the island of Hoy in the Orkneys. Here Hildr tried to make a reconciliation, warning her father that Hethinn was ready to fight. Högni 'answered his daughter curtly'. As the two sides draw up to each other, though, Hethinn makes a better and more courteous offer. But Högni refuses, saying: 'Too late have you made this offer of coming to terms, for now I have drawn Dáinsleif which the dwarves made, which must kill a man every time it is drawn, and never turns in the stroke, and no wound heals where it makes a scratch.' Unintimidated by words (like most Vikings), Hethinn shouts back that he calls any sword good that serves its master, and the battle is on. Every day the men fight, every night Hildr wakes them by witchcraft, so it will go to Doomsday.[7]

This story is one, evidently, of remorseless pride flaring only in taciturnity; its centre is Högni's decision to fight rather than look for a moment as if he could be bought; the 'objective correlative' of pride and decision is the sword Dáinsleif, the 'heirloom of Dáin', which the dwarves made and which knows no mercy. The sword Tyrfing in the *Saga of King Heidrek* edited by Christopher Tolkien is virtually identical—dwarf-made, cursed, remorseless, leading to murder between close relatives and the final lament, 'It will never be forgotten; the Norns' doom is evil'. These qualities, it seems, are those which Tolkien chose and developed for his dwarves. Thorin and company act out of revenge as well as greed in *The Hobbit;* the long and painful vengeance of Thráin for Thrór is the centre of what we are told of the dwarves in Appendix A of *The Lord of the Rings;* Dáin Ironfoot himself incarnates in Tolkien's Middle-earth the whole tough, fair, bitter, somehow unlucky character of the dwarvish race.[8] It is not too much to say that the 'inspiration' of their portrayal, as opposed to the more laborious element of 'invention', springs directly from Snorri and the *Hjaðningavíg* and 'Dáinsleif which the dwarves made'. To use Tolkien's phrase, this was a 'fusion-point of imagination', once met never forgotten.

As for the elves, their fusion or kindling-point would seem to be some twenty or thirty lines from the centre of the medieval poem of *Sir Orfeo,* itself a striking example of the alchemies of art. In origin this is only the classical story of Orpheus and Eurydice, but the fourteenth-century poet (or maybe some forgotten predecessor) has made two radical changes to it: one, the land of the dead has become elf-land, from which the elf-king comes to seize Dame Heurodis; two, Sir Orfeo, unlike his classical model, is successful in his quest and bears his wife away, overcoming the elf-king by the mingled powers of music and honour. The poem's most famous and original passage is the image of the elves in the wilderness, seen again and again by Orfeo as he wanders mad and naked, looking for his wife, but never certainly identified as hallucinations, phantoms or real creatures on the other side of some transparent barrier which Orfeo cannot break through. To quote Tolkien's translation:

> There often by him would he see,
> when noon was hot on leaf and tree,
> the king of Faerie with his rout
> came hunting in the woods about
> with blowing far and crying dim,

and barking hounds that were with him;
yet never a beast they took nor slew,
and where they went he never knew . . .
(*SGPO*, pp. 129–30)

Many hints from this took root in Tolkien's mind: the shadow-army with its echoing horns which was to follow Aragorn from the 'paths of the dead', the 'dim blowing of horns' as a 'great hunt' goes past the silent dwarves in Mirkwood in *The Hobbit,* and in *The Hobbit* again the image of the fierce, proud, impulsive, honourable elf-king who imprisons Thorin but will take no advantage in the end even of Bilbo. Stronger than anything, though, is the association of the elves with the wilderness — an idea corroborated to Tolkien by the many Anglo-Saxon compounds such as 'wood-elf', 'water-elf', 'sea-elf' and so on — and with the music of the harp, the instrument by which Sir Orfeo wins back his wife. It may even have seemed significant to Tolkien that in *Sir Orfeo* the elves freed and rewarded their harper-enemy for his skill, while in some versions of the *Hjaðningavíg* the dwarvish weapon Dáinsleif condemns Hjarrandi (the Northern Orpheus) not just to death but to death everlastingly repeated. A whole conflict of temperament between two species is summed up in the detail, and a conflict of style. However, the further one traces Tolkien's debt to ancient texts and fragments, in this matter, the more one realises how easy it was for him to feel that a consistency and a sense lay beneath the chaotic ruin of the old poetry of the North — if only someone would dig it out. To quote Shakespeare's observations on another Enchanted Wood which sensible people can make nothing of (in *A Midsummer Night's Dream* V i):

> But all the story of the night told over,
> And all their minds transfigured so together,
> More witnesseth than fancy's images,
> And grows to something of great constancy;
> But howsoever, strange and admirable.

I do not suppose Tolkien would have liked the downgrading of 'fancy', nor the comedy of Peaseblossom, Cobweb, Moth and Mustardseed. Bully Bottom, though, has a Tolkienish bravura;

and Hippolyta's feeling that 'there must have been *something* in it' was his own.

Creative Anachronisms

It was by similar processes of 'reconstruction' that Tolkien arrived at his 'orcs' and 'wargs', later his 'ents' and 'woses'.†
None of the foregoing, however, offers any help at all with 'hobbits'. If 'the word authenticates the thing', they are not authentic, for 'hobbit' is in no sense an ancient word. Nor indeed does their genesis seem to have had any element of 'invention' in it; it was pure 'inspiration', without any trace of thought at all. The moment of the word's arrival has in fact been recorded by Tolkien, and subsequently by Humphrey Carpenter:

> It was on a summer's day, and he was sitting by the window in the study at Northmoor Road, laboriously marking School Certificate exam papers. Years later he recalled: 'One of the candidates had mercifully left one of the pages with no writing on it (which is the best thing that can possibly happen to an examiner) and I wrote on it: *"In a hole in the ground there lived a hobbit."* Names always generate a story in my mind. Eventually I thought I'd better find out what hobbits were like. But that's only the beginning.' (*Biography*, p. 175)[9]

---

† 'Orcs' go back to the *orcnéas*, the 'demon-corpses' of the *Beowulf*-poet, and to another Old English word, *orcþyrs*, 'orc-giant'. 'Wargs' are a linguistic cross between Old orse *vargr* and Old English *wearh*, two words showing a shift of meaning from 'wolf' to 'human outlaw'. For the 'ents' see below, p. 131. The 'woses' are perhaps primarily an apology for *Sir Gawain* line 721, where *wodwos* is offered as a plural, though historically a singular derived from Old English *wudu-wása*. It would not have escaped Tolkien, though, that his office at Leeds University (like mine) stood just off 'Woodhouse Lane', which crosses 'Woodhouse Moor' and 'Woodhouse Ridge'. These names may preserve, in mistaken modern spelling, old belief in 'the wild men of the woods' lurking in the hills above the Aire. See further Tolkien's notes on 'Orc' and 'Woses' in 'Guide'.

The incident seems a perfect example of the creative unconsciousness: the boring job, the state of combined surface concentration and deeper lack of interest, the sudden relaxation which allows a message to force its way through from some unknown area of pressure. It is reminiscent of the flashes of insight which solve scientists' problems in dreams (like von Kékulé the chemist and the snake with its tail in its mouth). But what has philology to do with an event so mysterious and so personal?

Tolkien had no opinion to offer himself. In a letter in the *Observer* (20 February 1938), he answered speculation by saying, 'I do not remember anything about the name and inception of the hero', and denied (without total certainty) that the word 'hobbit' could have come from prior reading in African exploration or fairy-tale, as had been suggested. He thought that earlier writers' hobbits, if they existed, were probably 'accidental homophones', i.e. the name was the same but the thing was not. Much later, in a letter he seems never to have posted (*Letters,* pp. 379–87), he observed that though he could often remember acquiring names, this process played little part in the construction of stories. It is somehow typical that the *OED* should have claimed (*Times,* 31 May 1977) to have identified Tolkien's 'source' and 'inspiration' in J. Hardy's edition of *The Denham Tracts,* Vol. II (1895), which declares that 'the whole earth was overrun with ghosts, boggles . . . hobbits, hobgoblins'. The word 'hobbit' is there, but in a run of distinctly insubstantial creatures which hardly correspond to Tolkien's almost pig-headedly solid and earthbound race. Words are not things: the name 'hobbit' may seem to be, for the researcher, a dead-end.

Even dead-ends have their uses, though (see p. 71 below). This particular one prompts several thoughts. One is that although Tolkien accepted the word as coming from outside, not being rooted in antiquity at all, he nevertheless did not rest until he had worked out an acceptable etymology for it. 'In a hole in the ground there lived a hobbit' is of course the first sentence of *The Hobbit.* Not quite the last sentence, but on the last page of the last appendix of *The Lord of the Rings* is the note on the word 'hobbit' which gives its derivation, viz. from Old English **hol-bytla,* 'hole-dweller' or 'hole-builder'. *Holbytla* is an 'asterisk word'. It was never recorded, but nevertheless could, is even on the whole likely to have existed, like *dvairgs*. Furthermore it makes the magic sentence of inspiration into a tautology: 'In a hole in the ground there lived a hole-liver . . .' What else would you expect? The implication is that the inspiration was a memory of something that could in reality have existed, and that anyway conformed to the inflexible rules of linguistic history: as a word 'hobbit' was more like 'dwarves' than 'elfin'.

The next point is that Tolkien did admit one possible source in Sinclair Lewis's novel *Babbitt* (1922), the story of the near-disgrace and abortive self-discovery of a complacent American businessman; to this theme the journey and the nature of Bilbo Baggins show some correspondence. But the source that Tolkien emphatically rejected is the word 'rabbit', of which so many critics have been reminded. 'Calling Bilbo a "nassty little rabbit" was a piece of vulgar trollery', he wrote, 'just as "descendant of rats" was a piece of dwarfish [*sic*] malice' (*Observer*, 20 February 1938). 'Certainly not rabbit,' he affirmed later. Internal evidence runs against him here, however, for it is not only the trolls who think simultaneously of Bilbo and rabbits. Bilbo makes the comparison himself in chapter 6 of *The Hobbit*, when he sees the eagle sharpening its beak and begins 'to think of being torn up for supper like a rabbit'. Three pages later the same thought occurs to the eagle: 'You need not be frightened like a rabbit, even if you look rather like one.' Thorin shakes Bilbo 'like a rabbit' in chapter 16, and much earlier Beorn — admittedly a rude and insensitive character — pokes Mr Baggins in the waistcoat and observes 'little bunny is getting nice and fat again' (p. 144). He is in a sense repaying the insult Bilbo offered earlier (p. 127), when he thought Beorn's 'skin-changing' meant he was 'a furrier, a man that calls rabbits conies, when he doesn't turn their skins into squirrels'. But the multiplicity of names gives a further clue to Tolkien's real thoughts, incubating since 1915 and the neologism 'coney-rabbits' in 'Goblin Feet'.

The fact is that 'rabbit' is a peculiar word. The *OED* can find no ultimate etymology for it, nor trace it back in English before 1398. 'Coney' or 'cunny' is little better, going back to 1302, while 'bunny' is a pet-name used originally for squirrels, as it happens, and not recorded till the seventeenth century. The words for 'rabbit' differ in several European languages (French *lapin*, German *kaninchen*), and there is no Old English or Old Norse word for it at all. These facts are unusual: 'hare', for instance, is paralleled by Old English *hara*, German *hase*, Old Norse *heri*, and so on, while the same could be said for 'weasel' or 'otter' or 'mouse' or 'brock' or most other familiar mammals of Northern Europe. The reason, of course, is that rabbits are immigrants. They appeared in England only round the thirteenth century, as imported creatures bred for fur, but escaped to the wild like mink or coypu. *Yet they have been assimilated*. The point is this: not one person in a thousand realises that rabbits (no Old English source) are in any historical way distinct from mice (O.E. *mýs*) or weasels (O.E. *weselas*), while the word is accepted by all as familiar, native, English. The creature has further established itself irreversibly in the folk-imagination, along with wise owls (O.E. *úlan*) and sly foxes (O.E. *fuhsas*). But if an Anglo-Saxon or Norseman had seen one he would have thought it alien, if not bizarre. Rabbits prove that novelties can be introduced into a language and then *made to fit*—of course as long as one exhibits due regard to deep structures of language and thought. 'If a foreign word falls by chance into the stream of a language', wrote Jacob Grimm, 'it is rolled around till it takes on that language's colour, and in spite of its foreign nature comes to look like a native one.'[10]

Now this situation of anachronism-cum-familiarity certainly has *something* to do with hobbits. The first time that Bilbo Baggins appears in close focus he is 'standing at his door after breakfast smoking an enormous long wooden pipe'. Smoking later appears as not just a characteristic of hobbits, but virtually the characteristic, 'the one art that we can certainly claim to be our own invention', declares Meriadoc Brandybuck (*LOTR*, p. 8). But what are they smoking besides pipes? *'Pipeweed*, or *leaf'*, declares the *Lord of the Rings* Prologue firmly. Why not say 'tobacco', since the plant is 'a variety probably of *Nicotiana*'? Because the word would sound wrong. It is an import from some unknown Caribbean language via Spanish, reaching English only after the discovery of America, sometime in the sixteenth century. The words it resembles most are 'potato' and 'tomato', also referring to new objects from America, eagerly adopted in England and naturalised with great speed, but marked off as foreign by their very phonetic structure. 'Pipeweed' shows Tolkien's wish to accept a common feature of English modernity, which he knew could not exist in the ancient world of elves or trolls, and whose anachronism would instantly be betrayed by a word with the foreign feel of 'tobacco'. Actually Bilbo *does* use 'tobacco' on page 14 of *The Hobbit,* and Gandalf mentions 'tomatoes' not much later. *In the first edition.* The third changes 'cold chicken and tomatoes' to 'cold chicken and pickles',[11] and after that the foreign fruit is excluded. 'Potatoes' stay in, being indeed the speciality of Gaffer Gamgee, but his son Sam has a habit of assimilating the word to the more native-sounding 'taters' — Tolkien notes elsewhere that the word was borrowed into colloquial Welsh from colloquial English as *tatws,* in which form it sounds much less distinctive ('EW', p. 34). But in fact the scene in which Sam discusses 'taters' with Gollum (*LOTR,* p. 640) is a little cluster of anachronisms: hobbits, eating rabbits (Sam calls them 'coneys'), wishing for potatoes ('taters') but out of tobacco ('pipeweed'). One day, offers Sam to Gollum, he might cook him something better — 'fried fish and chips'. Nothing could now be more distinctively English! Not much would be *less* distinctively Old English. The hobbits, though, are on our side of many cultural boundaries.

That, then, is their association with rabbits. One can see why Tolkien denied the obvious connection between the two: he did not want hobbits classified as small, furry creatures, vaguely 'cute' just as fairies were vaguely 'pretty'. On the other hand both insinuated themselves, rabbits into the homely company of fox and goose and hen, hobbits into the fantastic but equally verbally authenticated set of elves and dwarves and orcs and ettens. One might go so far as to say that the absence of rabbits from ancient legend made them not an 'asterisk word' but an 'asterisk thing' — maybe they were there but nobody noticed. That is exactly the ecological niche Tolkien selected for hobbits, 'an *unobtrusive* but *very ancient* people' (*LOTR,* p. 1, my italics). It is not likely that this role was devised for them before the arrival of the inspired 'In a hole in the ground there lived a hobbit', any more than the etymology from *holbytla*. Still, the amazing thing about that sentence, looking back, is the readiness with which it responded to development. The first half of it helped to anchor hobbits in history, via *holbytlan,* the second to characterise them in fiction, via the anachronisms associated with the rabbit-analogy. Such complexity could be the result of prior unconscious cogitation or later artistic effort. Either way, 'hobbit' as word and concept threw out its anchors into Old and modern English at once: 'grammarye' at work once more.

Breaking Contact

This preamble makes it easier to say what Tolkien was doing in *The Hobbit.* Like Walter Scott or William Morris before him, he felt the perilous charm of the archaic world of the North, recovered from bits and scraps by generations of inquiry. He wanted to tell a story about it simply, one feels, because there were hardly any complete ones left; *Beowulf* or *The Saga of King Heidrek* stimulated the imagination but did not satisfy it. Accordingly he created a sort of 'asterisk-world' for the Norse *Elder Edda.* The dwarf-names of 'Thorin and Company', as well as Gandalf's, come from a section of the Eddic poem *Völuspá,* often known as the *Dvergatal* or 'Dwarves' Roster'. This is not much regarded now, and has been called a 'rigmarole', a meaningless list; *The Hobbit* implies, though, that that meaningless list is the last faded memento of something once great and important, an Odyssey of the dwarves. As for the landscape through which Gandalf, Thorin and the rest move, that too is an Eddic one; 'the pathless Mirkwood' is mentioned in several poems, while 'the Misty Mountains' come from the poem *Skírnismál,* where Freyr's page, sent to abduct the giant's daughter, says grimly to his horse:

> 'Myrct er úti, mál qveð ec ocr fara
>   úrig fiöll yfir
>   þyrsa þióð yfir;
> báðir við komomc, eða ocr báða tecr
>   sá inn ámátki iotunn.

'The mirk is outside, I call it our business to fare over the misty mountains, over the tribes of orcs *(þyrs = orc*; see note to p. 65 above); we will both come back, or else he will take us both, he the mighty giant.'

All that Tolkien has done, in a way, is to make place-names out of adjectives, to turn words into things.

But there is one very evident obstacle to recreating the ancient world of heroic legend for modern readers, and that lies in the nature of heroes. These are not acceptable anymore, and tend very strongly to be treated with irony: the modern view of *Beowulf* is John Gardner's novel *Grendel* (1971). Tolkien did not want to be ironic about heroes, and yet he could not eliminate modern reactions. His response to the difficulty is Bilbo Baggins, the hobbit, the anachronism, a character whose initial role at least is very strongly that of mediator. He represents and often voices modern opinions, modern incapacities: he has no impulses towards revenge or self-conscious heroism, cannot 'hoot twice like a barn-owl and once like a screech owl' as the dwarves suggest, knows almost nothing about Wilderland, and cannot even skin a rabbit, being used to having his meat 'delivered by the butcher all ready to cook'. Yet he has a place in the ancient world too, and there is a hint that (just like us) all his efforts cannot keep him entirely separate from the past.

His name, thus, is Baggins, and he lives in Bag End. This latter name had personal and homely associations for Tolkien (see *Biography,* p. 180). But it is also a literal translation of the phrase one sees often yet stuck up at the end of little English roads: *cul-de-sac. Cul-de-sacs* are at once funny and infuriating. They belong to no language, since the French call such a thing an *impasse* and the English a 'dead-end'. The word has its origins in snobbery, the faint residual feeling that English words, ever since the Norman Conquest, have been 'low' and that French ones, or even *Frenchified* ones, would be better. *Cul-de-sac* is accordingly a peculiarly ridiculous piece of English class-feeling—and Bag End a defiantly English reaction to it. As for Mr Baggins, one thing he is more partial to than another is his tea, which he has at four o'clock. But over much of the country 'tea', indeed anything eaten between meals but especially afternoon tea 'in a substantial form' as the *OED* says, is called 'baggins'. The *OED* prefers the 'politer' form 'bagging', but Tolkien knew that people who used words like that were almost certain to drop the terminal *g* (another post-Conquest confusion anyway). He would have found the term glossed under *bœggin, bœgginz* in W. E. Haigh's *Glossary of the Dialect of the Huddersfield District* (London: Oxford University Press), for which he had written an appreciative prologue in 1928. Mr Baggins, then, is at the start of *The Hobbit* full of nonsense, like modern English society as perceived by Tolkien: he takes pride in being 'prosy', pooh-poohs anything out of the ordinary and is almost aggressively *middle* middle-class in being more respectable than the Tooks, though rather 'well-to-do' than 'rich'. If he went much further in this direction he would end up like his cousins the 'Sackville-Bagginses' — they, of course, have severed their connection with Bag End by calling it *cul-de-sac(k)* and tagging on the French suffix *-ville*! Yet Bilbo's heart is in the right place (also like modern English society as perceived by Tolkien). He likes flowers; he is proud of his ancestor the Bullroarer; if not quite 'as fierce as a dragon in a pinch' he is at any rate no coward; and like his name he is ample, generous, substantial, if undeniably plain and old-fashioned. He has therefore not entirely lost his passport into the ancient world, and can function in it as our representative, without heroic pretensions but also without cynical ironies. He is admittedly a bourgeois. That is why Gandalf turns him into a Burglar. Both words come from the same root (*burh* = 'town' or 'stockaded house'), and while they are eternal opposites, they are opposites on the same level. By the end of *The Hobbit*, though, Bilbo as burglar has progressed so far as to rub shoulders with heroes, even to be (just) considerable as one himself.†

---

† I do not know the origin of the personal name 'Bilbo', but can record that on one occasion I found myself using Ordnance Survey map no. 161, of S. Herefordshire, to locate churches of similar date to *Ancrene Wisse* and preserving fragments of the early Anglo-Norse style of stonework. As I did this my eye moved west from Kilpeck to Wormbridge to Abbey Dore to a hill called 'Great Bilbo'. The *Place-Name Survey* has not done Herefordshire yet, and I have no explanation for the name; maybe Tolkien had one of his own.

The early moves of *The Hobbit* depend very much on this tension between ancient and modern reactions. It begins almost as satire on modern institutions, with Mr Baggins's language particularly taking some shrewd knocks: the more familiar it seems, the more fossilised it is. Thus Bilbo's 'Good morning' is no longer a wish offered to another person, but either that, or an objective statement, or a subjective statement, or all of them together, or even a gesture of hostility. '"What a lot of things you do use *Good morning* for!" said Gandalf. "Now you mean that you want to get rid of me, and that it won't be good till I move off."' His 'not at all' means 'yes', his 'my dear sir' means nothing, and when he says 'I beg your pardon' he no longer has any sense that he is asking for anything or that 'pardon' might be a valuable thing to receive. Against this the dwarves' ceremonious style of salutation — 'At your service!' 'At yours and your family's!' 'May his beard grow ever longer!' 'May the hair on his toes never fall out!' — may seem pompous and indeed be insincere, but at any rate it is *about* something, not just semantically empty. Similarly Bilbo, trying to be business-like, flees to abstractions, only to have the narrator expose them: '"Also I should like to know about risks, out-of-pocket expenses, time required and remuneration, and so forth" — by which he meant: "What am I going to get out of it? And am I going to come back alive?"' Thorin, though long-winded enough, does not talk about calculations, but about *things*[†]: the dwarf-song which opens their conclave centres on the misty mountains cold and grim, on harps, necklaces, twisted wire, pale enchanted long-forgotten gold. No wonder the hobbit feels 'the love of beautiful things made by hands and by cunning and magic moving through him, a fierce and a jealous love, the desire of the hearts of dwarves'. In the first clash between ancient and modern, 'ancient' wins easily; in an entirely proper sense (*res* = 'thing') it seems much realer.

---

† The contract he finally does deliver on p. 33 is typically more practical than Bilbo at his most business-like had thought. It covers profits, delivery, travelling expenses, but also defrayal of funeral expenses, 'by us or our representatives, if occasion arises and the matter is not otherwise arranged for'. This means, 'you or all of us may die, and also be eaten'.

In any case the narrator has his thumb firmly on the balance. His voice is very prominent throughout *The Hobbit* (as it is not in *The Lord of the Rings*), and as has been said it provides 'a very firm moral framework by which to judge'[12] — elves are good, goblins bad, dwarves, eagles, dragons, men and Beorn all in different ways in between. Besides building up morality, though, it more interestingly tears down expectation. The narrator's favourite phrase is 'of course', but this usually introduces something unexplained or unpredictable: 'That, of course, is the way to talk to dragons', or 'He knew, of course, that the riddle game was sacred', or 'It was often said . . . that long ago one of the Took ancestors must have taken a fairy wife. That was, of course, absurd'. Sometimes these and similar remarks introduce information. More often they create a sense that more information exists round the edges of the story, and that events are going according to rules only just hinted at, but rules just the same. Adjectives like 'the *famous* Belladonna Took' or 'the great Thorin Oakenshield *himself*' imply a depth of history, statements like 'no spider has ever liked being called Attercop' one of experience. The frequent remarks about legendary creatures of the 'Trolls' purses are the mischief' kind furthermore blur ordinary experience into the magical, while the question 'what would you do, if an uninvited dwarf came and hung his things up in your hall?' is very much in the style of 'have you stopped beating your wife?' The child reader senses, perhaps, the sportiveness of all this, and delights in it; the adult, as he goes along, finds himself succumbing to the ancient principle that 'redundancy is truth' — the more *unnecessary* details are put in, the more lifelike we take fiction to be. The underlying point, though, is that the narrator is there cumulatively to express a whole attitude to the archaic-heroic setting: casual, matter-of-fact, even unimpressed, but accordingly lulling. He gets the landscape, the characters, and the 'rules' through the modern barriers of disbelief and even, potentially, of contempt.

The way *The Hobbit* works in fact shows up well in any comparison of Chapter 2, 'Roast Mutton', with its analogue in the Grimms' folk-tale of 'The Brave Little Tailor'. In this latter a tailor (the trade was synonymous with feebleness, as in Shakespeare's *Henry IV Part II* III ii) kills seven flies at a blow, and is so emboldened that he starts a career of violence and monster-killing. He bluffs his way through a contest of strength with one giant, and frightens off a whole gang of them: 'each of them had a roast sheep in his hand and was eating it'. Sent by the king to catch two more, he hides up a tree and throws stones at them till they quarrel and kill each other: 'they tore up trees in their agony and defended themselves', he says airily when he shows the bodies, 'but all that does no good when a chap like me comes along who can kill seven with one blow!' Bilbo starts off very much as a 'little grocer', but he never shows anything like the 'little tailor's' resource or effrontery; an omni-competent character would destroy any modern story's action. Instead he is presented very much as a reader-surrogate, driven on by shame to try to be 'The Master Thief' (like the character in Asbjörnsen and Moe's Norse folktale) but hampered by utter ignorance of the rules of the game. He is caught by one 'fact' which neither he nor the reader could have predicted — trolls' purses talk — and saved by two more: wizards can ventriloquise, and 'trolls, as you probably know, must be underground before dawn, or they go back to the stuff of the mountains they are made of, and never move again'. 'As you probably know' is here the final blow in Tolkien's strategy of 'counter-realism'. Nobody knows that; indeed it isn't true; in a traditional tale no narrator could get away with so shamelessly exploiting the gap between his world and his listener's, because of course there wouldn't be one! However, in *The Hobbit* the combined assurance of Gandalf, the narrator, the trolls and the dwarves outweighs the ignorance of Bilbo, and the reader. As it happens, the belief about being underground before dawn is as traditional as belief in trolls and dwarves at all, going back to the *Elder Edda* and the end of the *Alvíssmál,* where Alvíss the dwarf is kept talking till daylight by Thórr, and so turned to stone.[†] Inventive resource is very strong in *The Hobbit,* over

---

[†] There is a further weak analogue in the Grimms' tale no. 195, 'The Grave-Mound', and a much stronger one in C. S. Lewis's *That Hideous Strength* (London: Bodley Head, 1945), end of chapter 16. There, though, the tale is given a moral significance, a little like Tolkien explaining 'elf-time' in Lothlórien.

words and races and characters and events. The book's *distinguishing* characteristic, though, is its sense that all these things come from somewhere outside and beyond the author, forming a *Zusammenhang* as solid as every day's and on occasion no more irrational.

The Ring as 'Equalizer'

This 'illusion of historical truth and perspective' is, of course, as Tolkien himself said of *Beowulf,* 'largely a product of art' ('Monsters', p. 247). And sometimes the art ran out. Tolkien himself admitted (*Observer,* 20 February 1938) that twice he got stuck. He did not say where, leaving that for later researchers to make fools of themselves over, but it may be argued that the first few chapters of *The Hobbit* consist mostly of disengagement and playing down the readers' collective sense of doubt. As late as the start of chapter 4 the company is halted again (for the third time), and there is a sense of the author groping for intellectual justification. In the mountain-storm Bilbo looks out and sees that 'across the valley the stone-giants were out, and were hurling rocks at one another for a game, and catching them, and tossing them down into the darkness where they smashed among the trees far below'. Giants never enter the Tolkien universe again — Gandalf accepts their existence for a second in chapter 7 — and the passage is a failure of tone; it reads like an old interpretation of giants as 'nature-myth', i.e. as personifications of the avalanche, like Thórr and his hammer personifying thunder and lightning. This is too allegorical for Middle-earth. But the story takes off very shortly afterwards, with the capture by the goblins (incidentally still too close to munitions workers as the trolls were to labourers), the escape, the goblin runners pursuing 'swift as weasels in the dark', and Bilbo's forcible detachment from the dwarves. As he crawled along the tunnel hours later, 'his hand met what felt like a tiny ring of cold metal lying on the floor of the tunnel. It was a turning point in his career', comments Tolkien, 'but he did not know it.' A turning-point in Tolkien's career too, for from this came most of his subsequent inspiration — Gollum, Sauron,[13] eventually *The Lord of the Rings* itself.

But no more than Bilbo did Tolkien realise this at the time. As he testified later (*LOTR*, p. xv), glimpses in *The Hobbit* 'had arisen unbidden of things higher or deeper or darker than its surface: Durin, Moria, Gandalf, the Necromancer, the Ring'. The ring changed its significance even between editions of *The Hobbit*.[14] In the first, matters were relatively straightforward: Bilbo found the ring, met Gollum, they agreed to hold a riddle-contest, the stakes being Bilbo's life against Gollum's 'precious'. Bilbo won, but since by accident he'd acquired Gollum's 'precious' already, he asked to be shown the way out instead. The sequence works, it excuses Bilbo of any charge of theft (he'd won the ring fair and square), but as anyone familiar with the Ring in its later manifestations will see, the amazing thing is Gollum's readiness to *bet* his 'precious', bear the loss of it, and then offer to show the way out as a *douceur*. 'I don't know how many times Gollum begged Bilbo's pardon. He kept on saying: "We are ssorry; we didn't mean to cheat, we meant to give it our only pressent, if it won the competition"' (*Hobbit*, first edition, p. 92). In the second and subsequent editions, his last words are 'Thief! Thief! Thief! Baggins! We hates it, we hates it for ever!' Furthermore Gollum's charge is arguably true, since in *this* version the deal was Bilbo's life against any nominated service, such as showing the way out. In both versions Bilbo gets the ring and the exit, but in the latter one it is his claim to the ring which is shaky.

Now, Tolkien integrated this second thought into his story marvellously well, even keeping the first version as an excuse Bilbo had told with uncharacteristic dishonesty to put his claim to the 'precious' beyond doubt. However, it is the first thought one should keep in mind while considering the genesis of *The Hobbit*. And here the obvious point, surely, is that the ring is just a prop: a stage-prop, like the marvellous devices common in fairy-tales or legends (there is a wish-fulfilling ring in the Grimms' 'The King of the Golden Mountain', and a cloak of invisibility), but also a prop for Bilbo's status with the dwarves. It is a kind of 'Equalizer'. After acquiring it Bilbo remains in most ways as out of touch with Wilderland as before: he cannot dress meat or dodge wargs, and when in chapter 15 Balin asks if he can make out the bird's speech, he has to reply, 'Not very well' — the narrator, still maximising the distance between him and everyday Middle-earth normality, adds '(as a matter of fact, he could make nothing of it at all)'. He cannot even tell when crows are being insulting. But the ring makes up for this. Before he had it he was essentially a package to be carried, his name as a 'burglar' nothing but an embarrassment even to himself. With the ring he can take an active part. He uses it straightaway to get past the dwarves' look-out and raise his prestige — they 'looked at him with quite a new respect' — and then to save his companions first from the spiders and second from the elvish dungeons. The problem after *that* is in a way to maintain his status without simply reducing it to the accident of owning a magic ring. Tolkien takes some trouble over this, observing in the wood-elves' dungeon that 'one invisible ring was a fine thing, but it was not much good among fourteen' — so that credit for that escape is Bilbo's — and after the fight with the spiders that 'knowing the truth about the vanishing did not lessen [the dwarves'] opinion of Bilbo at all; for they saw that he had some wits, as well as luck and a magic ring — and all three were useful possessions.' There is something provocative in this last statement, for it seems to deny that owning a magic ring *could* be an accident. Still, the very arguability of Bilbo's status shows how the ring changed *The Hobbit:* it brought a new possibility of action which would be simultaneously 'heroic' and credible, it developed the opposition of ancient and modern motifs into something like a dialogue.

The main subject of that dialogue is courage. Few modern readers of *Beowulf,* or the *Elder Edda,* or the Icelandic 'family sagas', can escape a certain feeling of inadequacy as they contemplate whole sequences of characters who appear, in a casual and quite lifelike way, not to know what fear is. How would we manage in such a society? With our culture's characteristic 'softness, worldliness, and timidity',[15] would we be fit for anything but slavery? To this self-doubt Bilbo Baggins makes a sober but relatively optimistic response. *His* style of courage shows up when he is in the dark and alone. He faces fear first in the escape from Gollum, when he takes a 'leap in the dark' rather than kill a defenceless enemy (this comes only in the second edition). A more significant scene is when he faces the giant spider and kills it 'all alone by himself in the dark without the help of the wizard or the dwarves or of anyone else'. A third is as he creeps down the tunnel to his first sight of Smaug, but stops as he hears dragon-snoring ahead. Tolkien lays great stress on this:

> Going on from there was the bravest thing he ever did. The tremendous things that happened afterwards were nothing compared to it. He fought the real battle in that tunnel alone, before he ever saw the vast danger that lay in wait. At any rate after a short halt go on he did . . . (p. 233)

Such scenes remind us that even Samuel Colt's 'Equalizer' did not make all men heroes: it only made them all the same size. They also provide a behaviour-model which is not quite beyond emulation (no one can fight a dragon, but everyone can fight fear). Mainly they place in a kindly light that style of courage—cold courage, 'moral courage', two-o'clock-in-the-morning courage—which our age is most prepared to venerate.

They further expose the dwarves to something like the satire turned on Mr Baggins's modernisms at the start of the story. Thorin Oakenshield, for all his heroic name, sends Bilbo down the tunnel, and the rest do little but look embarrassed. The narrator insists (p. 231) that 'they would all have done their best to get him out of trouble . . . as they did in the case of the trolls', but he may not carry entire conviction. When he escaped from the goblins, Bilbo had just decided he had to go back into the tunnels and look for his friends when he found his friends deciding just the opposite about him! 'If we have got to go back into those abominable tunnels to look for him, then drat him', is their last word. Maybe Gandalf would have talked them round. But before this begins to sound like treason against the images of the ancient North (the 'great contribution' of whose early literature, Tolkien had said, was 'the theory of courage'; 'Monsters', p. 262), it needs to be said that *The Hobbit*'s dialogue contains many voices. There is something splendid in the narrator's reversion to laconicism at the end, when he says (as a matter of course) that since Thorin is dead, Fili and Kili are too; they 'had fallen defending him with shield and body, for he was their mother's elder brother', a motif immemorially old. Much can be said too for Thorin Oakenshield, while for some considerable stretch of the story, say chapters

6 to 8, one can see Tolkien exploring with delight that surly, illiberal independence often the distinguishing mark of Old Norse heroes. Gandalf's own reaction to being treed is just to kill as many enemies as possible; the rescuing eagles are, the narrator says euphemistically, 'not kindly birds'; there is a fine scene of sullen insolence between Thorin and the elf-king; but the centre of the whole sequence is Beorn.

He is in a way the least invented character in the book. His name is an Old English heroic word for 'man', which meant originally 'bear', so that naturally enough he is a were-bear, who changes shape, or 'skin' as Gandalf calls it, every night. He has a very close analogue in Böthvarr Bjarki (= 'little bear'), a hero from the Norse *Saga of Hrólfr Kraki,* and another in Beowulf himself, whose name is commonly explained as Beowulf = 'bees' wolf' = honey-eater = bear, and who breaks swords, rips off arms, and cracks ribs with ursine power and clumsiness. Beorn keeps bees too; is surly in disposition, not to be trusted after dark, and 'appalling when he is angry', a description not altogether different from being 'kind enough if humoured'. The dwarves and Bilbo see both sides of him, but perceive them as one. On their second morning they find him in a good mood, telling 'funny stories' and apologising for having doubted their word—it has been confirmed by two prisoners:

> 'What did you do with the goblin and the Warg?' asked Bilbo suddenly.
>
> 'Come and see!' said Beorn, and they followed round the house. A goblin's head was stuck outside the gate and a warg-skin was nailed to a tree just beyond. Beorn was a fierce enemy. But now he was their friend . . . (p. 145)

'The heart is hard, though the body be soft', said Tolkien of fairy-tale readers. But actually in context Beorn's ferocity is attractive. It goes with his rudeness and his jollity, all projections of that inner self-confidence which, as Tolkien knew, lay at the core of the 'theory of courage'. 'What do you believe in?' ask whole sequences of kings to Icelandic wanderers in sagas. *'Ek trúi á sjálfan mik',* runs the traditional response, 'I believe in myself'. Killer-Glúmr, an axeman like Beorn, widens this to believing in his axe and his moneybag and his storehouse as well. Both characters have the air of men who have 'been into' a crisis of existentialism — and straight out the other side, leaving the crisis sadly tattered.

The solitary conquest of fear: the fierce denial of it. These two conceptions, one modern, one archaic, circle round each other most of the way through *The Hobbit*. It would be wrong to say they are ever resolved, but they do at least reach climaxes of anachronism and clash of style near the end; first in the death of Smaug, then around the Battle of the Five Armies.

To take these in order, it may be said that killing Smaug is the basic problem of *The Hobbit,* and not just for the dwarves. Tolkien had few models to work from: Beowulf kills his dragon in plain fight, but without surviving, as is also to happen at Ragnarök with Thórr and the Midgard Serpent. Sigurthr kills Fáfnir in the *Edda* by stratagem and via the notorious draconic 'soft underbelly'; Vítharr at Ragnarök again is to slay the monstrous Fenriswolf by putting foot on lower jaw and hand on upper and tearing the beast apart. This last is implausible for men or hobbits, Beowulf's case and Thórr's are depressing, and Sigurthr's frankly too obvious to be interesting: Tolkien thought of something like it to begin with, but if the dwarves are well up on 'stabs and jabs and undercuts', then probably Smaug would be too. In the end he had to use a variant on 'soft underbellies', but to it he adds a notion as anachronistic to old-style 'heroism' as are Bilbo's decisions in the dark. This new element is 'discipline'.

Like 'glamour', 'discipline' is a much-altered word. Its earliest English meaning, in the *Ancrene Wisse,* is 'flogging'; the lady anchorites, says its author, must well tame their flesh *mid herde disciplines.* Later on the word comes to mean teaching or training, especially military training or drill; by the eighteenth century it covered the whole complex business of priming, loading, cocking, presenting and firing the 'Brown Bess' infantry musket to the beat of drum, a ritual which if carried out perfectly left British redcoats invulnerable to direct assault (as at Culloden), but when bungled left them, as an *OED* citation says, 'fit only for the contempt and slaughter of their enemies' (as at Falkirk the year before). In Tolkien's day the word had come to signify the most prized of all British imperial qualities, a specialised cold-bloodedness and readiness to take punishment which the *OED* finds itself unable to define. Its classic case was perhaps the wreck of the *Birkenhead* troopship on 25 February 1852, when five hundred soldiers found themselves on a sinking ship with inadequate lifeboats in a shark-infested sea. They were drawn up on deck, maintaining, says the *Annual Register* for 1852, 'perfect discipline', and told eventually to jump overboard and make for the few boats which had been launched. But the ship's captain begged them not to, as the boats with the women in would inevitably be swamped. '"Not more than three," he reported, "made the attempt." Under this heroic obedience to discipline the whole mass were engulphed in the waves by the sinking of the ship.'[16] The event became a part of British mystique, as did the quality. Lord Kitchener asked Tolkien's army of 1916 to show 'discipline and steadiness under fire', with typical attention to passivity. Nothing like this can be seen in early Northern literature; the analogue to the *Birkenhead* disaster in *The Saga of Eirik the Red* has indeed a Norseman giving up his place in a lifeboat, but he does it with characteristic personal bravura (and rudeness).[17] Nevertheless, Tolkien had been taught to value discipline, and it solved his problem over Smaug.

It is Bard the Bowman who kills Smaug, heroically enough with a lost arrow saved as a family heirloom for generations. Before that, though, Bard has figured as a nameless participant in a crowd scene about the giving and taking of orders. He has the trumpets blown, the warriors armed, the pots filled with water and the bridge to the land thrown down; it is this last precaution which daunts Smaug for a moment as he sweeps in over the cold fire-quenching lake. Then the dragon is faced with 'a hail of dark arrows' from platoons of bowmen, urged on by 'the grim-voiced man (Bard was his name), who ran to and fro cheering on the archers and urging the Master to order them to fight to the last arrow'. Fighting to the last *round* is of course the traditional phrase; being a 'discipline' concept, it post-dates musketry. But Tolkien has here transferred the ethic of Waterloo or Albuera back to ancient days. He does it again as the dragon shatters the town and the townspeople break for *their* lifeboats: 'But there was still a company of archers that held their ground among the burning houses. Their captain was Bard . . .' The phrase 'hold one's ground' is not even recorded by the *OED* till 1856, though there is a parallel in the Old English poem *Maldon,* where the English are exhorted to 'hold their stead' (which they don't). Not that holding their ground does these particular archers any good, or Smaug any harm; he is killed by the last arrow, the one particular arrow shot heroically by Bard. Still, the whole pressure of the scene is towards modern coolness and preparation, not ancient 'berserk' fury (a 'berserk' being a 'bear-shirt', a man like Beorn). It is discipline that does for Smaug: discipline and that element of 'complacency' (*OED* 1650) which lets Smaug neglect his armour and so betray himself successively to hobbit, thrush and man.

The death of Smaug, like Bilbo in the dark, lets us see courage in a modern way. Their obverse is the Battle of the Five Armies (where Bilbo disappears from sight and heroic displays come from Thorin, Fili, Kili, Dain and especially Beorn), and the unusually complex scene of debate before it in chapter 15. Here Bard and Thorin oppose each other, and do so in highly unchildlike and ratiocinative style. To summarise Bard's proposition to Thorin, he says in essence: (1) I have killed the dragon, so I deserve a reward, (2) I am also the heir of Girion lord of Dale, and much of Smaug's treasure was his, so I should have it back, (3) Smaug's destruction of Laketown has left destitute the people who helped the dwarves, and they deserve repayment, especially as (4) the dragon-attack was the dwarves' fault (or actually Bilbo's). To these points — split up in the original by heavy rhetorical questions — Thorin replies in the same mode, though not the same order. He ignores (1), perhaps out of pride, rejects (2), on the ground that Girion is dead and so can have no claim, and half-accepts (3) and (4); in dwarvish style he agrees to pay a fair price for earlier assistance, but refuses compensation for the dragon-attack, since that was Smaug's business, not his own. Finally, he refuses to parley under threat and asks a rhetorical question himself: 'It is in my mind to ask what share of their inheritance you would have paid to our kindred, had you found the hoard unguarded and us slain'.

The laborious legalism of this is straight out of Icelandic saga: one thinks of the hero of *The Saga of Hrafnkell* ticking off the appropriate compensations for the murders he has committed, the hamstringing he has suffered, loss of goods during feud and even the natural increase of animals during periods of confiscation — all coexisting, of course, with an ethic of ruthless violence. It is clear that Tolkien was all but enchanted by that ethical and literary style. The whole scene is presented very much for our admiration, and when later on Dain and the dwarves of the Iron Hills appear, their stilted ceremoniousness — 'But who are you that sit in the plain as foes before defended walls?' — rings much more powerfully than the narrator's modernistic translation: 'You have no business here. We are going on, so make way or we shall fight you!' Nevertheless, between these two moments another scene has intervened, marked by the greatest cluster of anachronisms since chapter 1: Bilbo's delivery of the Arkenstone to Bard, the Elvenking and Gandalf.

Bilbo has all along been (nearly) immune to the paraphernalia of heroism. He would like to see himself in a 'looking-glass' when Thorin outfits him with mithril armour, but fears he looks 'rather absurd', especially when he thinks of his neighbours on The Hill back home. He also listens with dismay and disapproval to the proud speeches of Bard and Thorin, and takes his own steps to break heroic deadlock.

> 'Really you know', Bilbo was saying in his best business manner, 'things are impossible. Personally I am tired of the whole affair. I wish I was back in the West in my own home, where folk are more reasonable. But I have an interest in this matter — one fourteenth share, to be precise, according to a letter, which fortunately I believe I have kept.' He drew from a pocket in his old jacket (which he still wore over his mail), crumpled and much folded, Thorin's letter that had been put under the clock on his mantelpiece in May!
>
> 'A share in the *profits,* mind you,' he went on. 'I am aware of that. Personally I am only too ready to consider all your claims carefully, and deduct what is right from the total before putting in my own claim.' (pp. 292–93)

This speech and speaker could hardly be less like the ones that surround it. Bilbo's behaviour is solidly anachronistic, for he is wearing a jacket, relying on a written contract, drawing a careful distinction between gain and profit, and proposing a com- promise which would see Bard's claim as running expenses (al- most tax-deductible). Where Bard and Thorin used archaic words ('Hail!', 'foes', 'hoard', 'kindred', 'slain'), he uses mod- ern ones: 'profit', never used in English till 1604, and then only in Aberdeen; 'deduct', recorded in 1524 but then indistin- guishable from 'subtract' and not given its commercial sense till much later; 'total', not used as here till 1557; 'claim', 'inter- est', 'affair', 'matter', all French or Latin imports not adopted fully into English till well after the Norman Conquest. It is fair to say that no character from epic or saga could even begin to think or talk like Bilbo. But what is the effect here of this final sharp juxtaposition between Bard and Bilbo, 'hero' and 'busi- nessman'?

It does continue *The Hobbit*'s strong vein of comedy. It also leads to a sort of 'encatastrophe', to use Tolkien's own term, as Mr Baggins and the sympathetic reader with him find them- selves and the modern code of humility and compromise re- garded with gratifying wonder by the Elvenking and Gandalf himself. Still, the comedy is not all one way, for Bilbo remains faintly ridiculous; no one should see *The Hobbit* as a straight progression from satire against the modern world to satire against the ancient one. What chapter 16 and the scenes around it do most powerfully, perhaps, is to enforce a plea for tolerance across an enormous gap of times and attitudes and ethical styles. On the one hand there is Bilbo Baggins, with his virtue of 'moral courage' or readiness 'to encounter odium, disap- proval, or contempt rather than depart from what he deems the right course' (first recorded 1822); his corresponding vice is 'self-distrust' (1789). On the other we have Beorn, Thorin, Dain, whose virtue can only be described by such a non-Eng- lish noun as the Old Norse *drengskapr*—magnanimity, the awareness of being a warrior and so on one's dignity, the qual- ity Dain shows in ratifying Thorin's agreement even though Thorin is dead—and whose vice is a kind of selfish material- ism. Neither side is better than the other, or has any right to criticise. The contrast is one of styles, not of good and bad. Accordingly, though throughout *The Hobbit* there have been scenes where the pretensions of one have been exposed by the other (Bilbo sneering at Thorin's elevated language, p. 230; Gloin cutting Bilbo very short at p. 22), by the end even the two *linguistic* styles have become invulnerable to each other's ironies:

> 'Good-bye and good luck, wherever you fare!' said Balin at last. 'If ever you visit us again, when our halls are made fair once more, then the feast shall indeed be splendid!'
>
> 'If ever you are passing my way,' said Bilbo, 'don't wait to knock! Tea is at four; but any of you are welcome at any time!' (p. 316)

There is not much in common between the language of these two speakers; nevertheless it is perfectly clear that they are saying *the same thing*. Going on from his beliefs in 'the reality of language' and 'the reality of history', Tolkien was perhaps beginning to arrive at a third: 'the reality of human nature'.

The Bewilderment of Smaug

This is a slippery and dangerous concept. If there is one thing which twentieth-century anthropology has proved, it is that people are different, and that even matters which appear entirely natural or instinctive are so enmeshed in nets of custom as to make it impossible to detect 'human universals'. There is no sign that Tolkien took any notice of modern anthropology, but then he hardly needed to. Ancient texts would provide him with any number of examples of how what is now considered natural might be in another age unthinkable, or vice versa. People's behaviour all too evidently changes. But isn't there something underneath the nets of custom that remains the same? Something that would link modern Englishmen with their Anglo-Saxon ancestors just as philology sees, beneath a thousand years of change, essential continuity between the language of *Beowulf* and that of today?

Tolkien must have been brooding on this question for many years. In 1923 he published in *The Gryphon* (the magazine of Leeds's Yorkshire College) a poem called 'Iumonna Gold

Galdre Bewunden', the first version of what was to become in 1970 'The Hoard'. The first title is better, though, for it means 'the gold of ancient men, wound round with magic', it is line 3052 of *Beowulf,* and it points to a notorious difficulty in that poem over the hero's motives. When he went to fight *his* dragon he appeared to do so for the best of reasons, i.e. to protect his people. On the other hand he also showed a keen interest in the treasure, which the dragon was only trying to guard, having been provoked by the theft of a cup by a passing runaway (or 'burglar'). At one point indeed, in a violently-disputed passage, the poet seems to say that there was a curse on the gold, so that the man who plundered it 'should be guilty of sin, be shut up in devil's haunts, bound in hell-bands and tormented grievously. Yet by no means too eagerly had Beowulf before gazed upon its owner's treasure of gold with the curse on it.'[18] Was Beowulf guilty or not? Did the curse punish him or not? Certainly the hoard he wins brings death to him and disaster to his people. Maybe this is also a punishment for the spark of avarice the poet is hinting at. But then maybe the dragon-curse is *itself* avarice. So Tolkien suggested in the 1923 poem, tracing in successive stanzas the transmission of a treasure from elf to dwarf to dragon to hero and ending with the picture of an old and miserly king overthrown by his rivals and leaving his gold to oblivion. All the characters in it are the same: they begin with vitality, mirth and courage, they end in age, wealth and squalor. Their decline is caused by gold. Could their progress also be a kind of analogue of human history, beginning in heroic endeavour and ending in 'commercialism', 'materialism', 'industrialism', that whole series of distinctively modern concepts which nevertheless centre if not on gold, on that 'idolatry of artefacts' which C. S. Lewis called, in evident agreement with Tolkien, the 'great corporate sin of our own civilisation'?[19] If one does think that for a moment, there is a further corollary: just as old miser grew out of young hero eager for treasure, so the 'great corporate sin' of modernity must have had some ancient origin. This sinful continuity between ancient and modern must have been on Tolkien's mind as he finished *The Hobbit.*

There is in the final chapters a continuum of greed. Least

reprehensible is the Elvenking's: he likes artefacts, but for their beauty, and is satisfied in the end with the emeralds of Girion. Bard is more modern in tone, but is let off as well since his motives are so clearly constructive. Bilbo too, with his ethic of being 'well-to-do' rather than vulgarly 'rich', is relatively immune. The dwarves, though, have very strong feelings about treasure, especially their 'pale enchanted gold' or *gold galdre bewunden;* they even put 'a great many spells' over the trolls' hoard, just in case.[20] As soon as they come within range of Smaug's treasure, *its* spell starts to work on them. They send Bilbo down the tunnel; they rejoice prematurely; on first sight of the treasure they have to be dragged away from it by Bilbo, 'not without many a backward glance of longing'. Finally Thorin himself is obsessively determined to give nothing to Bard or elves or Lakemen, and when forced to disgorge by Bilbo's theft of the Arkenstone, thinks against normal dwarvish behaviour-patterns of breaking his word. 'So strong was the bewilderment of the treasure upon him, he was pondering whether by the help of Dain he might not recapture the Arkenstone and withhold the share of the reward.'

'Bewilderment' is a good word there. In modern parlance it means 'mental confusion', which is fair enough as a description of Thorin's state; he has no idea how he will reach his ends, or what these ends are, only that parting with treasure is not among them. The modern sense, however, arises from the physical one of being 'lost in the wild', and Thorin is that too, being stuck in the centre of the Desolation of Smaug with plenty of gold but little to eat; he could end up as literally 'bewildered' as the Master of Laketown, who, fleeing with his city's share of the treasure, 'died of starvation in the waste'. There is even a third sense of the word to remind us of the visible, tactile source of the treasure's power, the quality that makes the dwarves run their fingers through it: it means 'a tangled or labyrinthine condition of objects', says the *OED*, quoting (1884) 'What a bewilderment of light and color met her eyes'. When one thinks of the dim images of gold and jewels and 'silver red-stained in the ruddy light' which is Bilbo's first glimpse of the hoard, one sees that this sense for 'the bewilderment of the treasure' is appropriate too.

Thorin's 'bewilderment' is physical and mental and moral as well. The 'dragon-sickness' which he and the Master of Laketown catch is also simultaneously magical and moral. At the bottom of it there lies an old superstition which says that dragons are actually misers who have in greed and despair walled themselves up alive, 'lain down on their gold' as sagas say. Naturally the gold on which they have brooded (see *Hobbit*, p. 286) exudes a miasma of avarice. Yet one has the sense of an external force meeting an internal weakness, especially strong in the artefact-worshipping dwarves, and in the Master, whose mind was given 'to trades and tolls, to cargoes and gold', who despises old songs and speaks on occasion (pp. 272–73) with a distinctive post–Industrial Revolution modernity. This is in fact a complex and successful presentation of the motives behind a real historical change; one might usefully compare the scene at the end of Kurt Vonnegut's *Player Piano* (1952), where the revolutionaries against the Automated State turn obsessively, with their first success, to tinkering with machines. Both books are making the same sort of (not very liberal) point: things, metal things, are genuinely fun to play with, but it's very hard to stop the fun from getting out of hand, though only in the twentieth century have we become really aware of that. Hence the 'continuum of greed' from Elvenking to Master. Hence, too, the brooding from 1923 on the word *galdor*. Besides 'spell' and 'bewilderment' it also means 'poetry'; you could say that the 'enchantment' of the treasure is a kind of wicked equivalent of 'glamour'.

There is, however, another character in this continuum, indeed at one end of it, and that is Smaug. His name is another 'asterisk word', being the past tense **smaug* of a Germanic verb **smugan*, 'to squeeze through a hole', as Tolkien said in his 1938 *Observer* letter; also the Old Norse equivalent of an Old English magic word found in a spell *wið sméogan wyrme*, 'against the penetrating worm'. But he has a mental sense as well as a physical one, since O.E. *sméagan* also means 'to inquire into' and in adjectival form 'subtle, crafty'.[21] All round it is appropriate that Smaug should have the most sophisticated intelligence in *The Hobbit*.

Bilbo's conversation with him is indeed a brilliant stroke.

Like so much in the book it has a model in an Eddic poem, *Fáfnismál,* in which Sigurthr and Fáfnir talk while the dragon dies of the wound the hero has given him. Like Bilbo, Sigurthr refuses to tell the dragon his name but replies riddlingly (for fear of being cursed); like Smaug, Fáfnir sows dissension between partners by remarking on the greed that gold excites; the dissension actually breaks out when eating the dragon's heart helps Sigurthr to understand bird-talk (another prominent *Hobbit* motif). Nevertheless, *Fáfnismál* once again did not offer Tolkien enough. It drifted off into mere exchange of information; it contained, as Tolkien said of *Beowulf,* too much '*draconitas*' and not enough '*draco*', not enough of the 'real worm, with a bestial life and thought of his own' ('Monsters', pp. 258–59). Tolkien therefore set himself to repair this gap, and did so once more by introducing a strong dose of anachronistic modernity.

Thus the most remarkable thing about Smaug is his oddly circumlocutory mode of speech. He speaks in fact with the characteristic aggressive politeness of the British upper class, in which irritation and authority are in direct proportion to apparent deference or uncertainty. 'You have nice manners for a thief and a liar' are his opening words to Bilbo (their degree of irony unclear). 'You seem familiar with my name, but I don't seem to remember smelling you before. Who are you and where do you come from, may I ask?' He might be a testy colonel approached by a stranger in a railway carriage; why has Bilbo not been introduced? At the same time the 'bestial life' of the worm keeps intruding, as he remarks on Bilbo's smell and boasts parenthetically, 'I know the smell (and taste) of dwarf— none better', or when he rolls over, 'absurdly pleased' like a clumsy spaniel, to show the hobbit his armoured belly. One result is a frequent and vivid sense of paradox, which the ancient world, innocent of scientific rationalism, could hardly have developed: Smaug has both wings and weight, as we are reminded when he leaves his lair and '*float[s]* heavy and slow in the dark like a monstrous crow' (my italics); and in the cold reptilian belly he keeps hot fire, which peeps out from under his eyelids when he pretends to sleep and flashes 'like scarlet lightning' when he is amused. The paradoxes, the oscillations between animal and intelligent behaviour, the contrast between creaky politeness of speech and plain gloating over murder, all help to give Smaug his dominant characteristic of 'wiliness', and what the narrator calls with utter modernity (the noun dates in this sense from 1847) his 'overwhelming personality'.

All this gives great plausibility to another unexpected datum which the narrator springs on us, i.e. 'the effect that dragon-talk has on the inexperienced', the 'dragon-spell' which keeps prompting Bilbo to run out and confess. No ancient text contains any such motif, but as Smaug oozes confidentially on — 'I will give you one piece of advice . . . I suppose you got a fair price. Come now, did you? . . . Well, that's just like them . . . I don't know if it has occurred to you . . . Bless me! Had you never thought of the catch?' — he assumes the 'old experienced' end of the polarity so strongly that it is no surprise for Bilbo to find himself pressed towards the 'young innocent' one. Yet the combined magico-moral effect (is it 'spell' or is it 'personality'?) reminds one also of the 'dragon-sickness' that Smaug and his treasure between them seem practically and magically to generate. The character of Smaug is part of a *Zusammenhang:* nothing could be more archaic or fantastic than a dragon brooding on its gold, and yet the strong sense of familiarity in this one's speech puts it back into the 'continuum of greed', makes it just dimly possible that dragon-motivations could on their different scale have some affinity with human ones — even real historical human ones.

If one followed this line of reasoning too far *The Hobbit* could appear suddenly as a *roman à thèse,* or even an allegory, in which Bilbo Baggins as Modern Man embarks on his Pilgrim's Progress (or Regress) into Fantasy, only to find that at the very heart of his monsterworld there is none other than an embodiment of his own worst nature, Greed or even Capitalism itself, skulking on its gold like a fiercer Miss Havisham. The moral would be that all *bourgeois* must turn Burglar, or something of the sort. Of course such a reading would only be a joke. Still, if by no stretch of the imagination an allegory, *The Hobbit* does begin to show by its conclusion some flickers of the 'large symbolism' Tolkien saw in *Beowulf* and tried more positively to reproduce in *The Lord of the Rings*. In its last scene, the conversation between Gandalf, Bilbo and Balin, the wizard is allowed to make the point that metaphors can 'after a fashion' be true, that romance and reality are differences of presentation, not of fact. The logic of what he says is that if the matter behind old songs can contain someone as prosaic as Bilbo, then maybe even the prosaic events of today will sometimes be the matter of old songs. There is accordingly a reality, and a continuity, in human nature, even dwarf-hobbit-human nature.

Yet the reason why this hint should not be taken further is obvious enough. Most of *The Hobbit* suggests strongly that Tolkien did not work from ideas, but from words, names, consistencies and contradictions in folk-tales, things as localised as the dissatisfaction with *Fáfnismál* which produced Smaug, the brooding over the riddle-contests of *Vafðrúðnismál or The Saga of King Heidrek* which led (somehow) to Gollum. The two most powerful fragments of all ancient poetry for Tolkien at this time, I cannot help thinking, were the two similar bits from *Beowulf* and *Sir Gawain* which imply there are whole worlds the narrator simply cannot get round to. The Old English poet hints at the 'wide journeys' which Sigemund the dragon-slayer made, 'the wicked deeds and battles which the children of men' (but maybe not of monsters) 'never knew clearly'. His medieval successor says of Sir Gawain six centuries later that he would never even have reached his main adventure 'had he not been stalwart and staunch and steadfast in God', so many were his clashes with worms and wolves, with wood-trolls 'and with ogres that hounded him from the heights of the fells'. In exactly the same spirit we are told that even going home Bilbo 'had many hardships and adventures before he got back', since 'the Wild was still the Wild, and there were many other things in it in those days besides the goblins'. Some of them have been half-glimpsed already: eyes in the darkness, 'old castles with an evil look', 'startled ears' responding to the news of the death of Smaug. But in essence the plot of *The Hobbit* is a tour through darknesses, with no more connection between Gollum and the eagles and Beorn and the spiders than that of one-after-another. The true end of *The Hobbit,* as opposed to the last scene of chaos and tidying-

up,† is the regretful farewell to the Wild just before, as archaic
Took cedes to Edwardian Baggins:

> They came to that high point at morning, and looking
> backwards they saw a white sun shining over the out-
> stretched lands. There behind lay Mirkwood, blue in the
> distance, and darkly green at the nearer edge even in spring.
> There far away was the Lonely Mountain on the edge of
> eyesight. On its highest peak snow yet unmelted was gleam-
> ing pale.
> 'So comes snow after fire, and even dragons have their
> ending!' said Bilbo, and he turned his back on the adven-
> ture. (p. 319)

Adventure in Middle-earth embodies a modern meaning, but
does not exist to propagate it. Insofar as the two worlds are related it is because the 'inner consistency' of Secondary Art
must necessarily (in order to be consistent) be the same as that
of Primary Art or truth.

---

† Even this, I suspect, has a philological root. In the 1928 introduction he
wrote to W. E. Haigh's *Glossary of the Dialect of the Huddersfield District,*
mentioned above in connection with 'Baggins', Tolkien had said that it was
important to observe 'the changes in sense that take place when words of more
"learned" origin are adopted and put to everyday use in dialect (see *keęnsil,
okshęn, inséns)'.* But *okshęn* in Huddersfield dialect meant not 'auction' but
'mess'. 'Shu'z nout but ę slut; ęr eęs ęz ę feęr okshęn', quoted Mr Haigh, or for
non-natives, 'She's nothing but a slut; her house is a fair auction'. When he
gets home Mr Baggins finds his house a 'fair auction' in both senses. Not only
are they selling his goods, they are failing to wipe their feet on the mat! The
word has become a 'fusion-point' of outraged respectability.

CHAPTER 4

A CARTOGRAPHIC PLOT

Seventeen years went by between the publication of *The Hobbit* and that *of The Fellowship of the Ring*. It is true that in the interim a World War was fought, and Tolkien's family grew up, while Tolkien himself was committed to many professorial duties which, as he later insisted, he did not neglect. Nevertheless, the main reason for the long hiatus was the pace and nature of Tolkien's own creativity. He remained absorbed in Middle-earth; to it indeed he dedicated his 'years of authority' as a scholar; but he found the composition of *The Lord of the Rings* a matter which had to be allowed to obey its own laws. Thanks to the publication of (in particular) volumes VI to IX of 'The History of Middle-earth', we now know a good deal more about this process than we did when this book was first written.

To begin with, one can see that Tolkien was perhaps taken aback by, and was certainly not prepared for the success of, *The Hobbit* and the very natural demand by his publishers for a sequel to it. As we again now know much more clearly, and as is discussed in chapter 7 below, he had been working on what was to become *The Silmarillion* for many years, and had a great deal of material available from that. He sent selections from this corpus to his publisher, Stanley Unwin, in November 1937 (*The Hobbit* had been published in September of that year), only to have them politely rejected, probably on the basis of a partial reading, a month later.[1] Stanley Unwin wanted a sequel, not a prequel, and more about hobbits, not about elves. Between 16th and 19th December 1937 Tolkien accordingly began to write on from the end of *The Hobbit,* calling his initial chapter, as it was to remain right through to final publication, 'A long-expected party'. However, what is bound to surprise anyone familiar with *The Lord of the Rings* who then reads through Tolkien's early drafts in *The Return of the Shadow* is quite how little Tolkien had in the way of a plan, or even of a conception.

Bilbo's ring certainly came into the story. But it is (according to a note written perhaps a couple of months after starting) 'not very dangerous, when used for good purpose' (see *Shadow,* p. 42). As Christopher Tolkien points out, the ring remains for some time no more than a 'highly convenient magical device', the 'central conception of the Ruling Ring' being 'not yet present'; the moment when this 'central idea' came to Tolkien is still not clear (see *Shadow,* pp. 70, 87, 227). Meanwhile the character who was to become Aragorn, or Strider, begins his career as 'a queer-looking, brown-faced hobbit' called Trotter, who always wears wooden shoes, first encountered just like Aragorn in *The Prancing Pony* in Bree. 'Trotter' gave Tolkien immense trouble: at least three times he wrote 'Who is Trotter?' as a note to himself, and came up with repeated discrepant guesses — he was a cousin of Bilbo, he was a hobbit who was also a Ranger, he was an elf in disguise — only to fix eventually on him as a human and descendant of the Men of the North. Even after the character had become fixed as the tall and long-legged Aragorn, though, Tolkien stuck determinedly to the increasingly inapposite name 'Trotter', even writing the defence of it which was to survive into the finished version of *The Lord of the Rings* as the defence of 'Telcontar' (see respectively for the above *Shadow,* pp. 137, 210, 214, 223; *Treason,* p. 6; *War,* p. 390; and *LOTR,* p. 845). As Christopher Tolkien repeatedly notes, his father could be extremely tenacious in holding on to a scene through several revisions, while at the same time sharply altering its context and meaning. But in these early stages it would be truer to say that Tolkien was 'sleepwalking' his way towards a plot than that he was proceeding according to a plan. I look back with some shame (see 'Preface' to this edition) on my early attempt to diagnose one from Tolkien's finished product. No wonder the Professor would have liked to 'talk more' with me 'about design as it appears or may be found'! He would have told me that the design I was anxious to find simply wasn't there, not from the beginning and possibly not at all. Nevertheless, to quote Bilbo, 'Not all those who wander are lost'. While Tolkien did not have a grand design or central conception, had made no plans for a sequel to *The Hobbit,* and could not directly use his 'Silmarillion' material, he was not entirely without pre-existing resources. Something of what was going on in his mind is revealed by one of the major differences between *The Hobbit* and *The Lord of the Rings:* their use of maps and names.

Maps and Names

In *The Hobbit* names are astonishingly rare. There are of course the twelve dwarves, all taken from the *Dvergatal* poem, and apprehended I suspect by most readers as a homogeneous unit broken only by Fili and Kili, who are young, Bombur, who is fat, Balin, who is kindly, and Thorin, who is boss. There are few elf-names, and none of those which do occur — Bladorthin, Dorwinion, Girion, Galion, Moria, Esgaroth — is at all prominent in the story. The Elvenking remains anonymous in *The Hobbit* and is identified as Thranduil only in *The Lord of the Rings* (p. 234). The only hobbit surnames given are Baggins, Took and Sackville-Baggins (this last to prove an anomaly in Middle-earth and a failure of tone), with 'Messrs Grubb, Grubb and Burrowes' the auctioneers at the very end. Elrond, Azog, Radagast, the ravens' onomatopoeic Roäc and Carc — these all but complete *The Hobbit*'s list. A common practice for Tolkien at this stage was simply to make names out of capital letters. Thus Bilbo lives in a tunnel which goes 'not quite straight into the side of the hill — The Hill, as all the people for many miles round called it'. The stream at the foot of The Hill is called The Water, the hobbits' town on The Water is called Hobbiton (near Bywater), and so on into Wilderland, where we find the Misty Mountains, the Long Lake, the Lonely Mountain, a river called Running and a valley called Dale. Even 'Gandalf' is actually a name of this type. It also comes from the *Dvergatal,* where it is near Thráinn, Thorinn and Thrór, but Tolkien evidently regarded it with some suspicion since it con-

tained the element -*álfr*, while it was his opinion that elves and
dwarves cohabited only in the pages of the *OED*. So what was
'Gandalf' doing in a dwarves' roster, and anyway what was a
'gand-'? If Tolkien looked in the *Icelandic Dictionary* of R.
Cleasby and Gudbrand Vigfusson, he would have found the
opinions that the meaning of *gandr* was 'somewhat dubious'
but probably *'anything enchanted or an object used by sorcerers'*,
while *gandálfr* was either 'a wizard' or maybe a 'bewitched
demon'. He concluded, clearly, that this dictionary definition
was once again wrong, and that *gandr* meant 'wand' or 'staff'
(the common property of wizards, as one can tell even from
Shakespeare's Prospero or Milton's Comus). Accordingly,
when Gandalf first appears 'all that the unsuspecting Bilbo saw
that morning was *an old man with a staff*' (my italics).[2] He
turns out not to be an elf, but by the end of *The Lord of the
Rings* it is clear he comes from Elvenhome. 'Gandalf' is in fact,
then, not a name but a description, as with Beorn, Gollum, the
Necromancer, and other people, places and things in *The
Hobbit*.

Since *The Silmarillion,* with its developed nomenclature,
was already in existence, it would be wrong to say that Tolkien
in the 1930s was not interested in names. It does look, though,
as if he was not sure how to bring them into fiction, especially
if they were English names. Yet the point had caught his attention. As *The Hobbit* neared completion he focused on the problem with sudden clarity—as one can see from *Farmer Giles of
Ham,* not published till 1949, but composed apparently in the
period 1935–38, i.e. overlapping with the final production of
The Hobbit (see *Bibliography,* pp. 73–74). This throws many
interesting sidelights on Tolkien's fictional development. For
one thing, it is the only one of his stories set unmistakably in
England, and while its history is that of nursery-rhyme,[†] its

---

† At the bridge Chrysophlax the dragon sticks his claw into the king's white
horse and roars, 'There are knights lying cold in the mountain-pass and soon
there will be more in the river. *All the king's horses and all the king's men!'* (my
italics). There is also passing reference to (old) King Coel, and to King Lear,
who was responsible for the 'partition under Locrin, Camber, and Albanac'.
The world of the imagined 'editor' is that of the 'Brutus books', or fake his-

geography is remarkably clear. Ham is now Thame, a town in Buckinghamshire twelve miles east of Oxford. Worminghall is four miles away and Oakley, which had its parson eaten, five. The capital of the Middle Kingdom, 'some twenty leagues distant from Ham', sounds like Tamworth, the historical capital of the Mercian kings, sixty-eight miles from Thame as the crow flies (a league, N.B., is three miles). Farthingho in Northamptonshire, where once 'an outpost against the Middle Kingdom was maintained', is on a direct line between those two places about a third of the way from Thame — proof of the 'Little Kingdom's' lack of territorial ambition. Wales, where the giants live, and the (Pennine) mountains where the dragons live are on this parochial scale suitably far off. And when Farmer Giles refuses to listen to tales about the folk 'North over the hills and far away, beyond the Standing Stones and all', he means Warwickshire, probably, whose boundary with Oxfordshire runs by the Rollright Stones.

All in all it is extremely unfair of the imagined 'editor' of *Farmer Giles* to criticise its imagined 'author' for feeble geography; that 'author', like Tolkien, 'lived himself in the lands of the Little Kingdom' and knew what he was writing about. But what is the point of this sudden precision? Evidently, Tolkien wanted to re-create a timeless and idealised England (or rather Britain) in which the place and the people remained the same regardless of politics. The story of *Farmer Giles* is therefore largely the triumph of native over foreign (for in Giles's court 'the vulgar tongue came into fashion, and none of his speeches were in the Book-latin'), as simultaneously of worth over fashion and of heroic song and popular lay over pompous pernickety rationalistic scholarship. In all these ways *Farmer Giles* continues the vein of the 'Man in the Moon' poems and of *The Hobbit* — as it does also in its jibing at the *OED* with its arrogantly 'civilised' definition of 'blunderbuss'.[3] However, at the

---

tory of Britain accepted as true in medieval times (and later). He treats the author of *Sir Gawain and the Green Knight* as a 'historian', paraphrasing his 'Where . . . oft boþe blysse and blunder / Ful skete hatz skyfted synne' as, p. 7, 'the years were filled with swift alternations of war and peace, of mirth and woe'.

same time the story can be seen as one of the several works Tolkien wrote around this time with reference to his own switch from academicism to creativity (see pp. 43–54 above). Is *Farmer Giles*, like 'Leaf by Niggle', an allegory?

The main reason for thinking so is Giles's supporter the parson, 'a grammarian', note, who 'could no doubt see further into the future than most men'. His vital act is to remind Giles to take a long rope with him when he goes to hunt the dragon. Without that rope, one may say, there would have been no treasure, no tame dragon, no Thame, no Little Kingdom. Moreover the parson is also in a sense responsible for Tailbiter, Giles's sword. He guesses what the sword is while Giles and the Miller are still arguing, confirms the guess when it will not go into its scabbard with a dragon near, and in spite of his patter about 'epigraphical signs' and archaic characters does actually read the runes on the sword and declare its identity as Tailbiter (or as he prefers to call it, Caudimordax). By doing all this the parson puts heart into Giles. All round he deserves a lot of the credit—certainly much more than Augustus Bonifacius Ambrosius Aurelianus Antoninus, the proud tyrant who sent Giles the sword, though only because to him plain heavy things were out of fashion. It is very nearly irresistible to conclude that in his mixture of learning, bluff and sense the parson represents an idealised (Christian) philologist; in which case the proud tyrant of the Middle Kingdom who discards his most trenchant blade looks very like literary criticism taking no notice of historical language study! One could go on: Farmer Giles would be the creative instinct, the rope (like Tailbiter) philological science, the dragon the ancient world of the Northern imagination brooding on its treasure of lost lays, the Little Kingdom the fictional space which Tolkien hoped to carve out, make independent and inhabit. Of course such an allegory would be a joke;[4] but a joke in Tolkienian style, an optimistic counter-part to 'Leaf by Niggle' a few years later.

In the whole story linguistic humour is paramount, from the gloomy proverbs of 'Sunny Sam' and his pigheaded misprision of Hilarius and Felix—'Ominous names . . . I don't like the sound of them'—to Giles's own determined native errors of grammar. The real errors, though, Tolkien ends by remarking, come from later and more 'learned' history. Thus

Thame should be Tame, 'for Thame with an h is a folly without warrant'. In actuality, of course, the whole story that Tolkien tells to account for the names of Thame and Worminghall is based on nothing, is mere fiction. Still, even in actuality Thame-with-an-h *remains* a folly without warrant, part of the wave of Book-latinisms which have given us T*h*ames and T*h*omas and cou*l*d and de*b*t and dou*b*t and half the other non-sounded, unhistorical, un-English inserted letters that plague our spelling to this day. Tolkien would have liked them not to exist. He deplored the feeble modern understanding of English names, English places, English culture. In *Farmer Giles of Ham* one can see him brooding over problems of re-creation and of continuity — for names and places remain whatever people think about them. Though he joked about them, Thame and Worminghall are a long step on from The Hill and The Water. Farthingho set Tolkien thinking about the Farthings of 'The Shire'.

The further development into *The Lord of the Rings* is obvious. Where *The Hobbit* had some forty or fifty rather perfunctory names, the indices of *The Lord of the Rings* list over 600 names of 'Persons, Beasts and Monsters', almost as many places, with a couple of hundred unclassifiable but named objects for good measure. In the same way Thror's Map and the map of Wilderland in *The Hobbit,* which added nothing to the story but decoration and a 'Here be tygers' feel of quaintness, have ceded to the foldout map of Middle-earth in the first edition of *The Fellowship of the Ring,* the even more detailed map of the Marches of Gondor and Mordor in *The Return of the King,* the map of the Shire at the end of the 'Prologue', the still further elaborated map issued as a poster by Pauline Baynes in 1970: all of these based on Tolkien's own maps (see *Treason,* pp. 295–323), and all of them full of details never directly used in the text. Christopher Tolkien confirms the truth of his father's words to Naomi Mitchison, 'I wisely started with a map, and made the story fit'; see *Letters,* p. 177 and *Treason,* p. 315. But even the characters of *The Lord of the Rings* have a strong tendency to talk like maps, and historical ones at that. On p. 371, Aragorn begins 'You are looking now south-west across the north plains of the Riddermark . . . Ere long we shall come to the mouth of the Limlight that runs down from Fangorn to join the Great River.' A little before Celeborn had been tracing the course of Anduin 'to the tall island of the Tindrock, that we call Tol Brandir', where it falls 'over the cataracts of Rauros down into the Nindalf, the Wetwang as it is called in your tongue. That is a wide region of sluggish fen . . . There the Entwash flows in . . . About that stream, on this side of the Great River, lies Rohan. On the further side are the bleak hills of the Emyn Muil.' The flow of knowledge, and of names, seems irrepressible, and the habit is shared by Gimli, Gandalf, Fangorn, even Meriadoc. Why such elaboration?

The answer, oddly, lies as far back as *The Hobbit*. There Bilbo on one occasion screwed up his courage to ask why something was called 'The Carrock'. Because it *was*, replied Gandalf nastily (p. 126).

> 'He called it the Carrock, because carrock is his word for it. He calls things like that carrocks, and this one is *the* Carrock because it is the only one near his home and he knows it well.'

This is unhelpful, and not even true, since *carrecc* is Old Welsh for 'rock', preserved in several modern names like Crickhowell in Brecon (or Crickhollow in the Buckland). However, Gandalf has put his finger on one point about names, which is that they are arbitrary, even if they were not so in the beginning. Once upon a time all names were like 'Gandalf' or 'the Hill': thus (the) Frogmorton meant 'the town in the marshy land where the frogs are' (see 'Guide', p. 185); Tolkien was *der tollkühne or* 'the foolhardy one'; Suffield, Tolkien's mother's name, '(the one from the) south field'; and so on. However, *that is not how names are now perceived.* In the modern world we take them as labels, as things accordingly in a very close one-to-one relationship with whatever they label. To use a pompous phrase, they are 'isomorphic with reality'. And that means they are extraordinarily useful to fantasy, weighing it down as they do with repeated implicit assurances of the existence of the things they label, and of course of their nature and history too.

Tolkien's new equation of fantasy with reality comes over most strongly in his map, account and history of 'the Shire', an extended 'Little Kingdom', one might say, transplanted to Middle-earth. The easiest way to describe it is to say that the

Shire is 'calqued' on England, 'calquing' being a linguistic term to mean that process in which the elements of a compound word are translated bit by bit to make a new word in another language, as in French *haut-parleur* from 'loudspeaker' (*parler haut* = 'speak loudly'), or Irish *each-chumhacht* from 'horsepower' (*each* = 'horse', like *eoh, equus* on p. 21 above). The point about calques is that the derivative does not sound anything like its original: nevertheless, it betrays influence at every point. Thus historically the Shire is like/unlike England, the hobbits like/unlike English people. Hobbits live in the Shire as the English live in England, but like the English they come from somewhere else, indeed from the Angle (in Europe between Flensburg Fjord and the Schlei, in Middle-earth between Hoarwell and Loudwater). Both groups have forgotten this fact. Both emigrated in three tribes, Angles, Saxons and Jutes or Stoors, Harfoots and Fallohides, all since then largely mingled. The English were led by two brothers, Hengest and Horsa, i.e. 'stallion' and 'horse', the hobbits by Marcho and Blanco, cp. Old English **marh,* 'horse', *blanca* (only in *Beowulf*) 'white horse'.[5] All four founded realms which evolved into uncharacteristic peace: there was no battle in the Shire between the Greenfields, 1147, and the Battle of Bywater, 1419, an interval of 272 years very like the 270 between publication of *The Return of the King* and the last battle fought on English soil, Sedgemoor, 1685. Organisationally too the Shire, with its mayors, musters, moots and Shirriffs, is an old-fashioned and idealised England, while the hobbits, in their plainness, greediness, frequent embarrassments, distrust of 'outsiders'†and most of all in their deceptive ability to endure rough handling form an easily recognisable if again old-fashioned self-

---

† 'Outsiders' lead to one of Tolkien's weakest jokes. In early English a 'bounder' was someone who set boundaries, and so kept out 'outsiders'. However, in the slang of his youth a 'bounder' was, *OED* post-1889, 'a person who by his behaviour places himself outside the pale of well-bred society', i.e. an 'outsider'. Hence the joke in *LOTR,* p. 147. It seems that Tolkien had not decided early on how funny the hobbits were to be. Some of the parodic element of *The Hobbit* persists for a couple of chapters: 'eleventy-first', 'tweens', 'mathoms', etc.

image of the English. The calquing is most evident, however, on the map.

Here all that need be said is that Tolkien took most of his Shire-names from his own near surroundings. They sound funny but they ring true. Thus 'Nobottle' in the Northfarthing makes us think of glass containers, hardly plausible as features of the landscape, but the name comes from Old English *niowe* 'new', *botl* 'house' (as in *bytla,* cp. 'hobbit'). There is a Nobottle in Northamptonshire thirty-five miles from Oxford (and not far from Farthingstone). It means much the same as Newbury, also a town in England twenty-five miles south of Oxford and also a place in the Shire, or rather in the Buckland. Buckland itself is an Oxfordshire placename, common all over England since it has the rather dull etymology of *bócland,* land 'booked' to the Church by charter, and so different from *folcland* or 'folkland', which was inalienable. That derivation was impossible in Middle-earth, so Tolkien constructed the more satisfactory one that the Buckland was where the Buck family lived, was indeed a 'folkland' centred on Bucklebury, like the 'Tookland' centred on Tuckborough. As for 'Took', that too appears a faintly comic name in modern English (people prefer to respell it 'Tooke'), but it is only the ordinary Northern pronunciation of the very common 'Tuck'. Five minutes with the *Oxford Dictionary of Place-Names,* E. Ekwall's *English River Names* or P. H. Reaney's *Dictionary of British Surnames* will provide explanations for most hobbitic names of any sort, and the same is true, on a more learned scale, of the rest of Middle-earth. Thus Celeborn's 'Wetwang' is also a place in Yorkshire; the Riders' 'Dunharrow' has evident English parallels; the rivers Gladden, Silverlode, Limlight, etc., all have English roots or analogues; and so on outwards. The work that went into all these is immense. It also seems largely wasted, since for all the characters' efforts half the names never get into the plot! Still, Tolkien certainly thought, and very probably he thought rightly, that all this effort was not wasted. The maps and the names give Middle-earth that air of solidity and extent both in space and time which its successors so conspicuously lack. They mark an ambition much increased from *The Hobbit*'s opening scenes of parody and close of detached appreciation. They also quite simply provided grist for Tolkien's creative mill—one which, like the mills of God, ground slow but ground (in the end) exceeding small.

Getting Started

In a footnote to the 'Epilogue' of 'On Fairy-Stories', Tolkien noted, or confessed, that though every fantasy-writer aims at truth, 'it is seldom that the "inspiration" is so strong and lasting that it leavens all the lump, and does not leave much that is mere uninspired "invention".' One might think that authors start off with a flash of 'inspiration' and as it dies away keep things going with 'invention'. In Tolkien's case it looks very much as if he worked the other way round: he got started on relatively laborious 'inventions', and found as the story gathered way that the inevitable complications of these brought him 'inspiration'. Thus *The Hobbit* does not quite take off till Bilbo finds the ring, and even then the sense of events gaining continuity is not strong till the company reaches Mirkwood, on the other side of the house of Beorn. The same is true of *The Lord of the Rings*.

It is for one thing remarkable that Frodo has to be dug out of no less than five 'Homely Houses' before his quest is properly launched: first Bag End, then the little house at Crickhollow with its redundant guardian Fredegar Bolger, then the house of Tom Bombadil, then the *Prancing Pony,* and finally Rivendell with its 'last Homely House east of the Sea'. Each of these locations has of course its images and encounters to present, and some of them (like the meeting with Strider) turn out to be vital. Nevertheless there is a sense that the zest of the story goes not into the dangers but the recoveries—hot baths at Crickhollow, song and dancing at Bree, Goldberry's water that seems like wine, and Butterbur's 'small and cosy room' with its 'hot soup, cold meats, a blackberry tart, new loaves, slab of butter, and half a ripe cheese'. And this is to take no account of meals *en passant,* like Gildor Inglorion's pastoral elvish banquet and Farmer Maggot's 'mighty dish of bacon and mushrooms'! Meanwhile the Black Riders, for all their snuffling and deadly cries, are not the menace they later become, for though they may only be waiting for a better chance, as Aragorn insists, they could have saved themselves trouble several times in the Shire, in Bree and on Weathertop by pressing their attacks home. It seems likely that, as at the start of *The Hobbit*, Tolkien found the transit from familiar Shire to archaic Wilderland an inhibiting one. He broke through in *The Hobbit* with the trolls and then the ring. In *The Lord of the Rings* his invention came, to begin with, from a sort of self-plagiarism.

The hobbits' first three real encounters are with the Willow-man and Tom Bombadil in the Old Forest, and with the Barrow-wight on the Downs outside. All three could almost be omitted without disturbing the rest of the plot.[6] Willow-man is a forerunner of the Ents, or rather the Huorns, but Bombadil never comes back into the story at all: the Council of Elrond considers him for a moment; Gandalf stops for a chat when all serious work is over. The Barrow-wight does a little more in providing the sword that Merry uses on the chief Ringwraith in Book V, a sword specifically designed for use against the Witch-king of Angmar, which is what that Nazgûl turns out to be. Still, that is a by-product. All three of these characters furthermore go a long way back in Tolkien's mind, as far back as hobbits, probably, further than the Shire or the Ring; they are all in the poem 'The Adventures of Tom Bombadil', printed in the *Oxford Magazine* in 1934 (just as the song Frodo sings in the *Prancing Pony* is a revision from 1923). Tolkien was raiding his own larder, and one can in the end see why.

It is admittedly not so easy in the beginning. The thing we would like to know about Tom Bombadil is what he *is*, but this is never asked or answered directly. In chapter 7 Frodo raises the courage to ask instead who he is, only to receive the answers, from Goldberry, (1) 'He is', (2) 'He is, as you have seen him', (3) 'He is the Master of wood, water and hill', and from Tom himself (4) 'Don't you know my name yet? That's the only answer.' He seems in fact to be a *lusus naturae*, a one-member category; the hobbits are doubtful whether he can be called a man, though he looks like one apart from his size, which is intermediate between man and hobbit. More revealing is his main attribute, fearlessness, present in *The Lord of the Rings* but even clearer in the 1934 poem (and in its rewritten form as lead-poem of *The Adventures of Tom Bombadil* in 1962). The

action of that is simply four clashes between Tom and potentially hostile creatures: Goldberry, 'the Riverwoman's daughter', who pulls him into the river; Willow-man, who catches
him in a crack; the Badgerfolk, who drag him down their tunnel; and finally, as Tom goes home, the Barrow-wight behind
the door:

> 'You've forgotten Barrow-wight dwelling in the old mound
> up there atop the hill with the ring of stones round.
> He's got loose to-night: under the earth he'll take you!
> Poor Tom Bombadil, pale and cold he'll make you!'

But Tom reacts only with simple imperatives: 'You let me out
again . . . You show me out at once . . . Go back to grassy
mound, on your stony pillow / lay down your bony head, like
Old Man Willow.' And once the threats have been dismissed
Tom goes further, going back to seize Goldberry from her
nameless mother 'in her deep weedy pool', taking her back to
his house to be married. Their wedding-night is undisturbed
by the hags and bogles murmuring outside, and the poem ends
with Goldberry combing her hair and Tom chopping sticks
of willow. As Goldberry says to Frodo, Tom is 'the Master'.
What he *is* may not be known, but what he *does* is dominate.

Tom's other major quality is naturalness. Even his language
has something unpremeditated about it. A lot of what he says
is nonsense, the first thing indeed that the hobbits notice, even
before they see him. When it is not 'hey dol! merry dol!' and
the like, it tends to be strongly assertive or onomastic, mere
lists of names and qualities. From time to time it breaks
through to being 'perhaps a strange language unknown to the
hobbits, an ancient language whose words were mainly those of
wonder and delight'. But though they may not know the language, the hobbits understand it, as they understand Goldberry's rain-song without recognising the words; and when
Tom names something (as he does with the hobbits' ponies)
the name sticks—the animals respond to nothing else the rest
of their lives. There is an ancient myth in this feature, that of
the 'true language', the tongue in which there is a thing for each
word and a word for each thing, and in which signifier then naturally has power over signified—language 'isomorphic with
reality' once again.[7] It is this which seems to give Tom his

power. He is the great singer; indeed he does not yet seem to have discovered, or sunk into, prose. Much of what he says is printed by Tolkien as verse, but almost all of what he says can be *read* as verse, falling into strongly-marked two-stress phrases, with or without rhyme and alliteration, usually with feminine or unstressed endings; see for instance his last 'prose' speech, 'Tóm will give you góod advice, / tíll this day is óver / (áfter that your ówn luck / must gó with you and gúide you): / fóur miles alóng the road / you'll cóme upon a víllage, / Brée under Brée-hill, / with dóors looking wéstward.' The scansion-system (more complicated than I have marked) is a little like that of the Old English verse Tolkien was later to reproduce in the songs of Rohan, but more like that of much Old English 'prose', over whose claim to being 'verse' editors still hesitate. The point is though that while we appreciate it as rhythmical (unlike prose), we also do not mark it as premeditated or artificial (unlike verse). The hobbits fall into song themselves, 'as if it was easier and more natural than talking'.

Tom Bombadil, then, is fearless. In some way he antedates the corruptions of Art. According to Elrond he is 'Iarwain Ben-adar . . . oldest and fatherless'. Like Adam, also fatherless, 'whatsoever [he] called every living creature, that was the name thereof'. Unlike the descendants of Adam he does not suffer from the curse of Babel; everybody understands his language by instinct. It is odd, though, that Tom shares the adjective 'oldest' with another being in *The Lord of the Rings,* Fangorn the Ent, whom Gandalf calls 'the oldest living thing that still walks beneath the Sun' (p. 488). An inconsistency? It need not be so, if one accepts that Tom is not living — as the Nazgûl and the Barrow-wight are not dead. Unlike even the oldest living creatures he has no date of birth, but seems to have been there since before the Elves awoke, a part of Creation, an exhalation of the world. There are hints in old poems of such an idea. The Old English poem *Genesis B,* originally written in Old Saxon, at one point calls Adam *selfsceafte guma,* which could be translated calquishly as 'self-shaped man'. Modern translations prefer to say 'self-doomed' or something of the sort, while the Bosworth-Toller *Dictionary* prefers 'a man by spontaneous generation'. Adam of course wasn't spontaneously generated. But Tolkien may have wondered what the thing behind such a word could be. He must have also reflected on the strange Green Knight who comes to challenge Sir Gawain in the poem he had edited in 1925, like Tom Bombadil unflappable, a *lusus naturae* in size and colour, conveying to many critics a sense of identification with the wild wintry landscape from which he appears, called by the poet in respectful but uncertain style *an aghlich mayster*, 'a terrible Master'. The green man, the uncreated man, the man grown by 'spontaneous generation' . . . From what? Obviously, from the land. Tom Bombadil is a *genius loci*. But the *locus* of which he is the *genius* is not the barren land of the Green Knight's Pennine moors, but the river and willow country of the English midlands, or of the Thames Valley. He represents, as Tolkien said himself, 'the spirit of the (vanishing) Oxford and Berkshire countryside' (*Letters,* p. 26).

It is interesting that Tom's adversary from 1934 on is Willow-man. By *The Fellowship of the Ring* both have become attached to the River Withywindle, 'withy' of course being no more than the local word for 'willow', while 'windle' is O.E. **windol,* 'winding brook'. There is a Withybrook north of Oxford, in Warwickshire, while Windsor in Berkshire to the south could be derived from **windolsora,* 'the landing-place on the winding stream', in this case the Thames. As for the sudden striking description of the Withywindle in chapter 6, with its drowsy late-afternoon sunshine and through it winding lazily 'a dark river of brown water, bordered with ancient willows, arched over with willows, blocked with fallen willows, and flecked with thousands of faded willow-leaves', it would not do badly as a description of the stream that runs down to join the Thames at Oxford, the Cherwell — a 'very apt name', says Ekwall's *English River-Names,* meaning probably 'the winding river'.

The hobbits, to be brief, have got outside the Shire but not outside the boundaries of 'the Little Kingdom'. Tom is the spirit of pretty much their own land, and so like them in being slow, lavish, unbeautiful, but only stupid-seeming. Willowman is a narrower variant of the same idea, and Goldberry another in being 'the River-daughter', at first sight 'enthroned in the midst of a pool', with rippling hair and reed-green gown and flag-lilies round her waist and feet. Barrow-wight too springs from landscape, for barely fifteen miles from Oxford begins the greatest concentration of barrows in the country, where the green Berkshire downs rise from the plain. 'Wayland's Smithy' and the others must have called to Tolkien's mind the many Icelandic tales of the dwellers in the mounds, the *haugbúar* or 'hogboys' of dialect story. As for 'Bree on Bree-hill', it shows its conception in its name. Three miles from Worminghall and ten from Oxford the town of Brill sits on its hummock, betraying in its name a tale of ancient conquest.[8] 'Bree' *means* 'hill' in Welsh and Brill (from 'bree-hill') is therefore in a way nonsense, exactly parallel with Chetwode (or 'wood-wood') in Berkshire close by, exactly opposite to the 'capitalised' names of The Hill, The Water or The Carrock. Tolkien borrowed the name for its faint Celtic 'style', to make subliminally the point that hobbits were immigrants too, that their land had had a history before them. But for their first hundred-odd pages the hobbits seem to be wandering through a very closely localised landscape, one even narrower than their own travels; and that landscape and the beings attached to it are in a way the heroes.[9] They force themselves into the story. But while they slow its pace, appear strictly redundant, almost eliminate the plot centred on the Ring,[10] they also do the same job as the maps and the names: they suggest very strongly a world which is more than imagined, whose supernatural qualities are close to entirely natural ones, one which has moreover been 'worn down', like ours, by time and by the process of lands and languages and people all growing up together over millennia. In sober daylight no linguist would care to admit that places exhale their own names any more than English counties exude Tom Bombadils. Many people, however, feel that names fit; and that places have a character of their own. On this not entirely irrational opinion much of Middle-earth is based.

What has just been argued naturally says little about the story in *The Fellowship of the Ring* chapters 1–10, except perhaps that it was not the author's overriding interest. Still, much could be said about that too. Probably an analysis of the fantasy in those chapters would do well to start with the things that are not old in Tolkien's imagination and do *not* appear to fit. It is a great moment, for instance, when Merry wakes from the wight's spell and remembers only a death not his own. 'The men of Carn Dûm came on us at night, and we were worsted.

Ah! The spear in my heart!' He seems to have taken on the personality of the body in the barrow, but that warrior can hardly be the wight, for Bombadil remembers the dead lords and ladies with affection. So what did the wight intend, and what is it itself, human ghost or alien 'shadow' or sediment of death attaching itself to gold like the dragon-spell of avarice in *The Hobbit*? The uncertainty and the glimpses of an alien world that defies understanding (white robes, wriggling hand, sword across neck), these offer the special thrill of fantasy beyond study. However, that thrill is also related to the sense of solidity already mentioned. Without the feeling that he is at once independent, *sui generis,* and also related to a larger pattern that can take in the Ring and Farmer Maggot and the elves and the Dark Lord, even Bombadil would be a lesser creation.

Stars, Shadows, Cellar-doors:
Patterns of Language and of History

The basis of Tolkien's invention is unexpectedly earthbound and factual. However, he was also good at peripheral suggestion. '"Strider" I am', says Aragorn, 'to one fat man who lives within a day's march of foes that would freeze his heart, or lay his little town in ruin, if he were not guarded ceaselessly.' He does not say what the 'foes' are—wood-orcs? trolls? killer-Huorns? ettens from the high fells?—but the idea of glimpsed shapes in the sunless woods remains. In the same style Gandalf declares that 'far, far below the deepest delving of the Dwarves, the world is gnawed by nameless things', but does not particularise. The 'things' include Durin's Bane, the Balrog (maybe the same as the creature that replies to Pippin's stone with faint knockings, but maybe not), and such beings as Shelob, Gollum, the 'fell voices' and maniac laughter of the elementals like mad Bombadils who haunt the Dimrill Stair. Sometimes a veil is lifted for a moment, as when Gandalf tells the story of Gollum and takes Frodo back for a moment to Sméagol and Déagol and their quiet empty world of pools and irises and little boats made of reeds. However, more often stories are not told. Aragorn does not explain 'the cats of queen Beruthiel' (p. 303), he cuts off the tale of Gil-galad just before Frodo gets to the word 'Mordor' (p. 186), he offers only a selection from Beren and Tinúviel (pp. 187–90). Gandalf says similarly that if he were to tell Frodo all the story of the Ring 'we should still be sitting here when Spring had passed into Winter', and of Sauron's loss of the Ring 'That is a chapter of ancient history which it might be good to recall . . . One day, perhaps, I will tell you all the tale.' *Might* and *perhaps* are the operative words. It is a mistake to think these matters are settled by Appendices, or later publications (even if some of them eventually are). Their job in context is to whet the appetite and provide perspective: they do this, perhaps, less powerfully as history than as 'myth'.

The centre of Gandalf's account in 'The Shadow of the Past' is thus the little verse about the rings, which acts as epigraph to the whole work and also as final confirmation of the nature of the Ring itself. It concludes:

> One Ring to rule them all, One Ring to find them,
> One Ring to bring them all, and in the darkness bind them
> In the land of Mordor where the Shadows lie.

The last line is a kind of internal refrain for the verse. It is echoed oddly in the snatch of song that Sam repeats a hundred and forty pages later, about Gil-galad, which ends:

> But long ago he rode away
> and where he dwelleth none can say;
> for into darkness fell his star
> in Mordor where the shadows are.

The stanza is yet *another* pause on the brink of a story, but it acts also as a corroboration. What is the relationship between the one poem and the other? Nobody says, but there must be some relationship, some body of lore that has acted as stimulus for both; and this is not Gandalf's property alone, but something (once) widely dispersed in Middle-earth.

Bits of it keep turning up. Gildor and the other elves appear on p. 78 singing a 'hymn' to Elbereth which ends 'We still remember, we who dwell / In this far land beneath the trees, / Thy starlight on the Western Seas.' The implication is that the elves are exiles, themselves living in shadow though not in Mordor, looking up to a starlight from which they are now excluded. Bombadil evokes the same image of loss when he says sixty pages later 'Few now remember them, yet still some go wandering, sons of forgotten kings walking in loneliness, guarding from evil things folk that are heedless', and his words stir in the hobbits 'a vision as it were of a great expanse of years behind them, like a vast shadowy plain over which there strode shapes of Men, tall and grim with bright swords, and last came one with a star on his brow'. We realise eventually that this last is Strider, or rather Elessar 'the Elfstone'; but Bombadil's words just before are paralleled by Bilbo's gnomic and descriptive rhyme, heard before anything of Strider's lineage is revealed:

> All that is gold does not glitter,
> Not all those who wander are lost . . .

The echoes run off in many directions, but through them run the words 'remember', 'wander', 'dwell', most of all 'star' and 'shadow'. From all these references, together with others like Aragorn's song of Beren and Tinúviel with its heavy but elusive use of 'stars in shadow', 'trembling starlight', 'shadowy hair', one could further construct a kind of repeated pattern, allegedly historical, in which stars and shadows are always at strife, the latter nearer and more powerful, the former persisting in memory and in resistance.[11] Probably no reader actually does this, but all readers nevertheless perceive something, to be confirmed, reinforced, but not supplanted later on by fuller accounts from Gandalf and Elrond, from Galadriel's song on pp. 368–69, from the Appendices, eventually from *The Silmarillion* and the many versions of the latter in 'The History of Middle-earth'. Few readers also can fail to have resonances struck from their own familiar myths: the 'sons of Martha' story, maybe, in the grim unthanked indispensable Rangers, the Harrowing of Hell in Bilbo's 'A light from the shadows shall spring', Icarus or Prometheus or Balder Dead in the fall of Gil-galad. All these remain unfocused but not unfelt. Without extensive explanations they set the characters in a moral world as well as a geographical one, both of them like but not the same as our own.

'Gil-galad', then, has a function rather analogous to 'Nobottle'. Both offer the assurance that there is more to Middle-earth than can immediately be communicated. Among the many differences between the two names, though, is the fact that 'Gil-galad' is clearly something from an unfamiliar language; the effect of languages in Tolkien's world, as might be expected, is as great as those of maps or of myths. As might also be expected, Tolkien used them in an extremely peculiar, idiosyncratic and daring way, which takes no account at all of predictable reader-reaction. The 'myth of stars and shadows', for instance, is repeated in entirely characteristic style in a song sung in Rivendell (p. 231): 'O Elbereth who lit the stars . . . I will sing to you after having looked into far lands from here in tree-tangled Middle-earth . . .' However, no reader of *The Lord of the Rings* can actually know that, since it is sung in the elvish language Sindarin and not offered in translation till p. 64 of *The Road Goes Ever On,* the song-cycle published in 1968.[12] As they stand in *The Fellowship of the Ring* they are nonsense syllables: *A Elbereth Gilthoniel . . . Na-chaered palan-díriel o galadhremmin ennorath, Fanuilos, le linnathon.* What could any reader be expected to make of that?

Tolkien of course had an answer to the question, a private theory. It had been on his mind since 1926, when in his 'General Philology' chapter for *The Year's Work in English Studies* vol. 5 he had hinted there might be such a science as *Lautphonetik,* translatable as 'a phonology of sounds'. But all phonology is about sounds. Tolkien seems to have meant 'an aesthetics of sounds', a science that would explain why certain sounds or combinations of sounds produced different effects from others. Thirty years later he came back to the same idea in his last major learned work, the O'Donnell lecture on 'English and Welsh' given in Oxford in 1954 just after *The Fellowship of the Ring* came out. It is a discursive piece which covers many points, but one of them is a considered though not scientific attempt to say what makes a language beautiful. There is a pleasure, insisted Tolkien, 'in the phonetic elements of a language and in the style of their patterns'. More pleasure may come from 'the association of these word-forms with meanings', but that is a separate stage. Tolkien said that he had only needed to see a vocabulary-list of Gothic for his heart to be taken by storm. The same was true of Finnish; and all along something of the sort had flashed on him at the sight of Welsh names on English coal-trucks, or such simple inscriptions as *adeiladwyd 1887* on Welsh chapels.

What kind of pleasure was this? At the age of sixty-two Tolkien felt no urge to found a new branch of learning, and fell back on the word 'style': the pleasure comes from 'fitness . . . to a whole style', is felt in 'the reception (or imagination) of a word-form which is felt to have a certain style'. One feature of the Welsh 'style' might be 'the fondness for nasal consonants . . . and the frequency with which word-patterns are made with the soft and less sonorous *w* and the voiced spirants *f* and *dd* contrasted with the nasals: *nant, meddiant, afon, llawenydd, cenfigen, gwanwyn, gwenyn, crafanc,* to set down a few at random' (p. 40). The word and the theory were also in Tolkien's head when he wrote Appendix F to *The Lord of the Rings* and declared that he had used names like Bree, Combe, Archet and Chetwood because they contained non-English elements and he needed words to sound 'queer', to imitate 'a style that we should perhaps vaguely feel to be "Celtic"'. This was Tolkien's major linguistic heresy. He thought that people could feel history in words, could recognise language 'styles', could extract sense (of sorts) from sound alone, could moreover make aesthetic judgements based on phonology. He said the sound of 'cellar door' was more beautiful than the sound of 'beautiful'. He clearly believed that *untranslated* elvish would do a job that English could not.

Could he have been right? Tolkien's heresy was against the belief that language is only in a very limited way onomatopoeic, that we just happen from long habit to think 'pig' sounds piggish, while Danes (presumably) think *pige* sounds girlish. It was like him to think, Bombadil-style, that beneath all this there might be a 'true language', one 'isomorphic with reality', and that in any case there might often be a close connection between thing-signified, person-signifying, and language-signified-in, especially if the person who spoke the language lived on the thing. Legolas puts this view strongly in *The Two Towers* when he listens to Aragorn singing in Rohirric, a language he does not know, and then remarks (pp. 496–97), 'That, I guess, is the language of the Rohirrim . . . for it is like to this land itself, rich and rolling in part, and else hard and stern as the mountains. But I cannot guess what it means, save that it is laden with the sadness of Mortal Men.' He is right, but his is only one of many correct appraisals in the trilogy. The hobbits hear Gildor and the elves singing, and even the ones who know no Quenya find that 'the sound blending with the melody seemed to shape itself in their thought into words which they only partly understood' (p. 78). The dirge of Gléowine for Théoden has the same effect on p. 954. Gandalf uses the Black Speech of Mordor in Rivendell on p. 247 and his voice turns 'menacing, powerful, harsh as stone', so that the elves cover their ears and Elrond rebukes him, not for what he says but for the language he says it in. Conversely Merry 'felt his heart leap' at the songs of the Muster of Rohan (p. 775); and when Gimli sings of Durin Sam Gamgee — not a learned character — responds simply and directly to the ring of elvish and dwarvish names. '"I like that!" said Sam. "I should like to learn it. *In Moria, in Khazad-dûm!*"' Obviously his response is a model one.

One can see from all this why Tolkien made the seemingly wild assertion in 1955 that to him his work was 'largely an essay in linguistic esthetic' (*Letters*, p. 220). One can also see that he was convinced his heresy had worked, for at the end of his remarks on 'the Welsh linguistic style' in 'English and Welsh' he brought forward *The Lord of the Rings* not as fiction but as evidence, declaring: 'The names of persons and places in this story were mainly composed on patterns deliberately modelled on those of Welsh (closely similar but not identical). This element in the tale has given perhaps more pleasure to more readers than anything else in it.' 'Mainly' is a bit of an exaggeration; the Welsh-modelled names in Middle-earth are only those of Gondor and of Elvish, or more accurately of Sindarin, and these are precisely the most doubtful cases. Many English readers, however, accustomed to the linguistic map of England with its varying Anglo-Saxon, Old Norse and Welsh components, might in all sobriety be able to say 'Garstang sounds northern' or 'Tolpuddle sounds West Country', and be able to go on from there to cope with the varying styles of the Shire, the Riddermark and the dwarves. There must be much more doubt over how many readers grasp first-hand that the Rivendell song on p. 231 is in Sindarin but Galadriel's on p. 368 in

Quenya, and that these two languages are furthermore related. Still, it would be as wrong to say that readers understand nothing of alien songs as to say they understand everything. As with place-names, landscapes, mythic fragments, 'feel' or 'style' is enough, however much it escapes a cerebral focus.

Tolkien's linguistic map of Middle-earth furthermore shows exceptionally well the relation in his mind between 'inspiration' and 'invention'. One could argue that much of what he decided was forced on him: mere 'invention' to get out of difficulty. Thus it was inevitable that the story should be in modern English, and from the start of *The Hobbit* it was clear that the Bagginses at least were English by temperament and turn of phrase. Now Tolkien knew (none better) that logically this was impossible. He was committed then to a fiction in which 'hobbitic' was an *analogue* of English, was in fact a 'stylistically' neutral variant of a Common Speech. What then of dwarvish? Dwarf-names were already there in *The Hobbit,* and were in Old Norse, a language whose relationship to modern English was to Tolkien all but tangible. The dwarves then must have spoken a language analogous to the Common Speech in exactly the same way as Old Norse is to modern English; and since that was hardly likely in the case of two totally different species (men and hobbits are not really different species; see *LOTR,* p. 2), Tolkien found himself committed also to the notion that the dwarves spoke human languages and used human names for convenience, but had a secret language and secret names of their own, the latter not even to be carved on tombs (a belief which he no doubt enjoyed because of its corroboration in the Grimms' 'Rumpelstiltskin'). Having fitted in English and Norse, Old English could not be far behind: hence the Riders with their entirely Old English terminology, their names which are often Old English nouns capitalised (like Théoden King, a phrase of exactly the same type as Bree-hill),[13] the sense the characters occasionally indicate that 'hobbitic' is a worn-down variant of Rohirric in which words are changed but sound (p. 544) 'not unfitting'. But by this stage 'invention' has stopped and 'inspiration' taken over. In the conversation between Pippin, Merry and Théoden outside Isengard, Tolkien is no longer trying to explain old inconsistencies from *The Hobbit,* but writing ever deeper into a world with a life of its own.

This led him, indeed, into yet further inconsistencies, or rather disingenuousnesses. Tolkien was obliged to pretend to be a 'translator'. He developed the pose with predictable rigour, feigning not only a text to translate but behind it a whole manuscript tradition, from Bilbo's diary to the Red Book of Westmarch to the Thain's Book of Minas Tirith to the copy of the scribe Findegil. As time went on he also felt obliged to stress the autonomy of Middle-earth — the fact that he was only translating analogously, not writing down the names and places as they really had been, etc. Thus of the Riddermark and its relation to Old English he said eventually 'This linguistic procedure [i.e. translating Rohirric into Old English] does not imply that the Rohirrim closely resembled the ancient English otherwise, in culture or art, in weapons or modes of warfare, except in a general way due to their circumstances . . .' (note on p. 1110). But this claim is totally untrue. With one admitted exception, the Riders of Rohan resemble the Anglo-Saxons down to minute details. The fact is that the ancient languages came first.[14] Tolkien did not draw them into a fiction he had already written because there they might be useful, though that is what he pretended. He wrote the fiction to present the languages, and he did that because he loved them and thought them intrinsically beautiful. Maps, names and languages came before plot. Elaborating them was in a sense Tolkien's way of building up enough steam to get rolling; but they had also in a sense provided the motive to want to. They were 'inspiration' and 'invention' at once, or perhaps more accurately, by turns.

'The Council of Elrond'

The gist of what has been said in this chapter is that *The Lord of the Rings* possesses unusual cultural depth. 'Culture' is not a word Tolkien used much; it changed meaning sharply during his lifetime, and not in a direction he approved. Still, one can see a deep understanding of its modern meaning of 'the whole complex of learned behaviour . . . the material possessions, the language and other symbolism, of some body of people' in chapter 2 of Book II of *The Fellowship of the Ring*. This marks a jump-off point for the characters, whose objective is disclosed within it. It was also, I suspect, a jump-off point for Tolkien, since after that he was no longer writing his way through landscapes he had travelled before. It is therefore perhaps not surprising that as with the house of Beorn in *The Hobbit*, 'The Council of Elrond' should provide a sudden introduction to archaic and heroic worlds confronting and overwhelming modern, practical ones. The later work is, however, many degrees more complex than its earlier analogue, being indeed an interweaving of at least six major voices besides minor ones and reported ones; as well as telling a complex tale in complex fashion, what all these voices do is present, in our language, a violent 'culture-clash'.

This comes out most in the speeches and scripts impacted *inside* Gandalf's interrupted monologue of pages 243–58, the fifth and longest from a major speaker (the others coming from Glóin, Elrond, Boromir, Aragorn, Legolas). Within that monologue Gaffer Gamgee functions as a kind of base-line of normality — and, concomitantly, of emptiness. 'I had words with old Gamgee', Gandalf reports. 'Many words and few to the point':

> '"I can't abide changes," said he, "not at my time of life, and least of all changes for the worst." "Changes for the worst," he repeated many times.
>
> "Worst is a bad word," I said to him, "and I hope you do not live to see it."'

It is indeed a bad word, especially when all the Gaffer has to complain about is the Sackville-Bagginses; Denethor uses it as well, much later (p. 796), but again with ominous effect. As for 'abide', as used by Gaffer Gamgee it has almost no semantic content at all; in context it means 'bear, tolerate, put up with', but in that sense is simply untrue. The Gaffer can abide changes; he just has. He means only that he doesn't like them. But there is a moral for him in the history of the word, which has the frequent early sense of 'to await the issue of, to wait (stoically) for, to live to see'. In this last sense the Gaffer *could* 'abide' changes, and he does. Right at the end he moralises, stubborn as ever, 'It's an ill wind as blows nobody any good, *as I always say'* (my italics), 'And All's well as ends Better' (p. 999). At least he has learnt to eschew superlatives. But his language in Gandalf's monologue conveys an unwelcome reminder of psychological unpreparedness.

His son Sam re-establishes the hobbits slightly with his terminal comment, 'A nice pickle we have landed ourselves in, Mr Frodo', for though he is as obtuse as his father — Sam got himself into trouble, but Frodo did not — this blindness does coexist with a thoughtless courage, a relish for gloom, and a refusal to see Doomsday as more than a 'pickle', all adding up to the notorious Anglo-hobbitic inability to know when they're beaten. However, there is another modern voice in Gandalf's monologue to act as vehicle for cultural contrast: this is Saruman's. He has hardly been mentioned before, and the question whether he is good or bad is more difficult to decide than with most. But when he is introduced by Gandalf, we know what to think very soon; the message is conveyed by style and lexis. Saruman talks like a politician. 'We can bide our time', he says, using a fossilised phrase:

> 'we can keep our thoughts in our hearts, deploring maybe evils done by the way, but approving the high and ultimate purpose: Knowledge, Rule, Order, all things that we have so far striven in vain to accomplish, hindered rather than helped by our weak or idle friends. There need not be, there would not be, any real change in our designs, only in our means.' (p. 253)

What Saruman says encapsulates many of the things the modern world has learnt to dread most: the ditching of allies, the subordination of means to ends, the 'conscious acceptance of guilt in the necessary murder'.[15] But the way he puts it is significant too. No other character in Middle-earth has Saruman's trick of balancing phrases against each other so that incompatibles are resolved, and none comes out with words as empty as 'deploring', 'ultimate', worst of all, 'real'. What is a 'real change'? The *OED*'s three columns of definition offer nothing appropriate; the word has got below dictionary level. As we all know, 'real' is now a word like 'sincere' or 'genuine', a word whose meaning its speaker asks you to take for granted, a politician's word, an advertiser's word. 'Real change' shows Saruman up with even greater economy than 'changes for the worst' does Gaffer Gamgee.

By contrast with these familiar styles and voices several of the other participants in the Council come over as archaic, blunt, clear-sighted. Gandalf himself uses an older vocabulary than usual, as if to authenticate himself, and Elrond's speech (pp. 237–39), as is only suitable for one so old, is full of old-fashioned inversions of syntax and words like 'weregild', 'esquire', 'shards'. Its burden is to state the Northern 'theory of courage', as Tolkien called it in his British Academy lecture, whose central thesis is that even ultimate defeat does not turn right into wrong.† Elrond has seen 'many defeats, and many fruitless victories', and in a way he has even given up hope, at least for his adopted people the elves (see p. 262 and further p. 1006); but this does not make him change his mind or look for easy options.

The heroic note is struck most firmly, however, by the dwarf Glóin, or rather by his report of the dialogue between Sauron's messenger and that exemplar of stubbornness King Dáin. The messenger offers 'great reward and lasting friendship' in return for information about hobbits, or for the Ring. If Dáin refuses, he says:

'". . . things will not seem so well."

'At that his breath came like the hiss of snakes, and all who stood by shuddered, but Dáin said: "I say neither yea nor nay. I must consider this message and what it means under its fair cloak."

'"Consider well, but not too long," said he.

'"The time of my thought is my own to spend," answered Dáin.

'"For the present," said he, and rode into the darkness.'

---

† For all its age, this was evidently still a vital belief for Tolkien, and for other Inklings too. In C. S. Lewis's most Tolkienian work, *That Hideous Strength* (1945), Mark Studdock for all his failings reinvents it spontaneously at the end of chapter 15, section IV. The book also contains some fine Saruman-style speeches.

We get exchanges like this several times in *The Lord of the Rings,* mostly involving dwarves: Elrond and Gimli swap grim proverbs in the next chapter, Théoden King silences Merry in similarly abrupt style in Book V chapter 2, and Appendix A offers several dwarvish dialogues around the battle of Azanulbizar. Their unifying feature is delight in the contrast between passionate interior and polite or rational expression; the weakness of the latter is an index of the strength of the former. Thus the messenger's 'things will not seem so well' works as violent threat; 'not too long' means 'extremely rapidly'. In reply Dáin's 'fair cloak' implies 'foul body' and the obscure metaphor of spending the 'time of my thought' indicates refusal to negotiate under threat. Both participants seek to project a cool, ironic self-control. If Elrond's recommendation was courage, and Gandalf's hope, the dwarves' contribution to the ethical mix of the Council is a kind of unyielding scepticism. This virtue is no longer much practised, swept away by the tide of salesmanship, winning friends and influencing people, the belief that all aggression is dissolved by smiles. We no longer even have a name for it — except perhaps that people who call their tea their 'baggins' might recognise it in their approving use of 'bloody-mindedness' (not recorded by the *OED*). Whatever it is, it comes over in Dáin's speech as a force: words imply ethics, and the ethics of the spokesmen of Middle-earth fit together, beneath surface variation. None of them but Saruman pays any attention to expediency, practicality, *Realpolitik,* 'political realism'.

Any one of the counsellors in this chapter would bear similar analysis. Gandalf's account of Isildur makes a point through its combination of ancient words and endings ('glede', 'fadeth', 'loseth', etc.) with sudden recall of the words of Bilbo and Gollum. 'It is precious to me, though I buy it with great pain'; the 'reality of human nature' persists. More subtly, Aragorn and Boromir strike sparks off each other through their ways of speech as well as their claims, Aragorn's language deceptively modern, even easy-going on occasion, but with greater range than Boromir's slightly wooden magniloquence. There is even significance in Aragorn letting his rival have the last word in their debate, with a clause which is perfectly in line with modern speech — 'we will put it to the test one day'—

but also relates easily to the vaunts of ancient heroes, like Ælf-wine's *nú mæg cunnian hwá céne sý* in *The Battle of Maldon,* 'now who is bold can be put to the test'. Still, the overriding points are these: the 'information content' of 'The Council of Elrond' is very high, much higher than can be recorded by analyses like this; much of that information is carried by linguistic mode; nevertheless most readers assimilate the greater part of it; in the process they gain an image of the 'life-styles' of Middle-earth the solider for its occasional contrasts with modernity. Language variation gives Tolkien a thorough and economical way of dramatising ethical debate.

The Horses of the Mark

This virtue is easily missed by critics or reviewers skimming through for the plot; and perhaps we have now reached one reason for the enormous difference of opinion between Tolkien's admirers and his detractors. The whole of *The Lord of the Rings* is on its larger scale like 'The Council of Elrond'. Through both there runs a narrative thread, but just as the single chapter relies for a great part of its effect on the relishing of stylistic variation, so the work as a whole depends very largely on *tableaux:* separate images of places, peoples, societies, all in some way furthering the story, but sometimes (as with Bombadil or Willow-man) not furthering it very much, there mostly or largely for their own sake. Someone not prepared to read slowly enough — Tolkien thought his books were best read aloud — might paradoxically write off the story as 'slow' or 'nerveless'; and there would be a basis of truth for the observation *as long as it confined itself to the story*. But this is a poor way to appreciate the whole.

Any one of Tolkien's *tableaux* would stand analysis, and the obvious one to choose is perhaps Gondor. However, I prefer to start with the Riders of Rohan, not the first children of Tolkien's imagination but the ones he regarded with most affection and also in a sense the most central. In creating them Tolkien was once again playing with his own background and his home in 'the Little Kingdom'. Thus 'Rohan' is only the Gondorian word for the Riders' country; they themselves call it 'the Mark'. Now there is no English county called 'the Mark', but the Anglo-Saxon kingdom which included both Tolkien's home-town Birmingham and his *alma mater* Oxford was 'Mercia' — a Latinism now adopted by historians mainly because the native term was never recorded. However, the West Saxons called their neighbours the *Mierce,* clearly a derivation (by 'i-mutation') from *Mearc;* the 'Mercians" own pronunciation of that would certainly have been the 'Mark', and that was no doubt once the everyday term for central England. As for the 'white horse on the green field' which is the emblem of the Mark, you can see it cut into the chalk fifteen miles from Tolkien's study, two miles from 'Wayland's Smithy' and just about on the borders of 'Mercia' and Wessex, as if to mark the kingdom's end. All the Riders' names and language are Old English, as many have noted;[†] but they were homely to Tolkien in an even deeper sense than that.

As has already been remarked, though, the Riders according to Tolkien did not resemble the 'ancient English . . . except in a general way due to their circumstances: a simpler and more primitive people living in contact with a higher and more venerable culture, and occupying lands that had once been part of its domain'. Tolkien was stretching the truth a long way in asserting that, to say the least! But there is one obvious difference between the people of Rohan and the 'ancient English', and that is horses. The Rohirrim call themselves the *Éothéod* (Old English *eoh* = 'horse' + *þéod* = 'people'); this translates into Common Speech as 'the Riders'; Rohan itself is Sindarin for 'horse-country'. Prominent Riders call themselves after horses (Éomund, Éomer, Éowyn), and their most important title after 'King' is 'marshall', borrowed into English from French but going back to an unrecorded Germanic **marho-skalkoz,* 'horse-servant' (and cp. the name of the hobbits' Hengest). The Rohirrim are nothing if not cavalry. By contrast the An-

---

† Not many have noted that they are not in the 'standard' or 'classical' West Saxon dialect of Old English but in what is thought to have been its Mercian parallel: so Saruman, Hasufel, Herugrim for 'standard' Searuman, Heasufel, Heorugrim, and cp. *Mearc* and **Marc.* In *Letters,* p. 65, Tolkien threatens to speak nothing but 'Old Mercian'.

glo-Saxons' reluctance to have anything militarily to do with horses is notorious. *The Battle of Maldon* begins, significantly enough, with the horses being sent to the rear. Hastings was lost, along with Anglo-Saxon independence, largely because the English heavy infantry could not (quite) hold off the combination of archers and mounted knights. The *Anglo-Saxon Chronicle* entry for 1055 remarks sourly that at Hereford 'before a spear was thrown the English fled, because they had been made to fight on horseback'. How then can Anglo-Saxons and Rohirrim ever, culturally, be equated?

A part of the answer is that the Rohirrim are not to be equated with the Anglo-Saxons of history, but with those of poetry, or legend. The chapter 'The King of the Golden Hall' is straightforwardly calqued on *Beowulf*. When Legolas says of Meduseld, 'The light of it shines far over the land', he is translating line 311 of *Beowulf, lixte se léoma ofer landa fela*. 'Meduseld' is indeed a Beowulfian word (line 3065) for 'hall'. More importantly, the poem and the chapter agree, down to minute detail, on the procedure for approaching kings. In *Beowulf* the hero is stopped first by a coastguard, then by a doorward, and only after two challenges is allowed to approach the Danish King; he and his men have to 'pile arms' outside as well. Tolkien follows this dignified, step-by-step ceremonial progress exactly. Thus in 'The King of the Golden Hall' Gandalf, Aragorn, Legolas and Gimli are checked first by the guards at the gates of Edoras (= 'enclosures'), and then by the doorward of Meduseld, Háma. He too insists on the ceremony of piling arms, though Tolkien's characters object more than Beowulf does, largely because he is a volunteer and in any case fights by choice bare-handed. There is a crisis over Gandalf's staff, indeed, and Háma broods, reflecting rightly that 'the staff in the hand of a wizard may be more than a prop for age'; he settles his doubts with the maxim 'Yet in doubt a man of worth will trust to his own wisdom. I believe you are friends and folk of honour, who have no evil purpose. You may go in.' In saying so he echoes the maxim of the coastguard of *Beowulf* (lines 287–92), 'a sharp shield-warrior must know how to tell good from bad in every case, from words as well as deeds. I hear [from your words] that this warband is friendly . . . I will guide you.'

The point is not, though, that Tolkien is once more writing a 'calqued' narrative, but that he is taking advantage of a modern expansive style to spell out things that would have been obvious to Anglo-Saxons — in particular, the truths that freedom is not a prerogative of democracies, and that in free societies orders give way to discretion. Háma takes a risk with Gandalf; so does the coastguard with Beowulf. So does Éomer with Aragorn, letting him go free and lending him horses. He is under arrest when Aragorn re-appears, and Théoden notes Háma's dereliction of duty too. Still, the nice thing about the Riders, one might say, is that though 'a stern people, loyal to their lord', they wear duty and loyalty lightly. Háma and Éomer make their own decisions, and even the suspicious gate-ward wishes Gandalf luck. 'I was only obeying orders', we can see, would not be accepted as an excuse in the Riddermark. Nor would it in *Beowulf*. The wisdom of ancient epic is translated by Tolkien into a whole sequence of doubts, decisions, sayings, rituals.

One could go further and say that the Riders spring from poetry, not history, in that the whole of their culture is based on *song*. Almost the first thing Gandalf and the others see, nearing Meduseld, are the mounds covered in *simbelmynë* either side of the way. *Simbelmynë* is a little white flower, but also means 'ever-mind', 'ever-memory', 'forget-me-not'. Like the barrows it stands for the preservation of the memory of ancient deeds and heroes in the expanse of years. The Riders are fascinated by memorial verse and oblivion, by deaths and by epitaphs. They show it in their list of kingly pedigrees, from Théoden back to Eorl the Young, in the suicidal urges of Éomer and Éowyn to do 'deeds of song',[16] in the song that Aragorn sings to set the tone of the culture he is visiting:

'Where now the horse and the rider? Where is the horn that was blowing? Where is the helm and the hauberk, and the bright hair flowing?

Most of all it comes over in the alliterative dirges made for Théoden by Gléowine, for the dead of Pelennor by an anonymous 'maker', even in the rhyming couplet made for the horse Snowmane. These preserve the sonority, the sadness, the feeling for violent opposites ('death' and 'day', 'lords' and 'lowly', 'halls' and 'pastures') integrated in the Riders' language and culture. Their visual correlatives, one might say, are the spears planted in burial-mounds by Fangorn and at the Fords of Isen; or perhaps the spears are the men and the mounds are poems, for Éomer says of one burial, 'When their spears have rotted and rusted, long still may their mounds stand and guard the Fords of Isen!' The men die and their weapons rust. But their memory remains, passes into *simbelmynë,* 'evermind', the oral heritage of the race.

One should see at this point how far Tolkien's imagination surpasses that of most fantasy-writers. Proud barbarians are ten a penny in modern fantasy. Hardly one of their creators grasps the fact that barbarians are sensitive too: that a heroic way of life preoccupies men with death and with the feeble, much-prized resistances to death which their cultures can offer. Of course Tolkien drew his knowledge from Old English, from that literature whose greatest monument is not an epic but the 'dirge' of *Beowulf;* 'The King of the Golden Hall' echoes that poem as closely as Aragorn's song above echoes the Old English *Wanderer.* However, Tolkien was trying to go beyond translation to 'reconstruction'. And this is what explains the horses. The feeling of Anglo-Saxon poetry for these was markedly different from that of Anglo-Saxon history. Thus the retainers of *Beowulf* joyfully race their *mearas* back from the monsters' lake as they sing their praise songs; the ancient gnomic poem *Maxims I* observes enthusiastically that 'a good man will keep in mind a good, well-broken horse, familiar, well-tried, and round-hoofed'; it has already been noted that the same poem declared that 'an earl goes on the arched back of a war-horse, a mounted troop (*éored*) must ride in a body', only for a historical Anglo-Saxon scribe to rewrite *éored* foolishly as *worod* or '(foot) body guard'. Tolkien may have known that the confusing Anglo-Saxon words for colour were once words for the colour of horses' coats, like Hasufel = 'grey coat', suggesting an early society as observant of horses as modern African tribes of cows.[17] Maybe the infantry-fixation of historical periods was the result of living on an island. Maybe the Anglo-Saxons *before they migrated to England* were different. What would have happened had they turned East, not West, to the German plains and the steppes beyond?

In creating the Riddermark Tolkien thought of his own 'Mercia'. He also certainly remembered the great lost romance of 'Gothia' (see pp. 13–19 above), of the close kin of the English turning to disaster and oblivion on the plains of Russia. No doubt he knew the dim tradition that the word 'Goths' itself meant 'Horse-folk'.[18] This is what adds 'reconstruction' to 'calquing' and produces fantasy, a people and a culture that never were, but that press closer and closer to the edge of might-have-been. The Riders gain life from their mixture of homely, almost hobbitic familiarity with a strong dash of something completely alien. Éomer is a nice young man, but there is a streak of nomad ferocity in the way he and his men taunt Aragorn and company with their narrowing circle of horses and Éomer's silent advance 'until the point of his spear was within a foot of Aragorn's breast'. They behave like mail-shirted Sioux or Cheyenne. And like a Middle-earth Deerslayer, Aragorn 'did not stir', recognising the nomad appreciation of impassivity. A certain craziness shows itself in the Rohirric psychology at other points, as Éowyn rides in search of death and Éomer, sure he is doomed to die, laughs out loud for joy. The Dunlendings have heard that the Riders 'burned their prisoners alive'. Tolkien denies it, but there is something in his description that keeps the image alive.

For all this there is, once more, a visual correlative, and it is the first flash of individuality Éomer is given; he is (p. 421) 'taller than all the rest; from his helm as a crest a white horsetail flowed'. A horsetail plume is the traditional prerogative of the Huns and the Tartars and the steppe-folk, a most un-English decoration, at least by tradition.† Yet it comes to prominence several times. Across the chaotic battlefield of Pelennor it is 'the white crest of Éomer' that Merry picks out from the 'great front of the Rohirrim', and when Théoden charges at last, opposing hornblast and poetry to horror and despair, behind him come his knights and his banner, 'white horse upon a field of

---

† The Assistant Curator of the Household Cavalry Museum, Mr C. W. Frearson, informs me that the now-familiar white horsetail plumes of the Life Guards are an innovation brought in by Prince Albert in 1842. The Prince was copying a Prussian style itself copied from Russian regiments.

green', and Éomer, 'the white horsetail on his helm floating in his speed'. As it happens, there is a word for both Éomer's decoration and the Riders' collective quality, but it is not an English word: it is *panache*, the crest on the knight's helmet, but also the virtue of sudden onset, the dash that sweeps away resistance. This is exactly the opposite of English 'doggedness', and is a virtue traditionally regarded with massive suspicion by English generals. However, *panache* in both the abstract and concrete senses help to define the Riders, to present them as simultaneously English and alien, to offer a glimpse of the way land shapes people. Théoden's kindly interest in herbs and hobbits (they would have had him smoking a pipe, given time) co-exists with his peremptory decisions and sudden furies. It is a strange mixture but not an implausible one. There must have been people like that once, if we only knew.

The Edges of the Mark

The Mark works on a system of contrasts and similarities. This is rationally based and even has a sort of historical integrity; but as with place-names and elvish songs no one can tell how much of the author's system is apprehended unconsciously by the unstudious reader. The evidence suggests, though, that it is quite a lot: that the difference between Tolkien and Robert E. Howard, say, or E. R. Eddison or James Branch Cabell, lies precisely in his intense and brooding systematisation, never analytically presented but always deliberately nurtured (if not deliberately conceived). The planning behind Tolkien's cultural *tableaux* shows in the further set of contrasts and similarities round the Mark — contrasts which work, it should be noted, both inside the story (i.e. contrasts between Rohan and Gondor, Rohan and the Shire, Éomer and Gimli, etc.) and outside it (i.e. the running inevitable comparison of all those societies and the real one, the one we ourselves live in). Tolkien obviously worked at these just as he worked at the stylistic clashes of 'The Council of Elrond', and for the same reason, to provide cultural solidity.

Thus there are three scenes at least where the men of the Mark are opposed to the men of Gondor. These are the two 'meetings in the wilderness', of Éomer and his men with Aragorn, Legolas and Gimli (pp. 419–28), and of Faramir and his men with Frodo and Sam (pp. 642–67); the two set-piece 'building descriptions' of Meduseld (pp. 500–501) and the great hall of Minas Tirith (pp. 737–38); the longer comparisons of the dotage, cure and death of Théoden with the corruption, relapse and suicide of Denethor — two old men who have both lost their sons. All these characterise cultures as much as people. To take the first one first, there are all manner of similarities between Éomer's position and Faramir's, for both men come upon lonely trespassers, both have orders to detain such people, both would gain something by doing so, whether Narsil or the Ring, and both in the end make up their own minds, let the strangers go and offer them assistance. Yet in the end difference is perhaps more prominent than likeness.

Éomer, for one thing, is compulsively truculent. It is compulsive, for when his men move away he becomes much easier, but he takes little care to be polite. A large part of the reason is ignorance, signalled by almost his first speech, 'Are you elvish folk?' The answer that one of them is surprises him, for 'elvish' to him as to the *Gawain*-poet just means 'uncanny'. Éomer and his men are sceptics, about the Golden Wood, about elves, about halflings; they are also in a way superstitious (a combination Tolkien thought common enough), for Éomer says Saruman is 'dwimmer-crafty', using an old word for 'nightmare' or 'illusion' to say that wizards are 'skinturners' like Beorn, which as far as we know they are not. By contrast Faramir comes over as wiser, deeper, older; but this is a function of his society, not himself. He keeps using the post–Anglo-Saxon word 'courtesy', which like 'civilisation' or 'urbanity' implies a post-nomadic and settled state of culture. Frodo's courteous speech is one reason why Faramir recognises in him 'an elvish air', the word used this time in a sense exactly opposite to Éomer's disapprobation. Faramir is patient, too, and though both he and Éomer assert strongly their hatred of lies, it is fair to say that Faramir allows himself a relatively oblique approach to truth. He asks fewer direct questions; he hides the fact that he knows Boromir is dead; he lets Sam change the subject when they get too close to Isildur's Bane and the Ring. He smiles as well. While the Gondorians are dignified and even say a kind of 'grace', they are not as much on their dignity as the Riders, or as stiffly ceremonious as Shire-hobbits. Faramir is self-assured, in a word, and he explains why in his account of the Kings and Stewards and Northmen, the High and Middle peoples. Both he and Éomer think Boromir was nearer the Middle than the High, but Éomer thinks that is all to the good, while Faramir does not. The two contrasted scenes are making a very strong assertion about cultural evolution.

The balance is redressed, maybe, by Théoden and Denethor. If one looks at their houses, the latter's is the greater achievement, but it is lifeless. 'No hangings or storied webs, nor any things of woven stuff or of wood, were to be seen in that long solemn hall; but between the pillars there stood a silent company of tall images graven in cold stone.' In this sentence the word that stands out is 'web', for it is Old English, the normal Anglo-Saxon word for 'tapestry' (cp. the name 'Webster'). The criticism of lifelessness is one a Rider might have made. By contrast the corresponding scene in Meduseld is dominated by the *fág flór,* the floor 'paved with stones of many hues', and by the sunlit image of the young man on the white horse, blowing a great horn, with yellow hair flying and the horse's red nostrils displayed as it smells 'battle afar'. Yet the bravura of the Riders' culture is also complemented by one odd word, the 'louver' in the roof that lets the smoke out and the sunbeams in. This is a late word, French-derived, not recorded till 1393. If the Anglo-Saxons had such things, they called them something else. One might say that the Riders have learnt from Gondor, but not vice versa. If that is too much to build on two words, one can certainly say that the behaviour of Denethor, indeed the very self-assuredness he shares with his son, points to the weaknesses of civilised cultures: over-subtlety, selfishness, abandonment of the 'theory of courage', a calculation that turns suicidal. Gandalf can cure Théoden; but Denethor almost makes me use the word 'neurotic' (first recorded in the modern sense five years before Tolkien was born).

Such ramifications are almost inexhaustible, but their core is history — real history, but history philological-style, not in the footprints of Edward Gibbon. That is why it was said earlier that the Riders were in a sense central. Whether one thinks of them as Anglo-Saxons or as Goths, they represent the bit that Tolkien knew best. Against them Gondor is a kind of Rome, also a kind of mythical Wales of the sort that bred King Coel and King Arthur and King Lear. On their southern border are the 'Woses', an Old English word and an Anglo-Saxon bogey, surviving misunderstood into *Sir Gawain* like the word 'elvish' and enjoying a last flicker of life in the common English name 'Woodhouse' (see note on p. 65 above). To the North are the Ents, another Old English word which had interested Tolkien since he first wrote on Roman roads in 1924, and identified them with the *orþanc enta geweorc,* the 'skilful work of ents' of the poem *Maxims II*. Anglo-Saxons believed in ents, as in woses. What were they? Clearly they were very large, great builders, and clearly they didn't exist any more. From such hints Tolkien created his fable of a race running down to extinction.

However, the point that should be taken by now is not just that Tolkien worked by 'reconstruction' or from the premise that poetry is in essence true; rather it is that his continual play with calques and cruxes gave *The Lord of the Rings* a dinosaur-like vitality which cannot be conveyed in any synopsis, but reveals itself in so many thousands of details that only the most biased critical mind could miss them all.[19] It is not a paradox to say further that this decentralised life is also at the same time 'nuggety', tending always to focus on names and words and the things or realities which lie behind them. The first Rohirric place-name we hear is 'Eastemnet', followed soon by 'Westemnet'. An 'emnet' is a thing in Middle-earth, also a place in Norfolk, also an asterisk-word, **emnmæþ* for 'steppe' or 'prairie', also the green grass which the Riders use as a touchstone for reality. Everything Tolkien wrote was based on fusions like that, on 'woses' and 'emnets' and *éoreds,* on 'elvish' or *orþanc* or *panaches*.

'Magyk natureel'

Like a goldfish in a weedy pool, the theme that flashes from much of Tolkien's work is that of the identity of man and nature, of namer and named. It was probably his strongest belief, stronger even than his Catholicism (though of course he hoped the two were at some level reconciled). It was what drove Tolkien to write; he created Middle-earth before he had a plot to put in it, and at every delay or failure of 'inspiration' he went back to the map and to the landscape, for Bombadil and the Shire, the Mark and the ents. Through all his work, moreover, there runs an obsessive interest in plants and scenery, pipeweed and *athelas*, the crown of stonecrop round the overthrown king's head in Ithilien, the staffs of *lebethron*-wood with a 'virtue' on them of finding and returning, given by Faramir to Sam and Frodo, the holly-tree outside Moria that marks the frontier of 'Hollin' as the White Horse of Uffington shows the boundary of the Mark, and over all the closely visualised images of dells and dingles and Wellinghalls, hollow trees and clumps of bracken and bramble-coverts for the hobbits to creep into. The *simbelmynë*, as has been said, is a kind of symbol for the Riders, and the *mallorn* does the same for Galadriel's elves. The hobbits are only just separable from the Shire, and Tom Bombadil not at all from the Withywindle. Fangorn is a name for both character and forest, and as character he voices more strongly than anybody else the identity of name and namer and thing. 'Real names tell you the story of the things they belong to in my language', he says, but it seems unlikely that anyone but an ent could learn Old Entish. With Bombadil the identity of name and thing gives the namer a kind of magic. With the hobbits much the same effect is created by simple harmony. They don't in fact practise magic, says the 'Prologue', but the impression that they do is derived from 'close friendship with the earth'. Earth and magic and non-human species are all in differing proportions very closely combined. The voices that explain this to us, Fangorn's and the narrator's, are authoritative and indeed, especially Fangorn, 'professorial'. They admit no denial.

There is a sense, even, in which the non-human characters of *The Lord of the Rings* are natural objects: a tenuous sense but one deeply ingrained. On his first appearance Fangorn is seen by Pippin and Merry but categorised as 'one old stump of a tree with only two bent branches left: it looked almost like the figure of some gnarled old man, standing there, blinking in the morning light' (p. 451). Gandalf a little later speaks of his struggle with the Balrog and asks himself how it would have seemed to outside observers; just thunder and lightning, he replies. 'Thunder, they heard, and lightning, they said, smote upon Celebdil, and leaped back broken into tongues of fire. Is not that enough?' (p. 491). As for the elves and Elrond and Gandalf, how would they have seemed to mortal senses? Near the end Tolkien replies:

> If any wanderer had chanced to pass, little would he have seen or heard, and it would have seemed to him only that he saw grey figures, carved in stone, memorials of forgotten things now lost in unpeopled lands. For they did not move or speak with mouth, looking from mind to mind; and only their shining eyes stirred and kindled as their thoughts went to and fro. (p. 963)

At the end they fade into the stones and the shadows.

'Fade', or 'turn'? The future fate of the elves is often mentioned in *The Lord of the Rings* but never becomes quite clear. Some will leave Middle-earth, some will stay. Those who stay, says Galadriel, will 'dwindle to a rustic folk of dell and cave, slowly to forget and to be forgotten'. 'Dwindle' could have a demographic meaning; there could be fewer of them. It could be physical too, looking forward to the 'tiny elves' of Shakespeare, and even moral, making one think of the detached, cruel, soulless elves of Scottish and Danish tradition. The best fate for the elves who stay, perhaps, would be to turn into landscape. There is a local legend of that kind attached to the Rollright Stones on the north edge of Oxfordshire, mentioned for a moment in *Farmer Giles of Ham*. These, says the story,[20] were once an old king and his men. Challenged by a witch to take seven strides over the hill and look into the valley below, the king found his view blocked by a barrow and the witch's curse fulfilled:

> 'Rise up, stick, and stand still, stone,
> For king of England thou shalt be none.
> Thou and thy men hoar stones shall be
> And I myself an eldern-tree.'

The stones are still there, mysterious and by tradition uncountable. And though it may seem hard-hearted to wish for people to be petrified, it does assure them a kind of existence, a kind of integrity with the land they come from.

It's hard to say, declares Sam Gamgee of the elves of Lothlórien, 'whether they've made the land, or the land's made them' (p. 351). And his perceptions are often deep, even if his education has been neglected. His further explanation may be taken to refer to *The Lord of the Rings* as well as to Lothlórien: 'Nothing seems to be going on,' he says, 'and nobody seems to want it to. If there's any magic about, it's right down deep, where I can't lay my hands on it, in a manner of speaking.' Yes, agrees Frodo, complementing Sam's style as often with his own. Still, 'You can see and hear it everywhere'.

CHAPTER 5

INTERLACEMENTS AND THE RING

A Problem in Corruption

Lothlórien has won many hearts, and even the most censorious of Tolkien's critics have accordingly been ready to grant him the ability to create nice settings. 'What is outstanding, though, is the scenery', declared the kindly reviewer for the *Bath and West Evening Chronicle* (7 December 1974).[1] However, good scenery is not one of the major virtues on the critical scale; many published opinions throw it in as a sop, a makeweight to balance what they see as much more serious flaws deep in the heart of the Tolkienian 'fable', in the essential story of *The Lord of the Rings*. The characters, it is often alleged, are flat; there is not enough awareness of sexuality; good and evil are presented as absolutes, without a proper sense of inner conflict within individuals; there is something incoherent in the 'main pattern' of the story, which prevents one from reading it as 'a connected allegory with a clear message for the modern world'. Most of all, *The Lord of the Rings* is felt not to be true to 'the fundamental character of reality', not to mirror 'an adult experience of the world', not to portray 'an emotional truth about humanity'. Professor Mark Roberts, speaking from the centre of the critical consensus, declared: 'It doesn't issue from an understanding of reality which is not to be denied, it is not moulded by some controlling vision of things which is at the same time its *raison d'être*.' The archaism of the settings, in short, goes along with an escapism of intention, a deliberate turning away from real life and from present-day experience.[2]

Now it is evident that some of these statements have gone beyond compromise. When people start appealing to 'truth', 'experience' and 'reality', still more to 'the fundamental character of reality', they imply very strongly that they know what these things *are,* an insight not likely to be shaken by argument. Probably at the bottom of the confrontation between *The Lord of the Rings* and its critics there lies some total disagreement over the nature of the universe, a disagreement surfacing in strong, instinctive, mutual antipathy. Nothing will cure this. However, it ought to be possible to bring the reasons for it out into the light, and by doing so to show that whatever may be said of Tolkien's view of reality, it was neither escapist nor thoughtless. A sensible place to begin this endeavour is with the mainspring of the story's action, the Ring (here capitalised to distinguish it from the relatively insignificant stage-prop or 'Equalizer' of *The Hobbit*).

The most evident fact to note about the Ring is that it is in conception strikingly anachronistic, totally modern. In the vital chapter 'The Shadow of the Past' Gandalf says a great deal about it, but his information boils down to three basic data: (1) the Ring is immensely powerful, in right or wrong hands; (2) it is dangerous and ultimately fatal to all its possessors — in a sense there are no right hands; (3) it cannot simply be left unused or put aside, but must be destroyed, something which can happen only in the place of its origin, Orodruin, Mount Doom. 'There is only one way', he says to Frodo, and it is essential to the story that this should be accepted as true: the Ring *cannot* be kept, it has power over *everybody,* it *has* to be destroyed. Spread over sixteen pages (45–60), these remarks function as part of a story, but as soon as they are put together it is a dull mind which does not reflect, 'Power corrupts, and absolute power corrupts absolutely'. That maxim, one could say, is the core of *The Lord of the Rings,* and it is reinforced from the start by all that Gandalf says about the way Ringbearers fade, regardless of all their 'strength' or 'good purpose', and further by his violent refusal to take the Ring himself:

'Do not tempt me! For I do not wish to become like the Dark Lord himself. Yet the way of the Ring to my heart is by pity, pity for weakness and the desire of strength to do good. Do not tempt me! I dare not take it, not even to keep it safe, unused. The wish to wield it would be too great for my strength . . .' (p. 60).

His renunciation makes sense in an age which has seen many pigs become farmers; no reviewer has ever balked at this basic opening move of Tolkien's.

Yet the opinion that 'power corrupts' is a distinctively modern one. Lord Acton gave it expression for the first time in 1887, in a letter which Tolkien might have been interested enough to read — it is in a strongly anti-Papal context.[3] William Pitt had said something similar a hundred years before, 'Unlimited power is apt to corrupt the minds of those who possess it', but before that the idea does not seem to have been attractive. It might even have been thought perverse. Lord Acton's actual words were: 'Power tends to corrupt and absolute power corrupts absolutely. Great men are almost always bad men . . .', and with this latter opinion no medieval chronicler, romancer or hagiographer would have been likely to concur. There is as it happens an Anglo-Saxon proverb analogous to Lord Acton's, but still significantly different. What it says is *Man déþ swá hé byþ þonne hé mót swá hé wile,* 'Man does as he is when he may do as he wishes', or more colloquially, 'You show what you're like when you can do what you like'.[4] This is certainly cynical about the ill-effects of power, but what it implies is 'power *exposes*', not 'power corrupts'. The idea that a person once genuinely good could be made bad merely by the removal of restraints is not yet present. Tolkien is certain to have felt the modernity of his primary statement about the Ring. One has to wonder then why he made it and how he related it to the archaic world of his plot. Does Lord Acton's Victorian proverb, in Middle-earth, ring true?

There is at least a plausible argument to say that it does not. Thus Gandalf says at the start that the Ring will 'possess' and 'devour' any creature who uses it, while Elrond later goes further and says, 'The very desire of it corrupts the heart' (p. 261). As has been said, these are essential data for the story, and some of the time they seem to be confirmed. Gollum, for instance, is presented throughout as very nearly enslaved to the Ring, with only fleeting traces of free will left, and those dependent on keeping away from it. Much higher up the moral scale, Boromir bears out Elrond's words. He never touches the Ring, but desire to have it still makes him turn to violence. Obviously his original motive is patriotism and love of Gondor, but when this leads him to exalt 'strength to defend ourselves, strength in a just cause', our modern experience of dictators immediately tells us that matters would not stay there. Kind as he is, one can imagine Boromir as a Ringwraith; his never-quite-stated opinion that 'the end justifies the means' adds a credible perspective to corruption. The same could be said of his father Denethor, to whom Gandalf again makes the point that even unhandled, the Ring can be dangerous: 'If you had received this thing, it would have overthrown you. Were it buried beneath the roots of Mindolluin, still it would burn your mind away.' With examples like these, it is easy to go further and accept, for the purposes of the story, that even Gandalf's good intentions would not resist the Ring, and that Galadriel too does right to refuse it at p. 357. While the Ring stays a veiled menace, one may conclude, it works perfectly well.

The problem comes from the apparent immunity of so many other characters. Frodo, after all, is in contact with the Ring nearly all the time, but shows little sign of being corrupted. He goes through great labours to get rid of it. Furthermore, when he *does* give way and claim it for his own, he loses it almost immediately to Gollum, who bites off Ring and finger with it. Gandalf had said much earlier that 'already you too, Frodo, cannot easily let it go, nor will to damage it. And I could not "make" you — except by force, which would break your mind.' But in the Sammath Naur we have force being used very strongly, in the shape of Gollum's teeth; yet Frodo's mind remains unaffected. Anyway, what about Sam, who takes the Ring but hands it back with only momentary delay; Pippin and Merry, who show no desire for it at all; Aragorn, Legolas and Gimli, who display the same indifference without the excuse of ignorance; and Boromir's brother Faramir, who realises the Ring is in his power but refuses to take it, with no more sign of mental turmoil than a 'strange smile' and a glint in the eye? One sees the beginnings of a serious criticism of the very basis of *The Lord of the Rings* here: the author appears to have presented a set of rules and then observed them only partially, reserving as it were the right to exceptions and miracles. This is what has made some people think that in this work the distinction between good and bad is simply arbitrary, residing not in the nature of the characters but in the needs of the plot.[5]

Actually all the doubts just mentioned can be cleared up by the use of one word, though it is a word never used in *The Lord of the Rings*. The Ring is 'addictive'. All readers probably assimilate Gollum early on to the now-familiar image of a 'drug-addict', craving desperately for a 'fix' even though he knows it will kill him. For the same reason they understand why Gandalf tells Frodo not to use the Ring (use always causes addiction); why Sam, Bilbo and Frodo nevertheless survive their use of it (addiction in early stages is curable); why Boromir succumbs to the Ring without handling it (use has to be preceded by desire); and why Faramir can shrug it off (a wise person is capable of stifling the desire to become addicted, though no wisdom will stifle addiction once contracted). As for the scene in the Sammath Naur, it is even more providential than it looks. What Gandalf said to Frodo at the start, we should realise, was that he might be able to give the Ring away or destroy it, though only with a struggle; he could not, however, be made to *want* to do so (except by some kind of dangerous thought-control). In the end Frodo does want to destroy the Ring but has not the strength. Gollum is accordingly necessary after all—a striking irony. Extending the parallel with heroin, one may say that addicts *can* be cured by the use of external force, and often they have to be, though their co-operation certainly helps. To expect them to break their syringes and throw away their drugs by will-power alone, though, is to confuse an addiction, which is physical, with a habit, which is moral. In this aspect of the Ring as in others Tolkien is totally consistent.

He is, however, once again being distinctively modern. The phrase 'drug addict' is not recorded by the *OED* till 1920; probably the concept was created by the synthesis of heroin in 1898. As for the term 'addictive', by some oversight the full *OED* did not recognise its existence till after Tolkien's death. Still, during Tolkien's lifetime the words and the realities behind them were becoming more and more familiar, bringing with them, one should note, entirely new ideas about the nature and limitations of human will. As with 'power corrupting', Tolkien was during the 1930s and 1940s reacting quite evidently to the issues of his time. These deliberate modernities should clear him of any charge of merely insulated 'ivory tower' escapism. They ought to suggest also that he thought more deeply than his critics have ever recognised about just those issues he is commonly alleged to ignore: the processes of temptation, the complex nature of good and evil, the relationship between reality and our fallible perception of it. Nothing can prevent people from saying that the answers he gave were not 'adult' or 'fundamental', but it should be obvious that such adjectives are as culture-biased as Saruman's 'real': by themselves they express only the prejudices of the user. Tolkien was, in short, trying to make Middle-earth say something, as well as conducting his readers on a tour of it. Decision on whether the message is right or wrong should at least come after working out what the message *is*. But proper understanding of that, as often, depends on comparing ancient things and modern ones, checking old texts against new understandings, and against timeless realities.

Views of Evil: Boethian and Manichaean

A good way to understand *The Lord of the Rings* in its full complexity is to see it as an attempt to reconcile two views of evil, both old, both authoritative, both living, each seemingly contradicted by the other. One of these is in essence the orthodox Christian one, expounded by St Augustine and then by Catholic and Protestant teaching alike, but finding its clearest expression in a book which does not mention Christ at all: Boethius's *De Consolatione Philosophiae,* a short tract written c. A.D. 522–525 by a Roman senator shortly before his execution by *Thiudoreiks (or Theodoric), king of the Goths. This says that there is no such thing as evil: 'evil is nothing', is the absence of good, is possibly even an unappreciated good — *Omnem bonam prorsus esse fortunam,* wrote Boethius, 'All fortune is certainly good'. Corollaries of this belief are that evil cannot itself create, that it was not in itself created (but sprang from a voluntary exercise of free will by Satan, Adam and Eve, to separate themselves from God), that it will in the long run be annulled or eliminated, as the Fall of Man was redressed by the Incarnation and death of Christ. Views like these are strongly present in *The Lord of the Rings*. Even in Mordor Frodo asserts that 'the Shadow . . . can only mock, it cannot make: not real new things of its own' (p. 893), and Fangorn has already corroborated him: 'Trolls are only counterfeits, made by the Enemy in the Great Darkness, in mockery of Ents, as Orcs were of Elves' (p. 474). What the difference is between a real thing and a 'counterfeit', one cannot tell, but anyway the idea of perversion as opposed to creation comes over. It goes with Elrond's firm statement even earlier that 'nothing is evil in the beginning. Even Sauron was not so' (p. 261). On these ultimate points Tolkien was not prepared to compromise.

Still, there is an alternative tradition in Western thought, one which has never become 'official' but which nevertheless arises spontaneously from experience. This says that while it may be all very well to make philosophical statements about evil, evil nevertheless is real, and not merely an absence; and what's more it can be resisted, and what's more still, not resisting it (in the belief that one day Omnipotence will cure all ills) is a dereliction of duty. The danger of this opinion is that it tends towards Manichaeanism, the heresy which says that Good and Evil are equal and opposite and the universe is a battlefield; however, the Inklings may have had a certain tolerance for that (see C. S. Lewis's *Mere Christianity*, Book 2, section 2). Furthermore one can imagine statements about the nature of evil which would go past Boethius but stop short of Manichaeus. Tolkien perhaps found such opinions in a work he knew well, King Alfred the Great's personal translation of Boethius into Old English.

This is a remarkable book, mainly because while King Alfred showed a decent regard for the philosopher he was translating, he was not too modest to add bits of his own. He had, moreover, unlike Boethius, had the experience of seeing what Viking pirates did to his defenceless subjects; and again unlike Boethius had taken such drastic measures against evil as hanging Viking prisoners, and rebellious monks, and in all probability cutting the throats of any wounded pirates so unlucky as to be left on the battlefield. All this did not stop Alfred from being a Christian king; indeed some of his recorded behaviour seems almost quixotically forgiving. Nevertheless his career reveals the strong point of a 'heroic' view of evil, the weak point of a Boethian one: if you regard evil as something internal, to be pitied, more harmful to the malefactor than the victim, you may be philosophically consistent but you may also be exposing others to sacrifices to which they have not consented (like being murdered by Viking ravagers or, as *The Lord of the Rings* was being written, being herded into gas-chambers). In the 1930s and 1940s Boethius was especially hard to believe. Still, his view could not just be set aside.

Tolkien's way of presenting this philosophical duality was through the Ring. It seems in several ways inconsistent. For one thing it is notoriously elastic, and not entirely passive. It 'betrayed' Isildur to the arrows of the orcs; it 'abandoned' Gollum, says Gandalf, in response to the 'dark thought from Mirkwood' of its master; it all but betrays Frodo in the *Prancing Pony* when it slips onto his finger and proves his invisibility to the spies for the Nazgûl then present. 'Perhaps it had tried to reveal itself in response to some wish or command that was felt in the room', thinks Frodo, and he is clearly right. For all that, it remains an object which cannot move itself or save itself from destruction. It has to work through the agency of its possessors, and especially by picking out the weak points of their characters — possessiveness in Bilbo, fear in Frodo, patriotism in Boromir, pity in Gandalf. When Frodo passes it to Gandalf so that its identity can be confirmed, 'It felt suddenly very heavy, as if *either it or Frodo himself* was in some way reluctant for Gandalf to touch it' (p. 48, my italics). Maybe the Ring is magically conscious of Gandalf's power: maybe, though, Frodo is already afraid that he will lose it. These two possible views of the Ring are kept up throughout the three volumes: sentient creature or psychic amplifier. They correspond respectively to the 'heroic' view of evil as something external to be resisted and the Boethian opinion that evil is essentially internal, psychological, negative.

The point is repeated in several scenes of temptation. Frodo puts on the Ring six times during *The Lord of the Rings:* once in the house of Tom Bombadil (which does not seem to count), once by accident in the *Prancing Pony,* once on Weathertop, twice on Amon Hen, once in the final scene in the Sammath

Naur. On several other occasions he feels an urge to, most strongly in the valley below Minas Morgul, as the Ringwraith leads out his army. Four of these scenes, at least, are highly significant. Thus on Amon Hen Frodo puts on the Ring, contrary to Gandalf's injunction, simply to escape from Boromir, and the narrator ratifies his decision: 'There was only one thing to do'. He keeps it on, though, goes to the summit of Amon Hen and sits on the Seat of Seeing. There the Eye of Sauron becomes aware of him and leaps towards him like a searchlight:

> Very soon it would nail him down, know just exactly where he was. Amon Lhaw it touched. It glanced upon Tol Brandir — he threw himself from the seat, crouching, covering his head with his grey hood.
>
> He heard himself crying out: *Never, Never!* Or was it: *Verily I come, I come to you?* He could not tell. Then as a flash from some other point of power there came to his mind another thought: *Take it off! Take it off! Fool, take it off! Take off the Ring!*
>
> The two powers strove in him. For a moment, perfectly balanced between their piercing points, he writhed, tormented. Suddenly he was aware of himself again. Frodo, neither the Voice nor the Eye: free to choose and with one remaining instant to do so. He took the Ring off his finger. (p. 392)

This is a scene which has puzzled and irritated critics. Dr C. N. Manlove writes 'the Voice' off as 'providential', and clearly thinks it one more example of the 'biased fortune' which in his opinion makes it impossible to take the story seriously. Actually the Voice is Gandalf's, as we might have guessed from its asperity, and as is anyway confirmed on p. 484: it may seem fair enough to let a wizard oppose a necromancer. More remarkable is the opposition between *Never!* and *I come to you.* Is this a struggle inside Frodo's soul, between his conscious will and his unconscious wickedness (the sort of wickedness which might earlier have made him reluctant to hand over the Ring to Gandalf)? Or is *I come to you* the voice of the Ring itself — or even a projection from the voice of the Enemy, saying to Frodo what he wants to hear, putting words in the mouth but not in the heart, creating ugly fictions as he does later with the phantasmal corpses of the Dead Marshes? Either view is possible. Both are suggested. Evil may accordingly be an inner temptation or an external power.

Similar uncertainty dramatises other scenes when Frodo puts on the Ring, or tries to, or is ordered to. In the valley of Minas Morgul the Ringwraith sends out a command for him to put it on, but Frodo finds no response to it in his own will, feeling only 'the beating upon him of a great power from outside'. The power moves his hand, as if by magnetism, but he forces it back, to touch the phial of Galadriel and be momentarily relieved. Perhaps the same thing happened to him on Weathertop, where he put the Ring on as the Ringwraiths closed in, but the words used there are 'temptation' and 'desire' — 'his terror was swallowed up in a sudden temptation to put on the Ring. The desire to do this laid hold of him, and he could think of nothing else.' He had felt a similar urge in the Barrow, as the wight's fingers came towards him, and there the temptation offered was to abandon his friends and use the Ring to escape. On Weathertop we are told he had no such conscious and immoral thought. Nevertheless it seems that there the external power is abetted by some inner weakness, some potentially wicked impulse towards the wrong side. In the chambers of Sammath Naur one's judgement must also be suspended. Frodo makes a clear and active statement of his own evil intention: 'I will not do this deed. The Ring is mine!' But at the same time we have been told that even the phial of Galadriel loses its virtue on Mount Doom, for there Frodo is at 'the heart of the realm of Sauron . . . all other powers were here subdued'. Are Frodo's will, and his virtue, among those powers? To say so would be Manichaean. It would deny that men are responsible for their actions, make evil into a positive force. On the other hand, to put the whole blame on Frodo would seem (to use a distinctively English ethical term) 'unfair'; if he had been an entirely wicked person, he would never have reached the Sammath Naur in the first place. There seems to be a mixed judgement on him. Frodo is saved from his sin by his own earlier repeated acts of forgiveness to Gollum, but in a sense punished by the loss of his finger. 'If thine eye offend thee, pluck it out . . .' As it happens, the quotation that ran in Tolkien's mind when he considered this scene very much implies the dual nature of wickedness, but comes from the Lord's Prayer: 'And lead us not into temptation; but deliver us from evil.'† Succumbing to temptation is our business, one might paraphrase, but delivering us from evil is God's. As for the questions of how far responsibility is to be allocated between us and our tempters, how much temptation human beings can 'reasonably' be expected to stand — these are obviously not to be answered by mere mortals. Tolkien saw the problem of evil in books as in realities, and he told his story at least in part to dramatise that problem; he did not, however, claim to know the answer to it.

One can see then a philosophical crux in the very nature of the Ring, one that was certainly apparent and deeply interesting to Tolkien, and one which he furthermore expressed with great care and deliberation. This is not important just for Frodo. The uncertainty over evil in a way dominates the entire structure of *The Lord of the Rings*. All the characters would find decisions much easier if evil were unquestionably either just Boethian or else just Manichaean. If evil were only the absence of good, for instance, then the Ring could never be anything other than a psychic amplifier; it would not 'betray' its possessors, and all they would need do is put it aside and think pure thoughts. In Middle-earth we are assured that would be fatal. However, if evil were merely a hateful and external power without echo in the hearts of the good, then someone might have to take the Ring to the Cracks of Doom, but it need not be Frodo: Gandalf could be trusted with it, while whoever went would have only to distrust his enemies, not his friends and not himself. As it is, the nature of the Ring is integral to the story.

---

† Tolkien wrote this in a letter of 12 December 1955 to Mr David I. Masson, who kindly showed it to me and has given me permission to quote from it here. Irritated evidently by the *TLS* review of 25 November 1955 (to which Mr Masson had written a reply, published *TLS* 9 December 1955), Tolkien remarked that the reviewer should not have made such a fuss over giving quarter to orcs. 'Surely how often "quarter" is given is off the point in a book that breathes Mercy from start to finish: in which the central hero is at last divested of all arms, except his will? "Forgive us our trespasses as we forgive them that trespass against us. Lead us not into temptation, but deliver us from evil", are words that occur to me, and of which the scene in the Sammath Naur was meant to be a "fairy-story" exemplum . . .' See also *Letters,* p. 252.

The story also repeatedly reflects back on the nature of temptation and of the Ring. When Gandalf says to Frodo of his wound on Weathertop, 'Your heart was not touched, and only your shoulder was pierced; and that was because you resisted to the last', he may be making a moral statement (Frodo was rewarded) or a practical one (he dodged, called out, struck back, put off the Ringwraith's aim). When he says of Bilbo that he gave up the Ring 'of his own accord: an important point', he may be saying only that Bilbo can't have become too badly addicted, or more moralistically that Bilbo's good impulse will help his cure. When Glóin describes the dwarves' urge to revisit Moria, we cannot be sure whether this is the prompting of Sauron from outside or dwarvish greed and ambition from inside. All one need say is that this is how things often are. Maybe all sins need some combination of external prompting and inner weakness. At any rate, on the level of narrative one can say that *The Lord of the Rings* is neither a saint's life, all about temptation, nor a complicated wargame, all about tactics. It would be a much lesser work if it had swerved towards either extreme.

Conceptions of Evil: Shadows and Wraiths

One word which for Tolkien expressed this distinctive image of evil was 'shadow'. Do shadows exist or not? It is an ancient opinion that they do and they don't. In the Old English poem *Solomon and Saturn II†* the pagan Saturn asks the Christian Solomon (he *is* a Christian in this text) 'what things were that were not?' The answer is oblique, but it contains the word *besceadeð*, 'shadows'. Shadows are the absence of light and so

---

† There is a text and translation of this poem, and an introduction to it, in my *Poems of Wisdom and Learning in Old English* (Cambridge, D. S. Brewer Press, and Totowa, N.J., Rowman and Littlefield, 1976). Tolkien certainly studied the poem, for it is the best riddle-contest in Old English, and most like the Old Norse ones from the *Elder Edda* and *The Saga of King Heidrek*. Gollum's 'Time' riddle in *The Hobbit* is based on Saturn's 'Old Age' one.

don't exist in themselves, but they are still visible and palpable just as if they did. That is exactly Tolkien's view of evil. Accordingly Mordor is 'Black-Land', 'where the shadows lie', or even more ominously 'where the shadows *are*' (my italics); Aragorn reports that 'Gandalf the Grey fell into shadow'; Gandalf himself says that if his side loses, 'many lands will pass under the shadow'. At times 'the Shadow' becomes a personification of Sauron, as in Frodo's remark about mocking and making quoted earlier; at times it seems no more than cloud and mirk, as when the Riders' hearts 'quailed under the shadow'. At times one does not know what to think: Balin goes off to Moria and disaster after 'a shadow of disquiet' fell upon the dwarves, and when Glóin says this it appears only a metaphor for mundane discontent. It is an ominous metaphor, though. Maybe the 'shadow' was a Mordor-spell; maybe Balin simultaneously fell and was pushed. In such phrases one sees a characteristic Tolkienian strength: his ideas were often paradoxical and had deep intellectual roots, but they appealed at the same time to simple things and to everyday experience. Tolkien could be learned and practical at once, a style common enough in Old English but (he probably reflected) less and less so as the Norman Conquest and the Renaissance wore on, seeing to it that 'education' meant increasingly 'education in Latin' and the creation of a distinctive literary caste.

Tolkien's other main source for his image of 'the shadow' was probably *Beowulf,* lines 705–7. Here Beowulf and his men are waiting (the latter without hope) for the appearance of Grendel the man-eater. They did not expect to get home, says the poet; still, they went to sleep. Then he adds with sudden confidence, 'It was known to men that the demon-enemy could not draw them under shadow *(under sceadu bregdan),* as long as God did not wish it.' This is a tough thought, for all its confidence. 'Draw them under shadow' may mean no more than 'pull them out of the hall and into the dark', but it implies also 'going we know not where', dying and being handed over forever to the powers of evil. As for the phrase about God not wishing it, that seems on the whole a benevolent assertion of divine power. But what if God *does* wish it? Notoriously He does sometimes wish things like that, for even in *Beowulf* they have happened before. Tolkien was perhaps attracted by the phrase *under sceadu*, and also by the tableau of silent, rather sullen Anglo-Saxon courage. He would not have disagreed either with the implications about the unfairness of Providence; we should note that a recurrent prospect in *The Lord of the Rings* is for Frodo to be taken by Sauron and tormented till he too goes 'under the shadow', worn out by addiction and privation and torture and fear to a state of nothingness like that of 'the haggard king' of Minas Morgul.[6] This doesn't happen, but no one says it can't. Indeed, Gandalf says explicitly that it can. If the Morgul knife had reached its mark, 'You would have become a wraith under the dominion of the Dark Lord' (p. 216). And Tolkien's second word for expressing his concept of the ambiguity of evil is 'wraith'.

As so often, this may well take its source from a philological puzzle, and an uncertain entry in the *OED*. If one looks up the word 'wraith' in that dictionary — it may be remembered that Tolkien worked on its 'w' entries in his youth; see *Biography*, p. 108 — one finds a striking contradiction. First the *OED* says that 'wraiths' are ghosts, are dead, sense 1, 'an apparition or spectre of a dead person: a phantom or ghost'. Then it says that they may be alive, sense 1b, 'an immaterial or spectral appearance of a living being'. These apparently irreconcilable opinions are backed up, even more surprisingly, by quotations from the same author, Gavin Douglas, the sixteenth-century Scottish translator of Virgil's *Aeneid:* for sense 1, entirely unambiguously, 'In diuers placis The wraithis walkis of goistis that are deyd', but for sense 1b, and note the alternative word offered, my emphasis, 'Thidder went this wrath *or schaddo* of Ene' (i.e. Virgil's hero Aeneas, who may be walking through the underworld but is definitely himself alive). According to Gavin Douglas and the *OED,* then, wraiths may be alive or dead, just as, in Tolkien, the chief Ringwraith is 'undead', while all the wraiths seem to be, like shadows, both material presences and immaterial absences: under their hoods and cloaks there is nothing, or at least nothing visible, but just the same they can wield weapons, ride horses, be pierced by blades or swept away by flood. Meanwhile, if there was one thing more stimulating to Tolkien than a modern authority failing to make sense of an early text, it was perhaps a modern authority confessing itself baffled by a problem in etymology; and for 'wraith' the *OED* can do no better than the phrase 'of obscure origin'. This is, frankly, weak. The word's early Scottish associations should have suggested that it has gone through similar sound-changes to the word 'raid', a Scottish word whose standard English equivalent is 'road'. And just as 'raid'/'road' derive from the Old English verb *rídan,* so 'wraith' presumably derives from Old English *wríðan,* 'to writhe'.[7] But why should 'writhing' create a 'wraith'?

One may detect here something of a crux in the thinking of the Inklings generally, for the word and the idea are common to both Tolkien and Lewis, and to some extent Charles Williams as well: one wonders which of them thought of it first. Tolkien, at least, is the most likely to have noted the words derived from *wríðan:* 'wreath' (a twisted thing, but also an immaterial twisted thing; see his phrase 'a wreath of snow', p. 285); 'wrath', a twisted emotion; 'wroth', the adjective from 'wrath'; and the regular past participle 'writhen', a very rare word but nevertheless used twice in *The Lord of the Rings.*[8] One underlying meaning in all this is 'bent', and 'bent' is the word which C. S. Lewis used in his 1938 novel *Out of the Silent Planet* to describe the Devil, Satan, Lucifer, who is the 'bent' Oyarsa or demiurge of Earth, the 'silent planet' itself. At very much the same time, and indeed, according to Christopher Tolkien (see *Lost Road,* p. 9), 'in the actual context of [Tolkien's] discussions with C. S. Lewis in 1936', Tolkien was using the word *wraithas,* by now translated back to its 'reconstructed' or 'asterisk' form in Proto-Germanic, to express his myth of the 'Lost Straight Road' to the Undying Lands, now lost precisely because the world has become 'bent'. *Westra lage wegas rehtas, nu isti sa wraithas* is the sentence which keeps recurring, 'A straight road lay westward, now it is bent' (*Lost Road,* p. 43). To return to the Ringwraiths, they are in origin 'bent' people, and people who have been bent, perhaps, into a perfect self-regarding 'wreath', 'wraith', or Ring.

The psychological observation which underlies this puzzle in etymology seems to me to be both acute and highly contemporary. One of the strange features of the twentieth century has been the curious bloodlessness of its major demonic figures, and the repeated origin of disaster in loudly proclaimed good intentions — reform and revolution turning again and again to terror and mass murder, and throwing up leaders who for all their cruelties seem to have gained little or nothing in the way of personal satisfaction from them. By comparison with the warlords of the past, Attila or Alaric or Genghis Khan, Hitler and Stalin and their henchmen do appear as wraith-like figures, dreadful shadows, bureaucrats of genocide,[9] their original impulses (to rescue their people? to throw off oppression?) as lost as Boromir's would be, or Denethor's, or Gandalf's, if any of these were to take the Ring. There is a terrible 'applicability' about the idea of the wraiths, which many if not most of Tolkien's readers have been well able to follow. Boethius, with his view that evil is above all an absence, and that the first victim of the evil person is himself, would have been well able to follow it too; and might also have noted Tolkien's occasional suggestions of the 'wraithing' process starting even in the most well-intentioned characters, signalled by careful choice of words.[10] At the same time there is no doubt that the wraiths have to be fought physically as well as psychologically, as in the Manichaean world of Tolkien's own war experience. The Boethian and Manichaean views of evil appear incompatible, but in Tolkien's work neither can be entirely discounted.

The Opposing Forces: Luck and Chance

Tolkien's image of good is as complex as his image of evil, but often appears on the surface to be weaker and more limited. Once more he pulled a hint for his fiction from an ancient Beowulfian mystery. That poem opens with the funeral of the ancestor of one of its characters — Scyld, the king of the Danes, who according to legend came drifting to land as a baby, naked on a wooden shield. Now at the end of his life the Danes send him back to the sea in an unmanned funeral barge laden with treasure. 'By no means did [the Danes] provide him with less gifts, less national treasure', says the poet with proud understatement, 'than those did *(þonne þá dydon)* who sent him out at his beginning, alone over the waves, being a child.' Who are 'those'? The line is a very odd one, both technically† and ideologically. The *Beowulf*-poet was a Christian. There should have been no room in his universe for sub-divine but superhuman powers, other than devils or angels; however, the senders of Scyld seem supernatural in knowledge and purpose, while showing no interest in the inhabitants of Denmark's souls. One might put Scyld down to divine Providence, except that the word is *þá,* 'those', not *he,* 'He'. In *Beowulf* the matter is then dropped for good, but it leaves behind the implication that there are powers at work in the world, possibly beneficent ones, which human beings are not equipped to understand.

The same is true of *The Lord of the Rings,* though there as in *Beowulf* the lurking powers are never allowed to intervene openly. From *The Silmarillion* we can infer that Gandalf is a Maia, a spiritual creature in human shape sent for the relief of humanity; much later than he finished the trilogy Tolkien indeed reportedly said, 'Gandalf is an angel'.[11] During the action of *The Lord of the Rings,* though, Gandalf never looks very much like an angel, or at least not one of the normal iconographic kind. He is too short-tempered, for one thing, and also capable of doubt, anxiety, weariness, fear. Obviously too strong a flurry of angelic wings, too ready recourse to miracles or to Omnipotence, would instantly diminish the stature of the characters, devalue their decisions and their courage. How then does beneficence operate; and has Gandalf superiors? 'Naked I was sent back', he says at one point (recalling the story of Scyld), but he does not say who sent him. 'May the Valar turn him aside!' shout the Gondorians as the 'oliphaunt' charges. But the Valar don't. Or perhaps they do, for the beast does swerve aside, though this could be only chance. Can 'chance' and 'the Valar' be equated? Is 'chance' the word which people use for their perception of the operations of 'those', the mysterious senders of Scyld and of Gandalf too?

---

† It is the only instance, out of sixty-three occurrences in the poem, where the word *þá* as an unsupported demonstrative takes alliteration and stress, so gaining unusual if not unnatural prominence.

Tolkien had, probably, been developing some such thought as this for many years. He uses the word 'chance' quite often in a suggestive way in *The Lord of the Rings*. 'Just chance brought me then, if chance you call it', says Tom Bombadil when he rescues the hobbits from Willow-man; ruin was averted in the Northlands, says Gandalf in Appendix A III, 'because I met Thorin Oakenshield one evening on the edge of spring in Bree. A chance-meeting, as we say in Middle-earth.' Obviously chance is sometimes meant, as Gandalf says of Bilbo's finding of the Ring, though even Gandalf can only recognise such 'meanings' retrospectively. However, 'chance' was not the word which for Tolkien best expressed his feelings about randomness and design. The word that did is probably 'luck'.

This is, of course, an extremely common English word. It is also rather odd, in that no etymology of it is known. The *OED* suggests, without conviction, that it might come from words like Old English *(ge)lingan*, '*to* happen', giving then a basic meaning of 'happenstance, whatever turns up'. Tolkien would have liked that, for it would make 'luck' a close modern equivalent of the Old English word usually translated 'fate' and derived in exactly the same way from the verb *(ge)weorþan*, 'to become, to happen'. The *Beowulf*-poet often ascribes events to *wyrd*, and treats it in a way as a supernatural force. King Alfred brought it into his translation of Boethius too, to explain why divine Providence does not affect free will: 'What we call God's fore-thought and his Providence,' he wrote, 'is while it is there in His mind, before it gets done, while it's still being thought; but once it's done, then we call it *wyrd*. This way anyone can tell that there are two things and two names, forethought and *wyrd*.'[12] A highly important corollary is that people are not under the domination of *wyrd*, which is why 'fate' is not a good translation of it. People can 'change their luck', and can in a way say 'No' to divine Providence, though of course if they do they have to stand by the consequences of their decision. In Middle-earth, one may say, Providence or the Valar sent the dream that took Boromir to Rivendell (p. 340). But they sent it first and most often to Faramir, who would no doubt have been a better choice. It was human decision, or human perversity, which led to Boromir claiming the journey, with what chain of ill-effects and casualties no one can tell. 'Luck', then, is a continuous interplay of providence and free will, a blending of so many factors that the mind cannot disentangle them, a word encapsulating ancient philosophical problems over which wars have been fought and men burnt alive.

As important to Tolkien, though, was that it is a word (like 'shadow') which people use every day, and with exactly the right shade of uncertainty over whether they mean something completely humdrum and practical or something mysterious and supernatural. When Farmer Giles of Ham fires his blunderbuss at the giant he hits him 'by luck', indeed 'by chance and no choice of the farmer's': thoughts of the Valar enter no one's mind. On the other hand, his advantageous position at the rear of the knightly column which Chrysophlax decimates came about when his grey mare went lame, 'as luck (or the grey mare herself) would have it'. It is not providence, but it may have been *meant* just the same. The browbeating of the dragon outside its den, however, is something even the grey mare's prudence would not stretch to. 'Farmer Giles was backing his luck', as people often do; and it is common knowledge that while this is irrational, it works much more often than mere 'chance' would dictate. People in short do in sober reality recognise a strongly patterning force in the world around them, and both in modern and in Old English have a word to express their recognition. This force, however, does not affect free will and cannot be distinguished from the ordinary operations of nature. Most of all it does not decrease in the slightest the need for heroic endeavour. 'God helps those who help themselves', says the proverb. '*Wyrd* often spares the man who isn't doomed, as long as his courage holds,' agrees Beowulf. 'Luck served you there,' says Gimli to Merry and Pippin (p. 550); 'but you seized your chance with both hands, one might say.' If they hadn't, 'luck' would no doubt by that time have looked very different.

In Middle-earth, then, both good and evil function as external powers and as inner impulses from the psyche. It is perhaps fair to say that while the balances are maintained, we are on the whole more conscious of evil as an objective power and of good as a subjective impulse; Mordor and 'the Shadow' are nearer and more visible than the Valar or 'luck'. This lack of symmetry is moreover part of a basic denial of security throughout

The Lord of the Rings. Repeatedly we are told that if its characters fail to resist the Shadow, they will be taken over, but if they do resist they may get killed; similarly, if they reject the vagaries of chance (if Frodo for instance had refused to leave the Shire with the Ring), it's likely something highly unpleasant will happen, but if they accept and obey, things could grow even worse. The benevolent powers offer no guarantees. The best recommendation Gandalf can make is not to think about such things. 'But let us not darken our hearts by imagining the trial of their gentle loyalty in the Dark Tower. For the Enemy has failed — so far' (p. 486). Since it hasn't happened, in other words, it isn't *wyrd,* and so need not be explained. Still, it is essential to the story that such thoughts be entertained, as indeed Gandalf also says to Pippin: 'If you will meddle in the affairs of Wizards, you must be prepared to think of such things' (p. 580). Without them the characters' courage would look smaller; and courage is perhaps the strongest element in the Tolkienian synthesis of virtue.

Apparent Paradoxes: Happy Sadness and Hopeless Cheer

This has been both resented and denied: resented, simply because courage is no longer a very fashionable part of virtue; denied, in that some have said things are too easy for Frodo and his companions all through. They do escape, after all. Only Boromir of the Nine dies during the course of the action, and he deserves it. Gandalf is resurrected. Pathos is created only by the sacrifice of a few members of the virtuous side, mostly old ones like Théoden or Dáin, or peripheral ones like Háma and Halbarad and the list of mere names in the Rohan dirge after the Pelennor Fields. In a review in the *Observer* (27 November 1955) — one which Tolkien very much resented; see *Biography,* pp. 225–26 — Edwin Muir propounded a thesis that the non-adulthood of the romance was shown by its painlessness: 'The good boys, having fought a deadly battle, emerge at the end of it well, triumphant and happy, as boys would naturally expect to do. There are only one or two minor casualties.' In this there is a kind of truth (for Tolkien was kind-hearted about things like the 'evacuation' of Minas Tirith and the survival of

Bill the pony), but also an evident falsehood. When all is over Frodo for one is neither 'well', 'triumphant' nor even 'happy'. And he only exemplifies a much stronger theme in the work as a whole: the failure of the good, one might even say a sense of 'defeatism'. In the strict or dictionary sense *The Lord of the Rings* evades that concept totally, for according to the *OED* 'defeatism' is a straight borrowing from French *défaitisme,* recorded in English for the first time in 1918 and meaning 'conduct tending to bring about acceptance of defeat, esp. by action on civilian opinion'. With his best friends dead in Flanders, Tolkien had cause to hate that idea like poison, and indeed no one in Middle-earth is allowed to voice it. Even Denethor's reaction to defeat is to commit ceremonial suicide, not negotiate for some 'Vichy' status, though that is what Sauron's mouthpiece offers on p. 872, in a speech full of the Middle-earth analogues of 'reparations', 'demilitarised zones' and 'puppet governments'. Gandalf rejects that proposal with particular violence, and at all times discussion of odds or probabilities turns him hard and obstinate: '"Still," he said, standing suddenly up and sticking out his chin, while his beard went stiff and straight like bristling wire, "we must keep up our courage. You will soon be well, if I do not talk you to death. You are in Rivendell, and you need not worry about anything for the present."' 'Sufficient unto the day is the evil thereof' seems to be his motto.

Yet Gandalf also on occasion, together with the other wise men and women of the story, accepts defeat as a long-term prospect, a prospect which *The Lord of the Rings* as a whole does not deny. Thus Galadriel says of her life, 'Through ages of the world we have fought the long defeat.' Elrond agrees: 'I have seen three ages in the West of the world, and many defeats and many fruitless victories.' Later he queries his own adjective 'fruitless', but still repeats that the victory long ago in which Sauron was overthrown but not destroyed 'did not achieve its end'. The whole history of Middle-earth seems to show that good is attained only at vast expense while evil recuperates almost at will. Thangorodrim is broken without evil being at all 'broken for ever', as the elves had thought. Númenor is drowned without getting rid of Sauron. Sauron is defeated and his Ring taken by Isildur, only to set in motion the

crisis at the end of the Third Age. And even if that crisis is sur-
mounted, it is made extremely clear that this success too will
conform to the general pattern of 'fruitlessness' — or maybe
one should say its fruit will be bitter. Destruction of the Ring,
says Galadriel, will mean that her ring and Gandalf's and Elrond's will also lose their power, so that Lothlórien 'fades' and
the elves 'dwindle'. Along with them will go the ents and the
dwarves, indeed the whole imagined world of Middle-earth, to
be replaced by modernity and the domination of men; all the
characters and their story, one might say, will shrink to poetic
'rigmaroles' and misunderstood snatches in plays and ballads.
Beauty especially will be a casualty. 'However the fortunes of
war shall go . . . ,' asks Théoden, 'may it not so end that much
that was fair and wonderful shall pass for ever out of Middle-
earth?' 'The evil of Sauron cannot be wholly cured,' replies
Gandalf, 'nor made as if it had not been.' Fangorn agrees when
he says of his own dying species, 'Songs like trees bear fruit
only in their own time and their own way, and sometimes they
are withered untimely.' The collective opinion of Middle-earth
is summed up in Gandalf's aphoristic statement: 'I am Gandalf, Gandalf the White, but Black is mightier still.'

The implications of that *could* be alarming. It sounds Manichaean. However, as has already been seen, Tolkien was careful
to voice rebuttals of Manichaeanism and assertions of the non-
entity of evil many times throughout. Why then the continuing pessimistic expectations of defeat? The answer, obviously
enough, is that a major goal of *The Lord of the Rings* was to
dramatise that 'theory of courage' which Tolkien had said in
his British Academy lecture was the 'great contribution' to humanity of the old literature of the North. The central pillar of
that theory was Ragnarök — the day when gods and men would
fight evil and the giants, and inevitably be defeated. Its great
statement was that defeat is no refutation. The right side remains right even if it has no ultimate hope at all. In a sense this
Northern mythology asks more of men, even makes more of
them, than does Christianity, for it offers them no heaven, no
salvation, no reward for virtue except the sombre satisfaction
of having done what is right. Tolkien wanted his characters in
The Lord of the Rings to live up to the same high standard. He

was careful therefore to remove easy hope from them, even to make them conscious of long-term defeat and doom.

Nevertheless Tolkien was himself a Christian, and he faced a problem in the 'theory of courage' he so much admired: its mainspring is despair, its spirit often heathen ferocity. One can see him grappling with the difficulty in his poem-cum-essay 'The Homecoming of Beorhtnoth Beorhthelm's Son', published in 1953, the year before *The Fellowship of the Ring*.[13] This is a coda to the Old English poem *The Battle of Maldon,* which commemorates an English defeat by the Vikings in A.D. 991, and celebrates especially the unyielding courage of the English bodyguard who refused to retreat when their leader was killed, but fought round his body till all were dead. The very core of the sentiment is expressed by an old retainer called Beorhtwold: 'Heart shall be bolder, harder be purpose, / more proud the spirit, as our power lessens . . .' These lines, said Tolkien, 'have been held to be the finest expression of the northern heroic spirit, Norse or English; the clearest statement of the doctrine of uttermost endurance in the service of indomitable will'. Nevertheless he felt uneasy about them. He thought they were old already in 991; he saw they could be said as well by a heathen as a Christian; he thought the fierce spirit they expressed was one of the reasons for Beorhtnoth's rash decision to let the Vikings cross the river and fight on level ground; they had led to defeat and the death of the innocent.

In Tolkien's poem, accordingly, the words are not given to Beorhtwold but form part of a dream dreamt by the poet Torhthelm:

'It's dark! It's dark   and doom coming!
Is no light left us?   A light kindle,
and fan the flame!   Lo! Fire now wakens,
hearth is burning,   house is lighted,
men there gather.   Out of the mists they come
through darkling doors   whereat doom waiteth.
Hark! I hear them   in the hall chanting:
stern words they sing   with strong voices.
(He chants) "Heart shall be bolder,   harder be purpose,
more proud the spirit   as our power lessens!

Mind shall not falter   nor mood waver,
though doom shall come   and dark conquer.'"

                                                  (*Reader*, p. 19)

Tolkien himself did not think the dark would conquer. The
voices Torhthelm hears are those of his pagan ancestors, no
better than the Vikings 'lying off London in their long vessels,
/ while they drink to Thor and drown the sorrow / of hell's
children'. They are as wrong as Gandalf, or even more so;
Tídwald rebukes Torhthelm for being 'heathenish' when he
wakes up, and the poem ends with the monks of Ely singing
the *Dirige* or 'dirge' from the Office of the Dead. However,
Tolkien admired the aesthetic impulse towards good beneath
the pride and sorrow. In Middle-earth he wanted a similar ultimate courage undiluted by confidence — but at the same time
untainted by rage and despair. One may say that the wise characters in *The Lord of the Rings* are often without hope and so
near the edge of despair, but they do not succumb. That is left
to Denethor, who will not fight to the last, but turns like a heathen to suicide and the sacrifice of his kin.

Tolkien needed a new image for ultimate bravery, one
milder but not weaker than Beorhtwold's. He centred it, oddly
enough, on laughter, cheerfulness, refusal to look into the future at all.[14] There are hints of this in Middle English — the
critical moment in *Sir Orfeo* comes when the king in his
madness sees ladies at falconry, and laughs — while there is a
modern analogue in Joseph Conrad's *The Shadow-Line* (1917),
where laughter is an exorcising force. In *The Lord of the Rings*
it can be expressed by such high-status characters as Faramir,
who says at one point that he does not hope to see Frodo ever
again, but nevertheless invents a picture of them in an unknown future 'sitting by a wall in the sun, laughing at grief'.
However, the true vehicle of the 'theory of laughter' is the
hobbits; their behaviour is calqued on the traditional English
humour in adversity, but has deeper semantic roots.

Thus it is Pippin who looks up at the sun and the banners
and offers comfort to Beregond, and Merry who never loses
heart when even Théoden appears prey to 'horror and doubt'.
But Sam on the road to Mordor goes beyond both. He has less
hope even than Faramir. Indeed, we are told, he had

never had any real hope in the affair from the beginning; but being a cheerful hobbit he had not needed hope, as long as despair could be postponed. Now they had come to the bitter end. But he had stuck to his master all the way; that was what he had chiefly come for, and he would still stick to him. (p. 624)

Is it possible, one might wonder, to be 'cheerful' without any hope at all? Certainly it seems hardly sensible, but the idea rings true — it is corroborated by several first-hand accounts of the First World War, perhaps especially by Frank Richards's *Old Soldiers Never Die* (published 1933, and written significantly enough by a ranker, not an officer). Sam's twist on semantics is repeated by Pippin. He describes Fangorn and the last march of the Ents: was it 'fruitless'? Evidently not, in the short term, but in the long term Fangorn knows his race and story are sterile. The realisation makes him, according to Pippin, 'sad but not unhappy', and to modern English semantics the phrase makes almost no sense, like hopeless cheer. However, an early meaning of 'sad' is 'settled, determined'; 'cheer' comes from Old French *chair*, 'face'. The paradoxes put forward Tolkien's theses that determination should survive the worst that can happen, that a stout pretence is more valuable than sincere despair.

However, the best delineation of Tolkien's new model of courage is perhaps at the end of Book IV, chapter 8, 'The Stairs of Cirith Ungol'. Here Sam and Frodo, like Faramir, have little hope but still think of others in the future maybe 'laughing at grief'. Frodo indeed laughs himself: 'Such a sound had not been heard in those places since Sauron came to Middle-earth. To Sam suddenly it seemed as if all the stones were listening and the tall rocks leaning over them.' But then they fall asleep, and Gollum returns, to see and for a moment to love and aspire to the 'peace' he sees in their faces. It is characteristic of a kind of hardness in the fable that on this one occasion when Gollum's heart is stirred and he makes a gesture of penitence, Sam should wake up, misunderstand, and accuse Gollum of 'pawing' and 'sneaking'. Gollum gets no credit for his minor decency. But then he gave Frodo no credit earlier for his decency in saving Gollum from Faramir and the archers, preferring to spit, bear malice, and complain about 'nice Master's little trickses'. This is no excuse for Sam, but it shows maybe where criticisms like Edwin Muir's break down. The good side in *The Lord of the Rings* does win, but its casualties include, besides Théoden and Boromir, beauty, Lothlórien, Middle-earth and even Gollum. Furthermore, the characters are aware of their losses all the time, and bear a burden of regret. They just have to make the best of things and not confuse 'sorrow' with 'despair';[15] even the hobbits' schoolboy humour has a point. Tolkien after all put forward his theses about courage and about laughter fairly clearly. The critical inability to see them comes partly from mere ideological reluctance; partly, though, from unfamiliarity with the basic structural mode of *The Lord of the Rings,* the ancient and pre-novelistic device of *entrelacement*.

The Ethics of Interlace

There is a minor mystery about this mode, for Tolkien might have been expected not to like it. Its greatest literary monuments are the sequence of French prose tales from the thirteenth century about King Arthur known as the Vulgate Cycle and transposed into English only in highly compressed form by Sir Thomas Malory; and the later Italian epics about the knights of Charlemagne, Boiardo's *Orlando Innamorato,* 'Roland in Love', and Ariosto's *Orlando Furioso,* 'Roland Run Mad', imitated in English by Spenser's *The Faerie Queene.* Hence, no doubt, the early reviewers' comparisons of Tolkien with Malory, Spenser, Ariosto. However, Tolkien disobligingly remarked that he hadn't read Ariosto and wouldn't have liked him if he had *(Biography,* p. 221), while Spenser exemplified much that he hated (see p. 56 above). As for King Arthur, Tolkien might well have seen him as a symptom of English vagueness. Why should Englishmen take interest in a Welsh hero committed to their destruction, and known anyway via a French rehash? Still, the fact remains that Tolkien did produce a narrative of *entrelacement*. He had read a good deal of French romance for his *Sir Gawain* edition, and may have reflected further that even *Beowulf* has a kind of 'interlace' technique.

He knew also that the Icelandic word for 'short story' is *þáttr*, 'a thread'; sagas often consist of several *þættir*, strands woven together. The image is in Gandalf's mind when he says to Théoden, 'There are children in your land who, out of the twisted threads of story, could pick the answer to your question.' To unravel *entrelacement* — that is at least one route to wisdom.[16]

The narrative of the great 'interlaced' romances is, however, by no means famous for wisdom. Malory's editor, Eugene Vinaver, comments:

> Adventures were piled up one upon the other without any apparent sequence or design, and innumerable personages, mostly anonymous, were introduced in a wild succession . . . The purpose of their encounters and pursuits was vague, and their tasks were seldom fulfilled: they met and parted and met again, each intent at first on following his particular 'quest', and yet prepared at any time to be diverted from it to other adventures and undertakings.[17]

The result was meaningless confusion. This is very much not the case with Tolkien. The basic pattern of the centre of *The Lord of the Rings* is separations and encounters and wanderings, but these are controlled first by a map (something no Arthurian narrative possesses), and second by an extremely tight chronology of days and dates. Along with this goes a deliberate chronological 'leapfrogging'.

To particularise: the narrative of *The Fellowship of the Ring* is single-stranded, following Frodo, with the exceptions of the 'flashback' narratives embedded in 'The Shadow of the Past' and 'The Council of Elrond'. The Nine Walkers themselves stick together from the leaving of Rivendell to the end of the volume, apart from losing Gandalf in Moria. But on Amon Hen, on the 26th February, the fellowship is dispersed. Boromir is killed. Frodo and Sam canoe away by themselves. Pippin and Merry are kidnapped by the Uruk-hai. Aragorn, left to choose between chasing the latter or following the Ring, decides to pursue the orcs, along with Legolas and Gimli. The fates of these three parties are then followed separately. Briefly, what happens is that chapters 1 and 2 of Book III take Aragorn, Legolas and Gimli from the 26th to the 28th February;

chapters 3 and 4 lead Pippin and Merry from the 26th February to the 2nd March; chapters 5–7 return to Aragorn and his companions and 'leapfrog' them past Merry and Pippin again to the 4th March; while in chapter 8 these two sub-groups of the fellowship meet again on the 5th, for Merry and Pippin to bring their story up-to-date again in recounted narrative. By chapter 11 they are splitting up again, Gandalf (who had returned from Moria in chapter 5) riding off with Pippin, Merry setting off with Théoden, Aragorn, Legolas and Gimli going together once more towards the Paths of the Dead. They will not gather again till chapter 6 of Book V, 'The Battle of the Pelennor Fields'. These, however, are not the only strands. All the time Frodo and Sam are spinning another, and doing it with the same chronological overlapping. They too depart on the 26th February, and have reached the 28th by the start of Book IV. By the end of that book, though, they have got to the 13th March, some eight days later than the last events of which we are told in Book III. Gandalf and the others do not 'catch up' with Frodo and Sam till chapter 5 of Book V, but then they continue once again to the 25th March, which the two hobbits do not reach for another three chapters.

Now this unnatural form of presentation works well for surprise and suspense. It is a shock to have the battle of Helm's Deep decided by the Ents and Huorns, who were last seen marching on Isengard, but whose powers have never come out in the open before. It is a good 'cliffhanger' scene at the end of Book V, as Pippin falls in the black blood of the troll, to have his fate decided by events of which we have no knowledge. But Tolkien meant more by *entrelacement* than that.

One example of a retrospective connection has already been given. As Frodo feels the pressure of the Eye on Amon Hen, a Voice speaks to him and gives him a moment of freedom to act. This voice is Gandalf's, though Frodo thinks he is dead and the reader does too. Gandalf says as much on p. 484, though he is laconic about it — 'I sat in a high place [the great tree in Lothlórien?], and I strove with the Dark Tower' — since Aragorn and the others he is addressing can have no idea what is being referred to. Gandalf remarks at the same time that he sent Gwaihir the eagle to watch the River; presumably he was the eagle Aragorn saw, but thought nothing of, as he stared out

from Amon Hen on the first page of *The Two Towers*. Other
cross-connections are frequent. Fangorn looks long at the two
hobbits when they tell him Gandalf is dead; he does so because
he doesn't believe them, having seen Gandalf himself a couple
of days before. But we do not realise this till Gandalf remarks
on their near-meeting some thirty pages later. Across the whole
breadth of the story, meanwhile, fly the Nazgûl. Frodo and
Sam feel their presence three times as they wander across the
Emyn Muil and the Dead Marshes, on pp. 593, 616 and 620,
i.e. on the 29th February, 1st March and 4th March. Gollum
feels sure this is no coincidence. '"Three times!" he whim-
pered. "Three times is a threat. They feel us here, they feel the
Precious. The Precious is their master. We cannot go any further this way, no. It's no use, no use!"' What he says sounds
plausible enough, but it's wrong. Three times is a coincidence,
and actually we can guess each time what the Nazgûl are doing.
The first was coming back from a fruitless wait for Grishnakh
the orc, dead and burnt that same day, with the smoke from his
burning 'seen by many watchful eyes'. The second was probing towards Rohan and Saruman. The third was heading for
Isengard, to alarm Pippin on its way with the thought that it
had somehow been despatched for him (p. 585). Meanwhile the
body of Boromir establishes a similar transverse thread as it
drifts down the Great River, to be seen by Faramir, to have the
workmanship on its belt noted and compared with the broaches
of Sam and Frodo eight days later. These references and allusions tie the story together, we would say, or, to use Gandalf's
image, show one thread twisting over another. They prove the
author has the story under control, and are significant to any
reader who has grasped the entire plot. However, that is not
how they appear to the characters, or to the reader whose attention has lapsed (as whose does not?). In this contrast between
half- and full perception lies the point of interlacings.

For to the characters the story appears, to repeat a term
used already, as a 'bewilderment'. They are lost in the woods
and plains of Middle-earth. They also do not know what is going on or what to do next. Aragorn has to choose between going
to Mordor or to Minas Tirith; delays, and then finds himself
choosing between Sam and Frodo or Merry and Pippin; picks
one quest, and then has to decide whether to rest or pursue by

night. Neither decision nor delay seems to pay off. 'All that I have done today has gone amiss', he says (p. 404); 'Since we passed through the Argonath my choices have gone amiss' (p. 415); 'And now may I make a right choice, and change the evil fate of this unhappy day!' (p. 409). Éomer's intervention does not help him much, for he and his companions cannot decide at the end of chapter 2 whether they have seen Saruman or not. It appears they did (we learn later, p. 487), but the next time they think someone is Saruman it is Gandalf. Furthermore, the appearance of Saruman to drive off the borrowed horses is coincidental with the arrival of Shadowfax — the note of joy in their whinnyings puzzles Legolas, though their eventual return with Shadowfax provides an equine equivalent for the unexpected return of Gandalf. Simultaneously, in Fangorn Forest, Gandalf, Saruman and Treebeard himself are wandering, meeting or not meeting seemingly at random. The effect as a whole is like that of *A Midsummer Night's Dream*, where pairs of lovers wander in another enchanted wood, their paths crossed and tangled by Puck, Oberon, Titania and the infatuating Bully Bottom. 'Infatuation' is indeed a word one might use as well as 'bewilderment'. It means following the *ignis fatuus*, the 'will o' the wisp' that traditionally leads travellers into bog or quicksand; an analogue to the multiple wanderings of Book III is Frodo staring at the corpse-candles in chapter 2 of Book IV, to be warned by Gollum not to heed them, or the dead, rotten, phantasmal faces in the marshes below: 'Or hobbits go down to join the Dead ones and light little candles. Follow Sméagol! Don't look at lights!'

Even though it comes from Gollum, this is good advice. For of course Aragorn and the others, including Frodo, are in their feelings of confusion and meaninglessness absolutely wrong — 'infatuated', 'bewildered', drowning in a bog of mere events, caught in a strangler's net of *wyrd*. They have good apparent grounds for despair. But as it turns out (as it happens, as 'chance' or 'luck' would have it), there are things in the web of story to refute those grounds. As Gandalf points out, all Sauron and Saruman and the orcs have done between them is 'bring Pippin and Merry with marvellous speed, and in the nick of time, to Fangorn, where otherwise they would never have come at all!' — and so, one might say, though it is beyond

Gandalf's knowledge at the time, to rouse the Ents, overthrow Saruman, save Rohan, and free Théoden to make his decisive intervention at Minas Tirith. There are still several things one can not say: for instance, that Saruman's treachery was accordingly a Good Thing, or that the rescue of Minas Tirith is a reward for Aragorn's persistence. After all, if Saruman had stayed loyal, things might have ended better; if Aragorn had abandoned the chase, Merry and Pippin would have stirred up Fangorn just the same. What one can be absolutely sure about is that giving up does the other side's work for them, and ruins all your own possible futures and other people's as well. The despair of Denethor killed Théoden, as predicted by Gandalf on p. 832.[18] While persistence offers no guarantees, it does give 'luck' a chance to operate, through unknown allies or unknown weaknesses in the opposition.

As a working theory this is impregnable, whether considered sceptically or superstitiously. To it the *entrelacements* contribute a recognisable attitude towards reality. Events in the world, they say, appear chaotic and unplanned, appear so all but unmistakably. But however strong that impression is, it is a subjective one founded on the inevitably limited view of any individual. If individuals could see more widely — as we can, by virtue of the narrative structure of *The Lord of the Rings* — they would realise that events have a cause-and-effect logic, though there are so many causes that perhaps no one but God can ever see them all at once. The world is a Persian carpet, then, and we are ants lumbering from one thread to the other and observing that there is no pattern in the colours. That is why one of Gandalf's favourite sayings is 'Even the wise cannot see all ends', and why he often demonstrates its truth himself. Thus it is ironic that he more than once offers a cold-hearted appraisal of the junior hobbits' utility. 'If these hobbits understood the danger', he says to Elrond, 'they would not dare to go.' But they would still *want* to, he concludes, and their wish should outweigh their ignorance. He says to Pippin later, 'Generous deed should not be outweighed by cold counsel'. In the end he is proved both right and wrong: Merry and Pippin between them rouse the Ents, save Faramir, kill the Ringwraith. The last deed is caused by the sheer chance of finding a dagger 'bound round with spells for the destruction of Mordor' in the wight's barrow. 'Glad would he have been to know its fate who wrought it slowly long ago', comments the narrator; and his comment shows that the ancient smith was not glad, did not know, was condemned to defeat and death and oblivion in the barrows. Still, even after thousands of years hope should not be lost: nor relied on.

It is Pippin too who looks in the *palantír* and so misleads Sauron into thinking Saruman may have the Ring. This may have helped draw on the Enemy's hasty stroke, thinks Gandalf on p. 747. More important is the fact that Aragorn has the stone available to him, and that Sauron (having seen a hobbit in the same stone) thinks Aragorn *also has the Ring:* it is because Aragorn showed himself to Sauron in the palantír that Sauron neglects his guard. 'The Eye turned inward, pondering tidings of doubt and danger: a bright sword, and a stern and kingly face it saw' (p. 902). But once more ironically, it is what the Eye does not see that matters. The bright sword and kingly face turn out not to be critical. It is the two ants creeping along the Ephel Dúath who are going to change reality. Indeed Frodo and Sam provide perhaps the strongest effects of the *entrelacement*. Their bewilderments, infatuations, sense of being lost and abandoned, are much stronger than those of Aragorn or Gimli or anyone else in the more active half of the story. But by the time we come to following their strand along we know that these are not *true*. 'All my choices have proved ill', says Frodo within a couple of pages of the start of his quest. But his words echo unmistakably those of Aragorn nearly two hundred pages earlier; and we know Aragorn was wrong. What counts, then, is that Frodo should go on choosing. We perceive his doubt and weariness simultaneously as a natural reaction to circumstances, and as a temptation, even a phantasm or illusion of the Dark Tower. Evil works, we realise, by sapping the will with over-complication. Like 'the Shadow', this is in fiction an external force with physical effects of which sensitive characters like Legolas can be aware; it appeals to a recognition of truth outside fiction, however, in its buried statements that clouds have silver linings, that fortune favours the brave, that even in reality things are not always as they seem.

There is indeed a corpus of proverbs scattered through *The Lord of the Rings,* which add weight to the implications of interlace. 'Oft the unbidden guest proves the best company', says Éomer, and later 'Twice blessed is hope unlooked-for'. 'Where will wants not, a way opens', says his sister, more solemnly but also more familiarly. 'Oft hope is born, when all is forlorn', says Legolas. He, Aragorn and Théoden also state proverbs about freshness, with respectively 'Rede oft is found at the rising of the sun', 'None knows what the new day shall bring him', and 'In the morning counsels are best . . .' Legolas adds a spatial metaphor with his 'Few can foresee whither their road will lead them . . .' It should be noted that most of these are neutral on the optimism/pessimism scale, while some of the characters' proverbs approach the meaningless. 'Strange are the turns of fortune', says Gandalf (which could be good or bad depending on context), and 'Hope oft deceives', says Éomer (also so true as to be non-predictive). Still, most of those quoted so far are real proverbs, as the place-names of the Shire are real place-names, and they have a similar function: to draw us in, to make connections between experience inside and outside the story. Within this continuum, however, other proverbs are planted, sounding much the same as the others but more original and so closer to Tolkien's own intention. 'Often does hatred hurt it-self', says Gandalf; 'Oft evil will shall evil mar', says Théoden; 'The hasty stroke goes oft astray', says Aragorn; 'A traitor may betray himself', Gandalf again. It takes the action of the whole of *The Lord of the Rings* to make these ring true, and there is a vein of proverbial wisdom (about God being on the side of the big battalions) which would utterly deny them. These invented sayings show in miniature the 'contrivance' of which the trilogy has often been accused. Only a fool, though, would deny that the contrivances have a point; only a very careless reader would think that the *entrelacements* of this romance are purely for variety, and have nothing to say about 'the fundamental character of reality' at all.

Just Allegory and Large Symbolism

Tolkien's proverbs edge, on the whole, towards the archaic. So does his use of omens and prophecies — a feature of *The Lord of the Rings* which may furthermore seem to deny the idea of free will being left intact by the forces of providence. Galadriel seems to know in advance that Aragorn will take the Paths of the Dead, Aragorn to know that he and Éomer will meet again, 'though all the hosts of Mordor should stand between'. *Someone* (or something) foreknew that the Ringwraith would not fall 'by the hand of man'. These cross-temporal flashes suggest, perhaps, that some things are bound to happen regardless of what people do or choose. Yet that would clearly be a false conclusion. The words of prophecies could be fulfilled after all in many different ways. We are left always at liberty to suppose that Aragorn and Éomer could have met once more as prisoners, say, that the Grey Company could have quailed and turned back. If Merry had failed to stab the Ringwraith, it might have died aeons later at the hands of some other woman, hobbit, elf-hero. As Galadriel says of her Mirror (p. 354): it 'shows many things, and not all have yet come to pass. Some never come to be, unless those that behold the visions turn aside from their path to prevent them.' She articulates a theory of compromise between fate and free will once more at least a millennium old: in the *Solomon and Saturn* poem Saturn asks which will be the stronger, *wyrd ge warnung,* 'fated events or foresight', and Solomon tells him that 'fate is hard to alter . . . And nevertheless an intelligent man can moderate all the things that fate causes, as long as he is clear in his mind'. It is important to realize, though, that antiquarian as Tolkien's motives often were,[19] and 'pre-scientific' as the opinions of Galadriel and Solomon seem, what Tolkien was writing about is still in a way a live issue. 'Every bullet has his billet' is a distinctively modern saying, first recorded in that form in 1765, and in use up to the present day to indicate that sometimes no precautions work; yet saying the proverb, and believing it, probably never stopped anyone from taking cover. 'God helps those who help themselves', to repeat a proverb mentioned earlier. Tolkien in other words never lost his belief in the reality and continuity not only of language and of history, but of human nature and of some intellectual problems.

This should be kept in mind when considering the much vexed question of allegory, or symbolism, in *The Lord of the Rings*. Tolkien's opinions here are clear only up to a point. As is well known, he wrote in the 'Foreword' to the second edition: 'I cordially dislike allegory in all its manifestations, and always have done so since I grew old and wary enough to detect its presence.' He went on, though: 'I much prefer history, true or feigned, with its varied applicability to the thought and experience of readers. I think that many confuse "applicability" with "allegory"; but the one resides in the freedom of the reader, and the other in the purposed domination of the author.' Some relation between fiction and fact might be perceived, then; and 'The Scouring of the Shire' had 'some basis in experience' though no 'contemporary political reference whatsoever', not even to Britain's Socialist 'austerity' government of 1945–1950. As Tolkien wrote of *Beowulf*, it was important to preserve a balance, to see that the 'large symbolism is near the surface, but . . . does not break through, nor become allegory'. 'Allegory' would after all imply, to Tolkien (see pp. 43, 46–47 above), that *The Lord of the Rings* had only one meaning, which would have to remain constant all the way through; he toyed contemptuously with the notion in the 'Foreword' as he sketched out a plan for his work as a *real* allegory with the Ring itself as President Truman's atomic bomb.[20] 'Large symbolism', however, should not be a matter of one imposed diagram, but of repeated offered hints. The hints would work only if they were true both in fact and in fiction. History, thought Tolkien, was varied in its applicability. But if you understood it properly, you saw it repeating itself.

Some of Tolkien's hints have been glanced at already. The Riders of Rohan, and the Rangers of Gondor, will not offer the excuse that they were 'only obeying orders'; one cannot avoid the contrast with the Nazis. When Gandalf tells Frodo about the Ring, Frodo replies 'I wish it need not have happened in my time', but Gandalf reproves him: 'So do I . . . and so do all who live to see such times. But that is not for them to decide' (p. 50). The rebuke is deserved by Frodo, but also by Neville Chamberlain with his now infamous promise that he brought 'peace in our time'.[21] Elrond, on p. 237, has learnt better. He remembers a moment when 'the Elves deemed that evil was ended for ever' but knows that 'it was not so'. Tolkien himself fought in 'the war to end all wars', but saw his sons fighting in the one after that. Other ironies are not hard to discover. As Gandalf and Pippin ride from the Anórien towards Minas Tirith, they find their way blocked by men building a wall (p. 732). It is Denethor's insistence on defending this (p. 798) that nearly kills Faramir, and all it does in practice is to obstruct the arrival of the Rohirrim (p. 819), by which time it is already a 'ruin', for all the 'labour' wasted on it at the start. Men of Tolkien's generation could hardly avoid thinking of the Maginot Line. Gandalf's advice, 'But leave your trowels and sharpen your swords!', has more than an immediate relevance. The hint is unmistakable, as are others in the trilogy, of Vichyism and quislings, of puppet governments and demilitarised zones. How well do they hang together, though? Did Tolkien go on from the exploitation of occasional scenes to the manipulation of plot, the creation of recognisably symbolic characters, the thing Alfred Duggan, the *TLS* reviewer, asked for so plaintively, 'a clear message for the modern world'? Of course Tolkien would have scorned 'message' as much as 'modern'. Still, he created two characters in *The Lord of the Rings* of particular suggestiveness, both of them originally on the right side but seduced or corroded by evil, and so especially likely to have analogues in the real world: these are Denethor and Saruman, each of them seen faintly satirically, almost politically.

To take the more obvious example first, Saruman shows many signs of being equatable with industrialism, or technology. His very name means something of the sort. *Searu* in Old English (the West Saxon form of Mercian *saru) means 'device, design, contrivance, art'. Bosworth-Toller's *Dictionary* says cautiously that often you cannot tell 'whether the word is used with a good or with a bad meaning'. When Beowulf walks into Hrothgar's hall the poet says appreciatively that 'on him his armour shone, the cunning net *(searo-net)* sewed by the crafts *(orþancum)* of the smith'. Jewellers are *searo-cræftig,* and wizards *snottor searu-þancum,* 'wise in cunning thoughts'. The word stretches from wisdom to plot and treachery, though. Beowulf denies he ever sought out *searo-niþas,* 'cunning malices'; Grendel's corpse-holding glove is *searo-bendum fæst,* 'fixed with cunning bands'. The word implies cleverness, but is nearly always linked with metal: iron in armour and clasps, but also silver and gold. The dragon's treasure is a *searu-gimma geþræc,* 'a heap of cunning jewels', in the *Riming Poem* the poet says obscurely *sinc searwade,* 'treasure played the traitor'. That means 'left its possessor', suggest Messrs Bosworth and Toller. To Tolkien, with his theory of dragonish 'bewilderment', it meant more likely 'stayed with its possessor', driving him insidiously to greed and cunning.

These cruxes all form part of Saruman's character. He is learned, but his learning tends to the practical. 'He has a mind of metal and wheels', says Fangorn. His orcs use a kind of gunpowder at Helm's Deep (p. 525); thirty pages later the Ents meet at Isengard, or 'Irontown', a kind of napalm — perhaps one should say, with closer reference to Tolkien's own experience, a *Flammenwerfer.* The implication is that Saruman has been led from ethically neutral researches into the kind of wanton pollution and love of dirt we see in 'The Scouring of the Shire' by something corrupting in the love of machines or in the very desire for control over the natural world. And for this there is a real-world connection, for Tolkien's own childhood image of industrial ugliness in the midst of natural beauty was Sarehole Mill, with its literally bone-grinding owner 'the White Ogre'; see *Biography,* p. 28. The *Oxford Dictionary of English Place-Names* takes the first element of this place to be a personal name *Searu,* or perhaps the word 'sere, withered'; Tolkien would automatically have corrected to Mercian *Saru,* but might well have seen all the proposed meanings as relevant, 'grey and withered', but also 'cunning and mechanical'. It is interesting, too, that Saruman's Orc-men call him 'Sharkey' or 'Old Man'. To a medievalist the name might well suggest the 'Old Man of the Mountains' or leader of the Assassins as described in *Mandeville's Travels.* 'Old Man' is simply Arabic *shaikh* (cp. Orkish *sharkû*). And Mandeville's Old Man ruled, of course, by feeding his followers hashish and deluding them with dreams of paradise. So, we might think, 'cunning man', or 'machine man', or 'technological man', keeps a Utopian carrot dangling in front of our noses, of a world of leisure and convenience where each new mill grinds faster than the one before. But as Ted Sandyman ought to have realised, 'you've got to have grist before you can grind'; machine-masters end up ma-chine-minders, and all for nothing, or rather for an insidious logic of expansion.

This may not be a totally convincing critique of modern so-ciety, but it has clear modern relevance and is more than mere dislike. There is something suggestive also in Saruman's no-torious 'voice', which always seems 'wise and reasonable', and wakes desire in others 'by swift agreement to seem wise them-selves'. Gandalf's harshness represents denial of Utopias and insistence that nothing comes free. Even Lotho 'Pimple', Frodo's relative, has a place in the argument because he is such an obvious Gradgrind — greedy and bossy to begin with, but staying within the law till his manipulators take over, to jail his mother, kill him and eat him too (if we can believe the hints about Gríma Wormtongue). Jeremy Bentham to Victorian cap-italists? Old Bolshevik to new Stalinist? The progression is fa-miliar enough, and it adds another modern dimension to Mid-dle-earth or rather a timeless one, for though in the modern age we give Saruman a modern 'applicability', his name, and the evident uncertainty even in Anglo-Saxon times over mechani-cal cleverness and 'machinations', shows that his meaning was ancient too.

Saruman nevertheless does have one distinctively modern trait, which is his association with Socialism. His men *say* they are gathering things 'for fair distribution', though nobody be-lieves them — a particularly strange compromise of evil with morality, for Middle-earth, where vice rarely troubles to be hypocritical. It is worth saying accordingly that Denethor, con-trasted with Saruman as he is in other ways with Théoden, is an arch-conservative. In almost his last speech he declares:

> 'I would have things as they were in all the days of my life
> . . . and in the days of my longfathers before me . . . But if
> doom denies this to me, then I will have *naught:* neither life
> diminished, nor love halved, nor honour abated.' (p. 876)

'I will have *naught*' is a particularly ominous expression. As *The Lord of the Rings* was coming to the end of its gestation it became possible for the first time for political leaders to say they wanted nothing *and make it come true*. Denethor clearly will not submit to the Enemy, as Saruman did, but he also cares nothing in the end for his subjects, while his love even for his sons would take them both to death with him. 'The West has failed', he says. 'It shall all go up in a great fire, and all shall be ended! Ash! Ash and smoke blown away on the wind!' He does not say 'nuclear fire', but the thought fits. Denethor breaks his own staff of office as Saruman does not. He mingles an excess of heroic temper — the ancient Ragnarök spirit, one might say, which Tolkien with significant anachronism twice calls 'heathen'[22] — with a mean concern for his own sovereignty and his own boundaries: a combination that unusually and in this one particular case makes no sense at all before 1945 and the invention of the 'great deterrent'.

It is a risky business finally to draw a Tolkienian 'inner meaning' from these various 'applicabilities'. Tolkien himself insisted that he had not intended one; and finding one need not be the ultimate necessity for the critic, since after all political messages add nothing to Tom Bombadil, or the Ents, or the Riders of Rohan, or the *entrelacements,* or most of the things discussed in this chapter and the ones around it. The real point is that Tolkien's theories about nature, evil, luck and our perception of the world generated as a sort of by-product modern applications and political ones. His attachment to the 'theory of courage' made him believe that the Western world in his lifetime had been short not of wit or of strength, but of will. His readings of heroic poems made him especially scornful of the notion that to say 'evil must be fought' is the same as saying 'might is right'.[23] He thought that England, in forgetting her early literature, had fallen into liberal self-delusions. Naturally all these 'morals' or 'meanings' can in themselves be accepted or rejected, depending very much on the varied experience of readers. What cannot be denied is that they emerge from much experience in the author, and much original thought, that they are moreover integrated in a fiction which has a power independent of them. Tolkien was not writing to a thesis. A good deal of what he wrote may be taken as a rejection of the 'liberal interpretation of history', and indeed of the 'liberal humanist tradition' in literature;[24] nevertheless the centre of his story is the Ring and the maxim that 'power corrupts', a concept unimpeachably modern, democratic, anti- though not unheroic.

Eucatastrophe, Realism, and Romance

It should be clear by this time that if there is one critical statement entirely and absolutely wrong, it is the one quoted at the start of this chapter, about *The Lord of the Rings* not being 'moulded by some controlling vision of things which is at the same time its *raison d'être'*. The 'vision of things' is there in the Ring, in the scenes of conflict and temptation, in the characters' words and attitudes, in proverbs and in prophecies and in the very narrative mode itself. Naturally this 'understanding of reality' can be 'denied': so can they all. But not to see that it exists shows a surprising (and therefore interesting) blindness. It is matched only by Alfred Duggan's insistence in the *TLS* that in *The Lord of the Rings* all the good and bad sides do is try to kill each other, so that they cannot be told apart: 'Morally there seems nothing to choose between them.'[25] The difference is at the very heart of the plot. As W. H. Auden saw, in his piece for *The New York Review of Books* (22 January 1956), it is vital that Sauron does not guard the Cracks of Doom and discover Frodo because he is sure Aragorn will take the Ring:

> Evil, that is, has every advantage but one — it is inferior in imagination. Good can imagine the possibility of becoming evil — hence the refusal of Gandalf and Aragorn to use the Ring — but Evil, defiantly chosen, can no longer imagine anything but itself.

Not to see points like that (and there are more obvious ones) is in a way shameful. The repeated blindnesses of critics can only be explained by a deep dissatisfaction in them with the very data of 'fairy-story', an inhibition against accepting the conventions of romance.

Of these the greatest must be the 'happy ending' (one brought about, more often than not, by 'hap' or 'chance' or 'luck'). Tolkien, of course, being a Christian, did in absolute fact believe that in the end all things would end happily, that in a sense they already had — a belief he shared with Dante, and a matter of faith beyond argument. It needs to be said, though, that he was capable of envisaging a different belief and even bringing it into his story. Frodo and Sam debate it after they have destroyed the Ring and are caught in the fall of the Dark Tower:

> 'I don't want to give up yet' [said Sam]. 'It's not like me, somehow, if you understand.'
> 'Maybe not, Sam,' said Frodo; 'but it's like things are in the world. Hopes fail. An end comes. We have only a little time to wait now. We are lost in ruin and downfall, and there is no escape.' (p. 929)

He does not change his mind, nor his perception of how 'things are in the world'. They are changed for him by the eagles who come and take him in his sleep to a new world—which Sam, with a resurrected Gandalf in front of him, very nearly perceives as Heaven. The difference between Earth and Middle-earth, one might say, is that in the latter faith can, just sometimes, be perceived as fact. And while this is an enormous difference, it is not the same as that between the adult and the child.

It cannot be denied that there *is* a streak of 'wish-fulfilment' in *The Lord of the Rings*. Tolkien would have liked to hear the horns of Rohan blow, and watch the Black Breath of inertia dissolve from his own country. If his work has an image inside itself, it is I think the horn that Éomer gives to Merry, only a small one, but one from the hoard of Scatha the Worm and brought from the North by Eorl the Young. It is a magic one, though only modestly so: 'He that blows it at need shall set fear in the hearts of his enemies and joy in the hearts of his friends, and they shall hear him and come to him.' When Merry blows it in the Shire the revolution against sloth and shabbiness and Saruman-'Sharkey' is on: no doubt Tolkien would have liked to be able in his own person to do the same. He got closer to his goal than many, however, at least when it came to bringing 'joy'. At the same time his portrayal of Frodo quietly sliding down to sleep, dismissal and an oblivion which would include ents, elves, dwarves and the whole of Middle-earth shows that he recognised the limits of his own wishes and their non-correspondence with reality. The last word on the relationship between his literary mode and that of realism may perhaps go to Professor Frank Kermode, who wrote:

Romance could be defined as a means of exhibiting the action of magical and moral laws in a version of human life so selective as to obscure, for the special purpose of concentrating attention on these laws, the fact that in reality their force is intermittent and only fitfully glimpsed.

Professor Kermode made those remarks, however, *à propos* of Shakespeare's *Tempest*.[26] And one has to say that while both Prospero and Gandalf are old men with staffs, Prospero brushes aside the oppositions of reality with an ease which Gandalf is never allowed to aspire to.

CHAPTER 6

'WHEN ALL OUR FATHERS

WORSHIPPED STOCKS AND STONES'

Stylistic Theories: Tolkien and Shakespeare

Mentioning Tolkien in the same breath with Shakespeare will seem to many rash, even perverse. If there is one image which biographical criticism has projected powerfully, it is that of Tolkien the Philistine, hater of literary mainstreams. He read little modern poetry and little modern fiction, taking 'no serious notice' even of what he read. He liked as much as anything the works of John Buchan. In 1931 he succeeded in eliminating Shakespeare from his part of the Oxford English syllabus. In childhood he found that he 'disliked cordially' Shakespeare's plays, remembering especially an early 'bitter disappointment and disgust . . . with the shabby use made in Shakespeare of the coming of "Great Birnam Wood to high Dunsinane hill"'.[1] Many critics have felt that these strongly anti-literary or antipoetic attitudes have found suitable reflection in Tolkien's own style, described variously as 'Brewer's Biblical', 'Boy's Own', irresistibly reminiscent of 'the work of Mr Frank Richards' (the creator of a sequence of school stories about a fat boy, Billy Bunter). It is a common critical stance to praise Tolkien's conception, often somewhat vaguely, or with even more vagueness his 'mythological' or 'mythopoeic' powers; but then to declare that the words do not live up to the things, the style 'is quite inadequate to the theme'.[2] There are, however, immediate reasons for thinking that this stance is imperceptive. Tolkien said that he 'disliked' Shakespeare 'cordially', but he used exactly the same phrase of allegory too, where it concealed an opinion of some subtlety. On a larger scale one might observe that his lifelong preoccupation with words gave him a kind of sensitivity to them, even if it was an unorthodox one; and further that it is strange that a myth should so make its way if enshrined and embodied in words as inappropriate as critics have made out. 'Style' and 'mythology' are in fact not to be separated, though they may be disentangled. A concept which helps one to see Tolkien's view of both is that of 'loose' or 'tight' semantic and dramatic 'fit'.

The beginnings of this idea emerge well from a passage in *The Lord of the Rings* which has been singled out for especially ferocious criticism: the parting of Treebeard from Celeborn and Galadriel in *The Return of the King*, p. 959:

> Then Treebeard said farewell to each of them in turn, and he bowed three times slowly and with great reverence to Celeborn and Galadriel. 'It is long, long since we met by stock or by stone, *A vanimar, vanimálion nostari!*' he said. 'It is sad that we should meet only thus at the ending. For the world is changing: I feel it in the water, I feel it in the earth, and I smell it in the air. I do not think we shall meet again.'
>
> And Celeborn said: 'I do not know, Eldest.' But Galadriel said: 'Not in Middle-earth, nor until the lands that lie under the wave are lifted up again. Then in the willow-meads of Tasarinan we may meet in the Spring. Farewell!'

These two paragraphs are quoted in his book *Modern Fantasy* by Dr C. N. Manlove, who then goes straight on as usual to spearhead the critical assault and declare:

> The overworked cadences, the droning, monotonous pitch, the sheer sense of hearts charged not with lead but gas, can offer only nervous sentimental indulgence or plain embarrassment to the reader.
>
> Compare this with, say, Ector's lament over Arthur in Malory, or the 'Survivor's Lament' in *Beowulf,* or this from 'The Wanderer' . . .

and Dr Manlove goes on to cite a well-known *Ubi sunt* passage from the Old English poem and to observe that 'this is real elegy, for it has something to be elegiac about'.[3] Considered as criticism, much of this is mere rudeness, but it does have the merit of introducing medieval comparisons: not on the whole good ground for a Manlove to fight a Tolkien on.

Exactly that passage from *The Wanderer,* for instance, is paraphrased by Aragorn in chapter 6 of *The Two Towers:* a candid mind might have looked to see what Tolkien could make of it. As for Ector's lament, it was in fact over Lancelot, not Arthur. If one reads even more attentively, one cannot help noting a curious stylistic feature not entirely dissociated from Treebeard. What Malory actually wrote was:

> 'And now I dare say,' sayd syr Ector, 'thou sir Launcelot, there thou lyest, that thou were never matched of erthely knyghtes hande. And thou were the curtest [i.e. most courteous] knyght that ever bare shelde! And thou were the truest frende to thy lovar that ever bestrade hors, and thou were the trewest lover of a synful man that ever loved woman, and thou were the kyndest man that ever strake with swerde.[4]

The kindest man that ever struck with sword?, modern readers reflect. The truest lover that ever bestrode a horse? In modern contexts phrases like this could only be funny. Strong belief in the virtues of stylistic and semantic consistency urge us to keep kindness and sword-strokes, loved women and bestridden horses, in separate mental compartments. But clearly Malory did not feel this urge towards exactness at all. Did Tolkien? Tolkien furthermore no doubt noted that Malory's insensitivity in this respect (a common thing in medieval writers) had not led necessarily to failure. His emulation of 'loose semantic fit' does, however, puzzle many modern readers — those especially who have been sophisticated by modern literary practice.

To go back to Dr Manlove and Treebeard: it is actually hard to make out what bits of the text have caused the irritation. It could be the boldly untranslated fragment of Quenya,[5] or the triple repetition of 'feel . . . feel . . . smell', or the sudden change to less plain language in Galadriel's speech, with its elvish place-name (and also its typical echo of wartime English popular song).[6] However, all these are easily defensible. If the paragraphs quoted do contain anything to gripe at seriously, it must be Treebeard's opening sentence, with its oddly redundant phrase, 'by stock or by stone'. What have stocks and stones got to do with the matter? Isn't the phrase just meaningless, flung in for the rhythm, meaning no more than 'by pillar or by post', 'by night or by day', 'by hook or by crook'? So one might feel. But it is exactly in phrases like this that one sees Tolkien playing with medieval notions of style, with 'loose semantic fit', with a personal view of poetry.

'By stock or by stone' is certainly a deliberate echo of the fourteenth-century poem *Pearl,* written by the author of *Sir Gawain and the Green Knight,* and probably the most powerful of all medieval elegies. Under its image of the jeweller who has lost his pearl in an orchard, this describes a father lamenting his dead infant daughter in the graveyard where she is buried. He falls asleep with his head on her grave mound, to be taken away in spirit to a strange land where all his grief suddenly fades — and where to his utter delight he sees his lost child facing him, on the other side of a river. But she has grown up strangely, and she treats him with a cold formality, calling him 'Sir' but correcting him almost every time he speaks. How sad he has been, he says; he had no need to be, she replies. Quite right, he agrees, for (praise God) he has found her and will live with her in joy from now on; no, she says, she is not there, he cannot join her, he cannot cross the river. Don't send me away again, he pleads, to 'durande doel'. Why are you always talking about sorrow? she asks fiercely. At that the father gives up his attempt to take an active role, humbles himself, but repeats his grief in his apology:

> 'My blysse, my bale, ye han ben bothe,
> Bot much the bygger yet watz my mon;
> Fro thou watz wroken fro vch a wothe,
> I wyste neuer quere my perle watz gon.
> Now I hit se, now lethez my lothe.
>
> And, quen we departed, we wern at on;
> God forbede we be now wrothe,
> We meten so selden by stok other ston . . .

The quotation here is based on the edition of *Pearl* by E. V. Gordon (Oxford: Clarendon Press, 1953), originally meant to be a co-operative venture with Tolkien; and I would translate it as follows:

> 'You have been both joy and grief to me, but so far sorrow has been much the greater; I never knew, once you were removed from earthly dangers, where my pearl had gone. But now I see it, my sadness is assuaged. And when we were separated, there was no strife between us. God forbid we should now be angry with each other — we meet so seldom by stock or by stone . . .'

In his version of *Pearl* published in 1975 Tolkien translated that last line as 'We meet on our roads by chance so rare', but probably 'We meet so seldom by stock or by stone' is better. The pathos lies in the characteristic early English understatement — 'so seldom' means 'never' or, worse still, 'just this once' — and also in the last phrase's suspense between precision and vagueness. 'Stok other ston' could mean nothing, be just a line-filler, like 'erly and late' a few lines afterwards. On the other hand it implies very strongly 'on earth', 'in reality', 'in flesh and blood'. Where *is* the dreamer-father? At the end of the poem he will realise that the water was Death, his daughter in Heaven, the strange land a premonition of Paradise. If at the moment he speaks he thinks he is meeting his child in a land of real stones and tree-stumps, he is sadly mistaken; if he realises he is not, then already a touch of grief is creeping back into consolation.

'By stok other ston' is great poetry, one should see; not a great *phrase*, but great poetry, in its context. Could the same effect be reached in modern English, with its much fiercer attitude towards phrasal looseness? Tolkien tried the experiment in Treebeard's farewell, and maybe he failed; though one might say that the image behind the phrase works well for Fangorn, whose sense of ultimate loss naturally centres on felled trees and barren ground. However, the real point is that Tolkien was trying continually to extend the frontiers of style beyond the barbed wire of modern opinion. In this endeavour he thought he had the backing of the great poets and romancers, like Sir Thomas Malory or the anonymous authors of

Pearl and *Beowulf* and *The Wanderer*. It was true that they had mostly been forgotten, left unappreciated. The tradition they stood for, though, had not. You could see it, thought Tolkien, even in Shakespeare, here and there.

It is thus quite clear that whatever he said about Shakespeare's plays, Tolkien read some of them with keen attention: most of all, *Macbeth*. Motifs from this play are repeated prominently in *The Lord of the Rings*. The march of the Ents to Isengard makes true the report of the frightened messenger to the incredulous Macbeth in Act V Scene 5: 'As I did stand my watch upon the hill / I looked toward Birnam and anon methought / The wood began to move.' The prophecy that the chief Ringwraith will not fall 'by the hand of man', and his check when he realises Dernhelm is a woman, similarly parallels the Witches' assurance to Macbeth and his disconcertment when told 'Macduff was from his mother's womb / Untimely ripped.' There is a more complicated echo of Shakespeare in the scene when Aragorn, as the true king, revives the sick in the Houses of Healing with his touch and the herb *athelas*. In *Macbeth* too there is a healing king, but offstage — it is Edward the Confessor, the last legitimate Anglo-Saxon king, who sends Siward Earl of Northumbria to assist the rebels. This seems to be a deliberate compliment by Shakespeare to James the First (of England) and Sixth (of Scotland), who had begun to touch for the 'king's evil' or scrofula by 1606. Tolkien probably did not approve, thinking this mere flattery. After all, James was of the Stewart dynasty, so called because his ancestor Robert had been High Steward of Scotland, and had succeeded to the throne on the death of David II in 1371. When Denethor says that stewards do not come to be kings by the lapse of a few centuries in Gondor, but only 'in other places of less royalty', the remark is true of Scotland, and of Britain — though not of Anglo-Saxon England, ruled from the legendary past of King Cerdic to 1065 by kings descended in paternal line from one ancestor. *The Return of the King* is in a way a parallel, in another a reproach, to *Macbeth*.

Tolkien, however, used the play for both more and less than motifs. There is a flash of minute observation in chapter 6 of *The Two Towers*. What shall we do about Saruman, asks

Théoden. 'Do the deed at hand', replies Gandalf, send every man against him at once. 'If we fail, we fall. If we succeed — then we will face the next task.' The jingle of 'fail-fall' echoes a famous crux in *Macbeth*, where the hero falters in front of his wife. 'If we should fail?' he asks. 'We fail?' replies she — in the Folio punctuation. Actresses have tried the line different ways: as a sarcastic question, a flat dismissal, a verbal slap. They were all wrong, implies Tolkien; it was a misprint, the word was 'fall', meaning 'die', and is a straight answer to a straight question. The reading might not seem very good, except for one thing. 'Alliterative assonances' such as 'fail' and 'fall' are very common in Old English poetry, and indeed in Middle English in the tradition which includes *Pearl*. *Macbeth* is the only one of Shakespeare's plays to include Anglo-Saxon characters; and by some odd stylistic response it too is full of this ancient (but still popular) rhetorical device. 'My way of *life* / Is fallen into the sere, the yellow *leaf*', says Macbeth; 'why do you start, and seem to *fear* / Things that do sound so *fair*?' asks Banquo; 'I see thee still', says Macbeth to the imaginary dagger, 'And on thy *blade* and dudgeon gouts of *blood*, which was not so before.' 'Fail' and 'fall' would then be one in a set of nearly forty — a part of the play's poetic texture. How strange that critics should not have remarked the possibility! Or how typical, thought Tolkien. Modern critics were not good at Anglo-Saxon echoes, especially at ones which hung on into modern times in phrases like 'mock' and 'make', 'chance' and 'choice', 'bullet' and 'billet', all mentioned already in this study.

Gandalf's adaptation of *Macbeth* also, of course, restates the idea of aggressive courage, a quality very strong in the play and expressed very much in Tolkienian style by Old Siward, 'Why then, God's soldier be he . . . And so his knell is knolled'; by Malcolm, 'The night is long that never finds the day'; by Macbeth himself, 'Send out more horses, skirr the country round, / Hang those that talk of fear.' To this Tolkien could not remain immune. However, the final and strongest influence of *Macbeth* on *The Lord of the Rings* is quite obviously in theme. If there is one moral in the interlacements of the latter, it is that you must do your duty regardless of what you think is going to happen. This is exactly what Macbeth does not realise.

He believes the Witches' prophecy about his own kingship, and tries to fulfil it; he believes their warning about Macduff and tries to cancel it. If he had not tried to cancel it (and so murdered Macduff's family), Macduff might not have killed him; if he had not killed Duncan, he might conceivably have become king some other way. Macbeth is a classic case of a man who does not understand about the cooperation between free will and luck. Galadriel's warning about the events in her mirror, 'Some never come to be, unless those that behold the visions turn aside from their path to prevent them', would have been well said to him. But he had no Galadriel. The only mirror he sees is controlled (Act IV Scene 1) by the Witches.

Tolkien was trying, then, to make Shakespeare more positive — a bold venture, but based on a clear insight itself based on very minute reading. If he disliked Shakespeare, other than in joke, it was because he thought Shakespeare, a true poet with a deep tap-root into old English stories and traditions, had too often neglected that root for later and sillier interests. *King Lear* stems from the gaudy fictions of Geoffrey of Monmouth, laughed at in *Farmer Giles,* and yet it contains one ancient and resonant line in the mad scene of 'poor Tom':

'Child Roland to the Dark Tower came.'

The line obviously comes from some lost ballad telling the story of how Child Roland went to Elfland to rescue his sister from the wicked King, a monster-legend, a Theodoric-story.[7] Now why couldn't Shakespeare have told *that,* Tolkien must have reflected, instead of bothering with *King Lear*! As things were, Tolkien had to tell the 'Dark Tower' story himself. Still, there was no doubt that Shakespeare knew something. Besides *Macbeth* and *Lear,* Tolkien was probably struck by *The Tempest* and *A Midsummer Night's Dream* (the two 'fairy' plays and the two whose plots were not borrowed but made up by Shakespeare). But he remembered less likely plays too. As the Fellowship leaves Rivendell, Bilbo says:

'When winter first begins to bite
  and stones crack in the frosty night,
 when pools are black and trees are bare,
  'tis evil in the Wild to fare.'

In rhythm and theme he echoes the magnificent coda to *Love's Labour's Lost:*

> When icicles hang by the wall,
>   And Dick the shepherd blows his nail,
> And Tom bears logs into the hall,
>   And milk comes frozen home in pail,
> When blood is nipped, and ways be foul,
> Then nightly sings the staring owl,
>   Tu-who . . .

Shakespeare's piece is better, but Bilbo's is good enough. Remarkably, every single word in both is ordinary if colloquial English; every single word is also (with the doubtful exceptions of 'logs' and 'nipped') rooted in Old English. Both poems would require little change to make sense at any time between A.D. 600 and now. Yet they are representatives of a tradition Tolkien thought, if not too short, very much too scanty.

The Poetry of the Shire

One can see Tolkien's attempt to extend that tradition in the hobbit-poems scattered through *The Lord of the Rings* — or, to be more accurate, in the new hobbit-poems. Near the start there are a couple of pieces which Tolkien had written up to thirty years before, both rewritten a little for their new context: Frodo's 'Man in the Moon' song in the *Prancing Pony,* Sam's 'Rhyme of the Troll' near Weathertop. Take these away and one is left with a little body of poems from the Shire, mostly in quatrains with alternate lines rhyming, in plain language and metre and with for the most part a gently proverbial quality. They look unambitious. They were all written for *The Lord of the Rings* alone. It is tempting to say that they have no function besides advancing the story or embellishing the characters, no value outside their immediate context. However, one check to this theory should be that, although the poems all do fit their settings in the story very tightly, there is a strong sense even so that the same words can mean different things in different places. As in *Pearl,* a stock phrase or cliché can at any moment be given new point.

Bilbo's 'Old Walking Song', for instance, is repeated three times in different versions. The first or basic text is this, sung by Bilbo as he leaves Bag End for the last time:

> 'The Road goes ever on and on
> Down from the door where it began.
> Now far ahead the Road has gone,
> And I must follow, if I can,
> Pursuing it with eager feet,
> Until it joins some larger way
> Where many paths and errands meet.
> And whither then? I cannot say.' (p. 35)

Many years later, as *The Return of the King* draws to an end, Bilbo gives a markedly different version sitting in Rivendell, having heard Frodo tell the story of the destruction of the Ring and, in his advanced old age, having failed to understand most of it:

> 'The Road goes ever on and on
> Out from the door where it began.
> Now far ahead the Road has gone,
> Let others follow it who can!
> Let them a journey new begin.
> But I at last with weary feet
> Will turn towards the lighted inn,
> My evening rest and sleep to meet.' (p. 965)

And with these words, we are told, 'his head dropped on his chest and he slept soundly'. This seems to be an obvious case of context determining words. The first time he sang the poem Bilbo had just handed over the Ring and was off to Rivendell; the words accordingly express a sense of abdication, of having been left behind, along with determination to accept this and make a new life somewhere as yet unknown. 'I must subordinate my own wishes to the larger world' would be a fair summary, highly appropriate to Bilbo at that time. By contrast the second version — almost a mirror-image of the first — expresses only justified weariness. Bilbo is no longer even interested in the Ring. He thinks the 'lighted inn' is Rivendell, as indeed it is in immediate context. All readers, however, perceive that it could as easily mean death.

In between these two variants Frodo has sung the song (p. 72). His version is identical with Bilbo's first one, except that it makes the significant change, in line 5, of 'weary feet' for 'eager feet'. 'That sounds like a bit of old Bilbo's rhyming', says Pippin. 'Or is it one of your imitations? It does not sound altogether encouraging.' Frodo says he doesn't know. He thinks he was 'making it up', but 'may have heard it long ago'. This uncertainty (over an issue to which the reader knows the answer) points to the great difference between Bilbo's position and Frodo's. Both are leaving Bag End, but the former cheerfully, without the Ring, without responsibility, for Rivendell, the latter with a growing sense of unwished involvement, carrying the Ring and heading in the end for Mordor. Naturally the poem does not mean the same thing for him as for Bilbo. But can the same words carry different meanings?

It depends on how one sees 'the Road'. The most obvious thought is that if the 'lighted inn' means death, then 'the Road' must mean life. It need not be individual life, since in Bilbo's second version others can take it up and follow it in their turn; however, in Frodo's and Bilbo's first version the image of the traveller pursuing the Road looks very like a symbol of the individual pursuing his moment of consciousness down the unknown road which is everyone's future life, to an end which no one can predict. There is a further point to add, made by Frodo but repeating Bilbo:

> 'He used often to say there was only one Road; that it was like a great river: its springs were at every doorstep, and every path was its tributary. "It's a dangerous business, Frodo, going out of your door," he used to say. "You step into the Road, and if you don't keep your feet, there is no knowing where you might be swept off to. Do you realize that this is the very path that goes through Mirkwood, and that if you let it, it might take you to the Lonely Mountain or even further and to worse places?"' (pp. 72–73)

In context this is just a reply to Pippin's remark that the song 'does not sound altogether encouraging'. Frodo does not know he is going to Mordor yet, and Pippin shrugs the whole thing off. However, looking back, and especially looking back after all the interlacements of Volumes Two and Three, one might well think that besides an image of life 'the Road' has crept up to being an image of Providence. After all, Bilbo is right about the road outside Bag End leading all the way to Mordor. On the other hand there are on that road, which Frodo takes, thousands of intersections, as also thousands of choices to be made or rejected. The traveller can always stop or turn aside. Only will-power makes the road seem straight. Accordingly, when Bilbo and Frodo say they will pursue it, eagerly or wearily, till it is intersected by other roads, lives, wishes, *and will then continue into the unknown, if they can,* they are expressing a mixture of doubt and determination — exactly the qualities Gandalf so often recommends. This has become much stronger and clearer with Frodo. Indeed it is not too much to say that the traveller walking down the branching road becomes in the end an image of 'the Good' in Tolkien, and one opposed to the endless self-regarding circuits of the Ring. By the time one comes to that opinion the immediate dramatic contexts of the poem — leaving Bag End, leaving the Shire — have not been dropped, any more than 'the Road' has lost its obvious literal quality, but they have come to seem only particular instances of a much more general truth.

The 'tight fit' of poems to characters and situations is accordingly illusory. There is a sense that the lines mean more than their composers know, may indeed not be their personal compositions at all; they may also be brooded upon, to be repeated with new understanding much later. Thus at the very end of Volume Three Frodo sings again 'the old walking-song, but the words were not quite the same'; he says not 'we may . . . take the hidden paths that run, / Towards the Moon or to the Sun', but 'I shall'.[8] And he does, leaving Middle-earth the next day. The song he is refashioning is another of Bilbo's, though it is 'to a tune that was as old as the hills'. Even in its innocent context near the start of Volume One, when the hobbits are using it only to help themselves along, it has an odd ring. 'Upon the hearth the fire is red,' they sing, 'But not yet weary are our feet'. If one goes by the 'inn and weariness' symbolism of Bilbo's Rivendell song, that means they still have a zest for life. Still, what the song celebrates are 'hidden paths', 'sudden tree[s]', 'A new road on a secret gate' — things which seem to be or to lead out of this world. The refrain of each stanza addresses the familiar sights of the landscape, the little homely trees of English hedgerows, but bids farewell to them:

> 'Apple, thorn, and nut and sloe,
> Let them go! Let them go!
> Sand and stone and pool and dell,
> Fare you well! Fare you well!' (p. 76)

Are the hobbits, even in their good humour, 'half in love with easeful death'? A better answer perhaps is that in some inherited way they carry the 'tune' of an ancient grief, lulled by earthly beauty but capable of being woken in Frodo in the end, as in Legolas by the cry of the gulls.

The elvish song which follows immediately on the 'Walking Song' indeed says just that, though probably few readers make the connection straight away. All it contains, apart from its invocations to 'Elbereth', are the two opposed images of the stars, seen as the flowers of the 'Queen beyond the Western Seas', and the wood in which the elves 'wander'. Of course the elves *are* in a wood at that moment, and they are looking at the early evening stars, but that is not what they mean. Their song is of regret and exile, its core the oxymoron of 'this far land' — 'this' land is the real land, Middle-earth, 'far land' ought to be the one Elbereth is in beyond the Seas. But the elves refuse to accept the fact, seeing themselves as strangers whose highest function is memory:

> 'We still remember, we who dwell
> In this far land beneath the trees,
> Thy starlight on the Western Seas.'

As for the wood, its beauty is a net and a barrier; starlight and memory alone pierce through 'to us that wander here / Amid the world of woven trees'.

The myth behind the song remains obscure in *The Lord of the Rings,* just as the Sindarin song of Rivendell remains untranslated, merging only with the Quenya one just quoted in the story's last few pages (p. 1005). However, the image of the Wood of Life breaks through to hobbit consciousness with increasing clarity. Frodo uses it in the Old Forest:

> 'O! Wanderers in the shadowed land
> despair not! For though dark they stand,
> all woods there be must end at last,
> and see the open sun go past:
> the setting sun, the rising sun,
> the day's end, or the day begun.
> For east or west all woods must fail . . .' (p. 110)

As usual we take the immediate point — Frodo and the others want to get out of the forest — while reading through to a kind of universality: the 'shadowed land' is life, life's delusions of despair are the 'woods', despair will end in some vision of cosmic order which can only be hinted at in stars or 'sun'. What does Frodo mean by the repeated contrasts of setting/rising, west/east, day's end/day begun? They can hardly avoid suggesting death and life; in that case his song says there can be no defeat — even if the wanderers die in the dark wood, the real Old Forest, they will in death break through to sunlight and out of a hampering shade. 'East or west all woods must fail' is then a statement of exactly the same class as 'The Road goes ever on and on': literally true, literally unhelpful or even banal, but in its literal truth making a symbolic promise. Sam Gamgee hits on the same thought when he takes up the 'Blondin' role of faithful minstrel in Minas Morgul, and sings 'words of his own' fitted to another old Shire tune:

> 'Though here at journey's end I lie
> in darkness buried deep,
> beyond all towers strong and high
> beyond all mountains steep,
> above all shadows rides the Sun
> and Stars for ever dwell:
> I will not say the Day is done,
> nor bid the Stars farewell.' (p. 888)

'Day is done' is of course another Shakespearean echo, like the Dark Tower: 'The bright day is done', says Iras to Cleopatra, 'and we are for the dark'. But Tolkien would no doubt instantly have felt that Shakespeare had no copyright on the phrase, which must be of immemorial antiquity in English, 'as old as the hills'. Sam's song is simple and obvious, coming from 'the voice of a forlorn and weary hobbit that no listening orc could possibly have mistaken for the clear song of an Elven-lord'. Still, it has the characteristic qualities of the Shire's 'high style': plain language, proverbial sentiment, a closeness to immediate context reaching out simultaneously to myth, a brave suggestiveness at once hopeful and sad.

As has been said, the Shire is a calque on England. Where then is the source in English poetry for the poetry of the Shire? One might point to Spenser, whose *Faerie Queene* (regarded by Tolkien with disapproving interest) often uses the image of the wandering knight lost in trackless woods, and whose Mer-lin-vision of Britain reviving underlies Bilbo's 'Riddle of Strider'.[9] An even closer parallel is John Milton's masque of *Comus,* which Tolkien must have admired partly for its theme — it is an analogue of 'Childe Rowland', a tale of a maiden lost in a dark wood and imprisoned by a wizard, till her brothers and her guardian angel come to the rescue — but even more for its hovering between fact and symbol. A herb will protect them, says the disguised angel to the brothers; a shepherd gave it to him:

> 'The leaf was darkish, and had prickles on it,
> But in another country, as he said,
> Bore a bright golden flower, but not in this soil;
> Unknown, and like esteemed, and the dull swain
> Treads on it daily with his clouted shoon . . .

Ugly, prickly, much-trampled, flowering only in 'another country': it sounds like Virtue. Maybe the shepherd lad was the Good Shepherd himself. As for the wood, the Younger Brother wishes he could hear something from outside it, bleat or whistle or cockcrow:

> ''Twould be some solace yet, some little cheering
> in this close dungeon of innumerous boughs.'

His Elder Brother would prefer a glimmer from moon or lamp or candle, to 'visit us / With thy long levelled rule of streaming light'. Again the wood sounds like life, the 'levelled rule' from the world outside like Conscience. But as Tolkien said of *Beo-wulf,* the 'large symbolism . . . does not break through, nor be-come allegory'. The plain, even rustic language appeals to everyday experience. Everyone has been lost and found again, everyone is lost, will be found again. The maiden who is the soul will be taken in the end from 'the perplexed paths of this drear wood . . . the blind mazes of this tangled wood . . . this close dungeon of innumerous boughs', or as the elves would say *galadhremmin ennorath,* 'the world of woven trees'.

The Elvish Tradition

Shakespeare, Spenser, Milton: the list could be spun out, to include for instance Yeats, whose poem 'The Man Who Dreamed of Faeryland' could stand as a Tolkienian epigraph. However, the point should be clear. Tolkien was not by any means cut off from the mainstream of English poetry, though the qualities he valued were not surprise, the *mot juste,* verbal complexity, but rather a slow probing of the familiar. That was not, however, the end of his ambition or of his thoughts on style: there is an elvish streak too in the poetry of *The Lord of the Rings,* signalled in complete contrast by barely-precedented intricacies of line and stanza.

The best example of this is the 'Song of Eärendil' composed and sung in Rivendell by Bilbo (pp. 227–30). What the song means and what story lies behind it are typically not explained in *The Lord of the Rings,* but remain in suggestiveness till *The Silmarillion.* That suggestiveness, though, is much aided by devices not of sense but of sound. Bilbo uses some five of these: one is rhyme, which everyone recognises, but the others are less familiar — internal half-rhyme, alliteration (i.e. beginning words with the same sound or letter), alliterative assonance (the *Macbeth* device), and a frequent if irregular variation of syntax. All appear in the first eight lines:

> 'Eärendil was a mariner
> that tarried in Arvernien;
> he built a boat of timber felled
> In Nimbrethil to journey in;
> her sails he wove of silver fair,
> of silver were her lanterns made,

her prow was fashioned like a swan,
and light upon her banners laid.'

The rhymes are obvious, on lines 2 and 4, 6 and 8 — '-nien/-ney in', 'made/laid'. The internal rhymes, however, operate not between even lines but between odd and even, 1 and 2, 3 and 4, and so on. They are furthermore not on the ends of words but in the middle: '*mariner* / *tarried in*', '*timber felled* / *Nimbrethil*', '*silver fair* / *silver were*', '*like a swan* / *light upon*'. Nor are they always complete. One might note that the full rhymes are similarly not always exact, some of them being 'masculine', i.e. on one syllable only, but some 'feminine', on more than one syllable, and tending towards similarity rather than identity, as in 'Arvernien / journey in', 'armoured him / harm from him', 'helmet tall / emerald', etc. These are too common to be the result of incapacity, and they are furthermore reinforced by the unpredictable but frequent use of the other devices of sound: alliteration in 'light laid', 'shining shield', 'ward all wounds', etc., alliterative assonance in 'sails of silver', 'Night of Naught', 'sight . . . he sought' and 'boat it bore with biting breath'. Typically, in between there are such doubtful cases as 'built a boat' — just alliteration, or assonance as well? — while over the whole poem there lies a web of grammatical repetitions and variations, also never quite exact — ' her *sails* (he wove) of *silver* fair, / of *silver* (were) her lanterns (made), or later 'his sword (of steel) was *valiant*, / (of *adamant*) his helmet tall'.

Describing the technique is difficult, but its result is obvious: rich and continuous uncertainty, a pattern forever being glimpsed but never quite grasped. In this way sound very clearly echoes or perhaps rather gives the lead to sense. Just as the rhymes, assonances and phrasal structures hover at the edge of identification, so the poem as a whole offers romantic glimpses of 'old unhappy far-off things' (to cite Wordsworth), or 'magic casements opening on the foam / Of perilous seas, in *faery lands forlorn*' (to remember Keats). Frodo indeed finds himself listening in highly Keatsian style:

Almost it seemed that the words took shape, and visions of far lands and bright things that he had never yet imagined opened out before him; and the firelit hall became like a golden mist above seas of foam that sighed upon the margins of the world. Then the enchantment became more and more dreamlike, until he felt that an endless river of gold and silver was flowing over him, too multitudinous for its pattern to be comprehended . . . (p. 227)

Romanticism, multitudinousness, imperfect comprehension: these are the poem's goals, achieved stylistically much more than semantically.

Yet the 'Song of Eärendil' does of course tell a story as well: how Eärendil tried to sail out of this world to a kind of Paradise, how he succeeded in the end by virtue of the 'Silmaril', how this in turn led to his becoming a star, or rather the helmsman of a celestial boat in which the burning Silmaril appears to Middle-earth as a star. Still, more questions are raised than answered. Why did Eärendil go, why was he kept, what is a Silmaril? More acutely, what is the relationship in the story between success and failure? Eärendil's star appears to be a victory-emblem, 'the Flammifer of Westernesse', and yet is associated with loss and homelessness, with the weeping of women on the 'Hither Shore'. The 'paths that seldom mortal goes' may recall fleetingly the 'hidden paths' of the hobbits' walking-song, and its similar oscillation between adventure and homesickness; in this sense the two stylistically quite different poems relate to each other like elvish assonances, hinting at a pattern but stressing change as much as identity. The overall effect of the song in Rivendell is perhaps to show Bilbo approaching a body of lore and of poetry higher than the normal hobbitic vein, higher indeed than mortals can normally comprehend. Aragorn sings his song of Beren and Lúthien some fifty pages earlier with a certain reluctance, explaining that it is 'in the mode that is called *ann-thennath* among the Elves, but is hard to render in our Common Speech, and this is but a rough echo of it'. 'Echo' is a useful word, for that in a way is what the poem's metric is based on; there is no immediate similarity of stanza-form to Bilbo's song, but once again the 'elvish' idea of poetry comes through in an unexpected subtlety.

Briefly, one can say that each stanza is in eight lines, rhyming abac/babc; and that the fourth and eighth lines at once in-

terrupt the flow of each stanza and hold the two halves together
by their strong 'feminine' three-syllable rhymes, on 'glimmer-
ing/shimmering', 'sorrowing/following', etc. More significant
is the fact that the actual rhyming *words* in each first half are repeated once or more in each second half, as for instance 'seen'
in the first stanza, 'leaves' in the second, 'feet' and 'roam' in the
third, and so on. The device is somehow congruous with the
repeated images of hair like a shadow, beauty flying, leaves and
years falling, through it all the hemlock-leaves of death. But
the last stanza of nine breaks the pattern. Its rhyme words are
all different: 'bare/grey/door/morrowless/lay/more/away/sorrow-
less'. What does this fact mean? All one can say is that the story
being told (or hinted at) is also one of gloom, death and parting, like that between Eärendil and Elwing, the mariner and the
weeping women of Middle-earth. The last words of the song,
'singing sorrowless', stand out against this current, but still
wherever the lovers go it is 'away', 'in the forest', maybe the
forest of mortality and final death. Aragorn indeed confirms
this thought with his gloss that not only has Lúthien died (as
many elves do), but 'died indeed and left the world'. Further
explanation has to wait till *The Silmarillion,* but in a sense is
not needed. A point has been made by a sudden (if barely per-
ceptible) breaking of pattern, an absence of echoes. Perhaps
that is the essence of *ann thennath.*[10]

Further stylistic and thematic variations could easily be
listed. Gimli's 'Song of Durin' on pp. 308–9 is dwarvishly
plain and active, but still carries on the sense of decay in Middle-earth opposed to ultimate hope; Legolas's 'Song of Nimrodel' a little later makes similar oppositions but ends on an opposite note, of faltering and ultimate defeat on the 'Hither
Shore'. Frodo's elegy for Gandalf ends on the word 'died'; but
Sam's coda prefers 'flowers', and turns out to be truer in the
end. Galadriel's song in the Common Speech ends with regret
and a question, 'What ship would ever bear me back across so
wide a Sea?', but her Quenya one on hope and an assertion,
'Maybe thou shalt find Valinor. Maybe even thou shalt find
it.'[11] As with the hobbit-songs, behind all these there lies some
story of a Sentence and a Great Escape, but an escape forever
hindered by loving involvement with Middle-earth itself; that
is the root of the disagreement between Fangorn, Celeborn

and Galadriel when the Ent half-voices his lament for the stocks and the stones. However, the surprise in this 'elvish tradition' of mythic poetry is how much of its stories is conveyed by purely formal devices, by verbal patterns with meaning as apparently inherent in them as elsewhere in place-names, in untranslated fragments, or in Bombadil. Tolkien's idea of poetry mirrored his ideas on language; in neither did he think sound should be divorced from sense.

In reality this 'elvish tradition' was an English tradition too. The ultimate source for much that has been discussed must certainly be *Pearl*, with its story of the (failed) escape from mortality, its heavily traditional phrasing, and its fantastically complex metrical scheme, of twelve-line cross-rhymed stanzas with alliteration, assonance, syntax-variation and (even Tolkien did not attempt this) stanza-linking and refrains.[12] However, the *Pearl* tradition did not last till Shakespeare and Milton and the Romantics, who are accordingly and to that extent impoverished. Tolkien obviously hoped in one way to recreate it. More generally, the link between the last three sections of this book is Tolkien's perception, from *Pearl* and from poems like it, that poetry does not reduce to plain sense (so far most critics would agree with him), but furthermore that this is because words have over the centuries acquired meanings not easily traced in dictionaries, available, however, to many native speakers and (this is where many critics part company) at times breaking through the immediate intentions of even poetic users. 'Loose fit', in a word, works better in poetry than 'tight fit'; there are roads to wisdom besides the painstaking perverse originality of twentieth-century writers.

Middle-earth and Limbo: Mythic Analogues

What has been said about Tolkien's poetry has an immediate bearing on that most attractive but least tractable subject, 'Tolkien's mythology'. In a sense the problems and intentions were the same. Tolkien wanted his poems to make good sense in their dramatic context, as part of the story of *The Lord of the Rings;* he also wanted them to suggest a truth independent of their context. 'East or west all woods must fail' therefore applies *both* to the Old Forest *and* to the symbolic woods of Life and Error. In the same way his legends of Eärendil and Lúthien, his central fable of Frodo and the Ring, must firstly and continually work as fiction, but also reach out towards non-fictional truths about humanity — and perhaps about salvation. Yet in this latter ambition there lies a danger. If *The Lord of the Rings* should approach too close to 'Gospel-truth', to the Christian myth in which Tolkien himself believed, it might forfeit its status as a story and become at worst a blasphemy, an 'Apocryphal gospel', at best a dull allegory rehearsing in admittedly novel form what everyone ought to know already. In that case *The Lord of the Rings* would look like one of Bilbo's poems removed from context and put without explanation in *The Oxford Book of English Verse* — fictionless and unhappy. Tolkien had to take a rather strict line over 'myth'.

One reason, no doubt, was that he had little tolerance for real pagan myths or for naive mythicizers. In his *YWES* chapter for 1924 (p. 58), he remarked that 'it will be a grievous shock to many an innocent sentimentalist, accustomed to see the one-eyed and red-bearded deities everywhere, to learn that Þórr and Óðin cannot be found in any Scandinavian place-name in England'.† Tolkien did not believe in 'old religions' or 'witch-cults'; C. S. Lewis wrote a paper called 'The Anthropological Approach' which damned the learned variety of that error beyond redemption. Probably a major cause for their intolerance was that both, but especially Tolkien, had some idea of what genuine old paganism was like. The earliest account of the English (Tacitus's *Germania*, A.D. 97–98) remarks on their habit of drowning sacrificial victims in bogs. Many such have been recovered from the preserving peat of Denmark and of 'the Angle'. It would be surprising if Tolkien had not looked at the calm face of Tollund Man, or the hideously frightened one of 'Queen Gunhild' (all too obviously still struggling as she

---

† Here, as a matter of fact, Tolkien was wrong. 'Roseberry Topping' in North Yorkshire preserves beneath pastoral euphemism the Viking name *Othines-beorg*, 'Odin's mountain'. But Tolkien could have replied that this name had been so sharply changed as to suggest a deliberate de-mythicizing policy in the Middle Ages, which would support his general point.

was pinned down alive), and reflected that *these* were the true lineaments of his pagan ancestors.[13] 'There, but for the grace of God, go I.' No statement could be more apposite. Tolkien had grounds to suspect simple views of 'the noble pagan'.

Virtuous pagans, however, were quite another matter. Indeed, it is not too much to say that the Inklings were preoccupied with them. C. S. Lewis offered the most daring statement in the final volume of the 'Narnia' series, *The Last Battle* (1956), in which we come across a young (dead) virtuous pagan, Emeth, who explains that all his life he has served Tash and scorned Aslan the Lion — earlier on it has been made clear that Tash is a bloody demon, Aslan, one might as well say, the Narnian Christ. But once he is dead Emeth meets Aslan and falls at his feet in instinctive adoration, as in terror, 'for the Lion . . . will know that I have served Tash all my days and not him'. But Emeth is saved, for good deeds done for Tash belong to Aslan, and bad deeds for Aslan to Tash; as if to say that God and Allah are different, but yet that virtuous Mohammedans will be saved rather than murderous Christians. Later on each of the souls pouring out of Narnia on Doomsday looks at Aslan as it comes through the Doorway of Death — to be saved if it loves, destroyed if it hates. Lewis here repeats the belief of the fourteenth-century friar Uhtred of Boldon, that each dying person has a 'clear vision' or *clara visio* of God, on his reaction to which depends his ultimate fate.[14] Uhtred's opinion was denounced as heretical at Oxford in 1367 — it tends to suggest no man needs the Christian Church to be saved. But Lewis, a Protestant, might have agreed with that.

Tolkien, a determined Catholic, would not. Still, he was doubtless interested. Uhtred after all was an Englishman, only one of a list of would-be savers of righteous pagans from the British Isles. Pelagius, the great opponent of St Augustine, was a Welshman, his real name probably 'Morgan'. The story of the salvation of Trajan, the virtuous pagan emperor, was first told by an Anglo-Saxon from Whitby about the year 710. The poem *St Erkenwald* is a variant of that tale; some people have argued it is by the author of *Sir Gawain* and *Pearl*. Above all, to Tolkien's mind, there must have been present the problem of *Beowulf*. This is certainly the work of a Christian writing after the conversion of England. However, the author got through 3182 lines without mentioning Christ, or salvation, and yet without saying specifically that his heroes, including the kind and honest figure of Beowulf himself, were damned — though he must have known that historically and in reality they were all pagans, ignorant even of the name of Christ. Could the Christian author have thought his pagan heroes were saved? He had the opinion of the Church against him if he did. Could he on the other hand have borne to consign them all to Hell for ever, like Alcuin, the deacon of York, in a now notorious letter to the abbot of Lindisfarne, written about A.D. 797: 'What has Ingeld to do with Christ?' he asked scornfully — Ingeld being a minor character in *Beowulf*. 'The King of Heaven wishes to have no fellowship with lost and pagan so-called Kings; for the eternal King reigns in Heaven, the lost pagan laments in Hell'.[15] The *Beowulf*-poet's dilemma was also Tolkien's. His whole professional life brought him into contact with the stories of pagan heroes, Englishmen or Norsemen or Goths; more than anyone he could appreciate their sterling qualities. At the same time he had no doubt that paganism itself was weak and cruel. Uhtred's and Lewis's individualistic beliefs did not appeal to him, any more than Alcuin's smugly intolerant one. If there was anyone in the twentieth century to resolve the dilemma, repeat the *Beowulf*-poet's masterpiece of compromise, and preserve 'the permanent value of that *pietas* which treasures the memory of man's struggles in the dark past, man fallen and not yet saved, disgraced but not dethroned' ('Monsters', p. 266), Tolkien must have thought it should be himself. Such activity was for one thing 'part of the English temper'. *The Lord of the Rings* is quite clearly, then, a story of virtuous pagans in the darkest of dark pasts, before all but the faintest premonitions of dawn and revelation.

Yet there is at least one moment at which Revelation seems very close and allegory does all but break through — naturally enough, a moment of 'eucatastrophe', to use Tolkien's term for sudden moments of fairy-tale salvation. This appears to different characters in different ways. As has been said, Sam and Frodo experience it as thinking for a moment they have died and gone to Heaven, when they wake up on the field of Cormallen. Faramir, however, in the next chapter feels it more physically. He and Éowyn sense the earthquake that is the fall of Barad-dûr, and for a moment Faramir thinks of Númenor drowning. But then like the father in *Pearl* he is overcome by an irrational joy, to be explained by the eagle-messenger in a song:

> 'Sing now, ye people of the Tower of Anor,
> for the Realm of Sauron is ended for ever,
>   and the Dark Tower is thrown down.
>
> Sing and rejoice, ye people of the Tower of Guard,
> for your watch hath not been in vain,
> and the Black Gate is broken,
> and your King hath passed through,
>   and he is victorious.
>
> Sing and be glad, all ye children of the West,
> for your King shall come again,
> and he shall dwell among you
>   all the days of your life.' (p. 942)

There is no doubt here about Tolkien's stylistic model, which is the Bible and particularly the Psalms. The use of 'ye' and 'hath' is enough to indicate that to most English readers, familiar with those words only from the Authorised Version. But 'Sing and rejoice' echoes Psalm 33, 'Rejoice in the Lord', while the whole of the poem is strongly reminiscent of Psalm 24, 'Lift up your heads, O ye gates, and be ye lift up, ye everlasting doors, for the King of glory shall come in.' 'Who is the King of glory?' asks the Psalm, and one traditional answer is Christ, crucified but not yet ascended, come to the city of Hell to rescue from it those especially virtuous pre-Christians, Moses and Isaiah and the patriarchs and prophets. Of course the eagle's song is *not about that*. When it says 'the Black Gate is broken' it means the Morannon, a place in Middle-earth described on pp. 622–23; when it says 'your King shall come again', it means Aragorn. Yet the first statement could very *easily* apply to Death and Hell (Matthew 16:18, 'and the gates of hell shall not prevail'), the second to Christ and the Second Coming. This is a layer of double meaning beyond that even of 'East or west all woods must fail' or 'The Road goes ever on and on'.

Approach to the edge of Christian reference was here deliberate, as one can tell from the date Gandalf so carefully gives for the fall of Sauron (p. 931), 'the twenty-fifth of March'. In

Anglo-Saxon belief, and in European popular tradition both before and after that, 25 March is the date of the Crucifixion; also of the Annunciation (nine months before Christmas); also of the last day of Creation.[16] By mentioning the date Tolkien was presenting his 'eucatastrophe' as a forerunner or 'type' of the greater one of Christian myth. It is possible to doubt whether this was a good idea. Almost no one notices the significance of 25 March, or of the Company setting out from Rivendell on 25 December; the high style of the eagle's song has not had much appeal; though Tolkien himself wept over the grandeur of the Field of Cormallen *(Letters,* p. 321), many other readers have found the delight, tears and laughter (of Sam especially) unconvincing. Tolkien did right normally to avoid such allusions, to keep like the author of *Beowulf* to a middle path between Ingeld and Christ, between the Bible and pagan myth. The care with which he maintained this position (highly artificial, though usually passed over without mention) is evident, with hindsight, on practically every page of *The Lord of the Rings.*

Consider for instance the Riders. As has been said, they resemble the ancient English down to minute detail — with the admitted partial exception of their devotion to horses. However, the real ancient English had some belief in divine beings, the **ósas* or 'godu' analogous to the Norse *æsir,* Gothic **unsós,* whose names survive in our days of the week (Tíw's day, Wóden's day, Thunor's day, Frige day). To this the Riders have no counterpart, or almost none. Their place-names sometimes suggest ancient belief *in something or other:* thus 'Dunharrow' in Common Speech presumably represents Rohirric *dún-harg,* 'the dark sanctuary', just as 'Halifirien' on the borders of Gondor must be *hálig-fyrgen,* 'the holy mountain'. In 'Drúadan Forest' the second element is Gondorian *-adan,* 'man', the first probably *drú-,* 'magic'. In the same way the Anglo-Saxons borrowed the Celtic element of 'Druid' to create the term *dry-cræft,* 'magic art'. The Riders, one may say, have a sense of awe or of the supernatural; but they do nothing about it. No religious rites are performed at Théoden's burial. His followers sing a dirge and ride round his barrow, as indeed do Beowulf's. The only real-life burial where this combination of song and cavalcade is reported is that of Attila the Hun, in

Jordanes's *Gothic History*. But there the mourners also gash their faces so their king will be lamented properly in human blood, and when he is in his tomb they sacrifice (i.e. murder) the slaves who dug it. That kind of thing seems very out of place in Middle-earth. The Riders, like most of the characters of *Beowulf* but unlike all we can guess of the real pre-Christian English, do not worship pagan gods; they also do not hold slaves, commit incest, practise polygamy.[17] Their society has in a word been bowdlerised. They are so virtuous that one can hardly call them pagans at all.

Certainly Tolkien never does. As has been noted before, he followed the *Beowulf*-poet in being very loath to use the word 'heathen', reserving it twice for Denethor and by implication the Black Númenoreans.[18] Nevertheless, his characters are heathens, strictly speaking, and Tolkien, having pondered for so long on the *Beowulf*-poet's careful balances, was as aware of this fact as he was of the opposing images of open Christianity poised at many moments to take over his story. The pagan counterpart of the eagle's song may be the death of Aragorn, relegated as it is to an Appendix. Aragorn is a remarkably virtuous character, without even the faults of Théoden, and he foreknows his death like a saint. Nevertheless he is not a Christian and nor is Arwen. He has to say then to her, 'I speak no comfort to you, for there is no comfort for such pain within the circles of the world' (p. 1037). When she still laments her fate he can only add, 'We are not bound for ever to the circles of the world, and beyond them is more than memory. Farewell!' Arwen is not comforted. She dies under the 'fading trees' of a Lórien gone 'silent', and the end of her tale is oblivion, 'and elanor and niphredil bloom no more east of the Sea'. Aragorn, then, has some hope of the future and of something *outside* 'the circles of the world' that may come to heal their sorrow, but he does not know what it is. This is a deathbed strikingly devoid of the sacraments, of Extreme Unction, of 'the consolations of religion'. It is impossible to think of Aragorn as irretrievably damned for his ignorance of Christianity (though it is a view some have tried to foist on *Beowulf*). Still, he has not fulfilled the requirements for salvation either. Perhaps the best one can say is that when such heroes die they go, in Tolkien's opinion, neither to Hell nor Heaven, but to

Limbo: 'to my fathers', as Théoden says, 'to sit beside my fathers, until the world is renewed', to quote Thorin Oakenshield from *The Hobbit,* perhaps at worst to wait with the barrow-wight 'where gates stand for ever shut, till the world is mended'. The whole of Middle-earth, in a sense, is Limbo: there the innocent unbaptised wait for Doomsday (when, we may hope, they will join their saved and baptised descendants).

Tolkien took different views of his own work's religious content at different times. In 1953 he wrote to a Jesuit friend:

> *The Lord of the Rings* is of course a fundamentally religious and Catholic work; unconsciously so at first, but consciously in the revision. That is why I have not put in, or have cut out, practically all references to anything like 'religion', to cults or practices, in the imaginary world. For the religious element is absorbed into the story and the symbolism. (*Letters,* p. 172)

Tolkien perhaps found difficulty in explaining to a Jesuit why a 'fundamentally' Catholic work should *cut out* references to religion, but the reason is clear: he thought, or hoped, that God had a plan for pre-Catholics too. Later in life Tolkien may have become more uncertain about his own originality, and wrote that the elvish song of Rivendell was a 'hymn', that 'these [invocations of Elbereth] and other references to religion in *The Lord of the Rings* are frequently overlooked' (*Road,* p. 65). On the whole the earlier statement that references have been cut out seems truer than the later one that they are in but 'overlooked'. The elvish song is only analogous to a hymn as Gandalf is analogous to an angel; Elbereth too is unlike (say) the Holy Ghost in remaining visible, to elves, and rememberable as a being by those elves like Galadriel who have been across the Sea and met her. Tolkien did best when he kept mythic invention on the borderline between literal story and a wider suggestiveness (Fangorn, Bombadil, Lúthien, Roads and Rings); too conscious an approach to 'mythopoeia' would have ended only in allegory. To repeat a philological point made already in this study, the Old English translation of Greek *euangelion* was *gód spell,* modern 'Gospel', the 'good news' of salvation. Besides 'news', however, *spell* meant 'spell' and also 'story'. The foundation of Gospel lies then in 'good story', though 'good story' ought to generate a spell (or glamour) of its own.

Fróda and Frodo: A Myth Reconstructed

If one thinks that a 'myth' is an 'old story containing within itself vestiges of some earlier state of religious belief' — like the Grail-legend with its hints of sacrificed kings and vegetation-rituals — then *The Lord of the Rings* definitely is not one. Tolkien was alert to all such echoes and did his best to eradicate them. If one thinks that a 'myth' should be a 'story repeating in veiled form the truth of Christ Crucified', then *The Lord of the Rings* does not qualify either. There is an evil Power in both stories, and a glorious Tree, but Frodo, to make only three of the most obvious points, is not sacrificed, is not the Son of God, and buys for his people only a limited, worldly and temporary happiness. Nevertheless there is at least one sense in which *The Lord of the Rings* can claim 'mythic' status, which is as 'a story embodying the deepest feelings of a particular society at a particular time'. If one can speak of *Robinson Crusoe* as a 'myth of capitalism' and of *Frankenstein* or *Dr Faustus* as 'myths of scientific man', then *The Lord of the Rings* could be claimed as a 'myth against discouragement', a 'myth of the Deconversion'. In 1936 Tolkien had warned the British Academy that the Ragnarök spirit had survived Thórr and Óthinn, could revive 'even in our own times . . . martial heroism as its own end'. He was quite literally correct in this, as he was also in his further prophecy that it would not succeed, since 'the wages of heroism is death'. Still, he wanted to keep something of that spirit, if only its dauntlessness in what looked like a hopeless future; for similarly contemporary reasons he wanted to offer his readers a model of elementary virtue existing without the support of religion. Perhaps most of all he wanted to answer Alcuin's scornful question, relevant again after 1150 years: 'What *has* Ingeld to do with Christ?'

To his intentions here Tolkien left two very strong clues. One is the name of the 'hero' of *The Lord of the Rings,* Frodo. The other is the note in Appendix F, which says that some hobbit-names have been retained by Tolkien without translation, 'though I have usually anglicized them by altering their endings, since in Hobbit-names *a* was a masculine ending, and *o* and *e* were feminine' (p. 1109). 'Frodo', in other words, is an English form of original 'Froda'. But what kind of a name is that? Most readers probably take it as explained by Tolkien's preceding remark, 'To their man-children [hobbits] usually gave names that had no meaning at all in their daily language . . . Of this kind are Bilbo, Bungo, Polo, Lotho . . . and so on. There are many inevitable but accidental resemblances to names that we now have or know . . .' If 'Frodo' strikes any chords, then, it could be accident. On the other hand 'Frodo', surprisingly, is never mentioned in the name-discussion of that Appendix. Maybe his name is not a Bilbo-type, but a Meriadoc-Peregrin-Fredegar-type. As Tolkien goes on to say:

> In some old families . . . it was, however, the custom to give high-sounding first-names. Since most of these seem to have been drawn from legends of the past, of Men as well as of Hobbits, and many while now meaningless to Hobbits closely resembled the names of Men in the Vale of Anduin, or in Dale, or in the Mark, I have turned them into those old names, largely of Frankish and Gothic origin, that are still used by us or are met in our histories.

'Frodo' could be one of these, like 'Peregrin'. It could still and at the same time be an anglicisation of 'Froda', a name 'meaningless' to hobbits by the time of the War of the Ring, and accepted by them as just another chance disyllable like 'Bilba, Bunga, Pola', but actually preserving in oblivion the name of an ancient hero from the Dale or the Mark. That would make Frodo's name something of a freak in hobbit-nomenclature. However, this seems only appropriate for the central figure, especially since his name is so strikingly left uncategorised.

'Froda' actually *is* a name from the dimmest reaches of Northern legend. It is mentioned once in *Beowulf* (not in the main story), when the hero, discussing politics, says that the king of the Danes means to marry his daughter *glædum suna Fródan,* 'to the fortunate son of Fróda'. By this means he hopes to heal the feud between the Danes and the 'Bards' over whom Fróda once ruled. His idea won't work, says Beowulf, for the pressure on heroes to take blood-revenge is too strong — it seems, though this is speculation from other sources, that Ingeld's father Fróda was killed by the Danish king who now wants to make alliance with his son. The likelihood is that in this as in other matters Beowulf is meant to appear a good prophet, since the unsuccessful, possibly treacherous but in heroic terms entirely praiseworthy attack which Ingeld made on his father-in-law is repeatedly mentioned in Northern story. Probably it was the subject of the Northumbrian songs which so scandalised Alcuin. When he asked, then, 'What has Ingeld to do with Christ?', he was using Ingeld as an example of the most extreme gap between good 'heroic' behaviour and good Christian behaviour; Ingeld took unforgivingness as far as it could go. There is no need, however, to think the son was exactly like the father.

Nothing else is ever heard of Fróda in Old English, but the Norse form of the word — it means literally 'the wise one' — is Fróthi, and round this there are several stories. The most persistent is that Fróthi was a contemporary of Christ, alleged by both Saxo Grammaticus (c. A.D. 1200) and Snorri Sturluson (c. 1230). During his reign there were no murders, no wars, no robberies, and gold rings lay untouched in the open, so that everyone referred to his age as the *Frótha-frith,* the 'peace of Fróthi'. But it came to an end because of greed, or maybe over-altruism. The peace really came from Fróthi's magic mill, turned eternally by two giantesses to grind out gold and peace and prosperity. Fróthi (perhaps fearing for his subjects' security) would never let them rest — and so one day they ground out an army to kill Fróthi and take his gold. The viking army also would not let the giantesses rest, but sailed away with them and set them to grinding salt; they ground so much that the boat sank and the mill with it, though still (adds folk-tradition) in the Maelstrom the giantesses grind their magic quern. And that is why the sea is salt.

This is a story, one can see, about the incurability of evil. Has it anything to do with *Beowulf*? There is no overt connection, but Tolkien was used to 'reconstructing' stories. The point that seems to have struck him is the total *opposition* between son and father, Ingeld/Ingjaldr and Fróda/Fróthi. The one is an example of the Ragnarök-spirit undiluted, of heroic conventionality at its worst; in the *Beowulf* lecture Tolkien called Ingeld 'thrice faithless and easily persuaded'. The other has about him a ring of nostalgic failure; in his time everything was good, but it ended in failure both personally (for Fróthi was killed) and ideologically (for Fróda's son returned to the bad old ways of revenge and hatred, scorning peace-initiatives and even apparently his own desires). Of course the *Fróthafrith* could have been just an accident, a result of the Incarnation which not even virtuous pagans knew about. For all these reasons the composite figure of Fróda/Fróthi became to Tolkien an image of the sad truth behind heroic illusions, a kind of ember glowing in the dark sorrow of heathen ages. In 'The Homecoming of Beorhtnoth', Tídwald says reprovingly to Torhthelm, who has just discovered his master's headless body:

> 'Aye, that's battle for you,
> and no worse today   than wars you sing of,
> when Fróda fell,   and Finn was slain.
> The world wept then,   as it weeps today:
> you can hear the tears   through the harp's twanging.'
>
> (*Reader*, pp. 11–12)

There is something grimly appropriate, further, in the fact that 'Ingjaldr' remained a common Norse name for centuries. 'Fróthi', however, was quickly forgotten.

All this sounds very much like Tolkien's 'Frodo'. He is a peacemaker, indeed in the end a pacifist. One can trace his progress from p. 316, when he stabs the Moria troll, to p. 600, when he threatens to but does not stab Gollum. On pp. 670–73 he saves Gollum's life from the archers, against Sam's strong inclination to keep quiet and let him die. He gives Sting away on p. 905, keeping an orc-blade but saying, 'I do not think it will be my part to strike any blow again.' He throws even that away ten pages later, saying, 'I'll bear no weapon, fair or foul'. In 'The Scouring of the Shire' his role is to forbid killing (pp. 983 and 986–87), and later, after a battle in which he has not 'drawn sword', to protect prisoners. He will not kill Saruman even after his mithril-coat has turned a treacherous stab. His self-control has been learnt, of course, while carrying the Ring; but there is a touch of witheredness about it. '"All the same," said Frodo to all those who stood near, "I wish for no killing . . ."' 'Those who stood near'? One might have hoped Frodo would get up on a block and speak to everybody, impose his will. But Wit is the opposite of Will, and as a figure of increasing wisdom, Frodo ('the wise one') seems to lose all desire, even for good. Merry puts forward his plans for dealing with the ruffians by force. '"Very good," said Frodo. "You make the arrangements."'

This sense of age perhaps motivates the general unconcern for Frodo shown by the Shire, his unfair though unintended supplanting by the large and 'lordly' hobbits Merry and Pippin, the rudeness or much-qualified respect shown to him by Sharkey's men and Gaffer Gamgee too. Saruman knows better, and so do some others, but 'Sam was pained to notice how little honour [Frodo] had in his own country'. It is prophets who proverbially have no honour in their own country, and Frodo is increasingly a prophet or a seer. However, even in other countries the honour he gets is the wrong sort. One may remember Ioreth repeating to her cousin in Gondor that Frodo 'went with only his esquire into the Black Country and fought with the Dark Lord all by himself, and set fire to his Tower, if you can believe it. At least that is the tale in the City.' A wrong tale, naturally, but a *heroic* tale. In Gondor as in the Shire one sees how all achievement is assimilated to essentially active, violent, military patterns — 'the better fortitude', as Milton said in *Paradise Lost,* 'Of patience and heroic martyrdom / Unsung'. The end of Frodo's quest, in the memory of Middle-earth, is nothing. Bilbo turns into a figure of folklore ('mad Baggins'), the elves and dwarves percolate through to our world as time-shifters and ring-makers, even 'the Dark Tower' remains as an image for 'poor Tom' in *King Lear.* Of Frodo, though, not a trace: except hints of an unlucky, well-meaning king eclipsed on the one hand by the fame of his vengeful son, on the other by the Coming of the true hero Christ.

What has Ingeld to do with Christ? Nothing. But Fróda had something to do with both. He was a hinge, a mediation, like *The Lord of the Rings* in its suspension between pagan myth and Christian truth. He stood, in Tolkien's view, for all that was good in the Dark Ages — for the heroic awareness of heroic fallibility which Tolkien thought he could detect in *Beowulf* and in *Maldon,* for the spark of virtue which had made Anglo-

Saxon England ripe for conversion (a process carried out without a single martyrdom). Maybe his story had been, in God's plan, an *evangelica praeparatio:* a clearing of the ground for the good seed of the Gospel. It is possible that Tolkien thought of *The Lord of the Rings* in the same way. He knew his own country was falling back to heathenism again (if only on the model of Saruman, not Sauron), and while mere professorial preaching would make no difference, a story might. Frodo presents then an image of natural man in native decency, trying to find his way from inertia (the Shire) past mere furious dauntlessness (Boromir) to some limited success, and doing so without the inherited resources of the heroes and *longaevi* like Aragorn, Gandalf, Legolas, Gimli. He has to do so furthermore by destroying the Ring, which is merely-secular power and ambition, and with no certain faith in rescue from outside the *géara hwyrftum,* 'the circles of the world'. 'Myth is alive at once and in all its parts, and dies before it can be dissected', declared Tolkien ('Monsters', p. 257), and his statement is more than usually true of *The Lord of the Rings,* as I have said on p. 134 above. Something like the last few sentences must, however, have been at least a part of Tolkien's intention.

The Styles of Romance

One can see that ancient story is used very differently in *The Lord of the Rings* from the way it is in, say, James Joyce's *Ulysses.* Not only is the relation in the latter between Homeric 'myth' and modern novel one of irony and transformation; in it the 'myth', oddly enough, is given a higher and more assured status as something less sophisticated, more archetypal, closer to the holy and the divine. Tolkien by contrast was pre-eminently aware of *his* source-texts, like *Beowulf,* or Snorri's *Edda,* or Laʒamon's *Brut,* as the works of individuals like himself, who used old stories for contemporary purposes just as he did. In his view *The Lord of the Rings* was not a derivative or a metamorphosis of them and *Pearl* and *Comus* and *Macbeth* and all the other works I have mentioned of 'mythic' or near-'mythic' status: instead all of them, including *The Lord of the Rings,* were splinters of a truth, transformations *on the same level* of something never clearly expressed, not even (in entirety) in the Gospels.[19] Human awareness of this truth, he may have concluded, was passed on with just the same loose and haunting persistence as the rhythms and phrases of English poetry, surviving from Anglo-Saxon times to Middle English and 'The Man in the Moon', and on again to Shakespeare and Milton and Yeats and nursery-rhyme, without intention as without a break. Middle-earth itself survived in song even after people had forgotten what it meant: 'O cocks are crowing a merry midd-larf, / A wat the wilde foule boded day.'[20] Should that ballad of 1776 be classified as a 'myth'? It has old roots and is about a supra-rational world; but it was also sung for immediate pleasure without claims to any specially transmitted truth. In all these ways 'Sweet William's Ghost' is analogous to *The Lord of the Rings,* and even more so to its embedded songs and verses.

There is another way of approaching the question of the trilogy's literary status, which has the further merit of concentrating attention on its prose style as well as on poetry. This is via Northrop Frye's now famous book, *the Anatomy of Criticism* (1957), a work which never mentions *The Lord of the Rings,* but nevertheless creates a literary place for it with Sibylline accuracy. Mr Frye's theory, in essence, is that there are five 'modes' of literature, all defined by the relationship between heroes, environments, and humanity. 'If superior in kind both to other men and to the environment of other men', declares Mr Frye, 'the hero is a divine being and the story about him will be a *myth*.[21] One sees immediately that this does not apply to Gandalf or Aragorn, still less to Frodo: Gandalf can feel fear and cold, Aragorn age and discouragement, Frodo pain and weakness. Two steps down from 'myth', according to the *Anatomy,* we find 'high mimesis', the level of most epic and tragedy, in which heroes are 'superior in degree to other men but not to [their] natural environment'. This looks more like *The Lord of the Rings,* where many of the characters—Éomer, Faramir, Aragorn again—are very much of the stamp of old Siward or Coriolanus or other Shakespearean heroes. But are they on a par with their natural environment? Aragorn can run 135 miles in three days; he lives in full vigour for 210 years, dying on his birthday. Around him cluster characters who are immortal, like Elrond or Legolas, who can make fire or ride on eagles, while he himself can summon the dead. Clearly the mode intended is the one below 'myth' but above 'high mimesis', the world of 'romance' whose heroes are characteristically 'superior in *degree* [not *kind*] to other men *and* to [their] environments'.

The main points of this mode are then displayed by Mr Frye in ways immediately applicable to *The Lord of the Rings*. In it, we are told, 'the hero's death or isolation has the effect of a spirit passing out of nature, and evokes a mood best described as elegiac'; 'passing out of nature' is of course the main theme of hobbit-poetry. Elegy is further accompanied 'by a diffused, resigned, melancholy sense of the passing of time, of the old order changing and yielding to a new one'; while true of *Beowulf* and *The Idylls of the King,* this is conspicuously truer of *The Return of the King* and its dissolution of the Third Age. However, the main merit of Mr Frye's analysis, at this moment, is that besides describing Tolkien's literary category so well, it further indicates, first, an inevitable problem associated with that category, and then, more indirectly, the terms in which to express a solution.

To take the problem first: it is caused by the fact that there are literary modes beneath romance and beneath epic or tragedy, i.e. 'low mimesis', this being the mode of most novels, in which the hero is much on a level with us — and lower still 'irony', where heroes turn into anti-heroes like Sancho Panza or Good Soldier Schweik or Leopold Bloom. 'Looking over this table', Mr Frye observes, 'we can see that European fiction, during the last fifteen centuries, has steadily moved its center of gravity down the list' — so much so that, as has been remarked of *The Hobbit,* the co-existence of 'romance' characters like Thorin Oakenshield with 'ironic heroes' like Bilbo Baggins is immediately comic and only after many adventures rises to gravity. Tolkien's problem all through his career lay in his readership's 'low mimetic' or 'ironic' expectations. How could he present heroes to an audience trained to reject their very style?

His immediate solution was to present in *The Lord of the Rings* a whole hierarchy of styles. In this the hobbits are, orcs apart, at the bottom. Their very pronouns are against them, for the Shire version of Common Speech, like English but unlike all other major European languages, fails to distinguish polite from familiar forms of 'you'; Pippin, Merry and the others accordingly talk in a style which appears to Gondorians as unnaturally assured (though it is in fact almost 'democratic'; see p. 1107). In a more obvious way they are prone to compulsive banter. Merry, in the Houses of Healing, asks immediately after his recall from death by the sacral king for 'supper first, and after that a pipe'. The resultant memory of Théoden is dissolved by jokes about tobacco, about his pack, and by friendly abuse from Pippin. 'It is the way of my people to use light words at such times', says Merry apologetically, but just the same he cannot stop. One sees what causes the unkind critical remarks about *Boy's Own* and Billy Bunter. However, the emergence of anti-heroes like Billy Bunter, the demotion of romance to children's literature, are obvious consequences of the Western world's fifteen-hundred-year-long climb down the ladder of literary modes. All the hobbitic jokes are doing, then, is to reflect and by intention deflect the modern inhibition over high styles which we and they share; if we were not embarrassed by the hobbits, in other words, we would be by the heroes.

Many people indeed manage to be embarrassed by both, and for the latter reaction there is more excuse. As he climbed to the top of his stylistic hierarchy, Tolkien on occasion *wrote in* the responses he wanted instead of evoking them. High style is accompanied by characters stepping back, swelling, shining. Aragorn puts down Andúril at the gate of the Golden Hall, and declares its name: 'The guard stepped back and looked with amazement'. A few lines earlier 'wonder' has come into his eyes at the mention of Lothlórien. In the same way the guards at the Great Gate of Gondor 'fell back before the command of [Gandalf's] voice', while at the last embassy near the Morannon 'before his upraised hand the foul Messenger recoiled'. At that moment 'a white light shone forth like a sword' from Gandalf, as many people see 'the light that shone' round Éowyn and Faramir as they come down to the Houses of Healing. Galadriel is 'illumined' by 'a great light' when Frodo offers her the Ring, and seems 'tall beyond measurement'. All these images together are used when Aragorn draws Andúril and declares himself to Éomer (p. 423):

> Gimli and Legolas looked at their companion in amazement, for they had not seen him in this mood before. He seemed to have grown in stature while Éomer had shrunk; and in his living face they caught a brief vision of the power and majesty of the kings of stone. For a moment it seemed to the eyes of Legolas that a white flame flickered on the brows of Aragorn like a shining crown.
> Éomer stepped back . . .

Obviously his reaction is meant to be ours. Equally obviously that reaction cannot be counted on, because of the surly distrust engendered in us (as in Éomer) by generations of realistic fiction. Nevertheless, it is a mistake to think that the only literary modes which exist are those one period is familiar with. By his continual switching from one level of style to another, and his equally continual use of characters as 'internal reflectors' of embarrassment or suspicion, Tolkien showed at least that he was aware of that very predictable mistake, and ready to do what he could to help his readers round it. The worst one can fairly say is that in some scenes — the Andúril ones, the Field of Cormallen, the eagle's song — Tolkien underestimated his audience's resistance and reached too hastily for the sublime or the impressive. The real difficulty, though, is not his but ours: in ordinary modern 'low mimetic' novels such qualities are simply not allowed.

In fact one can often feel Tolkien, between these 'low' and 'high' stylistic poles, breaking with complete success out of all the categories into which he should have been put, rising again from the edge of romance to what almost anyone might call 'myth'. Perhaps the best example occurs at the end of Book V, chapter 4, 'The Siege of Gondor'. Here many of the story's threads are about to intersect. Faramir lies critically ill within the walls. Pippin is rushing to fetch Gandalf to save him, while Merry and Théoden are simultaneously approaching from Anórien; but at the Great Gate the chief Nazgûl, the 'haggard king' himself to whom Frodo had almost surrendered in the vale of Minas Morgul, leads the assault. All this is presented simply as story, even as history, but supra-realistic suggestions keep crowding in. The battering-ram of Mordor has a 'hideous head, founded of black steel . . . shaped in the likeness of a ravening wolf; on it spells of ruin lay. Grond they called it, in memory of the Hammer of the Underworld of old' — as if to recreate some earlier unstated triumph of the chthonic powers. Meanwhile the Nazgûl himself goes even more than usual beyond the boundaries of even 'romantic' humanity: he *looks* like a man, and carries a sword, but it is a 'pale' or insubstantial one; he bursts the Gate not only by Grond but by a projection of fear and dread, 'words of power and terror to rend both heart and stone', which work like 'searing lightning'. On the one hand he turns almost to abstraction, 'a vast menace of despair', as also to an image of the unexistence of evil, a 'huge shadow' which Gandalf tries to send back to 'nothingness'. But though the Nazgûl ironically proves Boethius right by throwing back his hood — 'and behold! he had a kingly crown; and yet upon no head visible was it set' — his deadly laughter shows that 'nothingness' can still have power and control. At this moment he calls himself Death:

> 'Old fool!' he said. 'Old fool! This is my hour. Do you not know Death when you see it? Die now and curse in vain!' And with that he lifted high his sword and flames ran down the blade.
>
> Gandalf did not move. And in that very moment, away behind in some courtyard of the City, a cock crowed. Shrill and clear he crowed, recking nothing of wizardry or war, welcoming only the morning that in the sky far above the shadows of death was coming with the dawn.
>
> And as if in answer there came from far away another note. Horns, horns, horns. In dark Mindolluin's sides they dimly echoed. Great horns of the North wildly blowing. Rohan had come at last.

In this passage the key words are perhaps 'as if'. Within the world of romance everything that happens here is literally 'coincidence'. The cock means nothing by crowing; that he crows at this moment is mere happenstance. Nor are the horns replying — they only seem to. Nevertheless, no reader takes the passage like that. The cockcrow itself is too laden with old significance to be just a motif. In a Christian society one cannot avoid the memory of the cock that crowed to Simon Peter just as he denied Christ the third time. What did *that* cockcrow mean? Surely, that there was a Resurrection, that from now on Simon's despair and fear of death would be overcome. But then again, what of *Comus* and the cockcrow the Younger Brother wishes for? "Twould be some solace yet, some little cheering / In this close dungeon of innumerous boughs.' It would show there is a world elsewhere. Tolkien too might think of the Norse legend of the 'Undying Lands', the *Odáinsakr:* when King Hadding reached its boundary the witch who guided him killed a cock and threw it over the wall — a moment later he heard the cock crow before he himself had to turn away and go back to mortality.[22] Cockcrow means dawn, means day after night, life after death; it asserts a greater cycle above a lesser one.

And what of the horns? They too are just the horns the Riders happen to be blowing, but they carry meaning in a more complicated way as well. Their meaning is bravado and recklessness. When he sets out from Rivendell, Boromir blows his horn, the family heirloom, and is rebuked by Elrond for doing so; but he takes no notice. 'Always I have let my horn cry at setting forth, and though thereafter we may walk in the shadows, I will not go forth as a thief in the night.' He means that good is stronger than evil, and even if it is not, that makes no difference to him. Challenging horns echo through Northern stories, from the trumpets of Hygelac, Beowulf's uncle, coming to rescue his dispirited compatriots from death by torture, to the war-horns of the 'Forest Cantons', the 'Bull' of Uri and the 'Cow' of Unterwalden, lowing to each other across the field of Marignano, as the Swiss pikemen rallied in the night for a second suicidal assault on overwhelming numbers of French cavalry and cannon. Horns go back to an older world where surrenders were not accepted, to the dead defiant Roland rather than the brave, polite, compromise-creating Sir Gawain, whose dinner is served to 'nwe nakryn noyse' — the sound of chivalric kettledrums. Nor are these the 'horns of Elfland dimly blowing' of late Romanticism; their echoes may be 'dim', but they themselves are 'wild', uncontrolled, immune to the fear and calculation on which the Nazgûl is counting. The combination of horncall and cockcrow means, if one listens, that he who fears for his life shall lose it, but that dying undaunted is no defeat; furthermore that this was true before the Christian myth that came to explain why.

The implications of that scene are more than realistic, and more than romantic. Nevertheless, the style of the passage is deliberately neutral.[23] There are touches of alliteration in 'wizardry' and 'war', 'death' and 'dawn', 'dark' and 'dim', while the verb 'recking' is old-fashioned. However, the vocabulary as a whole could hardly be simpler, largely monosyllabic, mostly words from Old English or Old Norse, but with an admixture of French words taken into the language many centuries ago, and even one Classical one in 'echoed'. Like Bilbo's and Shakespeare's winter songs, the 'breaking of the Gate' would take little rewriting to seem comprehensible and even colloquial at any time over the last half-millennium. The power of the passage lies not in *mots justes* but in the evocation of ideas at once old and new, familiar in outline but strongly redefined in context: like 'stocks and stones'.

The way this works has been once more illuminated by Mr Frye, who notes that though the line from Charles Kingsley's ballad about the 'cruel, crawling foam' (which swallows a girl drowned by accident) could be censured by rationalistic critics as the 'pathetic fallacy' — thinking nature is alive — what the phrase actually does is to let realism aspire for a second to higher modes, to give to the drowned Mary 'a faint coloring of the myth of Andromeda'. That aspiration is true of Tolkien in many places. It seems only apposite that he should hover so often on the edge of the 'pathetic fallacy', as for instance in the assault on Caradhras, where Aragorn and Boromir insist the wind has 'fell voices' and that stone-slips are aimed, or on the bridge at Khazad-dûm, where Gandalf is 'like a wizened tree', but the Balrog a mixture of fire and shadow, a 'flame of Udûn' — checked only for a moment by Boromir's horn. A good example of open discussion of such ambiguities within the trilogy is Frodo's passage of the Dead Marshes in pp. 613–15. It is Sam who falls with his face to the mud and cries out, 'There are dead things, dead faces in the water'. Gollum explains them as materialistically as possible. The dead are from the great battle long ago; the marsh-lights are exhalations from rotting corpses; he dug down once to eat them, though he found them beyond reach. Frodo sees more in them than that, though he cannot explain what:

> 'They lie in all the pools, deep deep under the dark water. I saw them: grim faces and evil, and noble faces and sad. Many faces proud and fair, and weeds in their silver hair. But all foul, all rotting, all dead. A fell light is in them.'

He does not say that 'fair is foul', like the witches in *Macbeth*. But the fear of the vision comes from the way that all, elves and orcs, evil and noble, are reduced to weeds and foulness in the end. The image picks up Merry's awakening from the barrow pages earlier, with its unexplained juxtaposition of the noble dead in the barrow with the wight itself. Does all glory decompose? That is what makes Frodo stand 'lost in thought'. Later on Faramir is to dismiss the whole thing as a sending of the Enemy. But there remains a feeling that the Enemy is not telling *absolute* untruth, even so. The landscape itself reinforces that belief. 'Far above the rot and vapours of the world the sun was riding high and golden', but all the hobbits can see and hear is 'the faint quiver of empty seed-plumes, and broken grass-blades trembling in small air-movements that they could not feel'. The discharged seed, the breathless air are images of the discouragement and sterility the Enemy projects. Mordor-flies have red eyes on them; all Mordor-bushes have thorns.

Both characters and readers become aware of the extent and nature of Tolkien's moralisations from landscape in such passages. In the thematic opposite to Mordor and the Marshes, however, in and around Lothlórien, old poems, old beliefs and fictional geography are much more closely intertwined, with the combination much less readily identified as fallacious. The word associated with Lórien most often is 'stain' — an odd word, both French and Norse in origin, with an early meaning of 'to lose lustre' as well as 'to discolour'. Frodo perceives the colours of Cerin Amroth accordingly as at once 'fresh' and familiar, with a light on them he cannot identify: 'On the land of Lórien there was no stain.' A few pages earlier he had felt that 'on the land of Lórien no shadow lay'. Much later Gandalf in the 'Song of Lórien' confirms, 'Unmarred, unstained is leaf and land'. With this mysterious absence of 'stain' goes a forgetting of grief; though the Fellowship has just lost Gandalf in Moria, the fact is not mentioned for close on twenty pages (330–46), and indeed we are told that 'in winter here no heart could mourn for summer or for spring'. This is very like *Pearl*, where the visionary landscape he wakes in makes the dreamer-father forget even his bereavement, 'Garten my goste al greffe forȝete'. It should be noted though that the dreamer crosses one boundary, from graveyard to dream, but not the next; when he tries to swim the river to Heaven at the end of the poem he is halted and woken before he reaches the water. Frodo and the Fellowship, however, cross two rivers, deliberately described and distinguished. One is the Nimrodel, which consoles their grief and promises them partial security; as Frodo wades it 'he felt that the stain of travel and all weariness was washed from his limbs'. The next is Celebrant, the Silverlode which they cannot ford but have to cross on ropes. Here they are totally secure, for, though the orcs can splash across the Nimrodel — 'curse their foul feet in its clean water!' says Haldir — it seems they cannot wade or swim the Silverlode. Even Gollum, though seen by the elves, vanishes 'down the Silverlode southward', i.e. on the far bank, and according to Aragorn has followed the Fellowship only 'right down to Nimrodel'.

With *Pearl* in mind, one might easily conclude that the stretch between the two rivers is a sort of 'earthly Paradise' for Frodo and the others, though one still capable of violation and invasion from the outside world. The 'Naith' of Lórien, though, across the second river, is Heaven; the company undergoes a kind of death in getting there, while there is a feeling of significance in the fact that they may not touch the water, not even to have their 'stains' washed away. A determined allegorist (or mythiciser) might go on to identify the Nimrodel with baptism, the Silverlode with death. A force which holds one powerfully back from such opinions is, however, Sam Gamgee, who counterpoints the most solemn moments of crossing with banalities like 'Live and learn!' and chatter about his uncle Andy (who used to have a rope-walk at Tighfield). He, and Gimli and Gollum and Haldir, keep even Lórien tied down to the level of story, in which rivers are tactical obstacles and not symbols for something else. Nevertheless, even though the *Pearl* analogue may occur to few, the references to absence of 'stain' and grief and blemish, the assertion that Lórien is a place apart, have their effect and keep one finally uncertain about the section's proper mode. The best one can say is that in those chapters, as in *The Lord of the Rings* more generally, a work essentially of 'romance' manages to rise at times towards 'myth', and also to sink towards 'high' or even 'low mimesis'.

Even 'irony' is not always out of place, though it is beneficent. As Sam and Frodo struggle on in Mordor, they come on a streamlet, 'the last remains, maybe, of some sweet rain gathered from sunlit seas, but ill-fated to fall at last upon the walls of the Black Land and wander fruitless down into the dust'. 'Fruitless' (a significant adjective elsewhere)? The water seemed so, but turns out not to be. By refreshing the Ring-bearer it does the best that any water could. The 'streamlet', in its apparent failure and eventual success, becomes a kind of analogue to Frodo's pity for Gollum, say, to all appearances useless, in the end decisive. It is hard to say what mode such scenes are in. They could be (by themselves) anywhere in Northrop Frye's stylistic hierarchy. This resonance of passages which can be read with different levels of suggestion at once, with 'myth' and 'low mimesis' and 'irony' all embedded deeply in 'romance', is perhaps the major and least-considered cause for the appeal of *The Lord of the Rings*.

Some Contradictions Mediated

If the three volumes had a thematic heart (in fact their whole method defies centralisation), one might like to see it in the dialogue of Legolas and Gimli, walking through Minas Tirith on p. 855, and looking at the masonry. Gimli is critical:

> 'It is ever so with the things that Men begin: there is a frost in Spring, or a blight in Summer, and they fail of their promise.'
>
> 'Yet seldom do they fail of their seed,' said Legolas. 'And that will lie in the dust and rot to spring up again in times and places unlooked for. The deeds of Men will outlast us, Gimli.'

'And yet come to naught in the end but might-have-
beens, I guess,' said the Dwarf.
'To that the Elves know not the answer,' said Legolas.

The exchange makes a point about Gondorian history. It also
brings out further one character's *idée fixe* (stonework), and de-
velops the theme of racial tension / personal harmony which
has been a feature of this relationship in the story for some
time. Yet the characters' speech here reaches out from its immediate context to timelessness and universality. Their sentences sound like proverbs. The idea of seed lying in the dust is
furthermore likely to arouse memory of the parable (Matthew
13: 18–23) of the seed that fell on stony ground. With a shock
one may wonder whether these proverbially soulless creatures,
Elf and Dwarf, are here — *all unwittingly* — talking about the
Son of Man. It would be like the elves to know a Saviour would
come to men, without having the slightest or remotest idea of
the mingled horror and beauty with which that event would
come about. We get a glimpse of how history might seem to the
most virtuous, and most pagan, of virtuous pagans — an odd
effect in, but not at all a contradiction to, 'a fundamentally religious and Catholic work'. In this way *The Lord of the Rings* can
be seen mediating between Christian and pagan, Christ and
Ingeld and Frodo, as between myth and romance, large pattern
and immediate context.

It is at the same time hovering between styles. There is no
archaic word in the passage, except perhaps 'naught'. Nevertheless a strong archaic effect is produced, by inversion of
nouns and adjectives, careful selection of adverbs of time like
'yet' and 'seldom', and other less obvious linguistic features.
Tolkien could have given a lecture about all these at any time.
It would have been no trouble to him to write the exchange in
modern English: 'It's always like that with the things men start
off on . . . But they don't often fail to propagate . . . They'll still
come to nothing in the end . . . The elves don't know the answer to that one . . .' *The Lord of the Rings* would have offered
fewer hostages to criticism if it had been written like that. But
would it have been better? It seems very unlikely. The discrepancy between modern usage and archaic thought would simply
have sounded bogus, leading to a deep 'disunion of word and

meaning' (as Tolkien showed by rewriting a similar passage; see *Letters*, pp. 225–26). His prose style was carefully calculated, and had its proper effect, in the long run, and for those not too provoked to read carefully. One might say, in Aristotelian terms, that the trilogy succeeded in harmonising its *ethos*, its *mythos* and its *lexis* — the subjects, roughly speaking, of the last three chapters respectively.

By those three words Aristotle would have meant 'setting', 'plot' and 'style', all meanings intended in the sentence above. However, semantic change often gives an unexpected bonus, which one should accept in this case as in others. The sentence above would still be true if the Greek words meant 'ethics', 'myth' and 'lexis' (the technical term for what one gets from dictionaries or lexicons). Tolkien thought there was a truth in the vagaries of words independent of their users. He probably did not, for instance, personally admire either Milton or Wordsworth: the one was a Protestant, a divorcer and a spokesman for regicides, the other a tinkerer with medievalism and a linguistic critic of the most ignorant type. But both were English poets, and the language spoke through them. How nearly Wordsworth echoed *Pearl* in his famous elegy on 'Lucy':

> No motion has she now, no force,
>   She neither hears nor sees,
> Roll'd round in earth's diurnal course
>   With rocks, and stones, and trees!

He should have written 'stocks', not 'rocks'. But he preferred the alliteration on *r* (and the tautology). Milton meanwhile got the phrase right in his sonnet 'On the Late Massacre in Piedmont':

> Avenge, O Lord, Thy slaughtered saints, whose bones
> Lie scattered on the Alpine mountains cold,
> Ev'n them who kept Thy truth so pure of old,
> When all our fathers worshipped stocks and stones . . .

However, in Tolkien's view everything else in the poem would be wrong: its vengeful ferocity, its equation of God's truth with Protestantism, most especially its contempt for 'our fathers' before they were converted, for the Anglo-Saxons indeed. Milton knew very little about them, and his contempt was based on ignorance. Yet poetry which uses old phrases is not always bound down to its creator's intention. Reading that line, and adding to it his memories of Finn and Froda, of Beowulf and Hrothgar and the other pagan heroes from the darkness before the English dawn, Tolkien may have felt that Milton was more accurate than he knew. Perhaps 'our fathers' did worship 'stocks and stones'. But perhaps they were not so very bad in doing so. After all, if they had not Christ to worship, there were worse things, many worse things for them to reverence than 'stocks and stones', rocks and trees, 'merry Middle-earth' itself.

CHAPTER 7

VISIONS AND REVISIONS

The Shaping of 'The Silmarillion'

The Hobbit and *The Lord of the Rings* are the works which have made Tolkien's reputation. They were not, however, 'the work of his heart', as I have called it elsewhere (*Author,* ch. 5). This was the immense complex of stories, repeatedly told and retold in quite different forms, which I call 'the Silmarillion', but distinguish from *The Silmarillion,* which is the selection from that immense complex made by Christopher Tolkien and published in 1977, arranged as the latter explains 'in such a way as seemed to me to produce the most coherent and internally self-consistent narrative'. Tolkien worked on his hobbit-cycle for nearly thirty years, if one accepts that he began composing *The Hobbit* about 1929 and was still working on the Appendices to *The Lord of the Rings* in 1955 (see *Bibliography,* pp. 7, 96). He worked on 'the Silmarillion', however, for more than twice as long, for his unpublished 'Story of Kullervo', written in 1914, contains the seed of the story of Túrin Turambar, later to be one of the 'Great Tales' (*Letters,* pp. 7, 214–15), and he was still thinking and writing about these texts and their problems in the last year of his life, 1973 (see *Peoples,* pp. 377–92). These sixty years of development are now set out in Christopher Tolkien's 'History of Middle-earth', most particularly in volumes I–V and IX–XII (VI–VIII being concerned for the most part with the four parts of 'The History of *The Lord of the Rings*').

The best short account of these sixty years is that of

Charles Noad, in his essay 'On the Construction of "The Sil-marillion"' in *Legendarium*, pp. 31–68, of which I can give only a summary here.[1] Briefly: the first glimmerings of Tolkien's new mythology are contained in a series of poems, mostly un-published at the time and written while Tolkien was an Oxford undergraduate, 1914–1916 (a collection of these poems was re-jected by the publishers Sidgwick and Jackson in April 1916). For most of the rest of that year Tolkien was training as an of-ficer or on active service at the Battle of the Somme.[2] Late in October 1916, however, he was returned to hospital in England with 'trench fever', and he remained a convalescent with recur-rent bouts of fever for the next two years. During this time, and for the most part in 1917, Tolkien wrote the material eventu-ally published as *The Book of Lost Tales, Parts One and Two,* the first two volumes of 'The History of Middle-earth'. These sixteen chapters contain a great part of the material which was to become *The Silmarillion,* including (under different titles) the 'Great Tales' of Beren and Lúthien, of Túrin Turambar, the Fall of Gondolin and the Tale of Eärendil, as also the elvish tales of 'The Darkening of Valinor' and 'The Coming of the Noldoli' and the mythological tales of 'The Music of the Ainur', 'The Coming of the Valar' and 'The Chaining of Melko'. It is not too much to say that the outline of *The Sil-marillion* was visible by the end of 1917 — or would have been if it had found any readers. For some years thereafter Tolkien was no doubt preoccupied with earning a living, but once he had found stable employment at the University of Leeds and then the University of Oxford, he began to put the tale of Túrin into alliterative verse and the tale of Beren into rhymed verse as 'The Lay of the Children of Húrin' and 'The Lay of Leithian' respectively, both now published as *The Lays of Beleriand,* volume III of 'The History of Middle-earth'; the first task occupied him approximately from 1920 to 1925, the second from 1926 to 1931. In 1926, though, Tolkien decided to show some of his poems, including a part of 'The Lay of the Children of Húrin', to his former schoolteacher R. W. Rey-nolds, and wrote a brief epitome of the 'Lost Tales' to give him some necessary background. This 'Earliest "Silmarillion"' led on to a longer epitome, the 'Quenta' or 'Qenta Noldorinwa . . . drawn from the Book of Lost Tales', written in 1930, and to two sets of annals, the 'Annals of Valinor' and 'of Beleriand', written at roughly the same time. These would lead on in their turn to two later sets of annals and a further expanded epitome, the 'Quenta Silmarillion', written between 1930 and 1937. These two bodies of work, from 1926 to 1930 and 1930 to 1937, appear in volumes IV and V of 'The History of Middle-earth', respectively *The Shaping of Middle-earth* and *The Lost Road*. In 1937, furthermore, Tolkien was asked by Stanley Unwin, publisher of *The Hobbit*, if he had any other material suitable for publication, and he sent him several manuscripts, including 'The Lay of Leithian' and 'The Quenta Silmarillion'. The publisher's reader, Edward Crankshaw, seems to have been given only the former to read and some pages of the latter as background, and seems also to have been quite baffled by both, and by how they related to each other. Stanley Unwin accordingly gave Tolkien a polite rejection and urged him to start working on a sequel to *The Hobbit*. Tolkien took the rejection as a rejection of the 'Silmarillion' material — which had in fact hardly been read at all — and started work on the *Hobbit*-sequel which was to become *The Lord of the Rings*.

The ironies of this situation are well set out by Christopher Tolkien in *The Lays of Beleriand*, pp. 364–67, but one effect was that Tolkien ceased working on anything but the hobbit-cycle (with one significant exception, discussed below, pp. 295–303) for more than a decade. Once *The Lord of the Rings* was effectively completed, however, he turned back with renewed energy to 'the Silmarillion', and in the early 1950s wrote two further sets of annals, 'The Annals of Aman' and 'The Grey Annals', along with a yet longer epitome, 'The Later "Quenta Silmarillion"', all these published along with much else in volumes X and XI of 'The History of Middle-earth', *Morgoth's Ring* and *The War of the Jewels*. From this body of materials, dating from 1917, from the 1920s, the 1930s, and the 1950s, much of it written over and over again so as to become 'a chaotic palimpsest, with layer upon layer of correction and wholesale rewriting, of riders and deletions' (*Lost Road*, p. 199), Christopher Tolkien was eventually to extract the work published as *The Silmarillion* in 1977. In *Unfinished Tales of Númenor and Middle-earth* three years later he went on to give significant expansions of some of the 'Silmarillion' material, including the longest and most developed account of the Túrin story, 'The Narn i Hîn Húrin' or 'Tale of the Children of Húrin', as well as of the Second Age (that of Númenor) and the Third Age, which ran from the first defeat of Sauron by Elendil, Gil-galad and Isildur to the destruction of the Ring and the departure of Frodo over the sea.

These two works, *The Silmarillion* of 1977 and the *Unfinished Tales* of 1980, are the subject of the rest of this chapter. It is true, of course, as should be clear from the paragraphs above, that these are posthumous works which never reached the final shape intended by their author. But in the first place their author never reached a final intention, so his wishes are not being flouted; in the second place, he clearly very deeply wished to see the materials on which he had worked for so long at last published, as his son records (*Lost Tales 1*, p. 5); and in the third place, *The Silmarillion* has by now found millions of readers to confirm its existence as a substantial text. Many of those readers have furthermore found it a difficult and challenging text: as I remark below, it 'could never be anything but hard to read', so that some account of it is not only called for but likely to be actually useful. Meanwhile, the main reason for deciding to treat it and the *Unfinished Tales* here, instead of where (some would say) they belong, i.e. before *The Hobbit* and along with the 'Philological Inquiries' of chapter 2, is that that is the way most readers experience them. Probably ninety-nine people out of a hundred come to *The Silmarillion* and the *Unfinished Tales* only after reading *The Lord of the Rings,* while because of the uncompromising nature of the posthumously published works, it will probably always be hard for most readers to understand them *except* after reading *The Lord of the Rings*. In that work Tolkien had set himself to write a romance for an audience brought up on novels. In the others, whether we consider them as earlier or later, we are left with far less guidance. It is accordingly the main aim of this chapter to help people to read *The Silmarillion* (I use once again the phrase which Tolkien and Gordon used of their edition of *Sir Gawain*) 'with an appreciation as far as possible of the sort which its author may be supposed to have desired'. Subsidiary to that, though still important, are the issues of what it has to say and how it came to be: 'sources' and 'designs' once more, both things Tolkien disliked, but useful if not essential to a proper reading.

I am grateful, however, for the opportunity to correct much of what I wrote twenty years ago in the light not only of the published material discussed above, but also of Christopher Tolkien's comments on my initial version, for which see *Lost Tales 1*, pp. 1–4, 7, and *Lost Tales 2*, p. 57.

The Dangers of Going On

Before beginning any commentary, though, there is one very obvious question to ask, which is why Tolkien never saw *The Silmarillion* into print himself, and why the *Unfinished Tales* remained unfinished. There were, after all, nearly eighteen years between the appearance of *The Return of the King* and Tolkien's death on 2 September 1973 — as long an interval as that between *The Hobbit* and *The Fellowship of the Ring*. During most of that period Tolkien was furthermore relieved of distracting academic duties, while he was not putting his energies into other creative work: almost all the sixteen poems in *The Adventures of Tom Bombadil* (1962) had seen print before, his contribution to *The Road Goes Ever On* (1968) consisted mostly of explanation and footnote, and *Smith of Wootton Major* (1967) is on the same relatively small scale as 'Leaf by Niggle'. Besides, to repeat the point made above, *The Silmarillion* was very largely in existence from 1937 on; was also known to be in existence, and very much in demand! Why, then, could Tolkien not finish off his legends of the First Age?

An answer to this, of a personal kind, has been given by Humphrey Carpenter on pp. 241–42 of his *Biography*. There was in Tolkien's later life, he notes, 'a perpetual discontinuity, a breaking of threads which delayed achievement and frustrated him more and more'. Partly the causes were external — loss of friends, hosts of visitors — but partly temperamental: Tolkien could not 'discipline himself into adopting regular working methods' (a fault of which he had been aware since the time of 'Leaf by Niggle'). *The Silmarillion* was accordingly held up to a great extent, in Mr Carpenter's view, by procrastination and bother over inessentials, by crosswords and games of Patience, by drawing heraldic doodles and answering readers' letters — all compounded, one might add, by the failing energies of age (see *Letters*, p. 228). This is a convincing picture, and no doubt partly true. Yet it is not a picture of someone taking things easy: rather of continual, if misdirected, intellectual effort. One may remark that it is common experience to find that conscientious people who have a job to do that is too much for them (like writing a book) turn in their uncertainty to doing a succession of easier jobs instead (like answering their mail, drawing up syllabuses, or rationalising office organisation). Something like this seems to have been the case with Tolkien. He may have frittered his time away in constructing etymologies and writing kindly letters to strangers. But these activities occupied him, one may well think, because he could see he had painted himself into a corner: there were purely *literary* reasons for not finishing *The Silmarillion,* and these can be deduced not only from that work itself, but from almost the whole of Tolkien's professional career. For one thing, both *The Hobbit* and *The Lord of the Rings* can be seen as primarily works of mediation. In the former Bilbo acts as the link between modern times and the archaic world of dwarves and dragons. In the latter Frodo and his Shire companions play a similar part, though the world they move in has also and in more complex ways been 'mediated', turned into a Limbo. Outside these works, though, hobbits are not to be met with; it would be almost impossible for them to exist in the much more rarefied air of the legends of the First Age, and without their existence modern readers lack guidance and a secure point of comparison. The very success of the hobbit-cycle was bound to make a work without hobbits a disappointment, or a puzzle.

But there may have been a more complex reason for Tolkien's long hesitation. To go back to '*Beowulf*: the Monsters and the Critics': if this makes one thing clear, it is that the literary quality Tolkien valued above all was the 'impression of depth . . . effect of antiquity . . . illusion of historical truth and perspective' which he found in *Beowulf,* in the *Aeneid* or for that matter in *Macbeth, Sir Orfeo* or the *Grimms' Fairy Tales.*

In all these works there was a sense that the author knew more than he was telling, that behind his immediate story there was a coherent, consistent, deeply fascinating world about which he had no time (then) to speak. Of course this sense, as Tolkien kept repeating, was largely an illusion, even a provocation to which a wise man should not respond. The 'heroic lays' which the *Beowulf-* poet knew and alluded to sound very fine from his allusions, but if we had them we might discover that the fascination came from his art, not theirs. 'Alas for the lost lore, the annals and old poets that Virgil knew, and only used in the making of a new thing!', wrote Tolkien, and he meant it. However, he also meant everyone to realise that the 'new thing' was worth more than the 'lost lore'.

The application of this to his own career must (once *The Lord of the Rings* was published) have seemed all too obvious. One quality which that work has in abundance is the Beowulfian 'impression of depth', created just as in the old epic by songs and digressions like Aragorn's lay of Tinúviel, Sam Gamgee's allusions to the Silmaril and the Iron Crown, Elrond's account of Celebrimbor and dozens more. This, however, is a quality of *The Lord of the Rings,* not of the inset stories. To tell these in their own right and expect them to retain the charm they got from their larger setting would be a terrible error, an error to which Tolkien would be more sensitive than any man alive — though as Christopher Tolkien points out (*Lost Tales 1,* p. 3), the error would be in the expectation, not in the telling. Tolkien saw the problem and expressed his sense of it in a revealing letter dated 20 September 1963. He had clearly been asked for a sequel to *The Lord of the Rings,* and replied that he could give 'another volume (or many) about the same imaginary world'. But he had many other things to do, he feared 'the presentation will need a lot of work' and he saw that the legends had to be made consistent with each other and with what he had already published. He went on:

I am doubtful myself about the undertaking. Part of the attraction of The L.R. is, I think, due to the glimpses of a large history in the background: an attraction like that of viewing far off an unvisited island, or seeing the towers of a distant city gleaming in a sunlit mist. To go there is to destroy the magic, unless new unattainable vistas are again revealed. (*Letters,* p. 333)[3]

To go there is to destroy the magic. As for the revealing of 'new unattainable vistas', the problem there — as Tolkien must have thought many times — was that in *The Lord of the Rings* Middle-earth was already old, with a vast weight of history behind it. *The Silmarillion,* though, in its longer form, was bound to begin at the beginning. How could 'depth' be created when you had nothing to reach further back to?

The problem was not absolutely insoluble: Milton, after all, had managed to begin *his* epic very near the beginnings of time, in *Paradise Lost.* Furthermore, one can perhaps see the solution to which Tolkien, in his philological way, was drawn, namely to present the First Age 'as a complex of divergent texts interlinked by commentary' (*UT,* p. 1), the texts themselves being supposedly written by Men, of different periods, looking back across the ages to vast rumours of whose truth they knew only part, like Sam Gamgee responding to Gimli's song 'Of mighty kings in Nargothrond / And Gondolin' (see once more *Lost Tales 1,* p. 3). *The Silmarillion* might then have come to look like (for example) *The Saga of King Heidrek the Wise,* written late but preserving intensely moving fragments of verse from some much older time now lost; even the editorial matter would then reinforce the effect of age and darkness (a device Tolkien used on a much smaller scale for *The Adventures of Tom Bombadil*). However, that avenue was never explored to its end; and if it had been, one may doubt whether many readers would have grasped the total effect. A *Silmarillion* on that plan could have ended as merely a pastime for scholars. It is better, no doubt, to see it as it is now, 'a completed and cohesive entity' (*UT,* p. 1 again). But in any case *The Lord of the Rings* had created other problems for its author besides the issue of 'depth': these affected *The Silmarillion,* but show up more strongly in the *Unfinished Tales.*

One was the strong temptation towards explicitness and over-clarity. In *Letters,* p. 348, Tolkien noted the comic case of a Mr Shorthouse, who produced by accident a strange, queer, debatable book called *John Inglesant.* Slowly it caught on, became a best-seller, 'the subject of public discussion from the Prime Minister downwards'. Success, however, ruined its author, who took to strange clothes and beliefs and 'never wrote any more, but wasted the rest of his time trying to explain what he had and what he had not meant in *John Inglesant*'. 'I have always tried to take him as a melancholy warning', wrote Tolkien in 1964, so the danger was seen. Still, it was there.

It emerges, for instance, if one considers water. No scene, perhaps, in *The Lord of the Rings* is more moving or more suggestive than the one in which Sam and Frodo, in Mordor, see the wind changing and the darkness driven back, and then as if in answer to prayer come upon a trickle of water: 'ill-fated' and 'fruitless' in appearance, but at that moment seemingly a message from the world outside, beyond the Shadow. In *The Silmarillion* we learn that water is the province of the Vala Ulmo, and that from it (sea or river) there often comes assistance; the incident with Sam and Frodo begins to seem less and less like chance, more and more of a 'sending'. If this went too far, of course, the sense of supernatural assistance would destroy one's awareness of the companions' courage, as also the deeply felt implicit moral that this is the way to behave. None of *us* can expect assistance from a Vala; nevertheless in any kind of Mordor it is one's duty to go on. By the time *The Lord of the Rings* was finished, Tolkien *was* beginning to think of taking matters further. He had shown inspiration coming from Ulmo to Tuor, as the hero sat by a trickling stream, both in *The Silmarillion* (p. 238) and in 'Of Tuor and his Coming to Gondolin' (written c. 1951),[4] in the *Unfinished Tales,* p. 20. Clearly the idea of water as a sanctity and an unfailing refuge from the Dark Lord had started to appeal to him; and in 'The Hunt for the Ring', accordingly, a sort of coda to *The Lord of the Rings* written c. 1955, he wrote that all the Nazgûl save their chief 'feared water, and were unwilling, except in dire need, to enter it or to cross streams unless dryshod by a bridge' (*UT*, p. 343). How then had they crossed Wilderland to the Shire? Christopher Tolkien notes that his father saw 'the idea was difficult to sustain'. Besides that, it would have brought the Valar too far forward; at many points it would have destroyed the hobbits' highly realistic sense of loneliness and confusion.

One may think that Tolkien was rightly pushing towards

a clarification of his 'mythology'.[5] Yet at the same time he was edging back from his long concern with heroic valour, or hobbitic moral courage. It has been remarked already (pp. 154–55 above) that he was in minor matters kind-hearted. *As The Lord of the Rings* came to an end this temptation, too, grew upon him. Bill the pony is saved in *The Return of the King*. In the 'Epilogue' to that work, eventually printed in *SD* pp. 114–35, we learn that Shadowfax will be saved too, to be taken on the last ship from the Havens to Aman, simply because Gandalf could not bear the parting. This would be a failure of nerve in a work which had sacrificed Lórien, and Tolkien, having written it, wisely decided to leave it out. Still, the second edition of *The Lord of the Rings* cuts out some minor, but convincing, asperity on the part of a strained Aragorn; it seemed too tough.[6] More seriously, in the 'late' narrative of 'The Disaster of the Gladden Fields' (*UT,* pp. 271–87), one can see Tolkien reconsidering Isildur. His use of the ominous word 'precious' in *The Fellowship of the Ring* (p. 246) had been quite enough to suggest that he was already becoming 'addicted', that his death was in a way a mercy. In the later narrative, though, Isildur uses the Ring painfully and reluctantly, with much excuse and apology. The Ring seems to find no answer in him to its call. But this again is running against a crucial point in *The Lord of the Rings,* namely that no one can be trusted, not even 'the Keepers of the Three'. Tolkien, no doubt, would have seen this point and dealt with it somehow if he had published a full account. Still, one can see him becoming more loath to accept the evil in the good: and while this is charitable, it does not make for powerful story.

A final straw in the wind may be Tolkien's increasing desire to pull strands together. The Middle-earth of *The Hobbit* and *The Lord of the Rings* is full of chaotic half-glimpsed independent lives, ears in the forest, fell voices on the wind, enemy powers older than Sauron and unconnected with him. In a letter of 1955 Tolkien had rather laughed at the idea that Willow-man and the wights were agents of the Dark Lord: 'Cannot people imagine things hostile to men and hobbits who prey on them without being in league with the Devil!' (*Letters,* p. 278). But in manuscript B of 'The Hunt for the Ring' (written at much the same time) just this idea is being entertained. The Chief

Ringwraith stays on the Barrow-downs for some while before Frodo sets out, 'and the Barrow-wights were roused, and all things of evil spirit, hostile to Elves and Men, were on the watch with malice in the Old Forest and on the Barrow-downs' (*UT*, p. 348).

None of the points just mentioned is of any great significance in itself. As a whole, though, they do suggest an author looking back over his own work *and trying to reduce it to order*. The menace in that, as everyone knows, is that with system comes rationalisation and loss of vitality. There are moments when one fears that Tolkien, in the *Unfinished Tales* — and in fairness one must repeat that they *are* unfinished, were never finally 'passed' by their author — was turning against the sources of his inspiration. He tried to realign retrospectively things he had written many years before, for what at the time had been entirely adequate reasons. The point of making Bilbo both 'bourgeois' and 'burglar' has been explained above (see p. 72), and the scene in Bag End in chapter 1 *of The Hobbit* is completely successful as comedy. But by the time he wrote 'The Quest of Erebor' (perhaps around 1950), Tolkien had come to think it undignified. In repeated versions he explains laboriously that Gandalf forced Bilbo on Thorin out of some Valinorean 'foresight'; or because he knew hobbits were stealthy; or because he thought Bilbo had the right 'mix' of Took and Baggins; while as for the word 'burglar', it was all a dwarvish misunderstanding. The very multiplicity of reasons suggests doubt; and in romance it is a good rule that not everything should be explained.

In any case one may well think that the sheer effort of dotting 'i's and crossing 't's was draining. On one issue — the nature of the orcs — Tolkien seems very nearly to have arrived at a solution without quite being able to grasp it, a sign, perhaps, of exhaustion. There can be little doubt that the orcs entered Middle-earth originally just because the story needed a continual supply of enemies over whom one need feel no compunction — 'the infantry of the old war', to use Tolkien's phrase from 'Monsters' (p. 264). But several readers had pointed out that if evil could not create, was only good perverted, then presumably the orcs had been by nature good and might in some way be saved; Tolkien certainly balked at calling them 'irredeemable'; see *Letters,* pp. 195, 355. *The Silmarillion* accordingly expresses more than once the theory that orcs were in fact captured elves 'by slow acts of cruelty . . . corrupted and enslaved' (*S,* p. 50). One can only say that in that case there are an awful lot of them — 'the pits of Angband seemed to hold store inexhaustible and ever-renewed' (*S,* p. 157). They must have been bred, one thinks, and indeed we are told they multiplied 'after the manner of the children of Ilúvatar', i.e. sexually. But in *that* case one wonders (a) why what we would call 'brainwashed' creatures should breed true, and (b) why we never come upon female orcs. Tolkien shrank from that last, and recorded (*UT,* p. 385) a rival theory that the orcs were bred from something like the Drúedain, the Pûkel-men. I suspect that at the back of his mind there lurked a phrase from *Beowulf,* about those very similar monsters Grendel and his mother: *no híe fæder cunnon,* 'men know of no father for them'. It would be a good solution to see the orcs as multiplying 'like flies', as if by some manufacturing process in hatcheries in Barad-dûr or Moria or the pits of Angband — maybe they 'quickened in the earth like maggots', as Snorri Sturluson had written centuries before (see p. 61 above). Such beings would be 'creatures' of evil in a special sense, made and animated by their master in a way which falls just short of the heresy that evil can itself create. As Ilúvatar says of Aulë's dwarves, they would have no being of their own, 'moving when [he thinks] to move them, and if [his] thought is elsewhere, standing idle'. Tolkien saw the problem, and collected the parts of a solution. He did not, however, assemble the parts — perhaps because it would have involved, to be consistent, a complete revision of all his earlier work.[7]

The word underlying these last few pages is 'thrift'. All minds possess a drive towards consistency, towards reducing data, events, characters to some smaller set of principles or categories. Much of Tolkien's writing in *Silmarillion* and *Unfinished Tales* shows that urge, a strong and honourable one. It is fair to say, though, that against this basic drive all minds also possess a wish to ignore principles and concentrate instead on single entities regardless of their place in larger systems, to appreciate them simply for themselves. For most of his career Tolkien was a most extreme example of a man with this second urge strongly developed: he was fascinated by names, to give only one example, part of whose nature is that they are for one thing and one thing alone, very hard to reduce to system! Hence the supreme lavishness of Middle-earth in *The Lord of the Rings,* with its vast store of plants and races, names and languages and individuals and landscapes. As he turned towards thrift, consistency, classification, Tolkien forfeited much of what he had valued before; he was contracting, not expanding. In a way the very success of *The Lord of the Rings,* founded on its immense solidity and scope, made life difficult for him afterwards. Not only would *The Silmarillion* have to achieve the 'depth' it had already been used to create, it would have to do so without contradicting, and while if possible reinforcing, all the millions of details Tolkien had handed over to his readership already. For these two reasons it is hardly any wonder that Tolkien balked, and that the *Unfinished Tales* in particular show a mind searching in different directions. After 1955 many ways forward were blocked. The question was, whether the vitality of his original conceptions and compositions of the period before *The Lord of the Rings,* indeed from the 1910s on, could survive.

Here one must concentrate, not on those explanations of the Second and Third Ages which Tolkien wrote as background for *The Lord of the Rings,* but on his labour and preoccupation for nearly sixty years, the legends of the First Age: Tuor and Túrin in the *Unfinished Tales,* but beyond and around them the whole 'narrative structure' of *The Silmarillion.* To repeat questions posed earlier: what have these to say, and how did they come to be?

Philosophical Inquiries

The most obvious fact about the design of *The Silmarillion* is that, like the Shire, it is a 'calque', though on the history of *Genesis* rather than the history of England. In chapter X of *A Preface to Paradise Lost* (London: Oxford University Press, 1942), C. S. Lewis gave a summary list of doctrines of the Fall of Man common to Milton, to St Augustine and to 'the Church as a whole'. Most of them reappear with little change in the

'Ainulindalë' or 'Valaquenta'. Thus Lewis asserts that 'God created all things without exception good'; in Tolkien even Melkor begins with good intentions (p. 18). 'What we call bad things are good things perverted . . . This perversion arises when a conscious creature becomes more interested in itself than in God . . . the sin of Pride'; compare Melkor in the music of the Ainur seeking 'to increase the power and glory of the part assigned to himself'. Lewis again, 'whoever tries to rebel against God produces the result opposite to his intention . . . Those who will not be God's sons become his tools'; and Ilúvatar to Melkor, 'no theme may be played that hath not its uttermost source in me . . . he that attempteth this shall prove but mine *instrument* in the devising of things more wonderful, which he himself hath not imagined' (my italics). It seems very likely that Lewis and Tolkien co-operated in their analysis of Christian essentials; *The Silmarillion,* with its exile from paradise, its ages of misery and its Intercessor, is a calque on Christian story, an answer to *Paradise Lost* and *Paradise Regained.*

Is it a *rival* to Christian story? The thought clearly occurred to Tolkien, if only to be repudiated. Significantly, he left a gap in *The Silmarillion,* or designed a dovetail, for the Fall of Man as described in the Old Testament. In his work the human race does not originate 'on stage' in Beleriand, but drifts into it, already sundered in speech, from the East. There something terrible has happened to them of which they will not speak: 'A darkness lies behind us . . . and we have turned our backs on it' (p. 141). Furthermore they have met 'the Lord of the Dark' before they meet the Elves; Morgoth went to them as soon as they were created, to 'corrupt or destroy'. Clearly one can, if one wishes, assume that the exploit of Morgoth of which the Eldar never learnt was the traditional seduction of Adam and Eve by the serpent, while the incoming Edain and Easterlings are all descendants of Adam flying from Eden and subject to the curse of Babel. *The Silmarillion,* then, tells the story of the fall and partial redemption of the elves, without contradicting the story of the Fall and Redemption of Man.

There is no point, though, in merely repeating a known pattern. Tolkien, in his history of the elves, would not wish to go against what he accepted as doctrine universally true. He did, however, want to say something different: as with a linguistic 'calque', familiar structure has to join with strange or novel material. The alienness of Tolkien's elves, the thing which makes their whole history different from that of humanity, is obviously that (in the natural course of things) they *do not die*. Accordingly they do not have to be rescued from death by a Saviour; nor from Hell, for they are not judged at death to Hell or Heaven, but sent to 'the halls of Mandos', from which they may in time return. Orthodox correspondents of Tolkien worried about this, and thought he was overstepping the mark (see especially *Letters,* no. 153). To their doubts Tolkien could only reply that he was writing fiction, he had a right to use his imagination, and that after all his elves were only 'certain aspects of Men and their talents and desires, incarnated in my little world'. Romance, as Professor Kermode said (see p. 176 above), is a stripped-down form which enables one to concentrate.

What Tolkien wanted to concentrate on, obviously, was death: more precisely perhaps on why people love this world and want so strongly to stay in it when it is an inescapable part of their nature 'to die and go we know not where'. His imagination centred again on a kind of calque, a diagrammatic reversal. Since we die, he invented a race which did not. Since our 'fairy-stories' are full of the escape from death (as he remarked near the end of 'On Fairy-Stories'; *Reader,* p. 85), 'the Human-stories of the elves are doubtless full of the Escape from Deathlessness'. Certainly one was, his own tale of Beren and Lúthien as embodied in his 'Lay of Leithian, Release from Bondage', in which Lúthien alone of the elves is *allowed* as a favour to 'die indeed' and leave the world like a mortal. *Paradise Lost,* one might say, exists to tell us that death is a just punishment, and anyway (see *Paradise Regained*) not final. *The Silmarillion* by contrast seems to be trying to persuade us to see death potentially as a gift or reward — an attitude to which other authors in this sceptical age have felt drawn.[8] While the legends of the First Age are a 'calque', then, their resemblance to a known pattern directs us primarily to difference from that pattern; the elvishness of the elves is meant to reflect back on the humanity of man.

That seems, anyway, to be what Tolkien came to think. There must, however, be at least a suspicion that — as with the languages of Middle-earth — he created a structure of thought to justify a more primary urge, delight in language, delight in ancient story. Elves, like dragons, are embedded deeply in several different traditions of northwest Europe, and the inconsistencies of those traditions[9] may only have made Tolkien itch to create a *Zusammenhang*. Did elves have souls, for instance? Could they be saved? Anyone who had read Hans Christian Andersen's 'The Little Mermaid' would know that they did not and could not — not unless they married a mortal, as with Lúthien. Tolkien did know 'The Little Mermaid', though he did not like it (*Letters*, p. 311), probably because he thought it too sentimental. Older and tougher belief on the same issue is embodied in another tale Tolkien had probably read, the Scottish story of 'The Woman of Peace and the Bible Reader'[10]: in this an elf-woman approaches an old man reading his Bible and asks 'if there was any hope given in holy Scripture for such as she'. The old man replies kindly, but says there is no mention of salvation in the Good Book 'for any but the sinful sons of Adam' — at which the lady gives a cry of despair and hurls herself into the sea. The old man's answer is strict and orthodox but (as with the view that pre-conversion heroes like Beowulf or Aragorn could not be saved) hardly seems fair. Why should only the 'sinful' be saved? However, it was not Tolkien's way to deny orthodoxy: nor to abjure equally old and traditional belief in the allure of elves and their separation from evil. He looked for a middle path. And in this activity he had at least one model.

This is not, for once, the *Beowulf*-poet, who took a strong line on *ylfe* or elves, putting them into a list with 'ettens' and indeed with 'orcs' — a very stern view of all non-human and un-Christian species. But at least one other English poet preceded Tolkien in being less sure, the author of the legend of St Michael in *The Early South English Legendary*, written about 1250. Tolkien never mentions reading this, but it is unlikely that as a medievalist he did not. What the Middle English poet has to say, in essence, is that in the war between God and Satan for men's souls, there may perhaps be *neutrals*. In the War in Heaven not all the angels were whole-heartedly for God or for Lucifer. The ones who inclined toward the devils without actually joining them are accordingly confined in tempests till

Doomsday, when they will go to Hell. Correspondingly, those who wavered towards God have been sent from Heaven to Earth, where 'they will be in a certain pain up to the end of the world, but at Doomsday they shall return to Heaven. Others are still in the Earthly Paradise, and in other places on Earth, doing their penance.' Both good and evil spirits come to Earth to protect or corrupt men, but these neutrals can be seen too:

> And ofte in fourme of wommane: In many derne weye
> grete compaygnie men i-seoth of heom: boþe hoppie
>   and pleiȝe,
> Þat Eluene beoth i-cleopede: and ofte heo comiez to
>   toune,
> And bi daye muche in wodes heo beoth: and bi niȝte ope
>   heiȝe dounes.
> Þat beoth þe wrechche gostes: Þat out of heuene weren
>   i-nome,
> And manie of heom a-domesday: ȝeot schullen to reste
>   come.

And often men see great numbers of them, shaped like women, dancing and sporting on many dark paths. *These are called Elves* (my italics), and often they come to town, and by day they are usually in the woods, by night on high hills. Those are the wretched spirits that were taken from Heaven. And at Doomsday many of them shall still come to rest.[11]

It is surprising how much of these few lines finds an echo in *The Silmarillion*. Of course Tolkien could not accept the basic postulate that elves were angels; like the story of the fairy and the Bible-reader, that is the product of a strict Christianity with very little space for outsiders. However, his elves are very *like* fallen angels, quite similar enough for confusion in the minds of fallible men. They seem part of a hierarchy which goes from Valar (good and bad) to Maiar (good and bad) to Eldar; they are 'like in nature to the Ainur, though less in might and stature', close enough in one case (Melian and Elwë or Elu Thingol) to intermarry. For a man to say that Galadriel was an angel, for instance, might then seem natural enough.[12] Would she be a *fallen* angel? In a way the answer is 'No', for certainly the elves play no part in Tolkien's War in Heaven, when Melkor is shut out. On the other hand Galadriel has been expelled from a kind of Heaven, the Deathless land of Valinor, and has been forbidden to return.[13] One can imagine the expulsion to Earth (of Melkor) and the expulsion to Middle-earth (of Galadriel) coming, in a mind like Éomer's, to seem much the same thing. Furthermore one notes the *South English Legendary*'s interesting conviction that some 'neutrals', or elves, are still on Earth, and others in the 'Earthly Paradise'. In a way this too is made true by *The Silmarillion* and *The Lord of the Rings* combined; for the latter predicts that some elves will refuse to leave Middle-earth, however much they may 'dwindle', while the former shows that others remain in Valinor, once part of the Earth, though now in some mysterious way sundered from it. What Tolkien took from that passage (and others) was, in short, the ideas that elves were like angels; that they had, however, been involved in a 'Fall'; that their fate at Doomsday is not clear (for men 'shall join in the Second Music of the Ainur', elves perhaps not; *S*, p. 42), that they are associated with the Earthly Paradise and cannot die till the end of the world. No earlier source puts forward the idea of the Halls of Mandos, but that half-way house, like Limbo, seems almost to be demanded by the terms of the problem. Have elves souls? No, in that they are not free to leave the world; so far the Ross-shire Bible reader was right. Yes, in that they do not go out like a candle on death; so far natural justice is satisfied. One sees that, as well as *Genesis*, Northern folk-tradition has helped to frame *The Silmarillion*. Its story has a root in the puzzles of ancient texts.

Pride and Possessiveness: Another View

None of the foregoing says anything about the 'Silmarils' themselves, the jewels which give their name to *The Silmarillion,* and whose fate determines its plot. However, they do in a way fit the scheme already outlined. *The Silmarillion* was based on the Christian story of Fall and Redemption, whether one took it from *Genesis* or *Paradise Lost*. It was different from the

Christian story in being about a race which had not been punished by death, rather by weariness of life (see especially *Letters,* p. 236). A natural question is, what was their sin? To keep
the pattern consistent, it ought not to be the same as that of
Adam and Eve, by tradition Pride, the moment when, as Lewis
said, 'a conscious creature' became 'more interested in itself
than in God'. In fact the elves seem much more susceptible to a
specialised variety of pride not at all present in *Paradise Lost,*
not quite Avarice or 'possessiveness' or wanting to own things
(as has been suggested),[14] but rather a restless desire to *make*
things which will forever reflect or incarnate their own personality. So Melkor has the desire 'to bring into Being things of his
own'; Aulë, though subjecting himself to Ilúvatar, creates the
dwarves without authority; Fëanor forges the Silmarils. One
might rewrite Lewis's phrase to say that in Valinor, as opposed
to Eden, the Fall came when conscious creatures became 'more
interested in their own creations than in God's'. The aspect of
humanity which the elves represent most fully — both for good
and ill — is the creative one.

There could be several reasons why Tolkien chose to write
about fascination with the artefact (a theme present in his work
since chapter 1 of *The Hobbit*). The most obvious is that he felt
it himself: to him his fictions were what the Silmarils were to
Fëanor or their ships to the Teleri, 'the work of our hearts,
whose like we shall not make again'. Significantly, Fëanor
learns not from Manwë, nor Ulmo, but from Aulë, the smith of
the Valar and the most similar of them to Melkor; Aulë too is
responsible for the despatch of Saruman to Middle-earth (see
UT, p. 393); Aulë is the patron of all craftsmen, including
'those that make not, but seek only for the understanding of
what is' — the philologists, one might say, but also the *scopas,*
the 'makers', the *fabbri,* the poets. Tolkien could not help seeing a part of himself in Fëanor and Saruman, sharing their
perhaps licit, perhaps illicit desire to 'sub-create'. He wrote
about his own temptations, and came close to presenting the
revolt of the Noldor as a *felix culpa,* a 'fortunate sin', when
Manwë accepts that their deeds will live in song, so that
'beauty not before conceived [shall] be brought into Eä'; fiction, poetry, craftsmanship are seen as carrying their own jus-

tification and as all being much the same thing. Rightly, Tolkien must have thought, did the poet of *Pearl* call himself a 'jeweller'.

A more wide-ranging reason is that love of things, especially artificial things, could be seen as the besetting sin of modern civilisation, and in a way a new one, not quite Avarice and not quite Pride, but somehow attached to both. In that view *The Silmarillion* would have something like the distinctively modern 'applicability' of *The Lord of the Rings* and *The Hobbit*, for all its archaic setting. Yet Tolkien believed, to repeat a point made already, that modern sins had ancient origins. The fall of the Noldor (*S*, p. 69) repeats a phrase from the Old English poem *Maxims I* about 'inventing and tempering wounding swords': the Anglo-Saxon poet seems to have looked back to Cain and Abel for the origin of evil, rather than Adam and Eve, and to have seen evil's symptom in metallurgy. More deeply, the Silmarils themselves seem to stem from yet one more philological crux, this time from Finnish.

The influence of that language and literature on *The Silmarillion* is undoubted. Finnish was 'the original germ of *The Silmarillion*', Tolkien wrote in 1944 (*Letters*, p. 87), and he repeated the assertion twenty years later (*Letters*, p. 345). Quenya itself is similar to Finnish in linguistic 'style'; names like Ilúvatar and Ulmo recall the Ilmatar and Ilmo of the *Kalevala;* the Valar are the powers who have agreed to be 'bounded in the world', and *vala* in Finnish means 'bond'; many more connections can be made.† It is therefore almost inevitable that the great mystery of the epic of Finland, the *Kalevala,* should irresistibly recall the Silmarils: it is the riddle of the *sampo*. This object is described repeatedly in the *Kalevala* as the work of the master-smith Ilmarinen, handed

---

† The point is made much more explicitly in Jim Allan's *An Introduction to Elvish* (Hayes: Bran's Head, 1978): Quenya resembles Finnish in 'style', especially in its complex noun-declensions, Sindarin is close to Welsh in for instance its sound-changes. A philological point not made by Allan is that Finnish preserves several words borrowed from Early Germanic in their early (or *) form: *kuningas* for 'king', *var(k)as* for 'warg', *jetanas* for 'etten' or 'giant'. Tulkas, the warlike Vala of *The Silmarillion*, seems a similar formation, cp. the Norse word *tulkr* ('tolke' in *Sir Gawain*), 'man, fighting man'.

over as payment for a bride, but then stolen back, broken in the pursuit, surviving only in fragments; yet no one knows what it is — or rather, what it was, for its loss is irrevocable. The singers themselves are uncertain, often replacing *sampo* (a word without a referent) by some other nonsense-word like *sammas*. Meanwhile the philologists, putting together the various clues inside the *Kalevala* — it is bright, it was forged, it is a kind of mill, it brings luck, it made the sea salt — have come up with innumerable solutions, at once vague and pedantic: the *sampo* was the Golden Fleece, some fertility-cult object, a Lappish pillar-idol, an allegory of the sky. In recent years, despondently, they have concluded 'that questions about what the *sampo* was can never be satisfactorily answered and that even if they could, an answer would probably make little contribution to the understanding of the poems'.[15] Nothing could be more provocative to Tolkien than a word without a referent *(emnet, wodwos, Gandálfr, ent)*, except perhaps an ancient poem written off by modern scholars as hopelessly irrational. In this case he clearly decided that the *sampo* was at once a thing and an allegory, like the Silmarils: a jewel, bright, hypnotic, intrinsically valuable, but also the quintessence of the creative powers, provoking both good and evil, the maker's personality itself. Some Finnish singers thought the *sampo* was their own poetry; all agreed that its fragments were the true prosperity of Suomi.

If only the Silmarils could inspire a true prosperity for England! As is well known, Tolkien's grand design, or desire, was to give back to his own country the legends that had been taken from it in the Dark Ages after the Conquest, when elves and woodwoses and *sigelhearwan* too had all been forced into oblivion. For that to be possible, the Silmarils and their chain of stories would have to be multi-faceted indeed, leaving scope for 'other minds and hands' to add their own significances. Certainly Tolkien's own efforts to say what *The Silmarillion* was 'about' were never completely illuminating. Still, his borrowings and his changes do at least define his area of interest. In *The Silmarillion* Tolkien played through once more the drama of 'Paradise lost'; but he added to it a hint of 'paradise well lost' (for many of the elves preferred Middle-earth even to immortal life, like Arwen); and through the story there runs a delight in mutability, as languages change and treasures pass from hand to hand; the deepest fable is of beauty forged, stolen and lost forever in recovery. Though springing from Genesis, this is at once more ambiguous, more heroic and more humane.

Eärendil: A Lyric Core

The preceding section (as Tolkien would have been the first to declare) probably falls into the perennial academic vice of neatness, over-valuing system and 'invention' instead of 'inspiration'. To redress the balance, it is worth noting that Tolkien was capable of working in quite a different way. He said repeatedly and consistently (*Letters,* pp. 221, 345, 420) that the 'kernel' of his mythology in the story of Beren and Lúthien was not a thought, not a principle, not a calque, but the vision of 'a small woodland glade filled with hemlocks at Roos in Yorkshire', where he saw his wife dancing. Everything else might be changed by the demands of story and of ratiocination — there are clear differences, for instance, between the accounts of that scene in the 1925 poem 'Light as Leaf on Lindentree' and in Aragorn's song on Weathertop — but to the vision itself he remained true, working out from it as from the detailed paintings of Lake Mithrim, Nargothrond, Gondolin, etc., which he made in the 1920s (see *Pictures* 32–36 and further *Artist,* chapter 2). Probably Tolkien would have accepted the thesis (not unfamiliar to medievalists) that all great works of fiction should contain a kernel scene or a 'lyric core': to use the terminology of Marie de France, whose 'Breton lays' Tolkien imitated in 'Aotrou and Itroun' (1945), every *conte* or story comes from a *lai* or song. There is one very striking example in the *Unfinished Tales,* namely the tale of 'Aldarion and Erendis: the Mariner's Wife'. This may have some root in Tolkien's own experience, for it stresses the unwisdom of fathers leaving their children — Tolkien hardly knew his own father — and seems to be groping towards a statement about the incompatibility of men and women, users and providers, wasters and winners. However, as a story it reaches no conclusion. What it does is to create an image of total separation expressed in understatement. Having been left by her husband in his urge for voyages abroad, Erendis retreats to the centre of Númenor, away from the sea, where she hears only the bleating of sheep. '"Sweeter it is to my ears than the mewing of gulls", she said.' Tolkien must have been thinking of Njörthr the sea-god and Skathi, daughter of the mountain-giant, in Snorri Sturluson's *Prose Edda*. Obliged to marry, these two tried taking turns to live in each other's homes. But the marriage was a failure, marked in Snorri's account by sudden quotation from yet one more lost poem:

> 'Leið erumk fjöll,   vaska lengi á,
>   nætr einar niu;
> ulfa þytr   þóttumk illr vesa
> hjá söngvi svana.'

'Hateful to me were the mountains, I was there no longer than nine nights; the howling of wolves seemed ugly to me against the song of the swans.'

So Njörthr; his wife replies with a complaint about the noise of the sea-mews. Wolves and swans, gulls and sheep: the contrasts generate the Norse poem and Tolkien's story by themselves.

Other tales in *The Silmarillion* are better worked up into narrative, and yet seem to spring likewise from single scenes, single outcries. An obvious case is that of Eärendil, the first character to take shape in Tolkien's mythology. His 'invention', like that of hobbits, has been well-chronicled by Humphrey Carpenter (*Biography,* pp. 72 and 175); the two cases are in several ways similar. With Eärendil, what happened is that Tolkien was initially struck by several lines from an Old English poem in the *Exeter Book,* now known as *Christ I or The Advent Lyrics:*

> Eala earendel,   engla beorhtast,
> ofer middangeard   monnum sended . . .

'Oh, Earendel, brightest of angels, sent to men above Middle-earth . . .'

These form the start of a speech by the prophets and patriarchs in Hell, who appeal for an Ambassador — this is before Christ's Advent — to bring them rescue from the *deorc déaþes sceadu,* the 'dark shadow of death'. But the word *earendel* is strange, not ordinary Old English, and evidently pre-dating its context;

245

Tolkien was caught by a difference of texture, prompting his own verses on 'The Voyage of Earendel', in 1914, and the reply to G. B. Smith's question as to what they were about, 'I don't know. I'll try to find out.'

But actually Tolkien had no doubt already started finding out, taking the two obvious courses of looking up 'Earendel' in A. S. Cook's 1900 edition of *Christ* and in the index of Jacob Grimm's *Teutonic Mythology*. From the latter he would have learnt that Earendel-references appear in several Germanic languages. In the *Prose Edda,* for instance, Aurvandill is a companion of the god Thórr, who loses a toe to frostbite only to have it thrown into the sky to become a star; as one might have guessed from *Christ,* 'Earendel' is the old name of a star or planet. Grimm also referred, though, to the German poem of *Orendel,* written about 1200. In this Orendel is a king's son shipwrecked in the Holy Land, but rescued naked by a fisherman. He retrieves a grey robe from a whale they catch, and in it returns to his own land to convert his heathen countrymen. The *grawe roc* he wears is the seamless robe Christ wore to the Crucifixion; in the end Orendel becomes *der Graurock,* 'Greycloak' — is identified with his garment. What this may have suggested to Tolkien is that if the Old English and Old Norse sources agreed that 'Earendel' was a star, the Old English and medieval German ones agreed he was a messenger of hope to the heathens. Perhaps the hope-association was as old as the star one; perhaps 'Earendel' had contained a presentiment of salvation even for the old heroes (like Beowulf) who lived before Christianity was brought to them. The notes in Cook's edition would meanwhile have told Tolkien that the Old English lines were based on a Latin antiphon, 'O *Oriens . . .*' ('O Rising Light, splendour of eternal light and sun of justice: come and shine on those who sit in darkness and the shadow of death'). In a Christian context this appeal is to Christ; in a pre-Christian context they could be a pagan's appeal, to a forerunner of Christ, to a Saviour whose nature he did not know.

These thoughts frame both the poem of 1914 and the *Silmarillion* account written many years later. In the latter Eärendil is not a Redeemer, but an Intercessor, unlike the true Messiah in that it is not his own sacrifice which persuades the Valar to change the sad history of Middle-earth, but still 'a man of sorrows, and acquainted with grief', hailed by Eönwë with eagle-like ambiguity (see p. 200 above) as 'the looked for that cometh at unawares, the longed for that cometh beyond hope'. In the former, it is perhaps the inadequacy of Eärendel that is more prominent than his partial success; at the end of the poem his light is blotted out by the greater light of dawn. However, one image is common to all Tolkien's versions and to the Old English poem too. This, one might say, is the 'lyric core', the flashpoint of the imagination. It is the vision of people looking up from the depths, *de profundis,* from the 'dark shadow of death' and of despair, and seeing a new light: 'unlooked for, glittering and bright; and the people of Middle-earth beheld it from afar and wondered, and they took it for a sign, and called it Gil-Estel, the Star of High Hope'. What the star was, how it was connected to Eärendil, how the name could cover both star and man, from what danger it signalled deliverance, whether that deliverance was final for the soulless elves . . . all these questions, and others, could find answers in the inventions of later narrative, in the different viewpoints of *The Silmarillion* or Bilbo's song in *The Fellowship of the Ring.* However, the image and the emotions associated with it did not change. They were central; part of Tolkien's 'data'; of the same order of importance as those other early captured scenes of Tinúviel dancing in the woods, Túrin answered by the 'cold voice' of his own sword, Valinor beyond the 'sunless lands' and 'dangerous seas'. If 'philosophical inquiries' provided material for Tolkien to brood on, these 'lyric cores' gave him the stimulus to go on brooding, to keep philosophy from aridness.

Characters and Cobwebs

Aridness is, however, a vice of which *The Silmarillion* stands accused: partly, no doubt, from a (mistaken) disappointment in those who wanted a second *Lord of the Rings,* but largely, as was said at the start of this chapter, because of the absence from it of 'mediators' like the hobbits and a generally novelistic mode of presentation. Much can be said about the 'meaning' of *The Silmarillion,* and more about its 'origins'. But it is more important in the end to get some idea of how to read it. And there are ways to appreciate *The Silmarillion* better, always provided that one is prepared to make certain basic assumptions.

One of these is that 'character' is in a sense fixed, static, even diagrammatic. Such was the common assumption of earlier times; as has been noted above, the modern saying that 'all power tends to corrupt' (with its assumption that character changes) is prefigured in Old English only by the saying that 'a man shows what he's like when he can do what he wants' (which assumes that changes are only apparent). The convention of Norse saga, then, is to say what a man is like as soon as he comes into the story: 'He was very hard to manage as he grew up, taciturn and unaffectionate, quarrelsome both in words and deeds' (Grettir, in *Grettir's saga*), or 'he had a crooked nose and teeth which stuck out, looked rather ugly in the mouth and yet extremely warlike' (Skarphethinn, in *Njál's saga*). These statements are always true, though there is still an interest, and a suspense, in seeing how events will prove them so. In *The Silmarillion*, Tolkien follows this convention closely: Fëanor 'was tall, and fair of face, and masterful, his eyes piercingly bright and his hair raven-dark; in the pursuit of all his purposes eager and steadfast. Few ever changed his courses by counsel, none by force'; or, later, 'Húrin was of less stature than his fathers, or his son after him; but he was tireless and enduring in body, lithe and swift after the manner of his mother's kin, Hareth of the Haladin'.

This second 'character-sketch' furthermore introduces another point in which *The Silmarillion* follows Norse belief, if not Norse convention: this is the conviction, shared also by the *Beowulf*-poet, that people are their heredity. Sagas commonly introduce characters with a list of their ancestors, often significant in their distinction, wisdom, ferocity or unreliability. Tolkien did not trespass so far on the short patience of modern times, but he did supply diagrams and family-trees: it is essential that these should be borne in mind. Thus one could easily say that the central tragedy of the Noldor is one between *sámmoeðri* and *sundrmoeðri*,[16] between full brothers, half-brothers and cousins, a tragedy of mixed blood. The 'Elves of the Light' are divided into three groups, in order of seniority, or wisdom, or attachment to the Valar: the Vanyar, Noldor, Teleri. Fëanor is pure Noldor on both sides, as are his sons. After the death of his mother, though, his father marries again, so that Fëanor has two half-brothers (Fingolfin, Finarfin). It is vital to remember that *their* mother is not of the Noldor, but of the 'senior' race of the Vanyar. While junior to Fëanor in birth and even in talent, therefore, his two half-brothers are marked from the beginning as superior to him in restraint and generosity. Their children are then again differentiated by a further 'out-breeding', in that Finarfin, of mixed descent himself, marries a wife from the 'junior' elvish branch, the Teleri; *his* sons and daughters, who are only a quarter Noldor — they include Finrod, Felagund and Galadriel — are more sympathetic than their uncle Fingolfin's children, such as the reckless Aredhel (mixed Noldor/Vanyar), and markedly more so than their other, pure-blooded Noldor cousins, the sons of Fëanor. One needs, perhaps, to ponder the diagram on p. 305 of *The Silmarillion* to see this clear. However, once the picture is clear one can appreciate the significance of some of Tolkien's oppositions — between Galadriel and Aredhel, for instance (bold as against rash), or between Finrod and Turgon (both founders of Hidden Kingdoms, but the latter retaining a connection with the higher wisdom of the Valar which the former, related to elves who refused the crossing to Aman, has given up). Nor do the oppositions stay on the level of diagram; they go on to shape narratives, and individual scenes.

The whole story of the ruin of Doriath, for instance, might be said to run from the moment when Caranthir, fourth son of Fëanor, reacts angrily to the fact that his Teleri-descended cousins have been talking to their maternal great-uncle Elwë Singollo (in Sindarin, Elu Thingol or 'Greycloak'), to whom he is not related at all. He says (p. 112):

> 'Let not the sons of Finarfin run hither and thither with their tales to this Dark Elf in his caves! Who made them our spokesman to deal with him? And though they be come indeed to Beleriand, let them not so swiftly forget that their father is a lord of the Noldor, though their mother be of other kin.'

The last clause is weighted with contempt — an improper contempt, if one remembers that the 'sons of Finarfin' have both 'junior' Teleri and 'senior' Vanyar blood from their mother and grandmother. There is a further irony in the phrase 'this Dark Elf in his caves', for though Elwë is king of the Dark Elves, he himself is not one, since he was one of the three origi- nal ambassadors to the light of Valinor, though his love for Melian kept him from returning to it. Fifty-six pages earlier we were told that he alone of his people had seen 'the Trees in the day of their flowering, and king though he was of Úmanyar, he was not accounted among the Moriquendi, but with the Elves of the Light . . .' The reader who has forgotten his genealogies, or forgotten the original embassy to Valinor, or never realised the equation of 'Dark Elves' and 'Moriquendi', is left at a loss. The tension of the moment, the skewed relation between truth and whole truth, pass him by. And once the thread is lost, the bitter resentment of Angrod seventeen pages later, the cold mood in which Nargothrond is founded by Angrod's brother Finrod, the whole structure indeed of *The Silmarillion* lose their connections and begin to seem mere happenstance.

An underlying stasis has to be picked out from genealo- gies, positions on the order of march to and from Valinor, rela- tionships of all kinds. Yet once that has been done, it is possi- ble to see a kind of dynamism in *The Silmarillion,* a chain of causes and effects. As often with Norse saga, a good question to keep asking is, with each disaster, 'Who is to blame?' Answers are never simple. Take, for instance, the fall of Gondolin, the 'Hidden City' of which Tolkien had written as far back as 1917, and which had made its way even into *The Hobbit*. It was founded by Turgon under the direct guidance of the Valar, and from it comes in the end the stock of Eärendil, the Intercessor. How was it betrayed to Morgoth? Unfolding the answer takes in much of *The Silmarillion,* but one can say that again it turns on a 'lyric core', and a conflict of kinship.

The 'lyric core' is the single scene in which Húrin, 'mighti- est of the warriors of mortal Men', having sat twenty-eight years as Morgoth's prisoner observing the torments of his race, is released to wander. Neither elves nor men will take him in. He remembers his boyhood stay in Gondolin, as also the fact that he was captured, and his house destroyed, while covering the retreat of Turgon at the Fen of Serech. He goes there- fore towards Gondolin, hoping the eagles will carry him to it. But though the eagles see him and tell Turgon, the king of

Gondolin refuses to trust the man who saved him once; and when he changes his mind, after sitting 'long in thought', it is too late:

> For Húrin stood in despair before the silent cliffs of the Echoriath, and the westering sun, piercing the clouds, stained his white hair with red. Then he cried aloud in the wilderness, heedless of any ears, and he cursed the pitiless land; and standing at last upon a high rock he looked towards Gondolin and called in a great voice: 'Turgon, Turgon, remember the Fen of Serech! O Turgon, will you not hear in your hidden halls?' But there was no sound save the wind in the dry grasses. 'Even so they hissed in Serech at the sunset', he said; and as he spoke the sun went behind the Mountains of Shadow, and a darkness fell about him, and the wind ceased, and there was silence in the waste.
>
> Yet there were ears that heard the words that Húrin spoke, and report of all came soon to the Dark Throne in the north; and Morgoth smiled. (p. 228)

Obviously, everything in this scene is emblematic. Even narrative almost disappears, for the 'long' and thoughtful delay of Turgon seems to take no time at all. Húrin is in the same place, listening to the same 'hissing' wind, after the delay as before. In fact Turgon's pause is there only to allow him to make a fateful decision and then regret it — or, one might say, to prove the adjective 'pitiless' in the passage quoted. It is not the land which has no pity, but Turgon, and the elves and men who rejected Húrin earlier. By similar transference cliffs are 'silent', grasses 'dry', the red sunset and white hair stand for future catastrophe and present despair, while the sun behind 'Shadow' marks the beginning of the end for Gondolin, as it revives the memory of a past sunset of defeat. Over all hangs the implication that the real sunset is in Húrin's heart, a loss of hope to elvish, and natural, indifference. And yet the indifference is an illusion, the silence full of ears, the despair a fatal mistake . . .

The scene is a picture, a posed *tableau*. Yet it centres on an outcry of spontaneous passion (like so many scenes of medieval romance). Dynamism is generated from it as soon as one asks the question, 'Whose fault?' Húrin's, for despair? Turgon's, for suspicion? One could even blame the rulers of Do-riath, for the true embitterment of Húrin's heart lies in the death of Túrin his son, in which many were involved. A full answer would consist of the whole unhappy history of Middle-earth. Yet that general answer still has to be reinforced by indi-vidual weakness, which is the true irony and wretchedness of the single scene. And still this is only a part of the fall of Gondolin. A second strand leads from Maeglin, spun once more from the strains of mixed blood.

Maeglin is the son of Turgon's sister Aredhel, carried off by Eöl, 'Dark Elf' *par excellence*, one of those who never went to Valinor and saw all the elves who returned as disposses-sors. In a sense that dispossession is the ultimate source of all Maeglin's treachery, and yet it too has to be magnified by a chain of individual sins or errors. One is the forced detention of Aredhel by Eöl; this means that father is resented by son, son in the end cursed prophetically by father. Another, though, is the pride of the sons of Fëanor, who (as with Thingol) will not recognise kinship except by blood. Eöl's relationship to them by marriage is ignored. Curufin tells him, 'You have my leave but not my love . . . The sooner you depart from my land the better will it please me' (p. 135). The *Macbeth*-style play on words is returned by Eöl (with a memory indeed of *Hamlet*), 'It is good, Lord Curufin, to find a *kin*sman thus *kindly* at need' (my italics). But the sarcasm only provokes outright dis-claimer: 'Those who steal the daughters of the Noldor . . . do not gain kinship with their kin.' It is significant that Turgon, though more injured than Curufin, does not make the same mistake and opens his speech, 'Welcome, kinsman, for so I hold you . . .' But by this time Eöl is embittered and refuses the relationship in his turn. He was at fault to begin with; Curufin has made matters worse; finally one could simply put the blame on Aredhel. She left Gondolin pridefully, against advice, and turned away from her wiser brothers to her more dangerous cousins, prompted by desire in the heart (p. 131), the evil at-traction of Fëanorian fieriness. Her breach of the orders of Turgon is echoed by her son Maeglin 111 pages later, when he too goes illegally beyond 'the leaguer of the hills', to be caught by Morgoth and made a traitor. Even his motivation is multi-ple: fear, but also jealousy of Tuor the mortal, imperfect loyalty to a grandfather who killed his father, the ambitious desire for Idril which seems a last reflection of the Sindar desire to get their lands back from their supplanters. Húrin, Maeglin, Aredhel, Eöl, Curufin, Turgon: all interact to create the fall of Gondolin. In each case, one may say, character remains fixed, but its flaws (or strengths) are brought to light by the strains of action.

The Silmarillion is even more tightly constructed than The Lord of the Rings, and it would be easy to trace its entrelacements further: Gondolin, for instance, is only one of three Hidden Kingdoms, Gondolin, Nargothrond, Doriath, founded by three relatives (Turgon, Finrod, Thingol), each ruined and betrayed, each penetrated by a mortal (Tuor, Túrin, Beren), well-meaning but carrying a seed of destruction, and all three mortals related by blood (S, p. 307) and with their fates to some degree intertwined. The book is in fact a 'web'. But that word does not so readily take the meaning of 'woven tapestry' as it did in The Lord of the Rings (see p. 130 above). Rather it keeps its familiar sense of 'cobweb', a trap spun by a great spider. In spite of Eärendil, the later-published work feels blacker and grimmer than the earlier; the sense that 'chance' or 'luck' may contain a providential element is not so strong. Much of Tolkien's tonal intention for The Silmarillion can indeed be deduced by looking through its threads at his archaic alternatives for 'luck', the words 'fate' and 'doom'.

Etymologies and Ambiguities

Neither of these words is used in modern English any more, though phrases like 'fatal accident' or 'doomed to disaster' survive. The reason for their unpopularity lies in their etymology. 'Fate' is derived, as the OED says, from Latin fari, 'to speak', and means originally 'that which has been spoken', i.e. spoken by the gods. It has never been anything but a literary word in English. 'Doom' by contrast is native, the modern pronunciation of Old English dóm, a noun related to the verb déman, 'to judge'. It too meant in early times what was spoken, what people said about you (especially once you were dead), but it had also the meaning of a judicial sentence, a law or a decision. If the king sentenced you to death, that was his 'doom', his decision, but of course it was your doom too, your now-determined fate. Judgement Day, the day at the end of the world when all souls will be tried and sentenced, was accordingly in Old English *dómesdæg,* 'Doomsday', which only strengthened the sense of 'future disaster' attached to the word. However, common to both words, 'fate' and 'doom', is the idea of a Power sitting above mortals and ruling their lives by its sentence or by its speech alone. This sense is completely absent from 'luck' or 'chance'; and with the waning of belief in superior Powers the more neutral words have become the common ones.

In *The Silmarillion,* though (unlike *The Lord of the Rings*), the influence of the Valar for good or ill is prominent, so that 'fate' and 'doom' become once again etymologically appropriate words, to be used frequently and with a complexity which determines the tone of several of its component stories. To take the simplest example, 'fate' in the story 'Of Beren and Lúthien' seems to have two meanings, related but separable even by grammar. On the one hand fate is an external force, which could without difficulty be capitalised: 'fate drove' Carcharoth the wolf through the protecting spells of Melian, and Beren managed the same feat because he was 'defended by fate'. There are many more occasions, though, when 'fate' does not seem a proper name, a word for some external Power, but rather the personal possession of someone or something: to it must be attached *either* a personal pronoun ('my fate', 'his fate', 'your fate') *or* another noun in the genitive case ('the fate of Arda', 'the fate of a mightier realm', 'the fates of Beren and Lúthien') *or else* an identifying relative clause ('the fate that was laid on him', 'the fate that lies before you'). What all these uses suggest is that fate is not something external and organising, like Providence, but something individual, like 'life' — something, however, unlike 'life', which *has been organised.* The very use of the word thus brings up a question of free will.

The word 'doom', in *The Silmarillion,* is more complicated. It too can appear as an overmastering Power: when Lúthien first sees Beren 'doom fell upon her', a phrase also found in Aragorn's 'Lay of Tinúviel' in *The Lord of the Rings.* However, it can be something much more elementary, retaining its basic meaning of a sentence or a decision: in the *Narn i Hîn Húrin* in the *Unfinished Tales* we find Thingol holding 'a court of doom', waiting 'to pronounce his doom', and saying 'otherwise shall my doom now be', or to paraphrase 'I am now going to change my sentence'. Much more often, though, the reader cannot make a clear decision as to the word's meaning. The sense of 'future disaster' is present: when Thingol challenges Beren to recover a Silmaril, the narrator says, 'Thus he wrought the doom of Doriath', and means that Doriath will be ruined by Thingol's words. So, when Melian says to him a few lines later (p. 168), 'You have doomed either your daughter, or yourself', she could mean either that he has given a judicial decision on Lúthien (old sense), or condemned himself to death (modern sense), or of course both, since both are true. There is a sense also in which 'doom' is a personal attribute, like 'my fate' or 'my life', but blacker and more hostile: 'So their doom willed it', says the narrator, as Beren and Lúthien make the fatal decision to go home, and Thingol recognises when he sees them that 'their doom might not be withstood by any power of the world'. What does it mean, then, when Beren says, 'Now is the Quest achieved . . . and my doom full-wrought'? That sentence on him has finally been executed? Or that disaster has come at last? Or that his life has now reached a proper close, with all debts paid, promises and curses fulfilled? All these meanings are present, as they are in many instances in *The Silmarillion*; 'doom' and 'fate' determine the tone especially of the stories of Beren and of Túrin Turambar.

What these words imply is in a sense illogical or self-contradictory. They indicate the presence of controlling powers, in whose toils the heroes are 'caught', 'meshed', 'ensnared'; yet people can be told, as Túrin is, 'the doom lies in yourself'. 'Fate' and 'doom' may be 'wrought' or 'devised' by people, and yet can take on a volition of their own; they 'lie' on characters, 'fall' on them, 'lead' them, but can at least in thought be 'turned from' or 'denied'. Túrin calls himself 'Turambar', 'Master of Doom', only to have the boast thrown back in his epitaph *A Túrin Turambar turún' ambartanen,* 'Master of Doom, by doom mastered'. Are people free to determine their own fate, one might ask, or are they 'the stars' tennis-balls, struck and bandied/Which way please them'? To accept the second alternative would have been, for Tolkien, to go against an orthodox Christian doctrine; to state the first positively would have lost for him that sense of interlacing, of things working themselves out, of a poetic justice seen only in the large scale, to which he had been attached from near the start of his career.

The denial of logic, it may be added, is an ancient one, found in Old English, but part of the fibre of the Norse 'family sagas', which Tolkien had imitated in other ways. In the *Saga of Gísli Súrsson,* Gísli sends a warning to his brother-in-law Vesteinn to say if he comes home he will be killed. But the messengers ride along the top of a sandhill while he rides below it, and so miss him. When they catch up he says: 'I would have turned back if you had met me earlier, but now all the streams run towards Dyrafjord and I shall ride there. And in any case I want to.' He goes on, and is killed. In his decision there is a strand of volition, for he says he wants to; one of pride, for he would not like to be seen turning back; one of chance in the way the messengers miss him. However, the centre of his speech is the remark about watersheds, and while this could be taken as merely practical, expressing the difficulty of travel in mountainous Iceland, all readers automatically take it as a sign of surrender to some superior force of embroilment. 'The words of fate will be said by someone', Gísli had remarked earlier. Individual will and external force, in other words, notoriously cooperate.

One sees in all this an echo of that dualism which had produced the Ring as hostile presence and psychic amplifier, or Sauron as enemy and as tempter. However, it is enough to say that in his tales of heroes in *The Silmarillion* (and the *Unfinished Tales*), Tolkien was aiming at a tone, or perhaps better a 'taste', which he knew well but which had fallen outside the range of modern literature: a tone of stoicism, regret, inquiry, above all of awe moderated by complete refusal to be intimidated. The complexities of 'fate' and 'doom' show us the intention clearly enough. But, one must ask, how far is that intention realised: especially in those early and central tales of heroic mortals, 'Of Beren and Lúthien' in *The Silmarillion* and (in its two main prose versions in *The Silmarillion* and *Unfinished Tales*) 'Of Túrin Turambar'?

The Tale of Beren

Opinions here may vary: and I come now to one place where I feel that Tolkien would not have agreed with the opinions I express. He clearly valued the tale of Beren and Lúthien in some ways above anything else he wrote, and he wrote it many times over: in 1917, when it was 'The Tale of Tinúviel' *(Lost Tales 2)*; in 1925, as the poem 'Light as Leaf on Lindentree', rewritten as Aragorn's 'Song of Beren and Lúthien' in *The Fellowship of the Ring*; in the early 1930s as 'The Lay of Leithian' in *Lays of Beleriand,* and repeatedly (1926, 1930, 1937, and in the 1950s) in the earlier and later versions of 'The Silmarillion'. If one adds in all the annals and epitomes, we have more than a dozen versions of the story besides chapter 19 of *The Silmarillion,* the only full rendering to become familiar; some of their complex interrelations are discussed in chapter 9 below. The tale was furthermore one of Tolkien's first inspirations, based (see *Biography,* pp. 104–5) on a vision of his own wife; to that vision he remained loyal all his life, for through all the rewritings he never changed some essential features; he remained loyal to it even after death, for his tombstone and his wife's read 'Beren' and 'Lúthien', a striking identification. Yet the tale as it emerged eventually in *The Silmarillion* has several faults, perhaps indeed connected with its early conception and long incubation.

It contains, to begin with, a strong element of duplication. Thus Beren, once he knows he has to win a Silmaril from the Iron Crown, goes to get help, only to fail, to be captured with Finrod and to be rescued from the 'Isle of the Werewolves' by Lúthien and the hound Huan. He goes into the woods to spend an idyllic season with Lúthien. But then the pattern repeats itself. He leaves Lúthien again, to go into the enemy's country, but is overtaken by her and Huan once more. They gain the Silmaril, lose it to the wolf and then retire again to the woods and 'houseless lands', still with survival but without victory. The pattern is completed when Huan fights Carcharoth to recover the Silmaril, repeating his earlier battle against Carcharoth's sire Draugluin. Two wolf-fights, three scenes of the power of song (including Sauron's defeat of Finrod), three woodland idylls, two pursuits and rescues by Lúthien . . . Beren meanwhile is wounded three times, twice by Carcharoth, once by Celegorm, and interposes himself twice between dart and Lúthien, wolf's teeth and Thingol. Three times Huan speaks, to advise Lúthien, to advise Beren, to bid farewell. Simultaneously the plot is traversed by the evil sons of Fëanor, Celegorm and Curufin: they capture Lúthien by coincidence on p. 173, and meet her and Beren by coincidence once again, after the rescue from Tol-in-Gaurhoth. Though they provide the knife Angrist that would cleave iron 'as if it were green wood', the scenes they contribute cost a good deal in contrivance. In 'Beren and Lúthien' as a whole there is too much plot.

The other side of that criticism is that on occasion Tolkien has to be rather brisk with his own inventions. Celegorm wounds Beren, and the hound Huan turns on his master and pursues him: 'returning he brought to Lúthien a herb out of the forest. With that leaf she staunched Beren's wound, and by her arts and her love she healed him . . .' The motif of the healing herb is a common one, the centre for instance of the Breton lai of *Eliduc* (turned into *conte* by Marie de France). But in that it occupies a whole scene, if not a whole poem. In *The Silmarillion* it appears only to be dismissed in two lines, while Beren's wound is inflicted and healed in five. Repeatedly one has this sense of summary. Christopher Tolkien points out, indeed (*BLT 2*, p. 57) that 'summary' is exactly right, for *The Silmarillion* is a summary and was even designed to feel like a summary, a compilation made much later than the events by one looking back over a great gap of time. In 'The Lay of Leithian', by contrast, the scene of the healing herb takes up more than sixty lines and the best part of two pages; see *Lays,* pp. 266–67. Just the same, the sense of briskness remains, as does a feeling here and there (rather surprising in what is overall a gloomy tale) of easy victory. Carcharoth is the Red Maw and the Jaws of Thirst, but when Lúthien stands before him her inner power fells him 'as though lightning had smitten him'. The blindness, anxiety and dark dreams of Morgoth are built up better, as is the thawing of Thingol's heart when he sees Beren's mutilation. However, the scene in the Halls of Mandos, when Lúthien moves the Lord of the Dead to pity, was beyond attempting, as Tolkien realised. One might say that this tale, more than any other of *The Silmarillion,* depends for success on its 'lyric core', the songs of Finrod, Sauron, Beren and of Lúthien before Morgoth and before Mandos. However, these could not be provided. One has to take the will for the deed.

A further criticism, and perhaps a connected one, is that in 'Beren and Lúthien' Tolkien had not yet freed himself from his many sources — as if trying to bring in all the bits of older literature that he liked instead of forging a story with an impetus of its own. The framework of the tale is the legend of Orpheus, the singer who challenges the power of the Underworld to rescue his wife. To this the Middle English 'lay' of *Sir Orfeo* had added the motif of the Rash Promise, by which the king of the Underworld — in *Sir Orfeo* the elf-king — has to stand by an undertaking carelessly worded. Tolkien picked this up too, converting it into the oath of Thingol (which provokes a corresponding oath from Beren). But around this we have the wizards' singing-contests (from the *Kalevala*), the werewolves devouring bound men in the dark (from the *Saga of the Volsungs*), the rope of hair let down from a window (the Grimms' 'Rapunzel'), the 'shadowy cloak' of sleep and invisibility which recalls the **heoloðhelm of* the Old English *Genesis B.* The hunting of the great wolf reminds one of the chase of the boar Twrch Trwyth in the Welsh *Mabinogion,* while the motif of 'the hand in the wolf's mouth' is one of the most famous parts of the *Prose Edda,* told of Fenris Wolf and the god Tyr; Huan recalls several faithful hounds of legend, Garm, Gelert, Cafall. Of course old motifs often do their work, as when the Iron Crown rolls on the silent floor of Thangorodrim, or Lúthien's rope of hair sways with more-than-elvish 'glamour' above the heads of her guards. However, some of them could have been omitted. The effect is lavish where it ought to be spare.

The strength of the tale lies perhaps in its interweavings around the central fable. Its heart — as the tale stands in *The Silmarillion,* but see further pp. 314–17 below — is the 'rash promise' of Thingol, 'Bring to me in your hand a Silmaril from Morgoth's crown; and then, if she will, Lúthien may set her hand in yours', with the countervailing promise by Beren, to be fulfilled in letter only and not spirit, 'When we meet again my hand shall hold a Silmaril'. The tale works through to the ironic fulfilment of both. However, as it works other strands are drawn in, to raise, increasingly, retrospective questions. Oaths are commonly regretted in this story. Finrod's oath 'of abiding friendship and aid in every need to Barahir and all his kin' was made in gratitude and affection, but when it comes to redeeming it he is sad for others rather than himself. What makes matters worse is that he had foreseen his own rashness long before, saying to Galadriel, 'An oath I too shall swear, and must be free to fulfil it, and go into darkness. Nor shall anything of my realm endure that a son should inherit.' How great the gratitude to overcome that foreboding; how much greater the disaster to quench that gratitude! Spontaneous motivations come to seem weak, and by reflection from the case of Finrod one may begin to wonder about others. The reaction of the sons of Fëanor against Beren seems spontaneous, but the narrator adds as gloss, 'the curse of Mandos came upon [them]'. If one looks back one sees that that curse dictates failure 'by treason of kin unto kin', and the sons of Fëanor plot treason against their cousin Finrod, grandson of another mother. They remember also that since the rescue of Maedhros they have been 'the Dispossessed'. Jealousy of Finrod, then, creeps into their contempt for Beren. From that jealousy Doriath will fall, and the sons of Fëanor themselves die.

But since motivations are so opaque one may look back at the offer of Thingol, the very heart of the story. To demand a Silmaril for Lúthien could be a fair offer: so Beren pretends to take it, calling it a 'little price'. In fact, as everyone sees, it is an attempt to commit murder in circumvention of the earlier, regretted oath not to kill Beren himself. Beneath that, though, there may be a yet worse motive; the sudden 'desire' for a Silmaril could contain a genuine impulse of greed beneath a calculated impulse of hatred. In that case Beren's insulting suggestion that Thingol values his daughter no more than a 'thing made by craft' would be true, if unconscious. The end of that strand is 65 pages later, when the dwarves in their turn seek 'a pretext and fair cloak for their true intent' in 'desiring' the Silmaril, and Thingol, like Beren before him, answers scornfully. His desire is like theirs, though, not like Beren's. So his death 'in the deep places of Menegroth', far from the light which he alone of his kingdom had seen, becomes an analogue of his descent to greed and cunning.

Words overpower intentions. In any case intentions are not always known to the intenders. This is the sense of 'doom' which Tolkien strives to create from oaths and curses and bargains, and from the interweaving of the fates of objects, people and kingdoms. At moments in the tale 'Of Beren and Lúthien' it comes through strongly.

'Túrin Turambar turún' ambartanen'

For a successful striking of the note, however, one has to wait for the story 'Of Túrin Turambar' in *The Silmarillion,* or better still, for the longer version of it in the *Unfinished Tales,* the *Narn i Hîn Húrin.* The existence of these two variants immediately makes several points about Tolkien's way of working. One is that 'Of Túrin' has been selectively compressed with regard to its major features; the interest in 'doom' is proclaimed by Túrin's final nickname 'Master of Doom', yet in the *Silmarillion* version the word is used only some ten times in 29 pages, considerably less than in the slightly shorter chapter 'Of Beren and Lúthien'. The *Narn* adds many more references, some of them prominent. It makes one wonder what the tale of Beren would be like if we had a full or final version, developed to the same extent as the *Narn.* A second point is that both accounts of Túrin seem to have digested their source much more fully than the *Silmarillion* account of Beren. The basic outline of the tale owes much to the 'Story of Kullervo' in the *Kalevala,* which Tolkien had begun to work on perhaps as early as 1912. In both a hero survives the ruin of his family to grow up with a cruel, wayward streak in fosterage; in both he marries (or seduces) a lost maiden, only for her to discover she is his sister and drown herself; in both the hero returns from his exploits to find his mother gone and home laid waste, and to be condemned by his own associates. Kullervo's dog leads him only to the place where he met his sister, and like Túrin, when he asks his sword if it will drink his blood, it agrees scornfully:

'Wherefore at thy heart's desire
Should I not thy flesh devour,
And drink up thy blood so evil?
I who guiltless flesh have eaten,
Drank the blood of those who sinned not?'[17]

But for all these points of derivation, 'Túrin' goes beyond 'Beren' in neatness of structure. It is striking, though, that its true point becomes clear (to all but extremely perceptive eyes) only in the *Narn*.

The *Narn i Hîn Húrin* centres on Tolkien's favourite question of how corruption worked, how far evil had power over the resisting mind. Possibly the most important scene added to the *Narn,* and not present in *The Silmarillion,* is the one in which Morgoth debates with his captive Húrin on top of the 'Hill of Tears', looking out over the kingdoms of the world like Christ and Satan in *Paradise Regained*. Morgoth's temptation is perfunctory, however. His *threat* is that he will ruin Húrin's family and break them on his will 'though you all were made of steel'. He cannot do it, says Húrin, having no power to 'govern them from afar'. He has a power of clouds and shadows, asserts Morgoth: 'Upon all whom you love my thought shall weigh as a cloud of Doom'. Húrin refuses to accept this last intangible, and claims that whatever happens, Morgoth cannot pursue men beyond death and beyond 'the Circles of the World'. This is not denied, any more than it is denied that Húrin's family are free to resist. However, the scene leaves a feeling that Morgoth is not entirely a liar, and that when he says Húrin does not understand the power of the Valar (including himself) he may be telling the truth. The power of the Valar, however, as one may remember from the 'oliphaunt' scene in *The Two Towers,* is to be equated with 'chance'.

Chance indeed seems to control the tragedy of Túrin. He takes the seat of Saeros (in the *Narn*) 'by ill-luck'. This leads to Saeros's taunting, Túrin's violent reply, the death of Saeros and expulsion of Túrin; so, stage by stage, to the fall of Nargothrond and ruin of Doriath. It is likewise a coincidence that orcs come on Nienor as she is led back from meeting the dragon; 'Ill chance', says Melian. It is a further ill chance that Nienor meets her brother exactly on the spot where his sentiments are most stirred, the grave of the woman he betrayed. At the same place Túrin meets Mablung, the one person who can confirm the secret he has been told. 'What a sweet grace of fortune!' he cries, with hysterical irony. 'Some strange and dreadful thing has chanced', says Mablung. The plot of the *Narn* seems to work on coincidence.

But what *is* a coincidence (a question traditional in Oxford philosophy examinations)? Throughout the *Narn* there is a strong tendency, just as in *The Lord of the Rings* (see pp. 152–53 above), to give double explanations of what happens. Thus Túrin's boyhood friend Sador Lobadal has been lamed 'by illluck or the mishandling of his axe'. It might seem hardly material which it was; but if it were the latter, one might say his pain was his own fault, as Túrin's mother Morwen claims: 'He is self-maimed by his own want of skill, and he is slow with his tasks, for he spends much time on trifles unbidden.' Túrin's father puts in a plea for good intentions: 'An honest hand and a true heart may hew amiss'. Character is fate, says one; accidents will happen, says the other. The narrator keeps on expressing no opinion. Túrin escapes from Dor-lómin 'by fate and courage', Túrin and Hunthor cross the Teiglin 'by skill and hardihood, or by fate', Túrin survives the illness that killed his sister, 'for such was his fate and the strength of life that was in him'. 'Fate' can always be offered as an explanation, it seems; but the word may mean nothing, be just what people say when they cannot find a better one.

There is a third possibility, which is that Morgoth was exactly what he said he was, 'master of the fates of Arda'. *He* could have turned Sador's axe. He *did* send the plague that carried off Lalaith. He could have had *something* to do with Saeros. The latter's motivation is clearly largely his own, based on pride, jealousy, resentment of Beren and consequently all Beren's kin. However, after he has spoken the words that provoke Turin's outburst Mablung says, 'I think that some shadow of the North has reached out to touch us tonight. Take heed, Saeros son of Ithilbor, lest you do the will of Morgoth in your pride'. The 'shadow' is not the jealousy, but Saeros's accidental touching on Túrin's sorest spot, his sense of having deserted mother and sister. 'If the Men of Hithlum are so wild and fell, of what sort are the women of that land? Do they run like deer clad only in their hair?' Being hunted with hounds was Sador's explanation to Túrin of what it might be to be a thrall. It remains a possibility for Morwen and Nienor. The hunted woman with her clothes torn instantly sends Túrin into a fury among the Gaurwaith. And before the end Nienor *does* appear as a quarry, flying naked 'as a beast that is hunted to heart-bursting' — perhaps that is what stirs Túrin's pity into love. One might say that this image, this fear, haunts the whole tale. For Saeros to pick on it unwittingly seems indeed more than chance. Morgoth put the words in his mouth; they are 'the words of fate', which will be spoken by someone, exactly as the Icelandic hero Gísli said.

Responsibility for *saying* them, however, remains on Saeros, and Túrin's reaction too is largely his own fault. There is a cruel and morbid streak in the stripping and hunting of his enemy, even if it was meant to end short of death. Túrin repeatedly strikes too soon, at Saeros, Forweg, Beleg, Brandir, in the end himself. Where does this element come from? The *Narn* offers two answers, one reaching towards a kind of 'characterisation', the other more simply genetic. Like so many others in *The Silmarillion,* Túrin is a hybrid, his father of the house of Hador — fair, masterful, 'quick to anger and to laughter' — his mother of the house of Bëor, dark, clever, inveterate, 'moved sooner to pity than to laughter . . . most like to the Noldor and most loved by them'. One might use an ancient racial stereotype and say that the one line seems 'Germanic', the other 'Celtic'. Túrin, dark, taciturn and slow to forget, clearly takes after his mother, though he has his father's soft-heartedness. In a way his life is a struggle between two sets of impulses; and another fact clearer in *Narn* than *Silmarillion* is that the impulses that come from Morwen are wrong. If one starts to disentangle the threads of blame for the fate of Túrin, Morwen holds a considerable share. Her husband's advice to her was *'Do not wait!'* She remembers this after his defeat, but does not obey — partly from fear for her unborn child, partly from hope that Húrin will come back, but largely from pride: 'She would not yet humble her pride to be an alms-guest, not even of a king. Therefore the voice of Húrin . . . was denied, and the first strand of the fate of Túrin was woven.'

So mother and son are separated. Pride keeps up the separation, and separation generates the fear that turns Túrin savage. The pride which Túrin inherits from his mother also makes him refuse pardon; and with it comes, not cowardice, but something less than the dauntlessness of his father. 'My father is not afraid', says Túrin, 'and I will not be; or at least, as my mother, I will be afraid and not show it.' But he does show it. Glaurung the dragon, like Saeros, strikes the hidden fear when he calls Túrin 'deserter of thy kin'; and so Túrin abandons Finduilas to save Morwen, comes too late to do anything but doom Aerin and then falls into despair, rejecting the obvious solution of following his mother and sister to safety. 'I cast a shadow wherever I dwell. Let Melian keep them! And I will leave them in peace unshadowed for a while.' 'Shadow' is an ominous word; it may not come from Túrin. Similarly Morwen falls into despair and rushes from security to her own death and her daughter's abandonment. Pride and fear, then, combine in mother and son to separate them and keep them apart. The 'thought of Morgoth' may influence their 'fates' and 'dooms', but also they take after each other, they co-operate.

The other fatal element in Túrin's character centres on the perception that in him something is missing: he is only half a man. This idea Tolkien clearly took from Norse sources, for instance from the famous *Saga of Egill Skallagrimsson*. In that saga Egill's grandfather is Kveld-Úlfr ('Evening-Wolf'), not entirely human, 'a great shape-changer', very like Beorn in *The Hobbit*. Kveld-Úlfr has two sons, Thórólfr and Skalla-Grímr ('Bald-Grim'), and the latter has two sons as well, Thórólfr junior and Egill himself. In each generation there is one fair, handsome, cheerful brother — these are the two Thórólfrs — and one like Egill or Grímr who is big, bald, ugly, overbearing and greedy. As long as the handsome brother is alive the other can be kept in check, but when his own magnanimity kills him, the brother who carries the marks of ogre descent becomes worse. So, in the saga, Egill sits silent and morose at the feast after Thórólfr's death, half-drawing his sword and then slamming it back, alternately raising and lowering his eyebrows; his mood remains dangerous till the king of England quietly begins to load him with gold and silver. Túrin, admittedly, is not as bad as that. Nevertheless, he has lost something — his sis-

ter Urwen or Lalaith, an analogue of Thórólfr, an image of
Túrin's paternal side in her fairness, her merriment, her ability
to charm. Lalaith, we are told, means 'laughter'. When she dies
of the Evil Breath his nurse tells Túrin, 'Speak no more of
Lalaith . . . of your sister Urwen you must ask tidings of your
mother'. Obviously the capital letter could be removed, and in
that sense the sentence would still be true — 'speak no more
of laughter' — and be obeyed. Túrin hardly ever laughs, and
when he does it is 'bitter' or 'shrill': he is a fraction of a personality, bereft of 'fairness' or ability to see 'the bright side' (which
is why his second sister, Nienor, also golden-haired, has such
fatal attraction for him). Filling out this sense of an imperfect
humanity is Túrin's affinity with evil, made concrete in his
weapons — the Black Sword of Beleg, which kills him in the
end, and even more the Dragon-helm of Dor-lómin.

This too is clearly based on a Norse idea, or word. In the
Eddic poem *Fáfnismál* the dragon boasts of bearing an *ægishjálmr,* a 'helmet of fear', over all the race of men. Is this a
word for something intangible, awe or horror, or for some object that produces that effect, perhaps the 'dragon-mask' itself,
the sight of the dragon's face?† Certainly both Nienor and
Túrin are bespelled when they stare into the dragon's eyes and
feel his 'fell spirit'; it seems that Túrin's heirloom is designed
to counterfeit this effect, its image of Glaurung striking 'fear
into the hearts of all beholders'. But is it right for heroes to use
an *ægishjálmr?* Sigurthr in the Norse poem had thought not,
insisting that one would be no protection against true courage.
Húrin seems to agree, declaring, 'I would rather look on my
foes with my true face'. Túrin, however, is prepared to use the
tactics of the enemy, fear and 'terrorism', and by doing so plays
into Morgoth's hands. It seems clear (from p. 153 of the *Unfin-*

---

† For some reason, several medieval words mean both 'mask' and 'ghost':
Latin *mascha, larva,* but also the Old English word *gríma* (as in Gríma Wormtongue). *Gríma,* however, is also applied to helmets; the Anglo-Saxon helmet
found at Sutton Hoo is a mask as well. In conjunctions the words suggest a
buried memory of a fearsome, uncanny war-mask, linked with belief in dragons. See also the Nazgûl in *The Two Towers,* p. 691, 'helmed and crowned with
fear', and note 6 to chapter 5 above.

ished Tales) that Tolkien meant the acceptance of the name Gorthol, 'Dread Helm', to mark a stage in Túrin's corruption. Certainly the decision to reveal himself seems the last stage in a progress from pity to fear, to despair, to a compensating rashness and that 'Ragnarök-spirit' which Tolkien had condemned elsewhere, a sign of courage without self-confidence or that ultimate hope Húrin had expressed on top of the 'Hill of Tears'.

Túrin's tragedy is silently opposed by the actions and fate of his cousin Tuor, whose path intersects with Túrin's at one point (see p. 239 of *The Silmarillion,* and pp. 37–38 of *Unfinished Tales*). The one relies on himself, the other on the Valar; the one brings hope to Middle-earth by his descendant Eärendil, the other leaves nothing behind. Yet the moral of the tale of Túrin remains uncertain in all versions: much is his fault, much the fault of the 'malice' that emanates from Morgoth — a word used repeatedly in the *Narn,* a word which the *OED* interestingly notes as having a sense in English law as 'that kind of evil intent which constitutes the aggravation of guilt distinctive of certain offences'. Malice turns manslaughter into murder, turns accident into crime; in the same way one feels that the circumstances of Túrin's life would have been similar in any case, but that his resentful attitude makes matters qualitatively worse. Had he any right to call himself *Turambar,* 'Master of Doom'? In the sense that he had free will, that he could have changed his attitudes, yes. However, 'Doom' is equated in the Narn with 'the Dark Shadow', and that Shadow knows how to turn strength to weakness. That is why the 'Master of Doom' ends 'by doom mastered'; it is an inextricably blended process of temptation and assault. The ironies of the tale of Túrin, one is meant to see, are constructed by Morgoth.

In places in this tale Tolkien comes close to superstition — unlucky objects, inherited failings, changing one's name to change one's luck, and so on. To that extent the *Narn i Hîn Húrin,* like *The Lord of the Rings,* approaches fairy-tale. At the same time one ought to recognise that it is capable, in its most fully worked-up passages, of exposing exactly the type of subtle internal treachery which has been the staple of the English novel since its inception. 'What is fate?' asks Túrin as a child. He might as well have asked, 'How are the heroes betrayed?', a question as applicable to him as to that other victim of 'dark imaginings', Othello. Finally one should note that, just as *Hamlet* peeped out of the tale of Eöl, so *Macbeth* was once more in Tolkien's mind with Túrin. At the end Túrin comes to the gorge of Cabed-en-Anas, and sees 'that all the trees near and far were withered, and their sere leaves fell mournfully' (*UT*, p. 145, cp. *S*, p. 225). He might well have said, 'My way of life / Is fall'n into the sere, the yellow leaf'. Like Macbeth, he has been caught in a web of prophecy and inner weakness, has slid down the scale from 'man' to 'monster', and to murderer. The best epitaph he might have chosen for himself is Macbeth's vaunt:

> 'The mind I sway by, and the heart I bear,
> Shall never sag with doubt nor shake with fear.'

Both tales are about the hardening of the heart.

Some Conclusions

The Silmarillion as a whole (and by this I mean as well those variants of its component parts printed in the *Unfinished Tales*) shows two of Tolkien's great strengths. One is 'inspiration': he was capable of producing, from some recess of the mind, images, words, phrases, scenes in themselves irresistibly compelling — Lúthien watched among the hemlocks by Beren, Húrin calling to the cliffs, Thingol's death in the dark while he looks at the captured Light. The other is 'invention': having seen the vision, Tolkien was capable of brooding over it for decades, not altering it but making sense of it, fitting it into more and more extraordinary sequences of explanation. So the boat of Eärendil generates a disaster, a rescue, an explanation of why the rescue has had to be so long delayed. The processes are exactly the same as the generation of Bilbo Baggins from 'In a hole in the ground there lived a hobbit . . .', and the expansion of his story all the way to the last explanation of *holbytla* seventeen years and 1500 pages later.

Where *The Silmarillion* differs from Tolkien's earlier works is in its refusal to accept novelistic convention. Most novels (including *The Hobbit* and *The Lord of the Rings*) pick a character to put in the foreground, like Frodo and Bilbo, and then tell the story as it happens to him. The novelist of course is inventing the story, and so retains omniscience: he can explain, or show, what is 'really' happening and contrast it with the limited perception of his character, as Tolkien does with Frodo lamenting his ill choices in *The Two Towers* (we have seen that Aragorn's similar laments were unfounded), or as Joseph Conrad does when his Dr Monygham tells Nostromo if he had the treasure he would give it to their enemies (we know Nostromo has the treasure, but is bitterly offended to have his efforts made vain). Novels work on a mixture of suspense and special knowledge: there is about them, one may as well say, something wildly unrealistic.

Against this *The Silmarillion* tries to preserve something much closer to the texture of reality, namely, that the full meaning of events can only ever be perceived retrospectively. Its stories are full of ironies only grasped on second reading. 'False hopes are more dangerous than fears', says Sador in the *Narn*. Once we have realised how Morwen ruined her life and her son's by waiting for Húrin, we see that Sador is, unwittingly, a 'soothsayer', and read all his remarks with much greater attention. At first reading, though, that point is invisible. So are most of the moments that lead to future disaster, like Aredhel's turn southward outside Gondolin, or Finrod's ignorance of the Noegyth Nibin (on *S*, p. 114). 'Ominous' statements are common enough — 'Their swords and their counsels shall have two edges' (Melian, *S*, p. 128), or 'Not the first' (Mandos, 50 pages before) — but for their immediate meaning one has to wait, and their full meaning often depends on unravelling the entire book. *The Silmarillion* could never be anything but hard to read: that is arguably because it is trying to say something about the relationship between events and their actors which could not be said through the omniscient selectiveness of the ordinary novel.

None of this, however, waves away the very nearly prophetic remark by Frodo sitting on 'The Stairs of Cirith Ungol' in *The Two Towers*. Sam Gamgee has just given a summary of the tale of Beren and Lúthien, and remarked that he and Frodo appear to be in the same tale: perhaps some hobbit-child in the future will demand the story of 'Frodo and the Ring'. Yes, says Frodo, and he will demand 'Samwise the stouthearted' too: 'I

THE ROAD TO MIDDLE-EARTH

want to hear more about Sam, dad. Why didn't they put in more of his talk, dad? That's what I like, it makes me laugh.' This embryonic piece of literary criticism does make a point about *The Silmarillion,* which is that it is all on the level of 'high mimesis' or 'romance', with no Gamgees in it. Not only children find that a lack. There is a reason for the decision once more, in that Tolkien was quite clearly, in the *Silmarillion* stories, recommending virtues to which most moderns no longer dare aspire: stoicism, nonchalance, piety, fidelity. In *The Lord of the Rings* he had learnt — by mixing hobbits in with heroes — to present them relatively unprovocatively. In *The Silmarillion* feelings of antagonism or doubt are often accidentally triggered, as when Fingon 'dared a deed which is justly renowned' or we are told the same of 'the Leap of Beren'. 'Don't tell us, show us', is the reply. 'We are not impressed by scale so much as by effort — by Bilbo going on alone in the dark.'

But the debate between ancient and modern modes of presentation, and between ancient and modern theories of virtue, need not be protracted. In his maturity, from the scenes at the end of *The Hobbit* almost all the way through *The Lord of the Rings,* Tolkien was able to hold a balance between them. In youth he had not learnt it, and in his later years he was unable to recover it — especially as recovering that balance would have meant what is notoriously one of the hardest jobs in the literary world, namely making a radical revision of something which has already taken a fixed shape of its own. Tolkien did not solve the problem of 'depth'; nor of 'novelising' romance; and in ignoring the one, as in brooding over the other, he showed himself out of step with his time, and exposed himself even more to lack of sympathy and careless reading. His decision to bring back the modes of the past was, however, not indefensible (as this chapter ought to show). It was also his last and boldest defiance of all the practitioners of 'lit.'.

CHAPTER 8

'ON THE COLD HILL'S SIDE'

Of Birch Hats and Cold Potions

Writing twenty years ago, I began this chapter with the words, 'There is, in a way, no more of "Middle-earth" to consider.' This was tempting Providence with a vengeance, for there were twelve volumes of 'The History of Middle-earth' yet to appear and to be considered. Nor can I correct myself at this stage by suggesting, 'Tolkien wrote no more of Middle-earth', for the last three volumes of 'The History of Middle-earth' in particular show, like much of the *Unfinished Tales,* that Tolkien's creativity was indeed released by the completion of *The Lord of the Rings,* and that he continued writing within the framework of his Middle-earth mythology all through the last twenty years of his life. Some of this has been discussed already, and there is further comment throughout chapter 9. This chapter turns, however, to a more personal theme: 'the road to Middle-earth', or Tolkien's own attitudes to his work, as they emerge especially from the short pieces and poems of his later years. Tolkien might not have approved of such a study, for he valued his privacy. Still, the inquiry has much to do with the major theme of this book, namely the interlocking of philology and fiction. And here I, at least, cannot help looking at what I see as the third in Tolkien's triad of short stories about the sources of his invention, *Farmer Giles* (written 1938), 'Leaf by Niggle' (a few years later), and finally, written in 1965, *Smith of Wootton Major.*[1]

To me, this does not seem to be a difficult piece. I take

it that, as with 'Leaf by Niggle' quite certainly, and as with *Farmer Giles* more partially, its mode is allegorical, and its subject is the author himself, especially the relations between his job and his private sources of 'inspiration'. This assumption has, however, been the one which has drawn the most determined rebuttals from other commentators, especially Mr David Doughan and (twice) Dr Verlyn Flieger,[2] and it is only fair, then, to restate the arguments for and against it. Against taking *Smith* allegorically, we have Tolkien's own endorsement (*Letters*, p. 388) of a review by Roger Lancelyn Green which stated firmly that the meaning of *Smith* should be left alone: 'To seek for the meaning is to cut open the ball in search of its bounce.' This can be backed up by Tolkien's own stated dislike of allegory, discussed on p. 43 above, and indeed by an even firmer statement of his own specifically about *Smith*, 'This short tale is not "allegory"'. That would seem to settle the matter (for in cases like this I would scorn to fall back on the well-known critical get-out, 'You cannot trust what an author says about his own work'), if Tolkien had not gone on immediately to add 'though it is capable of course of allegorical interpretation at certain points'. Tolkien furthermore gave a lead for any such allegorical interpretation by saying, 'The Great Hall is evidently in a way an "allegory" of the village church; the Master Cook with his house adjacent, and his office that is not hereditary . . . is plainly the Parson and the priesthood'. Tolkien's own surviving commentary on his story, from which these statements, cited by Dr Flieger, are taken, is indeed, again according to Dr Flieger, 'a running argument with himself on the question of whether the story is or is not an allegory'.[3] If Tolkien himself could not decide, then the question can fairly be taken as open.

There is furthermore one element which seems to me a clear case of Tolkienian private symbolism, and that is the name of Smith's main antagonist throughout the work, the rude and incompetent Master Cook, Nokes. As I have said repeatedly, Tolkien was for some time perhaps the one person in the world who knew most about names, especially English names, and was most deeply interested in them. He wrote about them, commented on them, brought them up in conversation. With all the names in the telephone book to draw on, Tolkien is unlikely to have picked out just one name without considering what it meant: and 'Nokes' contains two clues as to its meaning. One is reinforced by the names of Smith's wife and son and daughter, Nell and Nan and Ned, all of them marked by 'nunnation', the English habit of putting an *n* in front of a word, and especially a name, which originally did not have one, like Eleanor and Ann and Edward.[4] In Nokes's case one can go further and observe place-names, as for instance Noke — a town in Oxfordshire not far from Brill — whose name is known to have been derived from Old English *æt þam ácum,* 'at the oaks'. This became in Middle English **atten okes,* and in Modern English, by mistake, 'at Noke' or 'at Nokes'. There is no doubt that Tolkien knew all this, for there is a character called 'old Noakes' in the Shire, and Tolkien commented on his name, giving very much the explanation above, in his 'Guide to the Names in *The Lord of the Rings*', written probably in the late 1950s. Tolkien there wrote off the meaning of 'Noakes' as 'unimportant', as indeed it is for *The Lord of the Rings,* but it would be entirely characteristic of him to remember an unimportant philological point and turn it into an important one later.

The second clue lies in the derivation from 'oak'. 'Oak' had a special meaning for Tolkien, pointed out by Christopher Tolkien in his footnote to *Shadow,* p. 145.[†] In his early career as Professor at the University of Leeds, Tolkien had devised a system of splitting the curriculum of English studies into two separate groups or 'schemes', the 'A-scheme' and the 'B-scheme'. The A-scheme was for students of literature, the B-scheme for the philologists. Tolkien clearly liked this system, and tried unsuccessfully to introduce it to Oxford in 1930 with similar nomenclature (see 'OES', p. 780). But in his private symbolism 'A' was represented by the Old English rune-name *ác,* 'oak', 'B' by Old English *beorc,* 'birch'. Oaks were critics and

---

† As often, I am amazed that I did not at first recognise this, for at the time of my first comments on *Smith* I was still holding Tolkien's former position at the University of Leeds, and was in charge of the B-scheme, still in existence (though now no more). The B = birch equation, however, was no longer current.

birches philologists, and Tolkien made the point perfectly clear in *Songs for the Philologists,* for which see pp. 353–56 below. As must surely be obvious from chapters 1 and 2 of this work, oaks were furthermore the enemy: the enemy of philology, the enemy of imagination, the enemy of dragons. I do not think that Tolkien could ever have forgotten this. Furthermore, it makes sense within *Smith,* and is not inconsistent with Tolkien's own equation of the Master Cook with the Parson and the priesthood.

The name 'Nokes', then, is my main reason for seeing a professional element in the fable's allegory, which I would develop as follows. First, Tolkien liked to bring 'philologist-figures' into his fiction: the parson of Farmer Giles, the Master of the Houses of Healing, even Gollum as Sméagol with his head turned down and his fascination with 'roots and beginnings'. There is something faintly recognisable in the first Master Cook, whose retirement prompts the rest of the story: 'He had been a kind man who liked to see other people enjoying themselves, but he was himself serious, and said very little'. His sojourn in Faërie made him merrier. Nevertheless, one might say that the man who knows a lot but does not communicate it, and gives a false and unfortunate impression of gravity, is a good image of the nineteenth-century philologist — the type of man who turned the subject into a bogy (see chapter 1). By contrast Nokes seems very clearly to be an unsympathetic picture of the propounders of 'lit.'. He has no idea of the charms of fantasy. He equates the supernatural with the childish, and both with what is sweet and sticky. His idea of elvish allure has dwindled to a doll with a wand, labelled 'Fairy Queen'. In particularly annoying fashion, having set up a feeble image of the charms of Faërie, he takes it for granted that the feebleness of the whole concept has been demonstrated: he behaves, in fact, exactly like the critics of *Beowulf* whom Tolkien had excoriated thirty years before, who, having pushed over the tower of the poem, 'said (after pushing it over), "What a muddle it is in!"'; or like the Oxford colleagues of whom Tolkien had said, in his somewhat embittered 'Valedictory Address', that he 'felt it a grievance that certain professional persons should suppose their dullness and ignorance [over philology] to be a human norm'; or, one may as well add, like so many of Tolkien's own critics in later years. As for what Nokes has to offer, his Great Cake is good enough, with no particular faults (Tolkien had nothing against literary study *per se*), 'except that it was no bigger than was needed . . . nothing left over: no coming again'. Not much food for the imagination, one might paraphrase. In any case much of the cake's goodness seems derived from the sly watch Nokes keeps on Alf Prentice, and from the 'old books of recipes left behind by previous cooks', which Nokes cannot understand, but from which he scrapes a few ideas. Literary criticism in England (one might translate) leapt forward from a springboard of old philology, without which even readings of Shakespeare would not get very far. But once it took over the Mastership from the old serious philologists it refused to give credit; this thwarted its own development and left great areas of its proper subject misunderstood.

The 'professional' interpretation given above, meanwhile, seems readily compatible with Tolkien's own equation of Cook with Parson. Nokes is, one should note, married. This is one of the reasons given for selecting him as a stopgap after the departure of the first Master Cook: he was 'a solid sort of man with a wife and children, and careful with money'. But if he is married he must surely represent a Protestant parson, in England probably an Anglican, whose house (the vicarage) would in deed stand next to the Great Hall (the village church). Tolkien, however, was a Catholic. He might well have felt that just as Nokes represented a degradation, a decline, from philologist to critic, so he also represented a dwindling from Catholic priest with the power to celebrate the Mass to Anglican vicar capable only of holding a communion. In each case, one could argue on Tolkien's behalf, something had got lost, something vital if undefinable. Within the story, this mysterious element, 'not [quite] invisible to attentive eyes', is represented by the faystar: left behind by the old Master Cook, baked into a cake by Nokes, swallowed by Smith, for whom it becomes the passport into Faërie, returned reluctantly to Alf Prentice, destined in the end for Nokes's great-grandson Tim. Whatever wording one chooses, this object must surely stand for, and be understood by all readers to stand for, something like vision, receptiveness to fantasy, mythopoeic power, ability to pass outside Wootton Major, Wootton being, of course, *wudu-tún*, 'the town in the wood', the 'wood of the world' in which so many of Tolkien's characters — elves, men and hobbits — wander temporarily or permanently 'bewildered'.

There are two further strange features in the story which seem to call for an explanation, and which should be noted before trying to come to a conclusion. One is, as mentioned above, that the fay-star will go in the end to Nokes's kin, not Smith's. Smith is the central character, the bearer of the vision; he has a much-loved son, Ned; it would be a natural and satisfying ending for the star to go to him when Smith has finally to relinquish it. But this comfortable conclusion is rejected. Though Nokes is, at almost the very end, satisfactorily squashed, it might be said that his family, at least, will have the last laugh over Smith's, as Nokes has the last word — rather like Councillor Tompkins's final and crushing victory over Niggle, in this world, in 'Leaf by Niggle'. The other strange feature is a kind of duality in the supporters of Faërie. Smith is the central character and the bearer of the star, but the real controller of the star is Alf Prentice, and he too is in a way a dual character. One of his names, Prentice, is a trade-name, just like Smith, but the other is Alf. And while Alf is common English short-for-Alfred (and so looks like Ned or Nan or Tim), it is also the modern spelling of Old English *ælf,* 'elf', which is what Alf is. He disguises himself as an ordinary person, but is revealed at the end as King of Faërie, to whom the Queen sends her cryptic message, *'The time has come. Let him choose.'* Alf/Prentice, Smith/Prentice: what did Tolkien mean by this (for him) novel double duality?

I would suggest that, if the old Cook is a philologist-figure, and Nokes a critic-figure, the suspicion must be that Smith is a Tolkien-figure. Smith himself never becomes Cook, never bakes a Great Cake. It is perhaps fair to remark that Tolkien never produced a major full-length work on medieval literature. Against that Smith's life is one of useful activity: pots, pans, bars, bolts, hinges, fire-dogs — or, one might say, lectures, tutorials, scripts, pupils. Furthermore, Smith has the ability to pass into Faërie, and the mark of his strangeness is not only on his brow but in his song: he brings back visions for others. These visions furthermore expand. The doll 'on one foot like a snow-maiden dancing', the maiden 'with flowing hair and kilted skirt' who drags Smith into the dance, the Queen 'in her majesty and her glory' — all three are avatars of the Queen of Faërie, representing successively the tawdry images of former fantasy which are all the modern world has left, Tolkien's own first attempts to produce something truer and better, his final awareness that what he had attempted had grown under his hand, from *Hobbit* to *Silmarillion*. The image of Smith apologising for his people, and being forgiven — 'Better a little doll, maybe, than no memory of Faery at all. For some the only glimpse. For some the awaking' — might be taken without too much strain as Tolkien forgiving himself for 'Goblin Feet'. But still one is left with Alf.

He, perhaps, is born of a kind of weakness. Defeat hangs heavy in *Smith of Wootton Major*. Smith has to hand over his star, and return to Faërie no more; though he gains the right to say who shall have the star, his choice falls on Nokes's blood, not his own. These points are hard to read except as a kind of valedictory, an admission of retirement — Smith is 'an old man's book', as Tolkien said in *Letters*, p. 389. But Alf is there *to put Smith into a longer history*. There were men who wore the star of inspiration before Smith; in a later age there will be others; in any case that star, that inspiration, is only a fragment of a greater world, a world outside the little clearing of Wootton. Alf is there to reassure. His 'message', to put it with deliberate bathos, is that if stories have a particular quality of conviction or 'inner consistency', then they must (as Tolkien had said before) in some sense be true. The star on Smith's brow that makes him sing is a guarantee of the existence of Faërie; by the same reasoning, Tolkien's drive to create a world came not from within him but from some world outside.

Of course Tolkien had no 'Alf' to reassure him or to ease his retirement. No doubt he wished very much that he had. Yet there is one further oddity to keep *Smith of Wootton Major* from being just a fable of self-justification. This comes from the story's centre, i.e. the sequence of Smith's Faërie visions. First he sees the great warship returning from the Dark Marches; then the Great Tree; then the lake of glass and fire-creatures; then the maidens dancing; finally the Faërie Queen.

In the third of these visions, though, we find an odd sequence of events. When Smith touches the lake he falls, while a great 'boom' raises a wild wind to sweep him away. He is saved by clinging to a birch:

> and the Wind wrestled fiercely with them, trying to tear him away; but the birch was bent down to the ground by the blast and enclosed him in its branches. When at last the Wind passed on he rose and saw that the birch was naked. It was stripped of every leaf, and it wept, and tears fell from its branches like rain. He set his hand upon its white bark saying: 'Blessed be the birch! What can I do to make amends, or give thanks?' He felt the answer of the tree pass up from his hand: 'Nothing', it said. 'Go away! The Wind is hunting you. You do not belong here. Go away and never return!' (*Smith*, pp. 29–30)

What is the birch that saves, the wind that threatens?

I have already suggested that while 'oak' and 'Nokes' in Tolkien's private symbolism stand for literature and literary critics, the birch stands for the 'B' scheme of study, for philology, for the defiance of mere 'literature'; and this is confirmed by two poems about birches in the 1936 collection *Songs for the Philologists,* given in the original and in translation in Appendix B below. One is in Gothic, 'Bagme Bloma', or 'Flower of the Trees': this hails the birch as defier of wind and lightning, *bandwa bairhta, runa goda, þiuda meina þjuþjandei,* 'bright token, good mystery, blessing my people'. The other is in Old English, 'Éadig béo Þu' or 'Blessed be you'. Its last stanza, in translation, reads: 'Let us sing a cheerful song, praise the birch and birch's race, the teacher, the student and the subject — may we all have health, joy and happiness. The oak shall fall into the fire, losing joy and life and leaf. The birch shall keep its glory long, shine splendidly over the bright plain.' The birch, it seems, represents learning, severe learning, even discipline. But those who subject themselves to serious study — the 'dull stodges' of the 'B'-scheme at Leeds University, perhaps; see p. 12 above — are under its protection.[5]

The birch has one further association Tolkien did not miss. He respected the *English and Scottish Popular Ballads* collected by F. J. Child as being (see p. 52 above) the last living relic of

Northern tradition; in what is perhaps the most famous ballad
of all, the birch takes on a special role. 'The Wife of Usher's
Well' is about a widow who calls her drowned sons back from
the dead:

> It fell about the Martinmass,
> When nights are lang and mirk,
> The carlin wife's three sons came hame,
> And their hats were o the birk.
>
> It neither grew in syke nor ditch,
> Nor yet in any sheugh,
> But at the gates o Paradise,
> That birk grew fair eneugh.

The 'birk' is the birch; its wearers come to Middle-earth from
another world; but they are not allowed to remain past dawn.
In Lowry C. Wimberly's *Folklore in the English and Scottish
Ballads* (Chicago: University of Chicago Press, 1928), Sir Walter Scott is quoted as having found a story of an apparition
who wore the birch 'to the end the wind of the world may not
have power over me'. Smith's Wind, then, could be the world;
the birch is its traditional opponent, scholarly study; but that
study, like the birch hats of the drowned sons, also acts as a
passport, into and out of Middle-earth. It is a kind of Golden
Bough; not between Earth and Hell, like Aeneas's bough, but
between Earth and Paradise.

All this has a bearing on Tolkien's fable, and on his state of
mind. The birch protects Smith, but is left naked and weeping.
Did Tolkien feel he *had exploited* philology for his fiction? It
also tells Smith to 'go away and never return', a command he
cannot obey. Why should he have included this embargo, from
within Faërie, against revisiting it? Did he feel, perhaps, that in
writing his fiction he was trespassing in a 'perilous country'
against some unstated law? The *Songs for the Philologists* again
contain two poems (in Old English, and again in Appendix B)
about mortals who trespass in the Other World and suffer for
it, 'Ides Ælfscyne', about the 'elf-fair maiden' who lures the
young man away only to return him to a land where he is a
stranger, and 'Ofer Wídne Gársecg', where a young man is
lured away by a mermaid, to the sea-bottom and (traditional

motif) the forfeit of his soul. It seems that at times, at least, Tolkien thought that getting involved with Faërie was deeply dangerous. Though *Smith of Wootton Major* offers a reassurance that imaginative visions are true, it also declares, in a concealed way, in private images, that mortal men cannot wander in these visions all the time without danger. They must give up and make their peace with the world.[6]

This thought is strengthened, if not confirmed, by Tolkien's longest published poem, 'The Lay of Aotrou and Itroun' of 1945.[7] Its kernel, interestingly, is also in Wimberly, who quotes the Breton song of 'Le Seigneur Nann et la Fée', about a childless lord who gets a fertility potion from a witch and promises her her own reward; later she leads him into the woods in the shape of a white hart, only to reveal herself and demand his love as payment. He refuses (unlike the young men in 'Ides Ælfscyne' and 'Ofer Wídne Gársecg'), preferring death.[8] To this story Tolkien has added a heavy weight of faith. The lord's defiance of the Korrigan is associated explicitly with home and Christendom; but his sin has been to despair of Christianity in his childlessness, and take 'cold counsel', the grey and frozen potion of the witch. He would have done better to trust in 'hope and prayer', even if the prayer were unanswered. As an anonymous voice comments, when the potion brings Aotrou twins:

> 'Would every prayer were answered twice!
> the half or nought must oft suffice
> for humbler men, who wear their knees
> more bare than lords, as oft one sees.'

The Tolkienian moral of the story is: be content; be resigned; we can't all have everything. One might note, coincidentally, that in the *OED*'s 1972 Supplement, 'escapism' is defined for the first time as 'the practice of seeking distraction *from what normally has to be endured*' (my italics). A fear of barrenness, of leaving no descendants, and with it a fear that the escape from forge or castle into fantasy may not be permitted — these are the themes of 'Aotrou' and of *Smith*, like goblin doubts padding through Tolkien's mind.

An End to 'Glamour'

The Adventures of Tom Bombadil, which Tolkien put together with unusual speed in 1961–1962, may seem to have little connection with the foregoing. It is one of his more light-hearted books, centring on a character essentially fearless and self-confident, and a good deal of it is evidently old material from a more cheerful period (poems 1, 3, 5–7 and 9–10), while more is in a similar mode and probably of similar age (poems 4, 8, 11–12). The collection did not, however, escape Tolkien's ponderings over 'depth'. A letter to Rayner Unwin (*Letters,* p. 315) shows him wondering how to create a 'fiction' which would enable him to draw early works into the world of *The Lord of the Rings,* and deciding to do it by means of a comic 'editorial' preface. He carried this out with great *finesse,* explaining for instance that the poem 'Errantry' (which he had really written in 1933, when he had no need to harmonise his rhymes with Quenya) was actually written by Bilbo after he had returned from the Lonely Mountain — and so had learnt something of elves — but before he retired to Rivendell and began to learn Elvish properly. Other poems are ascribed to Sam, or (no. 14,[9] reworked from 1937) given a link with the still unpublished 'Silmarillion'. But the collection also contains both old and new work which hints at a deep sadness in Tolkien, and at an old but growing uncertainty.

The most obvious case is no. 16, the last poem, called 'The Last Ship'. In this Fíriel — once more a name which is really a description, 'mortal woman', Everywoman — gets up in the morning to go to the river, hears 'a sudden music' and sees the vision of the last elvish ship leaving Gondor. Where are they going, she asks, to Arnor, to Númenor? No, the elves reply, they are leaving Middle-earth for ever to go to the Undying Lands. Come with them, they call, escape from the world:

> 'One more only we may bear.
> Come! For your days are speeding.
> Come! Earth-maiden elven-fair,
> Our last call heeding.'

She takes a step towards them, but her feet sink 'deep in clay'; she takes this as a sign.

> 'I cannot come!' they heard her cry.
> 'I was born Earth's daughter!'

She turns back to her home, but the life of the morning — cockcrow, sunlight, jewels of dew on her gown — has gone. She goes through the 'dark door, / under the house-shadow', puts on dull clothes, starts work. The last word of both the two last stanzas is 'faded', and in the last stanza Fíriel herself has disappeared. Clearly she is dead, and she condemned herself to it when she stopped with her feet in the clay. 'Earth to earth, ashes to ashes', says the Funeral Service, and in this poem 'Earth-maiden', 'Middle-earth' and death are all equated. The poem takes on even more point if one remembers the ballad-genre which Tolkien knew so well and imitated in his two early *Songs* just mentioned — the one in which the elves steal away a human man or woman to live with them in delight in 'elf-hill'. 'The Last Ship' is an unprecedented reversal of that genre, in which the maiden refuses to go. It is true that she then avoids the risk of returning 'disenchanted' like Keats's lover from 'La Belle Dame Sans Merci'. She also turns from glamour to dullness and oblivion. The cockcrow at the start of the poem may hint at resurrection, but it does not carry the bravura of the cockcrow and the horns of Rohan in *The Return of the King*. The sense of loss is only increased if one compares the poem with its earlier and little-known version of 1934, when it had the title 'Firiel'.[10] The tone of 'Firiel' is much more optimistic than that of 'The Last Ship'. Firiel here (I use the form with no accent to distinguish her from Fíriel in the later poem) is called to by the elves, fears to go with them and turns back to the 'dark door', just as in the later poem, but the fleeting sense of regret and lost opportunity is rapidly buried by bustle. It is 'a vision' which fades, not 'sunlight'; the last two stanzas are not of resignation but of cheerful activity; the last words are not 'their song has faded' but 'please pass the honey'. There is a strong sense that Firiel has made the right decision, not, as in 'The Last Ship', an inevitable decision.

Other poems in the *Bombadil* collection also end with emptiness. No. 2, 'Tom Bombadil Goes Boating' (written 1962), seems to have very much the same outline as no. 1, 'The Adventures of Tom Bombadil' (rewritten with only minor changes from the version of 1934): in it Tom good-humour-edly browbeats a succession of creatures — wren, kingfisher, otter, swan, hobbits and finally Farmer Maggot. In the end all help him, with a central scene of merry-making. Just the same, there is a suggestion that the whole thing is a dream:

Ere dawn Tom was gone: as dreams one half remembers, some merry, some sad, and some of hidden warning.

Even his footprints are washed away, his boat vanishes, and all that is left is a pair of forgotten oars, which by themselves mean nothing. It is as if Tom has gone back to his natural world, leaving Maggot and his mortal friends to meet their own fate, separate from his. Certainly 'Long they lay at Grindwall hythe for Tom to come and find them' is a more 'downbeat' ending than 'While fair Goldberry combed her tresses yellow': *Grindr* in the *Poetic Edda* is the name of the gate that separates the living from the dead.

An even more striking revision comes in poem 15, titled 'The Sea-Bell', but in the editorial 'fiction' at the start given another title and a highly suggestive placing within the world of *The Lord of the Rings* 'It is the latent piece [in the collec-tion]', surmises Tolkien's imaginary 'editor':

and belongs to the Fourth Age; but it is included here, be-cause a hand has scrawled at its head *Frodos Dreme*. That is remarkable, and though the piece is most unlikely to have been written by Frodo himself, the title shows that it was as-sociated with the dark and despairing dreams which visited him in March and October during his last three years. But there were certainly other traditions concerning Hobbits that were taken by the 'wandering-madness', and if they ever returned, were afterwards queer and uncommunicable. The thought of the Sea was ever-present in the background of hobbit imagination; but fear of it and distrust of all Elv-ish lore, was the prevailing mood in the Shire at the end of the Third Age, and that mood was certainly not entirely dispelled by the events and changes with which that Age ended. (*TB*, in *Reader*, p. 194)

So the hobbits, like Fíriel, turned Earth-fast and Sea-shy. Meanwhile, the remark that the piece could not have been by or about Frodo, but was about some other hobbit, is Tolkien's bow to the fact that 'The Sea-Bell' is a thorough reworking of a piece he had written and published in 1934, before Frodo was thought of, called 'Looney'.

Close comparison of the two shows, as with 'Firiel' and 'The Last Ship', an increasing darkness. Both are poems of 'disenchantment' (as 'The Last Ship' was not), and in both the speaker, who has been in a magic boat to a far land, finds himself hunted out of it by a 'dark cloud', and returned to lonely and ragged craziness, scorned by others. In 'The Sea-Bell', though, a whole series of significant changes has been made. For one thing, the boat is much more like the boat of Fíriel, the *last* boat; when he sees it the voyager calls out, 'It is later than late!' and leaps into it with a new haste. For another, the menacing elements in the far country have been much expanded, with 'glooming caves' seen beneath the cliffs as soon as the speaker lands; in 'Looney' the impression of paradise lasted for a couple of stanzas. The 'Sea-Bell' landscape also includes 'gladdon-swords' (i.e. of wild iris) and 'puffballs' in the mould. One may remember that it was in the Gladden Fields that Isildur died, and that 'puffballs' were associated by Tolkien — since his 'Preface' to Walter Haigh's *Huddersfield Glossary* of 1928, p. xviii — with 'Dead Sea apples' and the bitter fruit of the Cities of the Plain.

A more important change, though, is that in the later version the speaker seems in a way guilty, as 'Looney' did not. In both poems the 'black cloud' comes, but in the earlier it is for no reason, while in the later it appears to be called, or provoked, by the speaker presumptuously naming himself 'king'. It casts him down, turns him into a kind of Orfeo-in-the-wilderness, till eventually he realises he must find the sea: 'I have lost myself, and I know not the way, / but let me be gone!' And seemingly as a result of that guilt the end is different. In 'Looney' the man returned from Paradise still had a shell in which he could hear the voice of the sea, as a kind of witness to what he had seen. In 'The Sea-Bell' the shell is there at the beginning, and it contains a call from across the seas; but at the end it is 'silent and dead':

Never will my ear that bell hear,
   never my feet that shore tread,
never again, as in sad lane,
   in blind alley and in long street
ragged I walk. To myself I talk;
   for still they speak not, men that I meet.

In the later poem—as in *Smith*—the return to Faërie, even
in memory, is banned. As for the mistaken title *Frodos Dreme*,
what it suggests with great economy is, first of all, an age in
which only the sacrifices of the War of the Ring are remembered (for some scribe has associated gloom with Frodo), and
second, more indirectly, a sense of ultimate defeat and loss in
the hero of *The Lord of the Rings*. Frodo doubted his own salvation. This could be seen as a dark illusion born of losing the
'addictive' Ring, but one senses that Tolkien was doubtful too:
not of salvation, but of the legitimacy of his own mental wanderings. For many years he had held to his theory of 'sub-creation', which declared that since the human imagination came
from God, then its products must come from God too, must be
fragments of some genuine if other-worldly truth, guaranteed
by their own 'inner consistency' and no more the artist's own
property than the star from Elfland was Smith's.[11] But by the
1960s he was not so sure. It is hard not to think that by then he
saw himself (perhaps only at times) as Fíriel, Farmer Maggot,
Frodo, 'Looney' and eventually Smith—a mortal deserted by
the immortals and barred from their company. He no longer
imagined himself rejoining his own creations after death, like
Niggle; he felt they were lost, like the Silmarils.

The Lost Straight Road

Tolkien of course asked more than he had a right to. No one
can expect fantasy to turn real, and all hopes for a star or shell
or supernatural guarantee are bound to be disappointed. In any
case these late and gloomy reactions have no bearing on *The
Hobbit, The Lord of the Rings* or *The Silmarillion,* which keep
their own purely literary justification; the theory of 'sub-
creation' is not needed. If it is the function of works of litera-

ture to enlarge their readers' sympathies and help them understand what their own experience may not have taught them, then Tolkien's fictions qualify on all counts. Certainly they are about 'creatures who never existed'. Most novels are about 'people who never existed'. The cry that 'fantasy is escapist' compared to the novel is only an echo of the older cry that novels are 'escapist' compared with biography, and to both cries one should make the same answer: that freedom to invent outweighs loyalty to mere happenstance, the accidents of history; and good readers should know how to filter a general applicability from a particular story. So Tolkien need not have yearned so much for a justification in fact and truth, nor felt such a sense of loss as 'inspiration' receded. Nevertheless, the burden of his loss becomes greater if one realises how consistent and long-lasting Tolkien's visions had been, especially his visions of that 'earthly Paradise' from which 'Looney' is returned and which Fíriel never reaches.

He remarked in later life (*Letters*, pp. 213, 347) that he had a 'terrible recurrent dream' of Atlantis and 'the Great Wave, towering up, and coming in ineluctably over the trees and green fields'. He seems to have been haunted also by other visions which had to be expressed in narrative: of cities sculptured in lifeless stone (see the poem 'The City of the Gods', 1923, a forerunner of Pippin's sight of Gondor in *LOTR*, pp. 734–35), of towers overlooking the sea (everywhere from 'Monsters' to the Tower Hills), most of all of beautiful unreachable countries across the ocean. Fascination with this may explain why the poem *Pearl* so appealed to him: it contains a land where grief is washed away, and in his poem of 1927, 'The Nameless Land', Tolkien wrote sixty lines in the complex *Pearl*-stanza describing a country further 'than Paradise' and fairer 'than Tir-nan-Og', the Irish land of the deathless. In 'The Happy Mariners' seven years before — also translated into Old English as 'Tha Éadigan Sælidan' — he saw himself looking out from 'a western tower' to the sea and the 'fairy boats' going through 'the shadows and the dangerous seas' to 'islands blest', from which a wind returns to murmur of 'golden rains'. The longing for a Paradise on Earth, a paradise of natural beauty, was compelling and repeated and there before Tolkien took to fiction. But in the last poems the murmuring wind has ceased, and the sense of a barrier is much stronger.

There is a resolution of hope and prohibition, finally, in an extremely private poem by Tolkien, 'Imram', from 1955. This is based on the famous voyage by St Brendan ('the Navigator') from Ireland to the unknown countries of the West, found in many medieval versions and related to a whole Irish genre of *imrama* which includes the famous *Imram Brain mac Febail,* or 'Voyage of Bran son of Febal to the Land of the Living'. In the heavily Christianised Brendan-story, the saint hears of a Land of Promise in the West and sets sail, to find islands of sheep and birds, a whale-island (like 'Fastitocalon', poem 11 in *TB*), islands of monks and sinners, till in the end he reaches the Land of Promise—from which Brendan is sent back, to lay his bones in Ireland. In 'Imram' Tolkien assimilates this story very closely to his own fiction. His St Brendan can remember only three things from his journeys, a Cloud over 'the foundered land' (of Númenor), a Tree (full of voices neither human nor angelic but of a third 'fair kindred') and a Star, which marks the 'old road' leading out of Middle-earth 'as an unseen bridge that on arches runs / to coasts that no man knows'. Brendan says he can remember these things, but never reach them; at the end of the poem he is dead, like Fíriel.

However, there is in this poem an image of possible escape, drawn out further in *The Silmarillion*. There, at the end of 'Akallabêth', Tolkien records the Númenorean belief that once mariners had been able to sail from Middle-earth to Aman, but that with the drowning of Númenor the deathless lands were removed and the earth made round; though since ships still came and went from the Grey Havens,

> the loremasters of Men said that a Straight Road must still be, for those that were permitted to find it. And they taught that, while the new world fell away, the old road and the path of the memory of the West still went on, as it were a mighty bridge invisible that passed through the air of breath and of flight (which were bent now as the world was bent), and traversed Ilmen which flesh unaided cannot endure, until it came to Tol Eressëa, the Lonely Isle, and

maybe even beyond, to Valinor, where the Valar still dwell and watch the unfolding of the story of the world. And tales and rumours arose along the shores of the sea concerning mariners and men forlorn upon the water who, by some fate or grace or favour of the Valar, had entered in upon the Straight Way and seen the face of the world sink below them, and so had come to the lamplit quays of Avallónë, or verily to the last beaches on the margin of Aman, and there had looked upon the White Mountain, dreadful and beautiful, before they died.

For those that were permitted . . . by some fate or grace or favour. Tolkien was deeply attached to Middle-earth, and knew that his bones must lie in England as St Brendan's in Ireland. His last works are full of resignation and bereavement. Still, if he had an inner hope, it might possibly have been that he too could take 'the secret gate', 'the hidden paths', 'the Lost Straight Road', and find the Land of Promise which was still within 'the circles of the world'. It had happened to others. In the *South English Legendary* version of the 'Life of St Brendan', a maiden tells Abbot Beryn that he ought to thank Jesus Christ for leading him to the Paradise in the West, for:

'Þis is þat lond þat he wole: ȝuyt are þe worldes ende
his dernelinges an erþe ȝyue: & hyder heo schulle wende.'

'This is the country that [Christ] will give, before the end of the world, to his secret favourites on earth, and this is where they will come.[12]

That land would be both sanctified and earthly, an ideal 'mediation' for Tolkien. It must have increased his hope and longing to observe that the last line, about the 'dernelinges', is not in the text but (like 'Frodos Dreme') has been added in the margin by a later hand — as if some early but forgotten scribe had received a mysterious promise of his own. The promise lay in the philological detail; and the philology was true, even if the promise could not be expected to 'come true'.

CHAPTER 9

'THE COURSE OF ACTUAL
COMPOSITION'

The Bones of the Ox

In the introduction to his 1851 translation of Asbjörnsen and
Moe's collection of Norse fairy-tales, Sir George Dasent wrote
that the reader 'must be satisfied with the soup that is set before
him, and not desire to see the bones of the ox out of which it
has been boiled'.[1] Dasent's introduction was in fact one of the
nineteenth-century classics of popularising philology, a highly
revealing response to the situation described on pp. 6–13
above; it is full of laudatory references to Jacob and Wilhelm
Grimm, of cross-connections between Norse and Scottish, or
Norse and Sanskrit, and it makes a determined attempt to
press on from comparative philology to comparative mythology. In this setting, what Dasent meant by his image was that
he wanted his reader to accept his conclusions, and not demand
to see the philological 'workings' on which they were based.
Tolkien did not approve. Nevertheless, he was struck by the
image, and repeated it in his essay 'On Fairy-Stories'. Only
what *he* meant by it, he said, was this:

> By 'the soup' I mean the story as it is served up by the au-
> thor or teller, and by 'the bones' its sources or material —
> even when (by rare luck) those can be with certainty discov-
> ered. ('OFS', in *Reader*, p. 47)

In other words, critics should study stories in their final forms, as 'served up' or published, not in their intermediate stages. At the time Tolkien wrote these words,[2] much of 'the Silmarillion' at least had been written several times over, as *The Lord of the Rings* eventually would be. If Tolkien had had foresight into the future, one may wonder, would he have felt that his ban on wanting to see 'the bones of the ox' should have been extended from fairy-tale collections (which of course may well have had an especially complex history) to his own fictional works?

There are reasons why he might. A major danger must be that too much study of 'the bones' makes 'the soup' lose its savour. In other words again, it could destroy the appeal, or charm, or 'glamour' of a finished work to know that some particularly cherished feature of it was in fact only an authorial accident; while too much awareness of wrong turnings the author might have taken could blur one's final sense of the right turning he did take. The risks are manifold. In the case of *The Lord of the Rings*, one might fear that too much looking at intermediate stages (in this case volumes VI–IX of 'The History of Middle-earth') could blur the edges of one's perception of the final stage, or of the work as published (for even after publication Tolkien continued to have afterthoughts, as one sees from both the *Unfinished Tales* and volume XII of 'The History of Middle-earth'); while in the case of *The Silmarillion*—which in a real sense never reached a final stage at all—over-careful picking over of volumes I–V and X–XI of 'The History' could easily lead to the loss of any sense of structure whatsoever.

If that were all that could happen, this chapter would have remained unwritten. Nevertheless, one has to face the fact that much of 'The History of Middle-earth' demands to be taken as 'ox-bones'—though a proportion of it is unpublished original work, and some at least of the 'bones', like the *Book of Lost Tales,* are easy to read in their own right—and furthermore that the kind of reaction I have just suggested is at least a possibility, or, some of the time, a certainty. Yet one may reflect that much of the trouble (and here one loses contact with Dasent's image and with Tolkien's application of it) lies with the reader, and not with the author at all.

Other authors than Tolkien have, for example, created amazement in their readers by their seeming utter inability to understand the logic of what they were doing. Charles Dickens was upset and alarmed when it was called to his attention that many of his heroes or hero/villain pairs had names beginning with his own initials, C. D.; while his surviving worksheets for *David Copperfield* (this time D. C.) show that he got even the totally transparent name Murdstone—for the *murd*erous stepfather who replaces the dead father under the grave*stone*—simply by writing a string of names across a page till he got one that felt right: Hasden Murdle Murden Murdstone.[3] Dickens never asked himself, seemingly, *why* 'Murdstone' felt right. In exactly the same way Tolkien dealt with several important queries by writing out a string of names, like 'Marhad Marhath Marhelm Marhun Marhyse Marulf' (*Treason*, p. 390), or —these are for Aragorn—'Elfstone . . . Elfstan, Elcdon, Aragorn, Eldakar, Eldamin, Qendemir' (*Treason*, p. 276), or—these are for Shadowfax—'Narothal, Fairfax, Snowfax, Firefoot [,] Arod? Aragorn?' (*Shaping*, p. 351). It is a surprise to learn that Aragorn could ever have been a name for a horse; even more surprising, given what is said about the meaning of the name, in pp. 170–71 above, that Saruman could have been the meaningless 'Saramond' (*Treason*, p. 70). I do not think there is any doubt that Murdstone in *David Copperfield* does 'mean' what is said above, and there is even less doubt about Saruman, whose name is a philological crux. But neither Dickens nor Tolkien seems to have started off with meaning; rather with sound.

All this comes as a shock. It may also prove an irritation. At one point (*Lost Road*, p. 217) Christopher Tolkien remarks of a passage in the carefully prepared 1937 'Quenta Silmarillion', '*Elwë* here, confusingly, is *not* Thingol', with a paragraph of explanation to follow. 'Confusingly' is putting it rather mildly. It seems unlikely that anyone at all could ever keep in mind all the variations and permutations which Tolkien carried out on his elvish characters for *The Silmarillion*. Finrod becomes Finarfin; Inglor becomes Finrod; besides the Ellu/Elwë/Olwë alternatives, one finds Elwë 'Thingol' (more accurately Elu Thingol in Sindarin, Elwë Singollo in Quenya) at different times as Ellon, Tinthellon, Tinto'ellon, Tinwelint, Tintaglin. Some of these changes are there to show the processes of language-change which were a major part of Tolkien's creativity from the beginning (see *BLT 1,* p. 48, a passage written c. 1919). But there are also signs of a continuous and seemingly random fiddling, which generates for instance diagram after diagram of the relations between the various tribes, groupings or languages of the elves (see *BLT 1,* p. 50; *Shaping,* p. 44; *Lost Road* pp. 181–83, etc.). Just as with Finrod or Thingol, it is at best confusing, at worst irritating, to discover that the Teleri were at one time the senior, at another the junior branch of the 'Light-elves'; and that the change really does not seem to make much *difference!* I have used the term 'fiddling'. But Tolkien commented more accurately on this tendency in himself in an interesting passage in Part 2 of 'The Notion Club Papers', in *Sauron Defeated,* pp. 239–40. There the character Lowdham criticises the very activity of inventing languages, that 'secret vice' of which Tolkien accused himself in *Essays,* pp. 198–223. Lowdham says:

> 'Anyone who has ever spent (or wasted) any time on composing a language will understand me. Others perhaps won't. But in making up a language you are free: too free . . . When you're just inventing, the pleasure or fun is in the moment of invention; but as you are the master your whim is law, and you may want to have the fun all over again, fresh. You're liable to be for ever *niggling,* altering, refining, wavering, according to your linguistic mood and to your changes of taste.'

Lowdham goes on to say that the languages he finds coming to him are *not like that;* and I have also omitted a section in which Lowdham says there are constraints on any conscientious inventor. Yet the word italicised above — the italics are mine — is a significant one. Tolkien used it elsewhere as the name of the character in his self-descriptive allegory 'Leaf by Niggle' (see pp. 43–44 above). He knew that one of his temptations was 'to niggle', i.e. *(OED)* 'to spend work or time unnecessarily on petty details; to be over-elaborate in minor points'. He could not do this (so much) with real philology, because there the data were available to others. But where 'his whim was law', in inventing his own languages (geographies, genealogies), he was likely to give in to temptation. Of course we should never have known it if we did not have, in this case, 'the bones of the ox'. But the revelation could create unease.

There are other surprising criticisms of Tolkien latent in 'The History of Middle-earth'. Sometimes, and in contrast to the 'niggling' just discussed, he was stubborn to the point of pig-headedness about sticking to names, apparently in total incomprehension of their likely effect on contemporary readers. He kept using the term 'Gnomes' for the Noldor till at least 1937, in confidence that 'to some "Gnome" will still suggest knowledge', through its connection with Greek *gnome*, 'intelligence' (see *BLT 1*, pp. 43–44). To some, possibly. However, to all but a vanishingly small proportion of English speakers, 'gnome' has lost all connection with its Greek root, and means instead a small, vulgar garden ornament, very hard to take seriously. Similarly, as remarked above, p. 95, Tolkien stuck to the name 'Trotter' while the character who bore it changed from a wandering hobbit to a hobbit-Ranger to a human Ranger to the last descendant of the kings of old. Very late in the construction of *The Lord of the Rings*, Aragorn, or 'Strider' as he eventually became, is still declaring (*War*, p. 390), 'But Trotter shall be the name of my house, if ever that be established; yet perhaps in the same high tongue it shall not sound so ill . . .' Wrong! For 'trot', as the *OED* rightly says, implies 'short, quick motion in a limited area', and is quite inconsonant with dignity when applied to a tall Man. Tolkien (we can see with hindsight) should have dropped the idea much earlier, along with much else: his preference for 'hobbit-talk' over action (see *Shadow*, p. 108), his strangely hostile picture of Farmer Maggot (*Shadow*, p. 291), his inhibiting confusions over the number and names of the hobbits with the Ring-bearer, over Gandalf's letter via Butterbur, and the general 'spider's web' of argumentation near the start of *Lord of the Rings* (see *Treason*, p. 52).

Meanwhile and conversely, it is almost dismaying — at least to the critic — to see what seem to be absolutely essential elements both of *The Silmarillion* and *The Lord of the Rings* excluded sometimes till virtually the last moment. The Ring is 'not very dangerous, when used for good purpose', says a naive note in *Shadow*, p. 42, and cp. p. 77 above; 'It is indeed a remarkable feature of the original mythology', says Christopher

Tolkien, 'that though the Silmarils were present they were of such relatively small importance' (*BLT 1*, p. 156, and cp. p. 241 above). A harmless Ring, meaningless Silmarils: as one reads through 'The History of Middle-earth' it is possible to feel — and this applies *especially* to a reader who knows the finished works well — that Tolkien did not know what he was doing. Tolkien himself once imagined summoning the scribes of the *Ancrene Wisse* from the dead, to indicate silently to them minor errors of grammar (see p. 41 above). If we were to do this to the shade of Tolkien, it would be hard not to put one's finger on Aragorn's 'Trotter' sentence just quoted without, perhaps, a look of quizzical reproach.

Yet having said all this — and it has been said with deliber-ately unmitigated bluntness — one has to consider in the end exactly what one's criticism may be. It seems hardly fair to criticise an author for not writing the book one would have liked; even less fair to complain that he did write the book one would have liked, but failed to manage it on the first try! Per-haps the real danger in picking over 'the bones of the ox' is no more than this: it comes as a threat to our general notion of cre-ativity. In our often dimly-perceived 'model' of the author at work, there is a tendency to think of him or her as following a Grand Design to which only the author is privy, and which is both central inspiration and guiding star. Critics often search for this — certainly that is what I was doing in 1970 when Tol-kien wrote me the letter referred to in my 'Preface' to this vol-ume, and from which the title for this chapter is taken. Dis-covering that the author does not have a guiding star, and is trying things out at random, can be a disillusionment; as can the realisation that the Grand Design (the Silmarils, the nature of the Ring) was in fact one of the last things to be noticed. Yet such disillusionment is in a sense only in the reader's head, nothing to do with the work or indeed the author. And one thing that following the progress of a work through 'the course of actual composition' can do is provide one with a more truth-ful model of the way that authors work — Tolkien being in this case (one may well suspect) more representative of authors in general than one might suppose, except in two respects: the very long gestation period of all his works, and his deep reluc-tance ever to discard a draft.

Nor need one abandon absolutely the notions of guiding star and Grand Design. For all the many surprises, false roads and spiders' webs of 'The History of Middle-earth', it still demonstrates very conclusively that Tolkien did have an over-powering urge towards expressing something, something which kept on pulling him even if he had lost (or not yet gained) clear sight of it. Do we now have a better image of the something? And can we find a better 'model' of the way Tolkien's creativity worked? These questions are considered in the rest of this chapter.

Lost Road, Waste Land

Tolkien had a theory, at least, about the second of the two questions above, which he expressed in a repeated fiction, or fictional debate — one hesitates to call it a story. This exists in two main forms, 'The Lost Road', from c. 1937, printed in *The Lost Road*, pp. 36–104; and, written some eight or nine years later, at a time when he might have been expected to be fully occupied with *The Lord of the Rings*, 'The Notion Club Papers', printed in *Sauron Defeated*, pp. 145–327.[4] The fictions are close enough to each other almost to be described in Christopher Tolkien's term (see *Shadow*, p. 3) as 'phases'. They have at least strong common elements, if not a common root.

The most obvious of these, not at all surprisingly, is continuous playing with names. In 'The Lost Road' the key names are two from an ancient Germanic legend, written down by Paul the Deacon in the eighth century, but dealing with events of the sixth. This germinal story tells of a king of the Lombards — for their importance to Tolkien, see below, p. 351 — called Audoin. He refused as it were to 'knight' his son Alboin after a battle, because Alboin had not yet received arms from a neighbouring king, as was the custom of this people, evidently and rightly designed to avoid favouritism. Alboin accordingly went to the king he had just defeated, and whose son he had just killed, and asked him to grant him arms, with a kind of noble or quixotic confidence in King Thurisind's magnanimity. His confidence was not misplaced; Alboin received his arms and his 'knighthood'; though he repaid the favour only with a series of brutalities leading to his own later murder, for forcing his wife to drink a toast from her father's skull, accompanied by what one can only call the orcish pleasantry of inviting her 'to drink merrily with her father'.

What caught Tolkien's eye in this was evidently not the story but the names: Alb-oin = Old English Ælf-wine = 'elf-friend', Aud-oin = Old English Ead-wine = 'friend of prosperity, bliss-friend'. 'Elf-friend': why should people be given names like that, consistently, over many centuries from the sixth to the eleventh, and from countries as far apart as Italy and England, if there had not been some original conception behind it? Audoin meanwhile had survived even into modern times, via Ead-wine, as the modern English Edwin. Did this not suggest that there was still some form of *living* tradition in the names and their meanings? Another element was the Old English name Os-wine, or 'god-friend', also surviving, if not very often, in the name Oswin (cp. Oswald). From these survivals and indications of continuity Tolkien began to sketch out a story about progression: from a modern day three-generation family tree (which ran Oswin — Alboin — Audoin, all of its members philologically conscious of the forms and meanings of their own names), back to the Lombardic son and father, and then back further to the mythic Germanic past, to Irish legend, to the unrecorded men of the Ice Age, and through them to Númenor. But in Númenor the names would be of different form, though identical meaning: Elendil = 'elf-friend' = Alboin, Herendil = 'bliss-friend' = Audoin, Valandil = 'god-friend, friend of the Valar' = Oswin. Moreover in Númenor the meanings of the names would be much more pointed, even incipiently antithetic: for in Númenor just before its fall, to be a friend of the elves, or even worse a friend of the Valar, was to risk death by sacrifice to Morgoth. Elendil and his son Herendil are indeed in Tolkien's story of 'The Lost Road' almost on the brink of separation, for the son, less wise than his father, seeks 'bliss' rather than truth, and bliss seems to his generation to be best achieved by obedience to their rulers and rebellion against the gods.

Yet Tolkien never achieved a full story on this theme. 'The Lost Road' is, even in outline, only a sequence of oppositions; plus a thesis about how events of the past might come to be known, through dreams and through a sort of linguistic vision. A great part of 'The Lost Road' in fact consists of detailing how Alboin, the modern English son, later to become a professor, finds coming to him from outside — not via his own invention — snatches of languages, including the 'Elf-Latin' Quenya, as well as Old English and even Old Germanic (the *-ancestor of Old English, Gothic and Lombardic as well). This trail soon petered out, with Tolkien sending his narrative-less 'Lost Road' fragment to Stanley Unwin in 1937, after the success of *The Hobbit*, having it rejected (no doubt with utter incomprehension) and dropping the idea for eight years, during which he was writing the bulk of *The Lord of the Rings*. Yet when he revived it, as 'The Notion Club Papers', with an apology to Sir Stanley for ever having troubled him with 'The Lost Road', what he did, with remarkable stubbornness, was to persist in *not* inventing a story, and instead to expand on what one might now call his obsessive playing with names and brooding on the question of transmission.

Part One of 'The Notion Club Papers' opens with a rejection of C. S. Lewis's device of using mere machinery (a spaceship, an *eldil*-powered coffin) to get his characters to Mars or Venus. The right way to explore other worlds, says Ramer, the main speaker at this point, is via dreams and via the languages you hear in them. But then in a strange switch, one of the most sceptical and persistent of his hearers, Lowdham, starts to speak with tongues and to see visions even during the course of the Club's own meetings, while he also starts to record snatches of languages very similar to those of Alboin in 'The Lost Road'. Further, an undergraduate member of the Club, John Jethro Rashbold, begins to speak with tongues as well; while a fourth member, Wilfrid Trewin Jeremy, somehow joins Lowdham inside one of Lowdham's own dreams — a vision of Anglo-Saxon England in King Alfred's time — as Tréo-wine (another -wine name, this time 'pledge-friend').

All the characters who speak are, rather evidently, reflections of Tolkien himself. Ramer is a professor of philology, Lowdham a lecturer on English language; Rashbold's last name is a 'calque' of Tolkien's (from German *toll-kühn* = 'crazy-bold'), while his middle name, 'Jethro' is linked with Tolkien's third name, 'Reuel', in the Old Testament; and though Christopher Tolkien regards the theory as 'unlikely' (*Sauron Defeated,* p. 189), it seems plausible that 'ramer' is in fact meant to be the dialect word 'raver, babbler', and so to fit Tolkien's repeated self-image as one who sees visions and dreams and is accordingly stigmatised by others as a 'looney' (see his poem of that name from 1934 and its later revision, pp. 283–85 above). As for Alwin Arundel Lowdham and Wilfred Trewin Jeremy, Alwin and Trewin are variants on the 'x-friend' series with which this discussion started, while Arundel — normal English surname that it is — is also a modernised version of Anglo-Saxon Éarendel, or Eärendil, the great Intercessor between gods and Middle-earth of Tolkien's mythology. What these two fictional 'phases' tell us about the way Tolkien's creativity worked — or the way he thought it worked — is surely this: he thought that ideas were sent to him in dreams, and through the hidden resonances of names and languages. He thought that the dreams and the ideas did not come from his own mind but might — like the names, after all — be the record or memory of something that once might have had an objective existence. A sceptic would naturally say that this belief is just another illusion, that the conviction that a dream 'comes from outside' comes from the inside, just like the dream. In reply to this (or possibly in agreement with it) I would point only to my remarks on pp. 21–22 above about the disorienting effects of studying the history of early literature philologically, so that 'the thing which was perhaps eroded most of all was the philologists' sense of a line between imagination and reality'. Once one had got used to tracing linguistic correspondences with *absolute confidence that they did represent reality,* it was a rather easy step to assuming that the guide to reality was one's own sense of linguistic correspondences. Tolkien's creativity, as this book has said many times, came from somewhere between the two positions expressed in the last sentence.

But if his playing with words and names tells us something of how he worked, what was he working *on*? What do all these varied relationships between people mean, and what was the 'something' that pulled him on, whether he had a Grand Design or not? A major theme, at least, is signalled by the two separate fragments of Old English which Tolkien wrote, rewrote and worked into both 'Lost Road' and 'Notion Club Papers' as genuine 'transmissions' from the past. The first of these *is* genuine: that is to say, it comes from a real, surviving Old English poem, *The Seafarer*, though adapted by Tolkien in both versions he gave. In 'The Lost Road' the lines come to an Old English poet, Ælfwine, as he chants them to a crowded hall:

> Monað modes lust mid mereflode
> forð to feran, þæt ic feor heonan
> ofer hean holmas, ofer hwæles eðel
> elþeodigra eard gesece.
> Nis me to hearpan hyge ne to hringþege
> ne to wife wyn ne to worulde hyht
> ne ymb owiht elles nefne ymb yða gewealc.

'The desire of my spirit urges me to journey forth over the flowing sea, that far hence across the hills of water and the whale's country I may seek the land of strangers. No mind have I for harp, nor gift of ring, nor delight in women, nor joy in the world, nor concern with aught else save the rolling of the waves.' (*Lost Road*, p. 84)

The moment Ælfwine chooses to chant this is highly inappropriate. He is in a king's hall, full of Dane-hunters and experienced warriors. Their view is that if Ælfwine would rather go to sea than receive gifts in the hall, let him get on with it! His yearning for the rolling waves leaves him socially isolated, a 'raver', a 'looney'. In 'The Notion Club Papers' Alwin Lowdham the linguist appears to be Ælfwine come again. One windy evening in 1954 he 'picks up' the seven lines just quoted, except that (a) they are in the Old Mercian dialect, not Old West Saxon, and (b) lines 3 and 4 have become:

> obaer gaarseggaes grimmae holmas
> aelbuuina eard uut gisoecae

'that I seek over the ancient water's awful mountains Elf-friends' island in the Outer-world.' (*SD*, p. 243)

The other repeated passage of Old English verse in these two works — this time one entirely original to Tolkien — runs as follows:

Thus cwæth Ælfwine Wídlást:
Fela bith on Westwegum werum uncúthra
wundra and wihta, wlitescéne land,
eardgeard elfa, and ésa bliss.
Lyt ænig wát hwylc his longath sie
thám the eftsíthes eldo getwæfeth

'Thus said Ælfwine the far-travelled: "There is many a thing in the West-regions unknown to men, marvels and strange beings, a land fair and lovely, the homeland of the Elves, and the bliss of the Gods. Little doth any man know what longing is his whom old age cutteth off from return".'

This time the lines come in 'The Lost Road' (p. 44) to Alboin, a twentieth-century teenager, again in a dream, and he tells them to his father. Yet doing so is *still* socially inappropriate. The last two lines sound insolent when said by a young man to an old one — to one who is in fact about to die — and as soon as Alboin quotes them, 'He suddenly regretted translating them.' His father indeed remarks that he did not need to be told: for him there will only be a *forthsith*, the compelled journey of Death which both Bede and Niggle were sent on (see p. 43 above), no *eftsith*, no going back. Once again these lines recur to Lowdham in 'The Notion Club Papers', with only two words added: Ælfwine Wídlást is now *Eadwines sunu*, Edwin's (or Audoin's) son. But on this occasion Alwin Lowdham cannot wound his father: *his* father did not wait for *eldo*, old age, but put to sea in 1947 in his boat *The Eärendel* and was never seen again. Drowned, or killed by a floating mine? Or did he succeed, perhaps, in finding the *aelbuuina eard*, the *eardgeard elfa* which is the common theme of both poems, the 'Elf-friends' island, the homeland of the elves'?

The recurrent motifs in these repeated passages are: the existence of an Earthly Paradise somewhere in the West; it being known to a select body of 'Elf-friends', whether in Old or modern England; the knowledge leading to a state of baffled yearning, or *langoth*; but return to the Paradise being irrevocably cut off, whether by old age (as for the 'Lost Road' father), or by physical impossibility (the theme, in a way, of the long 'Notion Club' discussion of the devices of C. S. Lewis). Nor is it hard to interpret the motifs. No-one could avoid the thought that the frustrated visionaries (Ælfwine, Alboin, Alwin Lowdham) represent Tolkien himself. But to this one should surely add the reflection that so do the visionaries' fathers: the missing father of Lowdham, the father-about-to-die of Alboin. The repeated father-son pairings in these debates all attempt to convey a kind of dialogue within Tolkien himself, as indeed does the whole 'Notion Club' scenario with its revealingly-named members. One half of Tolkien, one might say, was urging his spirit out across the sea, to visions of Paradise and discontent with the world; another half was telling him this was a waste of time. And, surprisingly, was threatening him with the shadow of *eldo*, old age, before he himself had passed his forties. A further indication of a kind of 'split personality' surfaces in 'The Lost Road', when Elendil in Númenor hears a song sung by one Fíriel, and feels his heart sink. It is odd that this should be his reaction, for Fíriel is the name of the mortal maiden who, in another poem by Tolkien from 1934 (see pp. 281–82 above), *rejected* passage into the West, with the words 'I was born Earth's daughter'. It seems as if Fíriel has changed her mind and accepted passage to the West; though, it is true, only to Númenor, not to Valinor and the lands of true immortality. Fíriel, one should add (see *Lost Road*, p. 382), is also a name of Lúthien: the maiden who *chose* mortality.

The total significance of this complex of splits, doublings, transmissions and reincarnations cannot perhaps be grasped. Still, it is clear that Tolkien's major theme — or so it seemed to him in these self-reflective fictions — was Death: its pain and its necessity, the urge to escape from it, the duty and the impossibility of resignation. And Tolkien saw this theme not only in fiction or in dream, but also in history and archaeology. Lowdham's father tried to escape from Death physically in his boat *The Eärendel;* possibly he succeeded, but probably not. Tolkien suggested repeatedly that the well-known ship-burials of England and Scandinavia, real burials like the ones at Sutton Hoo or at Vendel in Sweden, were motivated by some similar urge to escape. The custom went back, he said, to a belief in — or memory of — a land ruled by the gods in the West to which:

in shadow the dead should come . . . bearing with them the shadows of their possessions, who could in the body find the True West no more. Therefore in after days many would bury their dead in ships, setting them forth in pomp upon the sea by the west coasts of the ancient world. (*SD*, p. 338)

Yet even then this belief can have seemed little more satisfying than the Númenorean success in achieving, not immortality, but the art of preserving corpses. To those who remained the wrong side of the 'Sundering Sea', the world came to be like the dreary land, the waste land, of Tréowine's song in *SD*, pp. 273–76, identical, except in being set out as prose rather than alliterative verse, with the poem of 'King Sheave' attached to 'The Lost Road' (pp. 87–90):

'No lord they had, no king, nor counsel, but the cold terror that dwelt in the desert, the dark shadow that haunted the hills and the hoar forest: Dread was their master. Dark and silent, long years forlorn, lonely waited the hall of kings, house forsaken without fire or food.'

For Tolkien there was no 'eucatastrophe' (to use his own term; 'OFS', *Reader*, p. 85). The sense of age and exclusion seems to have grown on him more and more strongly (see ch. 8 above, *passim*). Yet those feelings seem now to have been with him *from the very beginning,* while he was still a young man in his early twenties. Another phrase common to both 'Lost Road' and 'Notion Club Papers' is (in various languages) *westra lage wegas rehtas, nu isti sa wraithas,* 'a straight way lay westward, now it is bent'. But this thought, if not the geography behind it, had been with Tolkien since 1916. *The Book of Lost Tales* opens with 'The Cottage of Lost Play'. In the cottage, though, Eriol the wanderer is told of another cottage, in the past, in Valinor, to which the children of men could come by the Path of Dreams. Vairë, explaining this, says, 'It has been said to me, though the truth I know not, that that lane ran by devious routes to the homes of Men'. The routes are 'devious'; they were not then 'bent'. But even then taking the path was dangerous, for according to old tradition human children who had once seen Elfland were liable on return to become 'strange and wild'. That lane is blocked now, says Vairë. Yet it seems that the children of his cottage are able to travel the other way, to find lonely children in the Great Lands, i.e. our world, Middle-earth, or 'those that are punished or chidden', and comfort them.

There is a 'Peter Pan' element about all this which Tolkien almost immediately dropped and thereafter disliked, but one has to say that the Path of Dreams was one of the most stable elements of his thinking, from 1916 to at least 1946. It is easy enough to call it 'escapist', and indeed the idea of the Great Escape from Death surfaces in Tolkien's mythology again and again. Yet one has to say (and see further below) that he never gave way to it. No doubt it was a temptation for a young man, in the middle of a great war, with no close living relatives and most of his friends dead, to lose himself in dreams of a world where none of this need be true; to construct a myth as context for the dreams; and then to rake together from his learning an elaborate self-justification for the myth. But if Tolkien did this, one has to admit that he also gave equal space, equal prominence, to the loss and resignation. He had, moreover, more than purely personal motives in elaborating the complex stories which 'The Lost Road' and 'The Notion Club Papers' were attempting to authenticate.

A Mythology for England

A similar blend of fantasy and fact can be seen in Tolkien's attempt, not so much to create a 'mythology for England' — an intention and a phrase which have often been ascribed to him[5] — as a mythology *of* England. One extremely unexpected aspect of Tolkien's early writings is his determined identification of England with Elfland. As soon as this phrase is used it sounds implausible, as Tolkien would have sensed as acutely as anyone. Nevertheless, he persisted in trying to equate the two places. Tol Eressëa, the Lonely Isle, is England; Kortirion, the town of the exiles from Kor, is Warwick; Tavrobel on Tol Eressëa 'would afterwards be the Staffordshire village of Great Haywood' (*BLT 1*, p. 25). How can these equations be made out, and what is the point of them?

At their heart, perhaps, is awareness of the paradoxical nature of a 'mythology for England'. England must be the most demythologised country in Europe, partly as a result of 1066 (which led to near-total suppression of native English belief; see p. 38 above), partly as a result of the early Industrial Revolution, which led to the extinction of what remained rather before the era of scholarly interest and folk-tale collectors like the Grimms. If Tolkien was to create an English mythology, he would first (given his scholarly instincts) have to create a context in which it might have been preserved.

His earliest attempts to do this centre on the figure of Ottor 'Wæfre', Ottor the Wanderer, also known as Eriol: as it were a dual ancestral figure, a point from which two chains of transmission ran, the one authentic, the other invented, but both determinedly native and English. In Tolkien's thinking, Ottor/Eriol was by his first wife the father of Hengest and Horsa, in early but authentic legend the invaders of Britain and the founders of England. But by his second wife he was to be the father of Heorrenda, a harper of English (and Norse) legend, about whom nothing else is known — an image, therefore, of the fantastic 'lost' tradition which Tolkien was about to invent. Tol Eressëa too, the place where Eriol *learns* this lost tradition — to become *The Book of Lost Tales* and in time *The Silmarillion* — is an image of similar duality. Tolkien changed his story about Tol Eressëa, the Lonely Isle, almost as often as he changed his views about elvish languages, but one stable thing about it is that it is *un*stable. It is the island drawn repeatedly eastward and westward across the sea to convey the elves to Valinor; it is drawn across the sea also to bring the elvish expedition of rescue to Middle-earth. Even when it is 'in place', so to speak, as when it is visited by Eriol, it is not quite a part of Valinor, and still 'by devious ways' in touch with the world of men. It is in short a 'medial' or 'liminal' place, a place 'neither one thing nor the other', just as Eriol is a 'medial' person. In Tolkien's story, could one call Eriol an Englishman? Hardly. He was born in what is now Germany, just south of the Danish border. Yet he was the father of Englishmen, of the founders of England. He goes back to a time (just) before the beginnings of tradition. In the same way Tol Eressëa in Eriol's time is still off the coast of Valinor, not off the coast of Europe, but is (just) about to shift and enter the real world of true history. Sig-

nificantly it is *seo unwemmede ieg,* in Old English 'the unstained
land', with 'stain' used in the same sense as in the description
of Lothlórien; see p. 217 above. It is a place before the Fall, so
to speak, the Fall being in some way the start of English history. Tolkien was setting his tales in a context at once unaffected by the disappointments of English tradition (maimed
and mangled for us by time and neglect), and yet with a clear
channel into it.

There are many logical difficulties with this idea — where,
for instance, could one fit in the Roman occupation of Britain?
— and Tolkien did not try to follow it through. Indeed he
showed his dissatisfaction with it before very long by converting Eriol to Ælfwine (with evident connection to the themes
discussed above), and by setting the whole tale in a distinctly
later period, not the fifth century of Hengest and Horsa, but at
least four hundred years later. What advantage did Tolkien
think he might gain from this? Arguably, the move was one of
slight desperation. As has been said, almost nothing is known
of native English tradition, especially pre-Christian tradition.
There has accordingly long been an impulse among comparative mythologists, like Dasent, to seize on the cognate Norse
tradition, and either to say that the English are really half-
Norse, or else that they were really rather *like* the Norse, so
that you can argue back from the one to the other. Sometimes
Tolkien took the latter route: Christopher Tolkien notes in
BLT 1, p. 245, that his father took an Old Norse mythological
name, Askr, and 'anglicised' it philologically to Æsc. And while
Tolkien senior was not much taken by the former route, he retained at least an awareness of the Norse contribution to England. Ælfwine is thus, in Tolkien's second self-authenticating
story, actually a slave of the Forodwaith, the Men of the North
who have invaded England as they did in fact from the ninth
century on, 'and his boyhood knew evil days' (*BLT 2,* 314).
But after he has escaped, been wrecked and been rescued by
the strange, ancient, stone-shoed Man of the Sea, a further
storm casts up on his island a wrecked dragon-ship, with in it
the corpse of Ælfwine's former master. Ælfwine says, 'He slew
my father; and long was I his thrall, and Orm men called him,
and little did I love him'. The Man of the Sea, with his greater
knowledge, does not contradict Ælfwine, but he puts a differ-

ent view: 'And his ship shall it be that bears you from this Harbourless Isle . . . and a gallant ship it was of a brave man, for few folk have now so great a heart for the adventures of the sea as have these Forodwaith'. Norsemen, it seems, are at least ambiguous: enemies, but worthy of respect. Tolkien never lost this ambiguity about the Old Norse heathen tradition, as one can see from his manoeuvrings between English and Norse ascriptions in 'The Homecoming of Beorhtnoth', discussed on pp. 157–58 above. Yet the post-Viking setting of the Ælfwine story may have been felt by him as an excuse for bringing that tradition in; and indeed much of *The Book of Lost Tales* consists of evident borrowings, more or less 'anglicised', from Norse mythology. The chaining of Melko (*BLT 1*, pp. 100–4) recalls the chaining of Loki by the gods of Ásgarthr; in the same passage Tulkas is teased very much as Thórr is in the Norse poem *Þrymskviða;* the three weavers on p. 217, though labelled with words for time in Old English, strongly resemble the Norse Norns with their names Urthr, Verthandi and Skuld (or 'Past, Present, Future'); the dragon's heart, dwarf's curse and dwarvish necklace of *BLT 2* all have evident analogues from the *Eddas*. Yet once again what all this shows most clearly is how difficult it has become to create a 'mythology for England' out of pure English material! Tolkien tried a pre-English story with Eriol and a part-English story with Ælfwine, and saw a prospect of repair or liberation in both: yet neither was entirely adequate for the claim he would so much have liked to make, that the *Engle,* the English, after all 'have the true tradition of the fairies, of whom the *Iras* and the *Wéalas* (the Irish and Welsh) tell garbled things' (*BLT 2,* p. 290).

Tolkien, it can be felt, was jealous of the much better-preserved Welsh and Irish folk-traditions, as of the Norse. He did his best with scraps of native lore that survived the post-Conquest 'defoliation'. Who is the powerfully described 'Man of the Sea' in the passage discussed above? Clearly, one answer is Ulmo, the sea-god of Tolkien's mythology, as is hinted in *BLT 2,* 319–20. But another answer must be that he is 'Wade', the mythical sea-giant dimly mentioned in the furthest reaches of Old English tradition and still remembered by Chaucer, but otherwise entirely forgotten.[6] Elsewhere Tolkien toyed with a brief scrap of Old English verse about 'Ing', quoted and translated by Christopher Tolkien in *BLT 2*, p. 305. His aim seems to have been to see Ing, like Eriol, as an eponymous founder of the English, who was 'first seen by men among the East-Danes' (i.e. near where the English originated), but then went away 'eastwards over the waves' (Tolkien would probably have preferred this to be 'westwards'); but to make the semi-divine Ing, unlike Eriol, an elf and a lord of Valinor. Again, though Tolkien kept on flirting with elvish names like Ingwë, Ingil (lord of Tol·Eressëa; *BLT 1*, p. 16), or Ingolondë (later to be Beleriand; *Shaping*, p. 174), he could not quite make a satisfactory connection. Yet it is clear enough what he was looking for, or groping for: a mighty patron for his country, a foundation-myth more far-reaching than Hengest and Horsa, one on to which he could graft his own stories.

In this aim Tolkien was not successful, usually discarding his own explanations, whether of Eriol or Ælfwine or Ing, before they reached anything like a final shape. He was unsuccessful indeed in a further way, almost a comic way when one considers his own concern for 'ethnic' tone, when he eventually did submit a version of his 'mythology for England' for publication in 1937. We know now that Tolkien sent in to Allen and Unwin a bundle of material including his 'Lay of Leithian' and the 'Quenta Silmarillion', a close descendant of *The Book of Lost Tales*. But when the Allen and Unwin reader read them — or read the bits he was shown; see Christopher Tolkien's account in *Lays,* pp. 364–67, and further *Bibliography,* pp. 216–18 — he was totally perplexed, unsure whether what he was reading was 'authentic' or not (so far Tolkien would have felt he had succeeded), but regrettably quite clear that whatever its authenticity it certainly could not be English! His comment, 'It [sc. the *Silmarillion* section he was given] has something of that mad, bright-eyed beauty that perplexes all Anglo-Saxons in the face of Celtic art', has been much quoted. Yet its irony has not been fully perceived. Tolkien had done his best to root his *Silmarillion* story in what little genuine Anglo-Saxon tradition he could find. But the first time it found a reader, that reader was sure (a) that *he* was Anglo-Saxon, as indeed his name was (Edward Crankshaw), but (b) that the *Silmarillion* was not: one more sad testimony, Tolkien may have felt, to the complete deafness of modern English people, especially educated English people, to their own linguistic roots.

What Tolkien was certainly doing through all his attempts to construct a historical frame for *The Book of Lost Tales* and *The Silmarillion* was, we would now say, trying to find a 'space' in which his imagination could feel free to work. In this he was in the end successful, and even his failures may have been necessary steps on the road. As for creating a 'mythology for England', one certain fact is that the Old English notions of elves, orcs, ents, ettens and woses have through Tolkien been re-released into the popular imagination, to join the much more familiar dwarves (stigmatised by Tolkien as a Grimms' fairy-tale conception), trolls (a late Scandinavian import) and the wholly-invented hobbits.[7] More than that could hardly be expected. And yet, one might say, it was a pity that Tolkien did not get on with telling more stories, that he was — in the material discussed both in this and the last section — so preoccupied not with what was told, but with how the telling came to be transmitted. Was he ever to gain any advantage from these professional tangles?

Creating Depth

There is a one-word answer to that question, which is 'depth', the literary quality Tolkien valued most of all. But since 'depth' is not commonly recognised, or even noticed, in the sense that he intended, more explanation is required. Tolkien's views on the subject have also become a good deal clearer as a result of the publications of the last ten years.

In his essay on 'Sir Gawain and the Green Knight', for instance, delivered in 1953 but not published till thirty years later, Tolkien declared that the poem 'belongs to that literary kind which has deep roots in the past, deeper even than its author was aware. It is made of tales often told before and elsewhere, and of elements that derive from remote times, beyond the vision or awareness of the poet' — like *Beowulf*, Tolkien goes on to say, or like *King Lear* and *Hamlet*. Tolkien then

paused, digressing consciously from his major theme in the essay, to consider further the idea of 'deep roots' and how one
can detect them in a work (like *Sir Gawain*) of whose immediate sources we know, in fact, next to nothing:

> It is an interesting question: what is this flavour, this atmo-
> sphere, this virtue that such *rooted* works have, and which
> compensates for the inevitable flaws and imperfect adjust-
> ments that must appear, when plots, motives, symbols, are
> rehandled and pressed into the service of the changed
> minds of a later time, used for the expression of ideas quite
> different from those which produced them. (*Essays,* p. 72)

Regrettably, perhaps, Tolkien then caught himself digressing,
said that 'though *Sir Gawain* would be a very suitable text on
which to base a discussion of this question', it was not what he
meant to discuss that day — or, alas, any other day. Tolkien
turned, in other words, from the question of 'ox-bones' to the
flavour of the soup, and went on to consider problems only in
the surviving text itself. Yet he had made the point (using in
fact the word 'flavour') that deep roots for a text are not just
something incidental, to be studied by scholars: they also affect
the nature of the text itself, and can be detected by the sympathetic ear, possibly even the naive or unscholarly ear. How they
do this, as he said, is an interesting question, though one virtually never studied.

I considered the matter with reference to Tolkien's own
aims in writing *The Silmarillion* in a passage above, pp. 229–30,
laying particular emphasis on a letter by Tolkien dated 20 September 1963, in which he discusses the 'attraction' of *The Lord
of the Rings,* much of it created, one might say, by a skilful
counterfeiting of the effect of 'depth'. My arguments were replied to, in a thoughtful and courteous way, by Christopher
Tolkien in his 'Foreword' to *BLT 1,* pp. 1–7. Some points of
agreement can immediately be located, and other points now
conceded. Thus both Christopher Tolkien and I agree on the
critical role of the hobbits in 'novelising' Tolkien's later narrative — the 'collision' Christopher Tolkien points to between
Théoden King and Pippin and Merry being of very similar
type to the one I discuss between Bard and Thorin on one side

and Bilbo on the other, in chapter 3 above. We also agree entirely on the ill effects of too narrow a literary 'habituation'; while our comments on Sam Gamgee as an instructor on how to read Tolkien (and a case of the naive hearer nevertheless responding immediately to the effect of 'deep roots') are virtually identical; see *BLT 1*, p. 3, and p. 115 above. Meanwhile I concede freely, in note 3 to chapter 7 above, that I misunderstood Professor Tolkien's letter of 1963, and repeat the concession here. In the first two editions of this book I completed Tolkien's sentence 'I am doubtful myself about the undertaking' with the clause '[to write *The Silmarillion*]'. As is now abundantly clear, it had already been written, and written several times over! I should have looked back at the antecedent sentences of the letter, and realised that what was meant was something more like 'I am doubtful myself about the undertaking [to make *The Silmarillion* consistent both internally and with the now-published *Lord of the Rings*, and above all to give it "some progressive shape"]' — matters in a sense forced on Tolkien against his will. Yet with all that said, I still feel that Tolkien himself had recognised 'the problem of depth' and the difficulty of creating that quality (flavour, atmosphere, virtue) in *The Silmarillion* if published as a single book; while the solution Christopher Tolkien indicates, of providing the reader with a 'point of vantage *in the imagined time* from which to look back', while certainly right in theory, nevertheless does create striking problems of presentation and response. However, we now have more than a single-book *Silmarillion*. 'The History of Middle-earth' does make it possible to give a much more satisfying account of the nature and problems of 'depth'.

To see this clearly, one might begin by making a comparison with a work which Tolkien knew well, the Old Norse *Völsunga saga*, or *Saga of the Volsungs*, mentioned as a source on p. 345 below. This is certainly a work with deep roots; and as is not the case with *Sir Gawain*, some of those roots still survive and can be traced. The saga is in fact part of a complex or tradition of texts, which may be laid out as follows. (I base the diagram below on the work of Professor Theodore Andersson, in his *The Legend of Brynhild* [Ithaca: Cornell University Press, 1980].)[8]

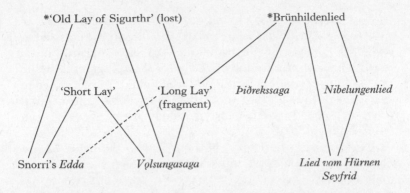

Among the things that this diagram means are the suggestions (a) that the author of *Völsunga* had access to a text which has since been largely lost, 'The Long Lay of Sigurthr', though we know it existed because of a gap in one surviving manuscript, and because Snorri Sturluson seems to have read it before it was lost; (b) that both that 'lost lay' and three other works are nevertheless similar enough to suggest a further reconstructable or *-poem behind them; (c) that even a late and poor-grade poem like the *Lied vom Hürnen Seyfrid* may nevertheless have a kind of value as a witness to something greater than itself.

But one further point one can make about *Völsunga,* independently of its own merits, is that framed in a context like this, even its *de*merits can create a kind of eerie charm. There is something very strange about a central aspect of the Brynhildr-story in *Völsunga.* Most of the texts above agree that Brynhild the Valkyrie was married to Gunnar king of the Burgundians as a result of deceit: she had sworn to marry only the man who could best her, and Gunnar could not manage it. Sigurd did it in his place and in his shape, handing Brynhild over to Gunnar only once she had been won. How did he tame her? Did he take her virginity — so in some way or other breaking a taboo and depriving her of her magic strength, as Delilah did by cutting Samson's hair? The German *Nibelungenlied,* its courtly author perhaps embarrassed by this aspect of the story, tells a confused tale. He declares that Sifrit (as he is called in that tale — one sees why Tolkien early thought it acceptable or even necessary to keep changing the forms of his character's names) did not deflower Prünhilt, though admitting that he was present in the marriage chamber. Yet later on Sifrit's wife, terribly jealous of Prünhilt, calls her a *kebse,* a paramour, and declares that it was her husband who took Prünhilt's maidenhead. For proof she has a ring which Sifrit took from Prünhilt when he overpowered her, and gave later to his wife. The accusation leads to Sifrit's death.

In *Völsunga* the story is even more doubtful. There Sigurthr releases an enchanted Valkyrie from her sleep and her coat of mail at once (is she Brynhildr?); promises to marry her, but leaves her; two chapters later meets her again, again promises to marry her and again leaves her; and is then given a potion of forgetfulness (which he hardly seems to need) and under its influence marries another woman. The story then goes on reasonably similarly to the *Nibelungenlied:* Sigurthr agrees to help Gunnarr win Brynhildr, rides through her magic wall of flame in Gunnarr's shape, lies with her for three nights (though with a sword between them), takes a ring from her and hands her over to Gunnarr. The 'quarrel of the queens' takes place, with the wife here telling Brynhildr that her husband was Brynhildr's *frumverr,* 'first man'. The ring is shown, Sigurthr is killed. Yet in this text there can hardly be any question of Brynhildr not knowing that it was really Sigurthr in disguise, and not her husband Gunnarr, who took her virginity — the obvious motive for her hatred and revenge — for Brynhildr herself declares that *before* she married Gunnarr she had already born a daughter to Sigurthr! It is impossible for this part of the *Völsunga saga* to make sense. If Brynhildr is to take offence, it can only be over the deceit, not over defloration. So how did she lose her strength? What is the significance of the ring? Why did Sigurthr put a sword between them, and if Brynhildr thought he was Gunnarr, why did she think he did it? One could imagine answers to these questions. But they lead you outside the saga, outside the text, into its complex frame of tradition.

Now this, I would suggest, is 'depth' as Tolkien understood it: to repeat his words on *Sir Gawain,* the quality 'which compensates for *the inevitable flaws and imperfect adjustments* that must appear, when plots, motives, symbols, are rehandled and pressed into the service of *the changed minds of a later time*' (my emphases added). It is a quality which may exist in one text, but is more likely to be produced by a complex of them. It is intensified by age, by loss, by reconstruction, by misunderstanding. A vital part of it is the sense that even the authors of texts like the *Völsunga* did not understand their own story, but were doing the best they could with it. And the charm of it, the sense of puzzlement, of a factual base, of a better and richer and truer story somewhere in the hinterland but never yet told, may in fact be created not by literary success but by literary failure. Even the 'inevitable flaws and imperfect adjustments' have an effect. For one thing, they may well urge later authors into retelling the story, to impose their own sense of how it should be told: sometime in the late 1920s or early 1930s Tolkien wrote a long poem called 'The New Volsung-Lay' ('Volsungakviða En Nyja'), probably to fill in some of the gaps in the diagram above, or as he put it 'to unify the lays about the Völsungs . . . to organise the Edda material dealing with Sigurd and Gunnar' (see *Letters,* pp. 379, 452). It will be interesting, when it appears, to see how it deals with the problems indicated.

What the widely variant texts of 'The Legend of Brynhild' do between them (and this includes even the latest, most faulty and inadequate works, like *Þiðreks saga* or the *Lied vom Hürnen Seyfrid*) is create once more an imaginative space in which later authors can work, a space moreover enriched by discrepancies, arguments, the sense of different opinions and different cultures, all in a way trying to interpret the same events. Perhaps the most important result of the publication of 'The History of Middle-earth' is that it has created, especially as regards *The Silmarillion,* a corpus in many respects similar to 'The Legend of Brynhild' and the diagram above. How many ancient versions of the Brynhild-story are there? Eight, with another hypothesised. How many extant versions are there of 'The Legend of Beren and Lúthien'? At least nine, as follows:

1) 'The Tale of Tinúviel' (*BLT 2,* pp. 4–41)
2) 'The Lay of Leithian', incomplete (*Lays,* pp. 154–363)
3) *The Silmarillion,* ch. 19
4) 'The Earliest Silmarillion', ch. 10 (*Shaping,* pp. 24–25)

5) 'The Quenta Silmarillion', ch.10 (*Shaping*, pp. 109–15)
6) 'The Earliest Annals of Beleriand' (*Shaping*, pp. 300–301, 307)
7) 'The Later Annals of Beleriand' (*Lost Road*, pp. 134–35)
8) (a) Aragorn's song in *Fellowship of the Ring*, Book I, ch.11, together with (b) its earliest version, published as 'Light as Leaf on Lindentree' in Leeds, 1925, and (c) its medial version, accompanied by a further paraphrase of the whole story, in *Shadow*, pp. 179–84.
9) 'The Grey Annals' (*Jewels*, pp. 61–71)

These versions vary very considerably in length (two pages to over two hundred), in completeness (the longest version is not the most complete), in intrinsic interest (the three 'Annals' versions are naturally annalistic), in literary merit and (not the same thing) in importance for understanding the development of the whole story. Yet the existence of all the versions together does more than merely provide one with more 'ox-bones' for study. It also radically alters the flavour of the soup, creating something of the 'flavour of deep-rootedness' which Tolkien so often detected and admired.

As with *Völsunga saga*, inconsistencies are a vital part of the new reading experience. Consider, for instance, the major versions of the critical event when Thingol, Lúthien's father, first meets Beren, hears Beren's demand for his daughter and imposes on him the task of bringing a Silmaril as bride-price.[9] If one had only the *Silmarillion* version of this scene, its logic and development would seem perfectly clear. One irreducible fact about Beren is that he becomes Ermabwed, or Elmavoitë, but anyway 'the One-Handed': he loses his hand to the wolf. Since this is an irreducible fact, surely it must all along have been part of the story that Beren, in the scene with Thingol, should find himself swearing an unknowingly ironic oath: in the words of the *Silmarillion* version, 'When we meet again my hand shall hold a Silmaril' — because of course when he and Thingol meet again his hand *will* be holding a Silmaril, but both will be in the belly of the wolf. With that established, it would seem to be only plain sense for Thingol to have provoked the oath by setting up a hand-for-hand, jewel-for-jewel exchange, as again he so clearly does in the *Silmarillion:* bring me a jewel (the Silmaril) in your hand, and I will put in your hand a compensating jewel (Lúthien's hand). All this seems, I repeat, to be virtually dictated by the essential core of the story: Beren's one-handedness, Thingol's imposition of a quest, the motif of the Rash Promise.

Yet a glance at the *BLT 2* version shows that in the beginning these connections were simply not there. Beren does say, in his *second* meeting with Thingol (there Tinwelint), 'I have a Silmaril in my hand even now', thus creating a kind of irony, but in the first meeting he does not make the corresponding promise. His exact words are only 'I . . . will fulfil thy small desire': which, of course, at the time of their second meeting he has still *not done.* The tone of the first scene is also entirely different, almost that of a joke which goes too far, without the edge of murder which creeps in later and the edge of hidden greed to be added later still. Meanwhile, in the medial version of 'The Lay of Leithian', the idea of ambiguous or ironic oaths has been brought very much into the foreground: Thingol swears to leave Beren free of 'blade or chain' but then tries unsuccessfully to make out that this oath need not apply to the mazes of Melian (*Lays,* pp. 188, 191). Yet even so there is still no sign of what one might have thought to be the critical phrase, 'My hand shall hold a Silmaril'. Version 8(c) above — the paraphrase accompanying 'Trotter's' poem in an early draft of *Lord of the Rings* — seems to have realised the potential of the 'hand' theme, for there Thingol at their second meeting reminds Beren that 'he had vowed not to return save with a Silmaril in his hand'. But the first meeting in that version is hardly described at all, so that the 'clear', the 'natural' version of this scene is still so to speak in 'imaginative space', like the true account of Brynhild's defloration.

An obvious point, once again, is that authors tend not to begin with Grand Designs which they then slowly flesh out, but with scenes and visions, for which they may eventually find intellectual justification.[10] In 'The Legend of Beren and Lúthien' (and by this I mean the collective body of texts, not any particular one) one notes also that there are scenes and images which persist regardless of their intellectual justification, or even in the absence of it. Tolkien never altered very much the dance before Melko/Morgoth, though early versions are more sexually suggestive than later ones; or the 'Alcestis' motif by which Lúthien rescues Beren from death and Mandos, regardless of whether he is Elf or Man. And he seems to have introduced the motif of the ring of Felagund before he knew precisely what to do with it. This does not exist at all in the *BLT 2* version, where the whole Nargothrond thread has yet to appear, but is fully developed in the *Silmarillion* account. Insulted by Thingol, Beren holds the ring on high, and says: 'By the ring of Felagund . . . my house has not earned such names from any Elf, be he king or no'. He seems here to be swearing a formal oath to the truth of his words, and swearing it *on the ring* — as Gollum wishes to do on the One Ring in *LOTR* Book IV, ch. 1, though Frodo will only allow him to swear *by* it; see the phrase quoted above. The corresponding scene in 'The Lay of Leithian' is very close to the *Silmarillion* one, even verbally, but it does not seem to contain the suggestion of an oath. All Beren means when he holds the ring aloft is that his inheritance and possession of it prove that he cannot be 'baseborn', or a spy or thrall of Morgoth. It is only a token or certificate.

Christopher Tolkien remarks in another context (*Shadow,* p. 430) how in his father's work, material he had had on paper for years could nevertheless suddenly acquire 'new resonance' on being shifted to a new context, and this is evidently true of much of the Beren material. The ring of Felagund was there *before* its purpose was known — just as the ring of Sigurd keeps on appearing in all texts of the Brynhild-legend, even when its particular point seems to have vanished, or is actively denied. Similarly a web of oaths and word-twistings takes shape in the Beren/Thingol scene before the point of the central oath is realised. Even what one would have thought utterly essential bits of narrative remain unsure after multiple retellings. How, after all, did Beren lose his hand? Did he strike at the wolf with the Silmaril (an unsuitable weapon, but see *BLT 2,* p. 34, or *Shaping,* p. 113)? Did he try to daunt the wolf with the sight of it, as in *Silmarillion,* p. 181? Or is it just something the wolf happened to do, as in *Shadow,* p. 183? The fact that there is no answer is now part of the story. An effect Tolkien valued very highly is what one might call the 'epicentric' one: the sense that once upon a time there had been a shattering event, never fully understood, with which a whole sequence of story-tellers had tried to cope, their failures and their partial successes all alike recording the force of the central event, like the needles jumping on seismographs unguessably far from the centre of the earthquake itself.

Tolkien wrote something to that effect in a passage of 'The Notion Club Papers', where Ramer says:

> 'I don't think you realize, I don't think any of us realize, the force, the daimonic force that the great myths and legends have. From the profundity of the emotions and perceptions that begot them, and from the multiplication of them in many minds — and each mind, mark you, an engine of obscure but unmeasured energy.' (*SD*, p. 228)

What Tolkien could not provide, of course, was the 'multiplication . . . in many minds', an effect which genuinely has to be created by the passage of time and generations. He may well have realised, though, as time went by and as the variant versions of his stories accumulated, that he was, at first by chance and then perhaps by design, building up a corpus of texts like those he was professionally used to. The thought may well have struck him that variant versions were nearly as good as 'many minds'. Certainly he was attracted by the thought of deepening what he had written by presenting it from an unfamiliar or half-comprehending perspective. That is what he was doing in the very late work of 'The Drowning of Anadûnê' (*SD*, pp. 329–440), a version of the Fall of Númenor clearly conceived of as being written by a Man of late date, sceptical temperament and limited information. He created the same effect, very successfully but on a much smaller scale, by putting his old poem of 'Looney' into a new context with 'new resonance' in *The Adventures of Tom Bombadil;* see p. 284 above. And there is a hint that Tolkien knew this was his chosen way of working in the essay on *Sir Gawain* quoted at the start of this section. Just after the passage quoted there, Tolkien says that his real subject in the lecture is not depth or rootedness, but 'the movement of [the poet's] mind, as he wrote and (I do not doubt) re-wrote the story, until it had the form that has come down to us'.

'Mere "Escapism" in Literature'

It would be possible, even tempting, to repeat the same exercise of comparative reading with several aspects of the Tolkien *legendarium:* to examine, for instance, the development of *draconitas* from Glorund through Glaurung to Smaug; to consider the developing but never determined theme of the 'dragon-helm' and its corruptions through the many versions of 'The Tale of Túrin' (more complex even than 'The Legend of Beren and Lúthien'); to see how the Silmarils and the Oath of the Sons of Fëanor develop from their early relative insignificance. And there are other topics which lead outside the *Silmarillion* corpus: the presentation of the nature of evil in the orcs (the ironies of which have never been pointed out, though the orcs have, interestingly, a concept of virtue);[11] Tolkien's development of his own poetic technique to something approaching Old English rigour, especially in his alliterative verse; or (a major theme and a major reason for his success) his surely in the end deliberate creation of a continuum of heroic figures ranging from the fierce and quasi-pagan (Helm Hammerhand, Túrin, Dáin) to the near-saintly, the almost-Christian (Tuor, Faramir, Aragorn). All these exercises would have their point, and could make interesting single studies. Yet I do not think any of them would alter anyone's overall view of Tolkien. And since this book hopes to do more than merely 'preach to the converted', it seems more important to return to the two questions asked at the end of the first section of this chapter, and see how adequately they have been answered.

How did Tolkien's creativity work? A good deal has been said above about self-reflection, 'sleepwalking' and creating 'imaginative space'. Yet there is one further thought generated powerfully by reading Tolkien's early drafts, though to elaborate it seems to concede advantage to some of his fiercest critics. This is — I put it candidly in the hope of an answering candour — that the drafts suggest his critics sometimes had the right idea; they detected in the finished work tendencies much more obvious in the medial stages, as also, on occasion and even more suggestively, motifs which remained forever buried to author and readers alike.

Thus Edwin Muir (see above, p. 154) said that the non-adult nature of *The Lord of the Rings* was proven by its lack of genuine casualties. Théoden, Denethor, Boromir — these are the kind of characters who can be picked out in every Western as to-be-dispensed-with before the end. I have replied to Muir above. Yet in all candour one has to say that the early 'phases' of *The Lord of the Rings* show Tolkien struggling hard to prove Muir right. He really did not like scenes of pain. So, in *The Treason of Isengard*, we find Frodo laboriously explaining to Sam that though the orc hit him with a whip, he was still wearing his mithril-coat and didn't feel it (p. 336, but cp. *LOTR*, p. 889). Much more seriously, the same volume shows a long and thorough attempt to pardon even Saruman and bring him back into the fold, thrusting all responsibility for the pollution of the Shire onto a mere walk-on 'baddie', and in the process eliminating (or rather aborting) the eerie death and ghostly rejection of Saruman in Book VI, ch. 8. Earlier on, in *The War of the Ring*, it is strange to see Tolkien toning down Denethor, trying very hard *not* to write the scene in which the father rejects the dutiful son in love and admiration for the absent prodigal (see *War*, pp. 327–34, and note Christopher Tolkien's comments on p. 332). And these last two cases are not just the kindheartedness over minor matters which I conceded to Muir in the passage just mentioned, one written before 'The History of Middle-earth' began to appear. If persisted in, they would have led to major differences in the plot; to a story of much narrower emotional range, with far less sense of irrevocable loss; to a situation much closer to what Muir detected. And yet, of course, Tolkien did not persist with them. He wrote them in, and then he wrote them out. It may well have gone against his own personal grain: I note elsewhere (p. 232 above) that as soon as Tolkien did reach a hard solution he was liable to begin to soften it, and we can see now that reaching it was for him a laborious business in the first place. Still, grain or no grain, labour or no labour, he did it. Comparison of *The Lord of the Rings* with its drafts shows that Muir detected a tendency; his criticism of the entire and finished work remains false.

In similar style, a more recent book, Christine Brooke-Rose's *A Rhetoric of the Unreal* (Cambridge University Press, 1981), strangely wraps a true perception in error. It has to be said that most of the time Dr Brooke-Rose merely continues the 'criticism of denial' already amply illustrated in the first few pages of this book; like so many professional critics, she resents her subject too much to read it fully. Thus on p. 247 she declares:

> Clearly LR is overcoded in this way [sc. as 'semiological compensation'], since the megatext, being wholly invented and unfamiliar, has to be constantly explained. Apart from the 'hypertrophic' redundancy in the text itself, the recapitulations and repetitions, there are long appendices, not only on the history and genealogy, but on the languages of elves, dwarves, wizards and other powers, together with their philological development, appendices which, though ostensibly given to create belief in the 'reality' of these societies, in fact and even frankly, playfully reflect the author's private professional interest in this particular slice of knowledge, rather than narrative necessity, since all the examples of runic and other messages inside the narrative are both given in the 'original' and 'translated'. Nor are the histories and genealogies in the least necessary to the narrative, but they have given much infantile happiness to the Tolkien clubs and societies, whose members apparently write to each other in Elvish. (op. cit., p. 247)

Much of this is so familiar as to be formulaic, the product of a small closed society of critics whose members too readily reach agreement with each other, not least by way of the 'automatic snigger' (to use Orwell's phrase). Thus, if happiness is conceded, it has to be 'infantile'; 'professional interest' in philology must *ipso facto* be playful (cp. pp. 25–26 above); the 'megatext', we are told, is 'wholly invented and unfamiliar' (a save-all footnote declares that even if there *are* sources in 'Old Norse and other materials', these have nothing to do with 'ultimate "truth"', a concept apparently securely in the critic's possession; see again p. 135 above). Much of the rest is just plain wrong, with the usual inference that the critic has been too angry or self-confident to read the book: wizards don't have a language, as it happens; and though it must have seemed a pretty safe bet to complain about all the 'runic and other messages'[12] given in the narrative being translated—for ninety-nine au-

thors out of a hundred would have felt obliged to do just that —
Tolkien, as it happens, was the hundredth (see pp. 113 and 179
above, and note 5 to chapter 6 below). As for 'Nor are the histories and genealogies *in the least* necessary to the narrative', that
ignores the whole question of 'depth' — the one literary quality, to say no more, which most certainly distinguishes Tolkien
from his many imitators.

And yet, and in spite of all this, Dr Brooke-Rose has a
point. She feels that *The Lord of the Rings,* viewed as fantasy, is
weighed down by 'hypertrophic' realism, by 'naive and gratu-
itous intrusions from the realistic novel'. Must genres always
practice *apartheid*? Evidently not. Still, reading the drafts of
The Lord of the Rings does make it clear what a temptation it
was for Tolkien to fall back on the familiar clichés of the realistic novel. Rayner Unwin, the young son of Tolkien's publisher,
noticed this at a very early stage indeed; his father wrote to
Tolkien that he had said chapters 2 and 3 had 'a little too much
conversation and "hobbit-talk" which tends to make it lag a little' (*War,* p. 108). Tolkien replied, 'I must curb this severely',
and he did: not totally, but a great deal more than in his first intention. In general, one may say that especially in the earliest
'phases', whenever the hobbits become the central figures of
the narration — the hobbits being obviously the most modernistic and novelistic characters in the book — Tolkien found
himself getting bogged down in sometimes strikingly unnecessary webs of minor causation. How many hobbits set out with
Frodo (originally Bingo), and what were their names and fami-
lies? Why did Farmer Maggot dislike Frodo/Bingo? How did
'Trotter' authenticate himself, was he an eavesdropper, and
how many letters did Gandalf write? Most of these questions
would now appear to be easily soluble, but they were not easily solved. What Tolkien's sometimes maddening hesitations
show is exactly how difficult he found that blend of ancient and
modern, realistic and fantastic, which in the end he developed
so successfully, and so much to his critics' disapproval. I repeat
that Dr Brooke-Rose's comments on Tolkien mostly strike me
as prejudiced to the point of wilful blindness. Like Muir, she is
a guide often only to what Tolkien was not. Yet like Muir, she
does see, with a certain insight, what he was *tempted* to be. The
final point to make, obviously, is that while Tolkien might not

have eradicated every trace of soft-heartedness (Muir) or 'realistic hypertrophy' (Brooke-Rose), he did nevertheless in the end and painfully fight off most of both temptations. Indeed, one could go further and say this: it seems an inherent temptation in romance to produce what is now called a 'cop-out' ending, an ending which defies the narrative logic of the story in the interests of popular sentiment or intellectual rationalisation. So Dickens gave *Great Expectations* a last-minute reconciliation; while the author of *Sir Gawain* tried to pass off all the events of his story as a totally unsuccessful practical joke on Guenevere. Tolkien too felt this temptation. He even wrote the ending: i.e., the 'Epilogue' (*SD*, pp. 114–35), with its strange similarity to the ending of George Lucas's *Star Wars* (medals, triumph, the gratifying elevation of the humble). But having written it, *he rejected it*. The rejection makes one realise that creativity involved for Tolkien not only invention, not only philological brooding and the discovery of self-licensing fictions: it also demanded self-knowledge and self-restraint.

The other question still 'hanging over' from p. 295 above is the (perhaps unanswerable) one of what—if it was not a Grand Design—was the urge which kept pulling Tolkien on to write through decades of discouragement. Here again a hostile critic may have a point to make. The critic on this occasion is one for whom I have considerably more respect than I do for Muir and Brooke-Rose. His name is Leonard Jackson, and he is the author of a distinguished trilogy of works considering the modern masters of literary theory, de Saussure, Marx, and Freud, and the way in which they have been continually distorted and misinterpreted. In the third of these works, *Literature, Psychoanalysis, and the New Sciences of Mind* (Harlow: Pearson Education, 2000), he makes the case for the Freudian argument that the power of literary works is created by their embodiment of unconscious fantasies: fantasy-patterns, unrecognised by the author, are present in the work and are transmitted to the readers, themselves unconscious of what it is they are receiving, but powerfully affected by them just the same. A textbook case of this, Jackson suggests, is *The Lord of the Rings*. Jackson remarks that all through the 1970s—and of course it must be happening again now—he found himself asking prospective students what they read, and being told '*The Lord of*

the Rings'. These prospective students were 'full of the fashionable opinions of the day: they lived in communes, were anti-
racist, and were in favour of Marxist revolution and free love'.
Jackson accordingly asked them 'why their favourite reading
should be a book about a largely racial war, favouring feudal
politics, jam-full of father-figures, and entirely devoid of sex',
but 'they never knew the answer'. One answer might have
been, though it would have been a bold prospective student
who told his interviewer this, that it was a bad question.[13] However, Jackson is certainly right in pointing to the total discrepancy, still marked, between Tolkien's own distinctly old-fashioned values and the radical attitudes of many of his admirers.
Is it just the case that a powerful story overleaps political barriers? And even if it is, where does the power come from?

Jackson's argument, set out on pp. 77–80 of the book just
mentioned, is that *The Lord of the Rings* is a classic Freudian
castration-fantasy. Its climactic scene, of course, is the biting
off of Frodo's finger with the Ring still on it, an image, says
Jackson, 'as clearly Freudian as one could ever hope to get. If
this scene is *not* a reference to the castration complex, then
there is no reference to castration anywhere in literature' (apart
from some entirely literal cases). To ensure that this option
feels right, Jackson continues, 'the book is stuffed with father-
figures', Gandalf, Fangorn, Bombadil and especially Sauron:
with the destruction of the Ring, the menacing father-figure
is removed from the scene, and Frodo abandons all possibility of growing up to be like him, while 'all the reassuring fathers are left behind'. One might add, pedantically, 'except for
Théoden', and wonder how Denethor fits in, but these objec-
tions could easily be accommodated. Jackson's main point is
that his teenage readers felt that 'the very lives they led . . . presented an enormous unconscious threat', and the removal of
that threat, beneath the surface of *The Lord of the Rings,* was
what drew them to the book. 'It was and is a very important
part of the appeal of *The Lord of the Rings* that its greatest
aficionados are quite incapable of noticing what it says.' Jackson
has the good grace to go on and add, 'Come to think of it, what
psychoanalysis suggests is that it is a very important part of the
appeal of all literature that its *aficionados* are quite incapable of
noticing what it says!'

There are several potential replies to Jackson's argument, and one is that it does not account for the work's strong appeal to groups outside his designated audience of young male students: women, children and middle-aged men, all well-represented in fan groups and fan audiences. Bits of what Jackson has to say are furthermore, and as usual, just *de haut en bas*, as in his extraordinary belief that literary critics (!) are good judges of emotional maturity. Nevertheless, I do feel he has a strong point, though I am not sure, whatever Freud may say, that it is solely and entirely to do with sex. One thing absolutely certain about *The Lord of the Rings* is that it is about renunciation: it inverts a very familiar narrative pattern, in that it is not a quest to obtain something, but an anti-quest, to get rid of it. The getting rid of it is furthermore something immensely difficult to do, perhaps in the very end impossible to achieve by will-power alone, because the Ring appeals to something deep in the fibre of everyone's being: these are the very ground-rules of the whole work. Even in Frodo, even in Sam, there is a response to evil deep in the heart. And this is not a criticism — since we are all at least as bad, no one has the moral authority to make such a criticism — just a statement of fact. Where the scene in the Sammath Naur reminded Tolkien (consciously) of the Lord's Prayer, however (see p. 145 above), one might put the case that (unconsciously) it plays out another verse of the Bible, already mentioned by me in the same context without prompting from Jackson: 'If thine eye offend thee, pluck it out'. There is something even in Frodo that responds positively to the Ring and to Sauron; to destroy the Ring, he has to lose a part of himself; having lost it, he is never the same again, nor can he be healed in Middle-earth.

But the 'it' that he loses does not have to be sex. If one considers the whole history of Tolkien's youth and middle-age, from 1892 to 1954, a period marked not only by two world wars and the rise of Fascism, Nazism and Stalinism, but also by — I give them more or less in chronological order — the routine bombardment of civilian populations, the use of famine as a political measure, the revival of judicial torture, the 'liquidation' of whole classes of political opponents, extermination camps, deliberate genocide and the continuing development of 'weapons of mass destruction' from chlorine gas to the hydrogen bomb, all of these *absolutely unthinkable* in the Victorian world of Tolkien's childhood,[14] then it would be a strange mind which did not reflect, as so many did, that something had gone wrong, something furthermore which could not be safely pushed off and blamed on other people. William Golding, author of *Lord of the Flies,* which came out in the same year as *The Lord of the Rings,* and like Tolkien a war veteran, remarked *à propos* of the meaning of his own works, 'I must say that anyone who passed through those years [of World War II] without understanding that man produces evil as a bee produces honey, must have been blind or wrong in the head'.[15] Now, if the evil-producing organ in the human brain could be identified, or if, less fancifully, some evil-generating urge in the human psyche could be identified, and if something had to be sacrificed to destroy it, would the sacrifice not be worthwhile? That seems to me to be a question raised by *The Lord of the Rings.* The answer is certainly something analogous to castration. Do the power and appeal of the work derive from the unconscious analogy? Since the process, if it exists at all, is unconscious, one naturally cannot say.

Jackson's argument furthermore brings into the foreground a major critical charge against Tolkien: that of 'escapism'. Like several of those just mentioned, this is an interesting word. It did not find its way into the *OED* till the 1972 Supplement, the year before Tolkien died; and even when it did the editors could find no citation earlier than 1933 (c.p. 'defeatism', discussed above, p. 155). The *OED* says that it means 'the tendency to seek, or the practice of seeking, distraction from what normally has to be endured'. And the *OED* has yet to find a citation which is not pejorative. In 1933 someone was complaining about the 'escapism' of Anacreon's 'bibulous, aphrodisiac lyrics' — at least the *Songs for the Philologists* were not aphrodisiac. Later on Louis MacNeice equated 'escapism' with 'blasphemy', while Joyce Cary informed his readers that 'Amanda had a great contempt for escapism'. As for the phrase at the head of this section, it comes from *Essays in Criticism:* where else? But if the *OED* is to be taken literally on 'escapism', it is hard to see how Tolkien can be convicted of it. Though he could be convicted (like most of us) of feeling an urge towards it.

I have put the case elsewhere (*Author,* pp. xxix–xxxii) for saying that the traditional opposition between 'escapist fantasy' and 'realist novel' was, throughout the twentieth century and beyond, 180 degrees in the wrong direction: it is the fantasists like Orwell or Golding or Vonnegut or Tolkien who have been confronting the fearful and horrible issues of political life, while the E. M. Forsters and John Updikes stayed within their sheltered Shires. However, there is a deeper, non-political and still more universal sense in which Tolkien rejects escapism, to which I now turn. Going back to the *OED* definition above, the experience which above all 'normally has to be endured' is Death. It has been suggested already (p. 302 above) that there would be no surprise in seeing Tolkien, the Lancashire Fusilier, survivor of the Somme, as deeply and early marked by fear of death, starting to write his fables of the Undying Lands and the potentially deathless elves in reaction or compensation. But did these *distract* him, and his readers? Or *focus their attention?* There is no doubt that Tolkien often dwelt on the *langoth,* the heartache endured by those who felt, or hoped, that there was an Undying Land at the other end of the Lost Road. If Tolkien was one of these (and if he was not, why write about it?), then the feeling itself might be called a search for 'distraction'. Yet in all Tolkien's fiction, from early to late, the point made again and again is that *langoth* has no power. No human reaches Valinor without at the least some major reservation or restriction: Frodo does, but it is not clear that he will be healed; he also loses Sam and the Shire. Eriol only reaches Tol Eressëa; Eärendil reaches Valinor, as a great exception, but is 'stellified'; the Númenorean attempt to conquer immortality kills all those who even sympathise; Fíriel turns back to clay and shadow, work and fading; Beren is resurrected, but only for a time. On a more personal note, few scenes in children's literature are more likely to make child-readers cry than the death of Thorin Oakenshield in *The Hobbit.* And death-scenes in Tolkien's fiction are, if not as common, then at least as carefully-worked as those of Dickens. Perhaps the most multivalent is the scene of Aragorn's death in one of the despised Appendices to *The Lord of the Rings.* It is true that one could say there is an element of romance, even of 'escapist' fantasy in Aragorn's immensely-extended life and quasi-saintly ability to choose the moment of his death. But by contrast there is a reverse 'anti-escapism' in the figure of Arwen, an immortal for whom death is emphatically *not* something which 'normally has to be endured', but who now realises she will have to endure it *without* the partner for whom she chose it. Aragorn says to her (it is a familiar *topos* of consolation in medieval literature)[16] that having accepted life one must accept death too, offering her also (not a familiar *topos*) a hint of escape; 'to repent and go to the Havens and bear away into the West the memory of our days together'. Arwen rejects the option and also the possibility. She puts into this narrative context a thought Tolkien knew was also universally true: 'There is now no ship that would bear me hence'. She speaks bitterly of her new sympathy for the 'escapist' Númenoreans, and all that Aragorn can say in reply is that sorrow need not be despair. Arwen does not believe him, and dies of despair herself.

Tolkien did not have a Grand Design, or a guiding star, or a single theme, but I would suggest that he was always a prey to two competing forces. One was the urge to escape mortality by some way other than Christian consolation: so far he was 'escapist'. The other was the total conviction that that urge was impossible, even forbidden. Just as much of his fiction may be seen as a tension between kind-heartedness and narrative logic, or between 'realistic hypertrophy' and the demands of romance, so the impossible attempt, to reconcile *langoth* and knowledge was for him an unfailing resource — the 'something' that kept on pulling him, but which of course he could never reach.

One final point may be made about 'escapism'. Many a classic novel (*Tom Jones, Emma, David Copperfield*) has hanging over its ending the invisible words, 'And so they all lived happily ever after'. This could be said of *The Lord of the Rings* as well — Bilbo has had it in mind as an ending from very nearly the start (see p. 32), and his wish does seem to come true. Sam gets married, Merry and Pippin become famous, the Shire enjoys a season of unnatural fertility, good weather and growth. But even inside the fiction many characters (Aragorn, Legolas, Gimli) know and say that all this is going to vanish, because such things always do. There is even a point in the deaths of Aragorn and Arwen being sent off to an Appendix. The Appendices prevent any sense of easy, happy closure, show the whole story fading into memory — and then, like the Third Age, into oblivion. Meanwhile, the actual ending is not the Field of Cormallen, nor in true cinematic cliché the ship sailing into the sunset, but the three companions riding home, along 'the long grey road' from the Grey Havens, where the ship sailed down 'the long grey firth' in 'the grey rain-curtain'. Sam returns, like Fíriel, to 'yellow light, and fire within', but something has gone out of the world just the same. Michael Swanwick, himself a brilliant writer of the fantastic, calls Sam's words, 'Well, I'm back', 'the most heartbreaking line in all of modern fantasy', and backs up his assertion with personal reminiscence.[17] More philologically, I would say that what hangs over the end of all Tolkien's fiction is not 'And so they all lived happily ever after', but the line from the Old English poem *Déor, Þæs ofereode, Þisses swa mæg*. This could be translated bluntly, 'That passed, this can too', but Tolkien translated it — see *BLT 2*, p. 323, for its importance to him and his writing — 'Time has passed since then, this too can pass'.

'So Deeply Stirred His Generation'

As the *OED* so masssively points out, words change meaning. They do so over the centuries, as a result of use, often as a result of error: from *burg* to 'burglar', from *grammatica* to 'glamour', from **hol-bytla* to 'hobbit'. But they can change also in another way, not shedding one meaning as they shift to another, but acquiring new meaning, 'new resonance' as Christopher Tolkien puts it, as a result of being placed in a new context. The poet of *Déor* could never have imagined his line of poetry being applied to a massive antiquarian romance a millennium or more after he had written it, by people who had all but forgotten his language and the stories he told. Nevertheless, it has happened: and the line, with its two demonstrative pronouns, 'that' and 'this', available as I translate it for whichever referent we choose to give them, takes on a new force no weaker for one's awareness that it was never intended.

I am sure this is the sort of fate Tolkien would have liked for his work: to be subsumed, to be taken into the unpredictabilities of tradition. For that to happen, its context would need to change; and already it is changing. As one looks at the development of Tolkien's work from 1916 and *The Book of Lost Tales* to 1967 and *Smith of Wootton Major*, one fact appears, which would, perhaps, not need saying if his critics had not been so dead sure his writing could not possibly have any relevance to the century he and they lived in. This is, as I suggest above, that *The Lord of The Rings* in particular is a war-book, also a post-war book, framed by and responding to the crisis of Western civilisation, 1914–1945 (and beyond). It is not at all clear why the response of several English and American writers, themselves personally involved in war, and deeply anxious to write about it, should have been to communicate their thoughts and experience via fantasy. Yet that is what they did: as mentioned above, William Golding, the naval officer, in *Lord of the Flies,* and subsequently in another fable of a non-human race, *The Inheritors* (1955); T. H. White, the neutralist, in *The Once and Future King,* written at much the same time as *The Lord of the Rings, nationibus diro in bello certantibus,* 'while the nations were striving in fearful war', the whole work appearing in 1958, four years after Tolkien's;[18] George Orwell, shot through the neck in Spain, in the fable/allegory *Animal Farm* (1945), and then in *Nineteen Eighty-Four* (1949); Kurt Vonnegut, the survivor of the bombing of Dresden, in *Slaughterhouse-Five* (1966). All these men were writing obviously, or even self-declaredly, about the nature of evil, which they thought had changed in their time, or about which the human race had gained new knowledge. Why did they have to write fantasy, or science fiction, if they had such an evidently realistic, serious, non-escapist, contemporary theme? No answer has been agreed, and the question has not often even been put. Still, one thing one can say is that Tolkien belongs in this group.

Or belonged. For books, like words, do not stay where they started. They may be put in new contexts, stir new feelings, have new results. I hope this is what happens to Tolkien, and think it is already happening, via his host of imitators, most of whom have no war experience and no clear sense of what he was writing about: what they get from him is different, not from what he put in, but from what he thought he put in. This is what happens to authors, if they are lucky. Tolkien evidently thought deeply about the story of the author Cædmon, not 'the father of English poetry' — Tolkien was quite sure, for reasons of his own, that he could not have been that — but allegedly the originator of Christian English poetry. His story begins near Whitby, near the year 680, when Cædmon, a North of England cowherd, went out to his byre to avoid having to sing at some festivity. There an angel appeared to him in a dream and told him what to sing. Fifty years later, his story was written down by the Venerable Bede in his *Ecclesiastical History of the English People*. Bede wrote in Latin, and gave only a translation of a part of Cædmon's first English poem. But at a very early subsequent stage someone else, not content with this, added to Bede's Latin nine lines of Old English verse, in Old Northumbrian — either remembering Cædmon's lines because they were famous, or else able to translate from Bede's Latin prose to poetry in his own dialect. The lines wandered all over Europe, as far as Russia: a major manuscript is now in Leningrad, where no doubt the Latin has long been readable, but where the Old Northumbrian must for centuries have been totally impenetrable. They were translated also into West Saxon; and two centuries after Cædmon, King Alfred of the West Saxons ordered the whole of Bede's Latin work to be translated into Old English — though he seems to have been unable to find a West Saxon to do it, the surviving translation showing signs of having been affected by Old Mercian. Probably the translator came from Worcester, very close to Tolkien. But then his translation too was forgotten for hundreds of years.

It has been rediscovered, and the whole story, from Whitby to Worcester, from Cædmon to Alfred, is once again made familiar to hundreds if not thousands of language students every year. In the process Cædmon's work itself has been totally lost, all but the nine lines written in by an early devotee, and maybe not even that. Tolkien accepted this with slight reluctance in his edition of *Exodus,* p. 34, conceding that 'none of this work [sc. what survives of Old English verse] can directly represent the moving poetry of the inspired peasant, which so deeply stirred his generation. Yet' — he went on — 'some of it evidently originated far back, not far from Cædmon's day, preserving the school or fashion of Cædmonian composition, and something of its spirit.' The words might have gone, but they stirred a generation, they transmitted a spirit.

Tolkien's words have not gone, but the rest is as true of him as of Cædmon. He would, I am sure, have liked to have applied to him — though the 'applicability' of course 'resides in the freedom of the reader', to use his own words — the words of the Worcester Bede-translator: 'Whatever he learned from scholars, he brought forth adorned with the greatest sweetness and inspiration, in poetry and well-made in the English language. And by his songs the minds of many men were kindled to contempt for the world and to fellowship with the heavenly life. And many others following him began also to make songs of virtue among the English people'. So far much of the Worcester translator's rendering could be applied to Tolkien: learning from scholars, well-made in English, minds kindled, contempt for the powers of the world, many emulators in the English language if not all within the British state. But the conclusion of his comments is apt without qualification. At the end of it all, the translator wrote, *ac nænig hwæðre him þæt gelíce dón meahte:* 'But just the same, none of them could do it like him.'

AFTERWORD

This book's main purpose has been to provide the material for a more thorough and appreciative reading of Tolkien. Closely associated with that, however, has been a desire to broaden the scope of criticism. Several writers have suggested recently that the toolkit of the professional critic at this time is too small: it does not work at all on whole genres of fiction (especially fantasy and science fiction, but including also the bulk of 'entertainment' fiction, i.e. what people most commonly read). Furthermore, it has a strong tendency to falsify much of what it *does* attempt to explain by assimilating it, often unconsciously, to more acceptable models.[1] Tolkien may be a peripheral writer for the theory of fiction. However, it seems time to pay more attention to the peripheries, and less to the well-trodden centre. If that extroversion were to encourage a greater interest in prenovelistic fiction and in 'philology' as a whole, I am sure that even 'literature', which within the British and American university systems has rejected 'language' for so long, would be the gainer.

There are still several reasons for thinking that happy issue unlikely, all of which have become clearer and clearer to me during the writing and rewriting of this book. For one thing, philology, in the sense that Tolkien meant it, has continued to lose its battle for survival in the universities of the English-speaking world. Like Galadriel, Tolkien spent his professional life fighting a 'long defeat', the stages of which one could follow by comparing, for instance, his hopeful letter of application for the Oxford Chair in 1925 (*Letters*, pp. 12–13) with his occasionally angry 'Valedictory Address' on retirement in 1959 (*Essays*, pp. 224–40, and see below). The 'long defeat' has only continued since his death. There is a violent and welcome irony, of course, in the fact that, like a vampire, philology has

sprung from its staked-out grave and into a wider world full of
complaisant victims, entirely as a result of Tolkien's fiction.
However, as one can see all too clearly from the first pages of
this work and the whole 'Foreword' to my 2001 book *Author of
the Century*, this success has not inspired as much rethinking in
the critical consensus as one might have hoped, for several reasons.

One is that, if you read very much at all of what has been
written on Tolkien, you cannot help concluding that there is
an enormous 'culture-gap' between him and his critics, which
they cannot bridge and usually have not noticed. The gap often
yawns most widely not between Tolkien and his detractors, but
between him and his admirers, at least when these happen to be
professors of English literature: in some ways it looks like a gap
not only of culture but also of temperament. Reference has
been made above (p. 234) to two opposing human urges: one
towards comprehension of wholes and classification of data
under principles and categories, the other towards a grasp of
single items, careless of their context or meaning as long as
they are there to be fully seen, explored, felt, tasted. The distinction aimed at is the famous one of William James between
'tender-mindedness' (interest in abstract schemes) and 'tough-
mindedness' (interest in concrete particulars).[1] In this James-
ian sense Tolkien was almost excessively 'tough-minded': his
temperament, his philological training and, it may be, something in the 'pragmatic' Anglo-Saxon tradition all drove him
to work out from single words, or cruxes, or kernels, or nug-
gets. There is a perfect example of this 'tough-mindedness' —
though it is not tough in any aggressive sense at all — in *Letters*
no. 312, which Tolkien wrote in 1969. This ponders mutation
in flowers, and remarks that just occasionally one can see a
plant which proves the taxonomies of scientists by not fitting
into them, by being (he mentions a particular example) 'fox-
glove' and 'figwort' at once. He goes on to trace the history of a
patch of garden daisies, in his flower-bed, then on the lawn,
finally on a patch of bonfire ash. The same seed, he observes,
came up different every time; and it was difference that in-
trigued and delighted him, not similarity.

Many of Tolkien's professional admirers do not write like
that at all, seeming to be 'tender-minded' excessively and with-

out qualification. The real horror for Tolkien would probably have come when he realised that there were people writing about him who could not tell Old English from Old Norse, and genuinely thought the difference didn't matter. If he got past that, he would have discovered writers contentedly using those cribs and 'substitutes for proper food' he had excoriated in his 1940 'Preface', tracing his thoughts through flattening, second-hand, language-less and usually wildly incorrect 'Encyclo-paedias of Mythology'. The end-product of book after book, meanwhile, is a scheme: *The Lord of the Rings* reduced to 'archetypes', related to solemn trudging plots of 'departure and return', 'initiation, donor and trial', hutching out banalities like 'for every good . . . there is a corresponding evil'. '*Every* good', Tolkien would no doubt have replied, his mind already turning to a list, 'maybe to beer there is alcoholism and to pipeweed lung cancer. But what about hot baths? starlight seen in a wood? the Eucharist? a round of hot buttered scones?' As for the other theses, he observed of W. P. Ker ('Monsters', p. 250) that if you read enough plot-summaries everything got to seem similar; but this told you nothing about any particular work. The critical remark for which Tolkien would have had least sympathy is finally Anne C. Petty's 'The mythogenetic zone for our times is the individual heart and psyche'. 'Blast our times!' (I can imagine Tolkien replying), 'and if that sentence means we should all try to get in touch with our insides, isn't it obvious myths need to come from *outside*?' As for 'mythogenetic zone', it sounds like Saruman: vague beneath a claim to precision.[3]

'Tough-minded' literature is as legitimate as 'tender-minded', and students of literature ought to have better ways of dealing with it. But even those who appreciate this quality, or say they do, have found Tolkien difficult. I cannot forbear from quoting once more the statement of Professor Mark Roberts (pp. 135, 174 above) that *The Lord of the Rings* 'is not moulded by some controlling vision of things which is at the same time its *raison d'être*'. Had Professor Roberts searched high and low for a work in which world-view and narrative were identical, he could not have found a clearer example! But Tolkien's detractors repeatedly seem blind to exactly those qualities in him which they had always said they were looking for. Thus Philip Toynbee — whose disobliging remarks on Tolkien were quoted at the start of this study — had preceded them only a little before (*Observer,* 23 April 1961) by a definition of 'the Good Writer'. 'The Good Writer', he declared, is a private and lonely creature who takes no heed of his public. He can write about anything, even 'incestuous dukes in Tierra del Fuego', and make it relevant. He 'creates an artifact which satisfies him' and 'can do no other', he takes 'certain perceptions to what would normally be regarded as excess', he 'knows much more about certain things than other people do', and when as a result his work appears it will be 'shocking and amazing . . . unexpected by the public mind. It is for the public to adjust'. This self-motivated and daemon-driven perfectionist sounds exactly like Tolkien — 'as easy to influence as a bandersnatch', said Lewis. And when one adds to it all Mr Toynbee's *sine qua non,* number 1 on his list of qualities, the assertion that 'the Good Writer is not directly concerned with communication, *but with a personal struggle against the intractable medium of modern English'* (my italics), all one can say is that it is a mystery how the critic failed to match such a clear blueprint to such a clear example in the flesh! 'It is for the public to adjust.' *But not too far.* Incestuous dukes in Tierra del Fuego, evidently, were much more acceptable as centrally humane than Sam Gamgee, or Théoden King, or Barad-dûr. Foreign, sexy, and above all gently snobbish: that was the kind of Good Writing the critical profession wanted, and if it shocked 'the public mind', so much the better. Shocking the critical mind, however, was definitely not acceptable.

It was no doubt partly Tolkien's generation which acted as a bar. Not that he was so much older than (the late) Mr Toynbee; rather that, unlike many men of his age, he had not been alienated even by the Great War from the traditions in which he had been brought up. Unlike Robert Graves, his near-contemporary and fellow-Fusilier, he never said 'Goodbye to All That'. As a result his elementary decencies — over patriotism, over euphemism, perhaps especially over sex and marriage — soon become an object of satire, provoking automatic derision from much of the literary world and preventing a fair reading. As I remark in *Author,* pp. 316–17, the English literary world from the 1920s on was dominated by the group labelled by Martin

Green as the *Sonnenkinder*, the circle of Evelyn Waugh and Cyril Connolly, frivolous, upper class, often Etonians, often Communists. Both Toynbee and the *TLS* reviewer Alfred Duggan, mentioned at the start of this work, were members of the circle, and descendants of the circle continue to be influential as editors and reviewers to this day. Their dandyism and romantic xenophilia are reflected exactly by Toynbee's longing for stories of delicious incest in far-off Tierra del Fuego. The thought stirs, naturally, that if Tolkien got through to so many people who would find no 'relevance' in 'incestuous dukes' at all, then possibly the preoccupation with licence and self-gratification which that example suggests is not a universal instinct at all, in fact just as culturally determined as Tolkien's Victorian pieties, if not more so. One of Tolkien's correspondents told him she had found in *The Lord of the Rings* 'a sanity and sanctity', and he prized the compliment perhaps more than any — though he replied that the 'sanctity' was not his, while 'of his own sanity no man may securely judge' (*Letters*, p. 413). He can judge others' sanity more fairly, though, and Tolkien thought (with good reason) that his reviewers' nausea and contempt for what he had done was so violent as to be proof of an unnatural one-sidedness: 'Lembas — dust and ashes, we don't eat that'.

Such ideological differences are even harder to bridge than the gap between 'tough' and 'tender' minds. There may be something more hopeful, though, in Mr Toynbee's remarks about 'modern English', that 'intractable medium' against which 'the Good Writer' is supposed to struggle. Finding English 'intractable' is certainly a common opinion, its *locus classicus* in recent times probably the passage from T. S. Eliot's Four *Quartets* (1944) about:

> Trying to learn to use words, and every attempt
> Is a wholly new start, and a different kind of failure
> Because one has only learnt to get the better of words
> For the thing one no longer has to say, or the way in which
> One is no longer disposed to say it. And so each venture
> Is a new beginning, a raid on the inarticulate
> With shabby equipment always deteriorating
> In the general mess of imprecision of feeling . . .[4]

With this one might compare Edmund Wilson's opinion in *Axel's Castle* (op. cit., p. 245) that the meaning of words depends on 'a web of associations as intricate and in the last analysis as mysterious as our minds and bodies themselves', while using words inevitably involves 'pouring them full of suggestion by our inflections, our pauses, our tones'. Wholly new, shabby equipment, mystery, suggestion, empty words being topped up by individual will-power: what these passages share is a conviction that since language is very complicated it is beyond the reach of reason. Inflections are private and personal; what one person means can never be fully understood by another; as in the paradox of 'Achilles and the Tortoise', you can only get closer and closer to what you want to say, but never be exactly *there*.

I do not think Tolkien would have agreed with this. He knew better than Edmund Wilson how hard words were to trace, but he also knew there were techniques for doing so; at the foundation of his art there was the perception of Grimm and Verner and Saussure and all the other old philologists, that in matters of phonology, at least, people were strictly controlled by laws of which they were not conscious. T. S. Eliot might not know why he said 'whole', 'heal', 'old', 'elder', but he *did*, and there was a reason for it which could be rendered (see p. 15 above). Semantic associations, too, could be traced, used and communicated: see 'glamour', spell', 'bewilderment', 'panache', 'worship', 'luck', 'doom' and all the rest.[5] Where 'lit.' quailed before English or felt discontented with it, in other words, 'lang.' could at least feel at home. Tolkien did not think his equipment was 'shabby', nor the Tree of Language leafless. As for modern English being 'intractable', that was a failure of education which had left its products historically deaf, deafer even than those uncorrupted ears which might be able to say — not knowing why — 'Garstang sounds northern' or 'Bree-hill and Chet-wood have the same sort of style'. All one can say is that this failure at least could be corrected. If there were a will, there would be a way.[6]

The problem remains 'misology', hatred of words, the opposite of philology. Tolkien used 'misology' and gave it this sense — it is in the *OED* under other senses — in his 'Valedictory Address to the University of Oxford': a technical piece, and addressed to a limited audience, but one which summed up much of his career experience. In 1959 he was looking back over thirty-nine years as a university teacher, all of it marked by the feuding between 'lang.' and 'lit.' which he had hoped to resolve, and his mood was not without a certain bitterness. He did not mind 'misologists' being dull or ignorant, he said, but he did feel

> a grievance that certain professional persons should sup-pose their dullness and ignorance to be a human norm, the measure of what is good; and anger when they have sought to impose the limitations of their minds upon younger minds, dissuading those with philological curiosity from their bent, encouraging those without this interest to be-lieve that their lack marked them as minds of a superior or-der. (*Essays*, p. 225)

Philology, in short, was a natural state; but where the Powers That Be were 'misologists', putting forward the views of Eliot or Toynbee or Wilson with the authority and prestige of 'mod-ern literature' behind them, nature could be deformed. From this both sides lost, falling into a state Tolkien labelled bluntly as '*apartheid*'. All he could do was go outside 'proper channels' and try to reach an unspoilt audience reading just to suit itself.

He did that successfully; his success goes far to proving his point about the naturalness of philology and the appeal of names, words and linguistic 'styles'; and in the wider sense of philology as that branch of learning which 'presented to lovers of poetry and history fragments of a noble past that without it would have remained for ever dead and dark' (*Essays*, p. 235), he showed that its appeal too was not confined to antiquity. I do not see how Tolkien can be denied the tribute of having en-larged his readers' apprehensions (of language), or their hu-man sympathies (with the disciplined, or the heroic, or the ad-dicted, or the self-sacrificing). But most of all I think his utility for the lover of literature lies in the way he showed creativity arising from the ramifications of words: unpredictable, cer-tainly, but not chaotic or senseless, and carrying within them-selves very strong suggestions of 'the reality of history' and 'the reality of human nature', and how people react to their world. Fawler, *saru-man*, fallow, Quickbeam: in each of these a word created a concept, and the concept helped to generate its own story.[7] In *The Road to Xanadu,* John Livingston Lowes's 1927 study of Coleridge and 'the ways of the imagination' (a book of a kind we need only one of, said T. S. Eliot stuffily), Lowes wrote that the 'hooks and eyes' of the memory 'will lead us to the very alembic of the creative energy'.[8] If he was wrong, it was because he thought too passively. Words, ancient words, do not have to be hooked together to make something. They have their own energy and struggle towards their own connections. Observing this impulse and co-operating with it is as good a guide for the artist as turning within oneself to the inarticulate.

APPENDIXES

·

NOTES

·

INDEX

APPENDIX A

TOLKIEN'S SOURCES: THE

TRUE TRADITION

Tolkien himself did not approve of the academic search for 'sources'. He thought it tended to distract attention from the work of art itself, and to undervalue the artist by the suggestion that he had 'got it all' from somewhere else. This appendix accordingly does not attempt to match 'source' to 'passage' in Tolkien. It does, however, offer a brief guide to the works which nourished Tolkien's imagination and to which he returned again and again; since many of them are not well known, this may give many people who have enjoyed Tolkien something else to enjoy. Whether that changes their reading of *The Lord of the Rings* or *The Silmarillion* is less important: though in fact comparison with 'the sources', in my experience, almost always brings out Tolkien's extremely keen eye for the vital detail.

He was also very quick to detect the bogus and the anachronistic, which is why I use the phrase 'true tradition'. Tolkien was irritated all his life by modern attempts to rewrite or interpret old material, almost all of which he thought led to failures of tone and spirit. Wagner is the most obvious example. People were always connecting *The Lord of the Rings* with *Der Ring des Nibelungen,* and Tolkien did not like it. 'Both rings were round', he snarled, 'and there the resemblance ceases' (*Letters,* p. 306). This is not entirely true. The motifs of the riddle-contest, the cleansing fire, the broken weapon preserved for an heir, all occur in both works, as of course does the theme of 'the

343

lord of the Ring as the slave of the Ring', *des Ringes Herr als des Ringes Knecht*. But what upset Tolkien was the fact that Wagner was working, at second-hand, from material which he knew at first-hand, primarily the heroic poems of the *Elder Edda* and the later Middle High German *Nibelungenlied*. Once again he saw difference where other people saw similarity. Wagner was one of several authors with whom Tolkien had a relationship of intimate dislike: Shakespeare, Spenser, George MacDonald, Hans Christian Andersen. All, he thought, had got something very important not quite right. It is especially necessary, then, for followers of Tolkien to pick out the true from the heretical, and to avoid snatching at surface similarities.

The single work which influenced Tolkien most was obviously the Old English poem *Beowulf*, written in Tolkien's opinion somewhere round the year 700. The best edition of this is by F. Klaeber (Boston: D. C. Heath, 1922, 3rd ed. 1950). There are many translations of it, including the one by J. R. Clark Hall and C. L. Wrenn to which Tolkien wrote the 'Preface' in 1940, and Tolkien's own, to be published, edited by Michael Drout, by Arizona State University Press in 2003. The reasons for the poem's appeal to him, however, seem to me to be expressed best in R. W. Chambers, *Beowulf: an Introduction* (Cambridge: Cambridge University Press, 1921, 3rd ed. with supplement by C. L. Wrenn, 1959). The first two chapters of this show with particular force and charm the way in which history and fairy-tale are in *Beowulf* intertwined. Other Old English poems which Tolkien used include *The Ruin, The Wanderer* and *The Battle of Maldon,* all edited and translated in Richard Hamer's *A Choice of Anglo-Saxon Verse* (London: Faber and Faber, 1970), and the 'Treebeard-style' gnomic poems *Maxims I* and *II,* edited and translated, along with *Solomon and Saturn II,* in my *Poems of Wisdom and Learning in Old English* (Cambridge: D. S. Brewer, and Totowa, N.J.: Rowman and Littlefield, 1976). Tolkien's own editions of *Exodus* and *Finn and Hengest* (see 'Abbreviations' at the start for publishing details) provide much insight into his views on history, heroic continuity and the relationship between Christian and pagan thought. I have discussed both in my review 'A Look at *Exodus* and *Finn and Hengest*' in *Arda* (the journal of the Swedish Tolkien Society), no. 3, 1982–1983, pp. 72–80. Very briefly one might say that Tolkien valued *Exodus* especially as an example of Christian material treated in an old-fashioned or heroic style: his own fiction being a similar mixture but the other way round.

The poem of *Solomon and Saturn* just referred to centres on a riddle-contest, a form with two other prominent examples, both in Old Norse. One is *Vafðrúðnismál,* one of twenty-nine poems in the *Elder* or *Poetic Edda,* a collection made in Iceland perhaps about A.D. 1200. Tolkien knew this collection well, drawing on the poem *Völuspá* for the names of the dwarves in *The Hobbit,* on *Fáfnismál* for the conversation with Smaug, and on *Skírnismál* for the 'tribes of orcs' and the 'Misty Mountains'. More generally, the whole collection gives a sharper edge than *Beowulf* to the ideal of heroism, and a stronger sense of a tumultuous history filtering down to echo and hearsay. Both points are well brought out in the old, now-superseded edition of the *Corpus Poeticum Boreale,* by Gudbrand Vigfusson and F. York Powell (2 vols., Oxford: Clarendon Press, 1883), as also in Ursula Dronke's much later partial editions, *The Poetic Edda, Volume I: Heroic Poems* and *Volume II: Mythological Poems* (Oxford: Clarendon Press, 1969, 1997). The best translation of the whole of *The Poetic Edda* remains *Norse Poems,* by Paul B. Taylor and W. H. Auden (London: Athlone Press, 1981). An earlier version of this last was dedicated to Tolkien, and Auden and Tolkien in the end became friends and correspondents.

The other major riddle-contest in Old Norse appears in *The Saga of King Heidrek the Wise,* edited and translated by Christopher Tolkien (London: Nelson, 1960). The relevance of this to all Tolkien's work, including *The Silmarillion,* should be obvious; the combination of pride, ferocity and sadness in the older poem of 'The Battle of the Goths and Huns' which has found its way into the saga seems to be the note that Tolkien often aimed at, and as often disapproved. Another *fornaldarsaga* or 'saga of old times' of much interest to Tolkien readers is the *Völsunga Saga;* William Morris's translation of it in 1870 was reprinted with an introduction by Robert W. Putnam (London and New York: Collier Macmillan, 1962); it has also been edited and translated by R. G. Finch in the same series as Christopher Tolkien's *Heidrek* (London: Nelson, 1965), while there is a recent translation by Jesse Byock, *The Saga of the Volsungs* (Berkeley: University of California Press, 1990). Meanwhile, the other great work of Old Norse mythology, later and more 'novelistic' in tone than the poems, is the *Prose Edda* of Snorri Sturluson, written in Iceland between 1225 and 1241. This too is a work of 'mediation', like Tolkien's; Snorri was a Christian trying to preserve pagan material for his countrymen and for the cause of poetry. In several ways, especially its combination of respect for antiquity with a certain detached humour, Snorri prefigures Tolkien. One of the 'lost' poems known only by its quotations was a model for 'Aldarion and Erendis' (see pp. 244–45 above); another poem added to a manuscript of Snorri's *Edda* by some well-wisher is *Rígsþula,* for the relevance of which see note 13 to chapter 4. There is a good translation of the whole of this work in the Everyman Classics series, Snorri Sturluson, *Edda,* trans. Anthony Faulkes (London: Dent, 1987).

It is a jump of many centuries to the great 'fairy-tale' collections of the nineteenth, but, as mentioned above (p. 62), Jacob Grimm at least thought the similarity between German fairy-tale and Scandinavian 'Edda' striking enough to prove that both were the debris of a greater unity. Whether this is so or not — the question is discussed intensively in the collection *The Shadow-walkers;* see note 16 to chapter 2 — the folk-tales of North-West Europe affected Tolkien profoundly. The major collections (from his point of view) certainly included that of the brothers Grimm, printed first in 1812, but expanded, revised and translated ever since: I have used *The Complete Grimm's Fairy Tales,* no translator named, published in London by Routledge and Kegan Paul in 1975, but Tolkien certainly read them in German — he relished the dialect forms of 'Von dem Machandelboom', quoting it in the original in 'On Fairy-Stories' (*Reader,* p. 56). Another work he refers to is *Popular Tales from the Norse,* collected by P. C. Asbjörnsen and J. I. Moe and translated by Sir George Dasent, published first in English in Edinburgh, 1851, but reprinted in London by The Bodley Head, 1969. In the same modern series (1968) is *English Fairy Tales* by Joseph Jacobs, a reprint from 1890; No. 21, 'Childe Rowland' is a 'Dark Tower' story (see p. 184 above). Tolkien also quoted from J. F. Campbell's *Popular Tales of the*

Western Highlands (4 vols., Paisley and London: Alexander Gardner, 1890–1893).

Parallel to the fairy-tale tradition collected by the Grimms and others is the ballad tradition, also preserved by collectors of the nineteenth century and containing much similar, and similarly archaic, material. The greatest collection of these is certainly F. J. Child's *The English and Scottish Popular Ballads,* first published in five volumes by Houghton Mifflin, Boston, 1882–1898, and reprinted by Dover Publications, New York, 1965. Particularly vital to this are the philological introductions to each ballad (see especially no. 19, 'King Orfeo', no. 60, 'King Estmere' and others); while Tolkien also almost certainly read Lowry C. Wimberly's commentary *Folklore in the English and Scottish Ballads* (Chicago: University of Chicago Press, 1928). Tolkien probably also knew the Danish collection begun by Svend Grundtvig, *Denmarks gamle Folkeviser,* out in twelve volumes from 1853 onwards, and partly available to English readers in *A Book of Danish Ballads,* ed. Axel Olrik, trans. E. M. Smith-Dampier (Princeton: Princeton University Press, 1939). The collection includes several elf-and-mortal or mermaid-and-mortal ballads like Tolkien's own poems mentioned or reprinted and translated in Appendix B below. The collector's father, Nicolai Grundtvig, was in my opinion the 'Beowulfian' whom Tolkien most respected—he appears in 'Monsters' as one of the 'very old voices' calling '"it is a mythical allegory" . . . generally shouted down, but not so far out as some of the newer cries'. Grundtvig senior was also remarkable for his efforts to reconcile his studies in pagan antiquity with his position as evangelistic reformer and 'apostle of the North', arguing for Óthinn as a 'forerunner', Earendel-like, of the Messiah, both 'sons of the Universal Father'.

But Tolkien was also interested in later traditions, and even in American traditions: anyone who reads the 'Introduction' to *English Folk-Songs from the Southern Appalachians,* collected by Olive D. Campbell and Cecil J. Sharp (New York and London: G. P. Putnam's Sons, 1917), will be struck by the strange resemblance of the mountain country of North Carolina before the First World War to 'the Shire' as Tolkien described it. Nor is this accident. A piece by Mr Guy Davenport in the *New York Times* (23 February 1979) records Tolkien grilling an

American classmate of his for 'tales of Kentucky folk . . . family names like Barefoot and Boffin and Baggins and good country names like that'. Old country names, one might add: in Kentucky and its neighbours, Tolkien obviously thought, there had for a time been a place where English people and English traditions could flourish by themselves free of the chronic imperialism of Latin, Celtic and French. In the same way Fenimore Cooper's hero Natty Bumppo prides himself on his English ancestry, while Tolkien recorded an early devotion to Red Indians, bows and arrows and forests ('OFS' in *Reader*, p. 63). The journey of the Fellowship from Lórien to Tol Brandir, with its canoes and portages, often recalls *The Last of the Mohicans*, and as the travellers move from forest to prairie, like the American pioneers, Aragorn and Éomer for a moment preserve faint traces of 'the Deerslayer' and the Sioux; see p. 127 above. The complaint in one of the sillier reviews of *The Lord of the Rings* that none of its characters (except Gimli) had 'an even faintly American temperament' is as imperceptive as irrelevant. The 'American temperament' has roots in many places, but England is not the least among them: *caelum non animam mutant qui trans mare currunt*.

The medieval or middle period between the high vernacular culture of North-West Europe and the collecting or 'reconstructing' era of Child and the Grimms was in several ways a disappointment to Tolkien, though of course he found much in its more traditional poems, such as *Pearl, Sir Gawain* and *Sir Orfeo*. His translations of these must be recommended (see 'Abbreviations' under *SGPO*), as also the edition of *Sir Gawain* by himself and E. V. Gordon *(SGGK)*, and of *Pearl* by E. V. Gordon alone (Oxford: Clarendon Press, 1953). Tolkien's assistance to the latter is acknowledged. Tolkien also lived for many years with the *Ancrene Riwle*, or *Ancrene Wisse*, and those concerned to seek out an influence on him might read *The Ancrene Riwle*, translated by Mary Salu, a pupil of his (London: Burns & Oates, 1955). That work was written c. 1225, in Herefordshire. Close by in both place and time was the *Brut*, an Arthurian Chronicle-epic by one Laȝamon. Tolkien certainly valued this as a repository of past tradition, borrowing from it, for instance, Éowyn's word 'dwimmerlaik'. At some stage he must also have noted that the stream by which the poet lived — it is a tributary of the Severn — was the River Gladdon. Part of the poem can be found in *Selections from Laʒamon's Brut,* ed. G. L. Brook with preface by C. S. Lewis (Oxford: Clarendon Press, 1963, 2nd ed. 1983), or in *Laʒamon's Arthur: The Arthurian Section of Laʒamon's Brut,* eds. W.R.J. Barron and S. C. Weinberg (Harlow: Longman, 1989), while the whole work is translated by Rosamund Allen as *Lawman's Brut* (London: J. M. Dent, 1992). I am also persuaded that Tolkien found stimulus in the slightly later legends of St Michael and St Brendan in *The Early South English Legendary,* edited by C. Horstmann for the Early English Text Society (London: Trübner, 1887).

Two other clear medieval English influences on Tolkien are *Mandeville's Travels,* written about 1375, and available in a modern translation by M. C. Seymour (London: Oxford University Press, 1968); and the *Lais* of Marie de France, also available in translation by Glyn Burgess and Keith Busby (London: Penguin Classics, 1986). The latter is a clear source for 'Aotrou and Itroun', the former perhaps the best guide to Tolkien's notions of the trees of Sun and Moon, the *Paradis terrestre* and the road to it encumbered by enchantments like those of the Dead Marshes. Many phrases from this book seem to have stayed in Tolkien's mind. One should add that for all their names and preferred languages, both Sir John Mandeville and Marie de France were certainly English by nationality.

Dealing with Tolkien's knowledge of other languages could protract this essay interminably, but a source of the highest importance was clearly the Finnish epic *Kalevala,* which Tolkien knew in the translation of W. F. Kirby (London and New York: Dent and Dutton, 1907). For a more modern and scholarly treatment, see note 15 to chapter 7 above. I would like to take the opportunity here (prompted by Dr Osmo Pekonen) of correcting the remark made on *Author,* p. xxxiv, that 'Lönnrot's *Kalevala* is now viewed with suspicion by scholars because . . . you cannot tell what is by him and what is "authentic"'. Dr Pekonen informs me that Lönnrot kept such careful scholarly records that this distinction can readily be made, and is made throughout in 'the flagship of Finnish philology', the thirty-four volumes of *Suomen Kansan Vanhat Runot,* 'The Ancient Runes of the Finnish People' (1908–1999). Dr Pekonen further cites Lönnrot's 'Preface' to the *Kalevala,* in which he declares that he felt he had 'the right to arrange the poems [he had collected] in such a way that they formed the best possible combination', just as the traditional singers did. This, perhaps, is a right Tolkien would also have wished to claim.

Also recommendable is the Irish *Imram, The Voyage of Bran Son of Febal,* ed. Kuno Meyer (2 vols., London: David Nutt, 1895–1897). Tolkien's wanderings in German romance, though probably considerable — see the remarks on *Orendel* and others on pp. 17, 246 above — are too complex for me to trace. Some guides through the wilderness of heroic legend can be found, however, in the philologists: and when it comes to it these were the men whom Tolkien probably followed with the keenest and most professional interest. Three major works may be cited, though they give the interested reader no more than a taste: *Grimm's Teutonic Mythology,* trans. J. S. Stallybrass (4 vols., London: George Bell, 1882–1888); R. W. Chambers, *Widsith, A Study in Old English Heroic Legend* (Cambridge: Cambridge University Press, 1912); and R. M. Wilson, *The Lost Literature of Medieval England* (London: Methuen, 1952). It should be noted that a vital part of this latter came out as early as 1941, in plenty of time for Tolkien to recall it in *The Lord of the Rings;* see note 19 to chapter 5 above.

The last major 'old' source for Tolkien which need be mentioned lies in history and chronicle. Gibbon's *Decline and Fall of the Roman Empire* certainly stayed in Tolkien's mind, though probably in the same compartment as Wagner; 'Radagaisus' may be found in its 'Index', if not 'Radagast', as also 'Fredegarius', though not 'Frodo'. Of the Latin histories which Gibbon used, the most interesting for Tolkien were probably Saxo Grammaticus's *History of the Danes,* of which Books 1–9 were translated by Oliver Elton, with an introduction by F. York Powell (London: David Nutt, 1894), now superseded by Peter Fisher's translation in two volumes, edited by Hilda Ellis Davidson (Cambridge: D. S. Brewer, and Totowa, N.J.: Rowman and Littlefield, 1979–1980); and *The Gothic History of Jordanes,* translated by C. C. Mierow (Princeton: Princeton University Press, 2nd ed. 1915). One has to add that Mr Mierow's grasp of Gothic, unlike his Latin, is feeble. The true opinions of Jordanes lie buried in Karl Müllenhoff's notes to Mommsen's edition of 1882. A final note on the Germanic tribes as they appealed to Tolkien's imagination may be found in Sir Charles Oman's classic, *A History of the Art of War in the Middle Ages* (London: Methuen, 1898). Its description on pp. 48–51 of the Lombards, that other Germanic 'horse-folk' *par excellence,* strongly recalls the Riders of the Mark.

When it comes to modern writers, Tolkien was notoriously beyond influence (though reports of his skimpy reading have been much exaggerated; see especially the start of Chapter 6 above). Three authors of his youth must remain prominent in any account. One is George MacDonald, whose influence Tolkien both admitted and minimized; see references in the 'Index' to *Letters:* besides *The Princess and the Goblin* of 1872 and *The Princess and Curdie* ten years later, one should note especially *Phantastes* (1858) and *Lilith* (1895). Tolkien also read William Morris, probably with more appreciation: Morris, after all, knew a good deal of Icelandic and had been stirred by heroic story, trying to reproduce its effects in three of the romances of his last years, *The House of the Wolfings* (1888), *The Roots of the Mountains* (1889) and *The Glittering Plain* (1891). The first is clearly about Goths; the second gave a hint for Gollum, as for Brodda the Easterling in *The Silmarillion;* the last is about a quest for the Undying Lands. In my introduction to the World's Classics 1980 reprint of Morris's *The Wood at the World's End* (1894) I suggest a slight connection between that and the bewilderments of Fangorn Forest. Finally —though Tolkien never mentions him in a letter—I cannot help thinking that Tolkien knew Kipling's stories well, especially the collections *Puck of Pook's Hill* (1906) and *Rewards and Fairies* (1910). In both the theme of an unchanging Englishness is strong, as is that of smithcraft; and Puck's dislike for the word 'fairies' and the 'sugar-and-shake-your-head' Victorian concepts attached is exactly that of Tolkien (see especially the story 'Weland's Sword').

I do not think Tolkien would have had much time for Kipling's 'Indian' works. The centre of all that has been mentioned in this essay is English tradition, though Tolkien was prepared to accept connections by blood with Iceland or Saxony or America, and (in a more gingerly way) by old proximity with the Irish or even the Finns. However, he was in some ways what would now be called an 'ethnic' writer, though the rule for 'ethnicity' nowadays seems to be that anyone can have it *except Anglo-Saxons* (Tolkien was not quite a WASP). Largely this restriction is a penalty of success; since English is international, the language naturally ceases to carry strong national sentiment. Behind that success, though, Tolkien was conscious of many centuries of discouragement which had suppressed native tradition in England more quickly, perhaps, than in any other European country. He valued what was left the more highly. In much of what he wrote and read one can see him trying to return to the time before confusion set in, when the traditions of the Shire and the Mark were uncorrupted.

A final word should be said about Tolkien criticism. Much of it, especially that written by professional literary critics, is quite remarkably short-sighted or perverse, for reasons of inner antipathy repeatedly discussed above. The best and most useful works are referred to in the list of 'Abbreviations' at the start of this volume, and in the 'Notes' at the end. Three overall surveys may also be recommended: first, Richard C. West's *Tolkien: An Annotated Checklist, Revised Edition* (Kent, Ohio: Kent State University Press, 1981); second, Judith A. Johnson's *J.R.R. Tolkien: Six Decades of Criticism* (Greenwood: Westport, Conn., and London, 1986); and, bringing matters up to the present day, the long bibliography by Michael Drout, Hilary Wynne and Melissa Higgins, 'Scholarly Studies of J.R.R. Tolkien and His Works (in English), 1984–2000," in *Envoi* vol. 9, no. 2 (Fall 2000), pp. 135–65.

APPENDIX B

———

FOUR 'ASTERISK' POEMS

Tolkien contributed some thirteen poems to *Songs for the Philologists,* according to Humphrey Carpenter in *Biography,* p. 269. Most are *jeux d'esprit,* either mildly satirical like 'Lit. and Lang.' (see p. 6 above), or else remarkable only for their linguistic dexterity (like 'Syx Mynet', an Old English rendering of 'I've Got Sixpence', or 'Ruddoc Hana', which is 'Who Killed Cock Robin?'). Four of them, however, seem to have something more personal to say, and I accordingly reprint them here by kind permission of the executors of Tolkien's estate. At some time after the production of *Songs for the Philologists* all four were furthermore carefully corrected and emended by Tolkien himself; I am grateful to Christopher Tolkien for showing me copies of the corrected texts, and have included, or noted, all such changes in the versions below. Since three of the poems are in Old English and one in Gothic, I have followed each text with a translation.

Two of the four may be described as 'birch' poems: for their relevance see pp. 273–74 above. The other two are poems in which a mortal is trapped in some way by an immortal. They are meant, I think, to appear as 'ancestors' for such ballads as 'Tam Lin' or 'The Queen of Elfan's Nourice' in the Child collection, or 'The Daemon Lover' in Sharp's, or 'Agnes and the Merman' in Svend Grundtvig's (see Appendix A above). The corrected version of 'Ofer Wídne Gársecg' indeed includes the note, in Tolkien's hand, 'An OE version of 'Twas in the broad Atlantic in the equinoctial gales That a young fellow fell overboard among the sharks and whales'.

The Birch Poems

(a) Bagme Bloma

Brunaim bairiþ Bairka bogum
laubans liubans liudandei,
gilwagroni, glitmunjandei,
bagme bloma, blauandei,
fagrafahsa, liþulinþi,
fraujinondei fairguni.

Wopjand windos, wagjand lindos,
lutiþ limam laikandei;
slaihta, raihta, hweitarinda,
razda rodeiþ reirandei,
bandwa bairhta, runa goda,
Þiuda meina þiuþjandei.

Andanahti milhmam neipiþ,
liuhteiþ liuhmam lauhmuni;
laubos liubai fliugand lausai,
tulgus, triggwa, standandei.
Bairka baza beidiþ blaika
fraujinondei fairguni. *(Gothic)*

Flower of the Trees

The birch bears fine leaves on shining boughs, it grows
pale green and glittering, the flower of the trees in
bloom, fair-haired and supple-limbed, the ruler of
the mountain.

The winds call, they shake gently, she bends her boughs
low in sport; smooth, straight and white-barked,
trembling she speaks a language, a bright token, a
good mystery, blessing my people.

Evening grows dark with clouds, the lightning flashes,
the fine leaves fly free, but firm and faithful the white
birch stands bare and waits, ruling the mountain.

(I am indebted to Miss Rhona Beare of Adelaide University for showing me her translation of this poem.)

(b) Éadig Béo Þu

Éadig béo þu, góda mann!
Éadig béo þu, léofe wíf!
Langre lisse ic þe ann —
hafa lof and líe líf!
Hé þe hér swa sáre swanc,
rúna rædde' and fyrngewrit,
hál beo hé, on sálum wlanc,
healde láre' and wis gewit!

Éadge béo we eft swa nú!
Dréam ne dréose, drync genóg
flówe on fullum síþ swa iú —
fyllaþ wæge, fyllaþ cróg!
Byrla! byrla! medu scenc!
Dóm is feor þeah dóm sie strang.
Swinc forlǽt and géot ús drenc!
Lust is lýtel, earfoþ lang.

Uton singan scírne sang,
herian Beorc and byrcen cynn,
láre' and láreow, leornungmann —
sie ús sǽl and hǽl and wynn!
Ác sceal feallan on þæt fýr
lustes, léafes, lífes wan!
Beorc sceal ágan langne tír,
bréme glǽme glengan wang! *(Old English)*

Good Luck to You

Good luck to you, good man, and to you, dear woman. I
give you lasting joy, have praise and pleasant life. He
who worked here so hard, expounded runes and
ancient texts, may he be happy too, merry at his
feasts, and keep up good sense and learning.

May we be happy later as we are now, may joy not fail,
and drink enough flow in the cups in times to come
as times gone by — fill the cups and fill the pitchers!
Waiter, waiter, give us mead! Doom is far though
doom be strong, give up work and pour us drink.†
Joy is little and labour long.

Let's sing a cheerful song, praise the Birch and birch's
race, the teacher, the student and the subject, may we
all have health and joy and happiness. The oak will
fall into the fire, losing joy and leaf and life. The
birch shall keep its glory long, shine in splendour
over the bright plain.

'Trapped Mortal' Poems

(a) Ides Ælfscýne

Þa ǽr ic wæs cniht, þa cóm ic on pliht:
  Sum mægden mé métte ond mælde:
'La, léofa, wes hál! Sceal uncer gedál
  ná nǽfre má weorðan on eorðan!'
Nó má weorðan on eorðan. (bis)
  Wá! ides ælfscýne, ond wá, wine míne!
Sceal nǽfre má weorðan on eorðan.

Héo cyste me sóna, þǽr lixte se móna;
  on clommum me clypte ond sǽlde;
on ofste me nóm mid hire' under glóm,
  þǽr sceadugong ǽfre wæs wǽfre,
    wælmist ǽfre wæs wǽfre. (bis)

---

† Tolkien wrote three versions of the fifth and seventh lines of this stanza.
The printed text of *Songs* reads *Byrla! byrla! medu briht . . . Swinc tomorgen,
drinc toniht!*, or 'Waiter! waiter! bright mead . . . work tomorrow, drink tonight!' Tolkien rejected this in his corrected version, writing at the bottom
'*briht* is not an OE form'. In the left-hand margin he wrote: *Byrla medu! Byrla
wín . . . Scenc nu his and scenc nu mín,* or 'Serve mead! Serve wine! . . . Now
give him his and give me mine'. In the right-hand margin, in a more careful
hand, he wrote the version used in text and translation above.

Wá! ides ælfscýne, ond wá, wine míne!
þǽr sceadugong ǽfre wæs wǽfre.

Hwǽr wǽre' hit ic nát: we stigon on bát,
   þǽr murcnede mere on mealme.
Ofer lagu ic láð, ond modes ic máð,
   ac ǽfre me strongode longað,
      Awa strongode longað. (bis)
   Wá! ides ælfscýne, ond wá, wine míne!
   Þǽr ǽfre me strongode longað.

Þǽr gréne wæs grund, ond hwít hire hund,
   ond gylden wæs hwǽte on healme,
on fyrlenum londe, on silfrenum stronde,
   þǽr darode dweorg under beorgum
      darode dweorg under beorgum. (bis)
   Wá! ides ælfscýne, ond wá, wine míne!
   Þǽr darode dweorg under beorgum.

To Gode' ic gebæd, elþéodunga sǽd
   be dimmum ond dréorigum wǽgum.
Þǽr sunne ne scán, ac micel ʒimstán
   on lyfte þǽr gléow mid his léomum,
      léohte gléow mid his léomum. (bis)
   Wá! ides ælfscýne, ond wá, wine míne!
   On lyfte þǽr gléow mid his léomum.

Ofer missera hund ic wǽdla ond wund
   eft cyrde to mennisce' ond mæʒum:
on moldan wæs nú se ðe cúðe me iú,
   ond hár ic nú waniʒe ána,
      sáre waniʒe ána. (bis)
   Wá! ides ælfscýne, ond wá, wíne míne!
   Ond hár ic nú waniʒe ána. (Old English)

Elf-fair Lady

Before I was so much as a boy, I came into danger; a
   maiden met me and said: 'Greetings, my darling,
   from now on the two of us must never be separated
   on earth'

—never be separated on earth. Alas! elf-fair lady,
and my friend, alas! must never more be separated on
earth.

She kissed me straight away, where the moon was shining, she embraced me and bound me in her grasp.
Quickly she took me with her under the gloom,
where the shadow-way always flickered
—where the death-mist always flickered. Alas! elf-
fair lady, and my friend, alas! where the shadow-way
always flickered.

I don't know where I was, we stepped in a boat, where
the sea moaned on the sand. I travelled over the
ocean, and hid my thoughts to myself, but always my
longing grew stronger
—always longing grew stronger. Alas! elf-fair lady,
and my friend, alas! where longing always grew
stronger.

There the ground was green, and her hound was white,
and the wheat on the stalk was golden—in the far-
off land, on the silver strand, where the dwarf lurked
under the mountains
—the dwarf lurked under the mountains. Alas! elf-
fair lady, and my friend, alas! where the dwarf lurked
under the mountains.

I prayed to God, tired of my exile by the dim and
dreary waves, where the sun did not shine, but a
great gem-stone glowed there in the sky with his
beams
—glowed brightly with his beams. Alas! elf-fair lady,
and my friend, alas! glowed there in the sky with his
beams.

Fifty years later I returned again, poor and hurt, to men
and my family. The one who had known me before
was now in the mould, and now I dwindle, grey and
alone
—dwindle alone and in pain. Alas! elf-fair lady, and
my friend, alas! and now I dwindle, grey and alone.

(b) Ofer Wídne Garsecg

Þa ofer wídne garsecg wéow unwidre ceald,
  Sum hagusteald on lagu féoll on nicera geweald.
He legde lást swa fýres gnást, he snude' on sunde fléah,
  Oþþæt he métte meremenn déopan grunde néah —

La! hwæt, ic Gárdena on geárdagum geseah
  þéodcyninga-ninga-ninga þrym and —
    brýdealoþ under brimfaroþ déopan grunde néah!

Þæt merewíf þá of stóle úplang héo gestód,
  Mid fágum fintan fægniendc: wæs hire grétung gód.
Héo smearciende smǽre' hie wende, tǽhte hire hand;
  'Nú, wilcuma, lá, hláford mín, on meremenna land!'

La! hwæt, ic Gárdena on geárdagum onfand
  þéodcyninga-ninga-ninga þrym and —
    brydealoþ under brimfaroþ on meremenna land.

'Hér leng ne mót ic bídan, gedǽle' ic nú wiþ þé!'
  Héo cwæþ: 'Ná, ná! ne biþ hit swál þu gewífast nú
    on mé.
Nú eft þú gá, and cweþ: "Nó má fare' ic on sunde héah;
  Gemæcca mín is meremann déopan grunde néah."'
      (First refrain)

On nacan his genéatas hine sohton wíde' ymb sund;
  Hi wéopon and hi hréopon and hi sméadon Þone grund.
þa úp he sprang and hlúde sang, and hearde helman hrand:
  'Gáþ eft ongen! me béodeþ cwén on meremenna land.'
      (Second refrain)

'Tódǽlaþ nú mín ágen, pannan, páde, préon!
  Gifaþ hrægelciste mínre nifte, méder míne méon!
Se stéorman stód on stefne wód, and he to brime béah;
  Cwæþ: 'Far nu wel! þe hæbbe Hel, déopan grunde
    néah!'
      (First refrain)
(Old English)

359

Across the Broad Ocean

When the cold blast was blowing across the broad
ocean, a young man fell into the sea, into the power
of the monsters. As fast as fire he made his way, he
swam along so quickly — until he met the mermen
near the deep sea-bottom.
— Listen, I have seen the power of the kings of the
people of the Spear-Danes in days gone by† — and
also the bridal beneath the sea, near the deep sea-
bottom!

The mermaid then stood up from her chair, fawning
with her shining tail: her greeting was good.
Smirking with her lip she turned and stretched out
her hand. 'Now welcome indeed, my lord, to the
mermen's land!'
— Listen, I have discovered the power of the kings
of the people of the Spear-Danes in days gone by —
and also the bridal beneath the sea, in the mermen's
land!

'I may not stay here any more, now separate from me!'
She said: 'No, no, it will not be so! Now you will
marry me. Now go back again and say: "I'll go on the
high sea no more. My wife is from the mermen near
the deep sea-bottom."'

His companions in the ship sought him far across the
sea. They wept and cried out and scanned the sea-
bottom. Then up he sprang and sang aloud and
thrust hard at the rudder: 'Go back again! The queen
makes me an invitation, from the mermen's land!'

---

† This is a quotation from the first few words of *Beowulf*. One might paraphrase the refrain as saying that Tolkien wished for other epics more firmly
centred on monsters.

'Share out my goods, my pots and coats and brooches,
give my clothes-chest to my niece and my shoes to
my mother!' The steersman stood angrily at the
prow, and turned towards the sea, said: 'Fare you
well, and may Hell take you, near the deep sea-
bottom.'

NOTES

Chapter 1

1   We now know that it was the historical novelist Alfred Duggan. Duggan, stepson of Lord Curzon, Viceroy of India, and in his youth immensely rich and well connected, was a contemporary of Evelyn Waugh and a member of his group at Oxford between the wars, as was Philip Toynbee, mentioned below. For the literary allegiances and antipathies implied, see 'Afterword', and further *Author*, pp. 316–17.

2   Edmund Wilson, *Axel's Castle* (New York and London: Scribner's, 1931), p. 252.

3   C. N. Manlove, *Modern Fantasy: Five Studies* (Cambridge: Cambridge University Press, 1975), p. 206.

4   For further, if barely credible, examples of the same phenomenon, see pp. 178–79 below, and in truly painful detail, Patrick Curry, 'Tolkien's Critics: A Critique,' in Thomas Honegger, ed., *Root and Branch: Approaches Towards Understanding Tolkien* (Zurich and Berne: Walking Tree, 1999), pp. 81–148.

5   See further note 5 to chapter 8, and the discussion on p. 273 below.

6   Holger Pedersen, *The Discovery of Language: Linguistic Science in the Nineteenth Century*, trans. J. W. Spargo, 1931 (reprinted ed. Bloomington: Indiana University Press, 1962), p. 79.

7   L. Bloomfield, 'Why a Linguistic Society?', *Language* vol. 1 (1925), p. 1.

8   J. C. Collins, *The Study of English Literature*, 1891, but quoted here from D. J. Palmer, *The Rise of English Studies* (London: Oxford University Press, 1965), pp. 83–84.

9   See L. Bloomfield, *Language* (London: George Allen & Unwin, rev. ed. 1935), p. 12 ff.

10   See Pedersen, op. cit., pp. 263–64.

11   See Pedersen, op. cit., especially chapters 1, 2 and 7.

12   Max Müller, 'Comparative Mythology', 1856, in *Chips from a German Workshop* (4 vols., London: Longmans, 1880), vol. 2, p. 26.

13   There is an account of the affair in Peter Ganz's 'Eduard Sievers', *Beiträge zur Geschichte der Deutschen Sprache und Literatur*, vol. 100 (1978), pp. 76–78.

14   See D. J. Palmer, op. cit., p. 97.

15 R. W. Chambers, *Man's Unconquerable Mind* (London: Jonathan Cape, 1939), pp. 342–43.

16 The phrase was coined by Sir Walter Raleigh, Professor of English Literature at Oxford 1904–29 and quoted as evidence in *The Teaching of English in* England (London: HMSO, 1921), p. 218.

17 Pedersen, op. cit., p. 108.

18 *Widsith: a study in Old English Heroic Legend,* ed. R. W. Chambers (Cambridge: Cambridge University Press, 1912), pp. 1–2.

19 *Die beiden ältesten Gedichte aus dem achten Jahrhundert,* ed. W. and J. Grimm (Cassel: Thumeisen, 1812), p. 31.

20 Axel Olrik, *The Heroic Legends of Denmark,* trans. Lee Hollander (New York: American-Scandinavian Foundation, 1919), p. 85.

21 *Corpus Poeticum Boreale,* ed. G. Vigfusson and F. York Powell (2 vols., Oxford: Clarendon Press, 1883), vol. 1, p. xcvii.

22 See Pedersen, op. cit., pp. 277–92, and O. Jespersen, *Language* (London: George Allen & Unwin, 1922), pp. 80–83.

23 Text and translation are those of Thomas Jones, 'The Black Book of Carmarthen "Stanzas of the Graves"', *Proceedings of the British Academy,* vol. 53 (1967), pp. 125–27.

24 See R. M. Wilson, *The Lost Literature of Medieval England* (London: Methuen, 1952), p. 15.

25 Palmer, op. cit., pp. 66–117.

26 Peter Ganz, 'Jacob Grimm's Conception of German Studies', Inaugural Lecture (Oxford: Clarendon Press, 1973), pp. 7–9.

27 J. Grimm, *Teutonic Mythology,* trans. J. S. Stallybrass (4 vols., London: George Bell, 1882–88), vol. 3, p. lv.

28 Remarks quoted in the preceding paragraph come respectively from Edmund Wilson in the review already cited, p. 312; Lin Carter, *Tolkien: A Look Behind The Lord of the Rings* (New York: Ballantine, 1969), pp. 93–94; Neil D. Isaacs, 'On the Possibilities of Writing Tolkien Criticism', in *Tolkien and the Critics,* ed. N. D. Isaacs and Rose A. Zimbardo (Notre Dame: University of Notre Dame Press, 1968), p. 7; and Robert J. Reilly, 'Tolkien and the Fairy Story', Isaacs and Zimbardo anthology, p. 137.

Chapter 2

1 J.R.R. Tolkien, 'For W.H.A.', *Shenandoah: The Washington and Lee University Review,* vol. 18, no. 2 (Winter 1967), pp. 96–97.

2 See W. Grimm, *Die deutsche Heldensage,* 3rd ed. (Gütersloh: Bertelmann, 1889), p. 383, and 'OFS', *Reader* p. 55. In conversation, Tolkien noted that his aunt Jane Neave's surname might derive from the heroname Hnæf, while that of Hnæf's avenger, the hero Hengest, might survive in the Oxfordshire place-name Hinksey *(Hengestes-ieg).* Legend was still preserved in perfectly familiar everyday surroundings, if no longer consciously.

3 J.R.R. Tolkien, 'Goblin Feet', in *Oxford Poetry 1915*, ed. G.D.H. C[ole] and T.W. E[arp] (Oxford: B. H. Blackwell, 1915), pp. 120–21. I quote from this first published version, which differs slightly from that used by Humphrey Carpenter, *Biography*, pp. 82–83. It is most conveniently found in *The Annotated Hobbit*, ed. Douglas A. Anderson (2nd ed., Boston: Houghton Mifflin, 2002), p. 113.

4 G. B. Smith, 'Songs on the Downs', *Oxford Poetry 1915*, p. 116.

5 See *Biography*, pp. 79–84, 97–102.

6 A list of published poems appears in *Biography*, p. 266 ff., though nothing in print has yet disclosed their serpentine intertwinings. Several poems were clearly rewritten several, or many, times.

7 J.R.R. Tolkien, 'The Name "Nodens"', Appendix I *to Report on the Excavation . . . in Lydney Park, Gloucestershire*, Reports of the Research Committee of the Society of Antiquaries, no. 9 (London: Oxford University Press, 1932), pp. 132–37.

8 Since writing this I have noticed that one of the Inklings, the Reverend Adam Fox, actually did write a narrative poem on *Old King Coel* (the proper spelling), which Tolkien knew; see *Letters*, p. 36.

9 There is an edition of it, with translation, in *Medieval English Lyrics*, ed. R. T. Davies (London: Faber and Faber, 1963), pp. 71–73.

10 J.R.R. Tolkien, *'Sigelwara Land:* Part II', *Medium Aevum* vol. 3 (1934), pp. 110–11.

11 Tolkien used allegory several times in his academic articles, to make a point, always a comic or satirical one, as for instance in the story of the man and the tower cited just below — a clear case of the *reductio ad absurdum*. Strict allegory, the sort in which every item in the story corresponds exactly to an item in the hidden meaning, is, however, notoriously hard to keep up for long, while moral allegory rapidly becomes dreary, which probably accounts for Tolkien's expressed dislike.

12 See *Biography*, pp. 142–43, 198–99, 241–43. He calls himself 'a natural niggler, alas!' in *Letters*, p. 313. See further *Author*, pp. 267–68, and p. 292 below.

13 There is doubt about the details here. The first version of 'Leaf by Niggle' seems to have been written in 1939 (see *Bibliography*, p. 348), at which point *The Lord of the Rings* might not have been advanced enough to be a convincing 'Tree'. Possibly the 'Tree' here should represent, as I remark in the preface to this book, 'something much more extensive' in Tolkien's growing mythology, the whole developing story of First, Second, and Third Ages including the many stages of the 'Silmarillion'. The idea of something growing unexpectedly as the artist works on it does sound, however, very like Tolkien's own experience with the hobbits, so I have let the equation stand.

14 I have to admit no source for this other than Oxford gossip. There is, however, a highly characteristic anti-Tolkien conversation presented in fictional form in J. I. M. Stewart's *A Memorial Service* (London: Methuen paperback, 1977), p. 176. In this a Regius Professor writes off

'J. B. Timbermill' — evidently Tolkien — as 'a notable scholar' who 'ran off the rails'.

15 I discuss its repeated revisions and reprintings in 'The Versions of "The Hoard"', published in *Lembas,* newsletter of the Dutch Tolkien Society, no. 100 (2001). The earliest version, from 1923, is again most readily available in Douglas Anderson's *Annotated Hobbit,* pp. 335–37. A revised version appears in *TB* as 'The Hoard'.

16 There are extensive accounts of the dragon concept in Joyce Lionarons, *The Medieval Dragon: The Nature of the Beast in Germanic Literature* (Enfield Lock: Hisarlik Press, 1998), and in Jonathan Evans's article '"As Rare as they are Dire": Old Norse Dragons, *Beowulf,* and the *Deutsche Mythologie,*' in *The Shadow-Walkers: Jacob Grimm's Mythology of the Monstrous,* ed. Tom Shippey (Tempe: Arizona State University Press, forthcoming 2003).

17 For the quotations above, see *The Saga of King Heidrek the Wise,* ed. and trans. C. Tolkien (London: Nelson's, 1960), pp. xxiii and 45.

Chapter 3

1 The gloss, to the poem 'June', was not written by Spenser himself, but by a friend known only as 'E.K.' — someone even prouder than Spenser of his Classical learning and so the more likely to make unbelievable errors over non-Classical matters.

2 'Elfin' is in the poem 'Light as Leaf on Lindentree', but has become 'elven' in the revision given to Aragorn, *LOTR,* pp. 207–9; 'fairy' occurs once in all editions of *The Hobbit,* 'gnome' in the first edition only. 'Goblin', a Latin-derived word, is used throughout *The Hobbit,* but relatively rarely in *LOTR.* For 'dwarfish', see the letter cited on p. 67 — another printer's correction?

3 This is a modernised form of a ballad recorded in *Danmarks Gamle Folkeviser* (12 vols., Copenhagen: Thiele, 1853–1976), Vol. II, 105–9, by Svend Grundtvig — son of the Beowulfian scholar Nikolai Grundtvig.

4 C. S. Lewis, *The Problem of Pain* (1940, London: Fontana Books reprint, 1957, p. 13). This was clearly an 'Inkling' theory, cp. Tolkien's 'supremely convincing tone of Primary Art' ('OFS', in *Reader*).

5 See the *Prose Edda* of Snorri Sturluson, *Skáldskaparmál,* sections 35 and 39. There is a full translation by Anthony Faulkes in the Everyman series (London: Dent, 1987).

6 Preface to J. and W. Grimm, *Haus- und Kindermärchen* (3rd ed., Göttingen: Dieterichische Buchhandlung, 1849), p. xxviii.

7 Snorri, *Prose Edda, Skáldskaparmál* section 49.

8 As a youth (by dwarvish reckoning) he kills Azog in revenge for his father, and looks into Moria, *LOTR* p. 1049; as an old man he is killed fighting, p. 1053. In between he is seen bandying words with Sauron's

messenger, p. 235, and sticking to the letter of Thorin's bargain in *The Hobbit*, p. 315.

9 Tolkien tells the same story in a letter to W. H. Auden, *Letters*, p. 215, and there is a more extensive account of what is known about the book's genesis in *Bibliography*, pp. 7–8.

10 Quoted in Ganz, Inaugural Lecture, p. 5.

11 I am indebted for this point to an article by Jessica Kemball-Cook, in *Amon Hen: The Bulletin of the Tolkien Society of Great Britain*, no. 23 (December 1976), p. 11. See also *Bibliography*, pp. 29–33.

12 See Paul Kocher, *Master of Middle-earth* (Boston: Houghton Mifflin, 1972), Penguin Books edition, 1974, p. 24.

13 As remarked in the 'Preface', this was a mistake as originally written. We now know that Sauron had come into Tolkien's fiction well before *The Hobbit*. However, *The Hobbit* does not make the equation between Sauron and 'the Necromancer' eventually made by Gandalf in 'The Council of Elrond', so once again I have let the comment stand.

14 See *Bibliography*, esp. pp. 21–24. It should be noted that *The Hobbit* continued to hold misprints and errors through many editions, caused sometimes by printers' 'corrections' at an early stage, sometimes by incomplete revision. Till the 1990s, for instance, Durin's Day had one definition at the end of chapter 3, 'last moon', and another at the start of chapter 4, 'first moon'. See further Douglas A. Anderson's *Annotated Hobbit*, pp. 384–86 and *passim*.

15 C. S. Lewis, *The Problem of Pain*, p. 42.

16 See 'The Wreck of the Birkenhead', *Annual Register* 1852, pp. 470–73.

17 See *The Vinland Sagas*, trans. M. Magnusson and H. Pálsson (Harmondsworth: Penguin Books, 1965), p. 104.

18 Since this is a contentious piece, I have not given my own translation but that of Clark Hall and Wrenn, to which Tolkien wrote the 'Prefatory Remarks' in 1940.

19 Lewis, *The Problem of Pain*, p. 62.

20 The phrase had had special meaning for Tolkien since 1923; see note 15 to chapter 2 and note 9 to chapter 8.

21 Gollum's original name, Sméagol, comes from the same root, as does modern 'smuggle'. Sméagol and Déagol could be translated as 'Slinky' and 'Sneaky'.

Chapter 4

1 The best account of what happened is given by Christopher Tolkien in *The Lays of Beleriand*, pp. 364–67.

2 This is another late change in the text; see once more *Bibliography*, p. 29. But in all editions Gandalf's staff appears in the first scene. He uses it to scratch the sign on Bilbo's door.

3 Paul Kocher, *Master of Middle-Earth*, p. 161, notes that the definition of 'blunderbuss' ascribed in Farmer Giles to 'the Four Wise Clerks

of Oxenford' is that of the *OED*, the Four Wise Clerks being the four editors, J.A.H. Murray, H. Bradley, W. A. Craigie and C. T. Onions. Giles's blunderbuss, like Tolkien's dwarves, does not fit the *OED* definition.

4 When I first thought of this, in my article 'Creation from Philology in *The Lord of the Rings*' in *Memoriam Essays,* I wrote it off as 'entirely adventitious'. It has grown on me since, which may be no more than *furor allegoricus,* or allegorist's mania. However, I did not at that time realise how well *Farmer Giles* fitted the other allegories of 1935–1943.

5 This point is also made by Paula Marmor, 'An Etymological Excursion among the Shire-Folk', in *An Introduction to Elvish,* ed. Jim Allan (Hayes: Bran's Head Books, 1978), pp. 181–84.

6 A point seen, of course, by Peter Jackson in his direction of the 2001 movie version, which skips from crossing the Brandywine to arriving in Bree. Tolkien noted that 'Tom Bombadil is not an important person — to the narrative' in *Letters,* p. 178, and again that he was put in because 'I . . . wanted an "adventure" on the way', *Letters,* p. 192. Both letters, however, then qualify what appears to be a dismissive view.

7 C. S. Lewis's *That Hideous Strength* once again offers a close parallel in the idea of language with meanings 'inherent in [its syllables] as the shape of the great Sun is inherent in the little waterdrop', p. 281. Later it appears that this is a language even beyond 'Numinor', as Lewis spells it.

8 The two towns from *Giles* and *LOTR* are linked in traditional rhyme: 'Brill on the hill, Oakley in the hole, dirty Ickford and stinking Worminghall.'

9 The point is taken further by Brian Rosebury, who remarks in his *Tolkien: A Critical Assessment* (Palgrave Macmillan: Basingstoke and New York, 1992) first that 'the circumstantial expansiveness of Middle-earth itself is central to the work's aesthetic power', and then that 'Middle-earth, rather than any of the characters, is the hero of *The Lord of the Rings*' (see pp. 8, 29).

10 In two letters written in 1954 Tolkien both conceded that Bombadil entered because 'I had "invented" him independently . . . and wanted an "adventure" on the way', and insisted that he nevertheless had a part to play as presenting 'a natural pacifist view', something 'excellent' in itself but incapable of surviving unprotected; see once more *Letters,* pp. 192, 179.

11 It is interesting that the first version of this song, 'Light as Leaf on Lindentree' in *The Gryphon* for 1925, does not use the word 'shadow': Tolkien rewrote it to bring it into line with his developing myth. The 1925 version is reprinted in *Lays,* pp. 108–10, supplemented by notes on pp. 121–22.

12 *Road,* p. 64. Even there it is not entirely clear. Tolkien gave first a word-for-word translation of the Sindarin and then a connected English one, but the two are not altogether consistent with each other. I have combined them.

13 It is perhaps worth noting that all the names in Théoden's pedigree from

Thengel back to Brego are Old English words for 'king', except for Déor and Gram, for reasons I do not understand, and excepting Eorl the Young, founder of the line, who looks back to a time before kings were created and when all men, as in the Old Norse poem *RigsÞula*, were 'earl', 'churl' or 'thrall'.

14 Though Tolkien did not know from the beginning where, or if, he was going to fit them in. A vital moment in the development of *The Lord of the Rings* is when Tolkien suddenly sketched out a note about language-relationships; see *Treason*, p. 424.

15 A phrase notoriously used by W. H. Auden in his 1937 poem 'Spain'. George Orwell commented scornfully that people who wrote like that had never encountered murder: they were playing with fire without realising it was hot; see his 1940 essay 'Inside the Whale'.

16 This even has an effect on Merry the hobbit. On p. 786 he begs Théoden to let him come with the Riders: 'I would not have it said of me in song only that I was always left behind!' The phrasing is ironic, but it is an attempt to find an argument that Théoden will accept. For remarks on how styles shape thoughts, see especially *Letters*, pp. 225–26.

17 See Nigel Barley, 'Old English colour classification: where do matters stand?' *Anglo-Saxon England*, vol. 3 (1974), pp. 15–28.

18 It is mentioned by C. L. Wrenn, 'The Word "Goths"', *Proceedings of the Leeds Philosophical and Literary Society* (Lit.-Hist. Class), vol. 2 (1928–1932), pp. 126–28.

19 Though there are such unobservant minds around; see for instance note 12 to ch. 9.

20 See Arthur J. Evans, 'The Rollright Stones and their Folk-lore', *Folklore*, vol. 6 (1895), pp. 6–51.

Chapter 5

1 Amusingly, in view of later events, he was Terry Pratchett, whose 'Discworld' comic fantasies have since made him Britain's best-selling domestic author. These began at least as part-parodies of Tolkien, and continue to include Tolkienian in-jokes.

2 These opinions are taken from the anonymous review in the *Times Literary Supplement* (25 November 1955); C. N. Manlove's *Modern Fantasy*, p. 183; an anonymous review in *Punch* (16 November 1966); a review by Mark Roberts in *Essays in Criticism*, vol. 6 (1956), p. 459. But the list could easily be extended.

3 See Louise Creighton, *The Life and Letters of Mandell Creighton* (2 vols., London: Longmans Green & Co., 1904), vol. 1, p. 372.

4 It is no. 14 of *The Durham Proverbs*, ed. O. S. Arngart (Lund: Lunds Universitets Arsskrift, 1956), vol. 52, no. 2.

5 These accusations are made most clearly in C. N. Manlove's *Modern Fantasy*, pp. 173–84 — a book I find often imperceptive and almost always unreflective, but certainly written with energy.

6 It is worth noting that not even the Ringwraiths were originally evil, though they have become absolutely so. The word 'haggard', used on p. 691, implies how this happened. It was first used as a noun, to indicate a hawk caught when fully fledged; later it came to mean 'wild, untamed', and to be applied with special reference to a look in the eyes, 'afterwards to the injurious effect upon the countenance of privation, want of rest, fatigue, anxiety, terror or worry'. At this stage it was influenced by 'hag', an old word for witch, and implied also gaunt or fleshless. The Ringwraiths are fleshless and 'faded' from addiction, and privation, and from being caught by Sauron. They are also witches, simultaneously victims of evil within and agents of evil without. Their leader is 'helmed and crowned with fear', i.e. he wears an *ægishjálmr* or 'fear-helm' like Fáfnir the dragon; dragons too were in some opinions misers transformed by their own wickedness; see pp. 88–89 above.

7 The singular past tense of *rídan* is *rád*. The long *a* in standard English was rounded to *o*, so both 'rode' and 'road'. In Northern English and Scottish it remained unrounded, but was changed by the early modern Great Vowel Shift to *ai*, so 'raid'. The same processes give us the old adjective 'wroth' = 'angry', and the noun 'wraith'. See further *Author,* pp. 121–28, and my article 'Orcs, Wraiths, Wights: Tolkien's Images of Evil', in George Clark and Daniel Timmons, eds., *J.R.R. Tolkien and his Literary Resonances* (Greenwood: Westport, Conn., and London, 2000), pp. 183–98.

8 See the entry in Richard Blackwelder's *A Tolkien Thesaurus* (Garland: New York and London, 1990) — a most invaluable work for checking points like this.

9 Dan Timmons has pointed out to me a piece by Robert Harris in the Canadian *National Post* for 24 January 2002, p. A 16. In this Harris notes the anniversary of the Wannsee conference, 20 January 1942, where fifteen senior civil servants, eight of them with doctorates, had lunch, conducted a meeting 'very quietly and with much courtesy', organised the Holocaust and then circulated the minutes for approval. Tolkien of course could not have known about the meeting, but the bureaucratisation of evil was already clear, as one can see from C. S. Lewis's strongly Tolkien-influenced novel *That Hideous Strength* (1945).

10 In the passage quoted on p. 143 above one might note the phrase, said of Frodo feeling the pressure of Sauron's Eye, 'he writhed, tormented'. At the death of Saruman, his spirit seems to look to the West (for forgiveness?), 'but out of the West came a cold wind, and it bent away, and with a sigh dissolved into nothing'. One might paraphrase that Frodo is still writhing, and so not yet a wraith, but Saruman has been bent past recovery.

11 Edmund Fuller says that Tolkien said this to him in a conversation in June 1962; see 'The Lord of the Hobbits: J.R.R. Tolkien', in *Tolkien and the Critics*, ed. Neil D. Isaacs and Rose A. Zimbardo, p. 35. I am sure Tolkien did say this; but he had perhaps grown accustomed to suiting his conversation to his interviewers' understanding. 'Angel' is anyway de-

rived from Greek *angelos,* 'messenger'; in that (recondite) sense Gandalf is 'an angel'.

12 *King Alfred's Old English Version of Boethius,* ed. W. J. Sedgefield (Oxford: Clarendon Press, 1899), p. 128, my translation.

13 I have discussed this work more extensively in an essay called 'Tolkien and "The Homecoming of Beorhtnoth"', in *Leaves from the Tree: J.R.R. Tolkien's Shorter Fiction,* ed. Alex Lewis (London: Tolkien Society, 1991), pp. 5–16. Tolkien began working on it more than twenty years before it was published; see *Bibliography,* p. 303, and *Treason,* pp. 106–7, where a fragment of an early version is quoted.

14 It is only fair to say that the orcs are great jokers too. What their humour seems to show, though, is that while the orcs at bottom have a sense of morality not dissimilar to our own — for evil cannot make, only mock — they are comically unable to apply it to themselves. In both *Author,* pp. 131–33, and the article 'Orcs, Wraiths, Wights' cited in note 7 above, I discuss the orcs with particular reference to the scene centred on 'old Ufthak' at the very end of *The Two Towers.* The theological status of the orcs continued to give Tolkien anxiety after publication of *LOTR;* see *Morgoth's Ring,* pp. 408–24.

15 The two concepts are distinguished with special sharpness by Aragorn in his death-scene in Appendix A1, p. 1038. It is not clear that Arwen appreciates the distinction.

16 Richard C. West, in 'The Interlace Structure of *The Lord of the Rings*', *A Tolkien Compass,* ed. Jared Lobdell (La Salle, Ill.: Open Court, 1975), pp. 77–94, also asks why Tolkien should for once follow Old French models, but gives a more abstract answer.

17 *The Works of Sir Thomas Malory,* ed. E. Vinaver, 3 vols. (Oxford: Clarendon Press, 2nd ed., 1967), vol. 1, pp. lxiv–lxv. The passage is a description of one 'Vulgate' romance specifically, but can be applied readily to others.

18 I discuss the ironies surrounding Denethor at greater length in *Author,* pp. 172–73. They become visible only if one follows Tolkien's very careful but unobtrusive cross-referencing of dates, but briefly, one may be fairly sure that Denethor despairs because he has seen, in the *palantír,* a vision of the captured Ring-bearer, and has concluded, wrongly, that Sauron now possesses the Ring.

19 Thus Galadriel's piece of advice to Legolas on p. 492, 'Legolas Greenleaf, long under tree / In joy thou hast lived. Beware of the Sea! . . .' echoes in rhythm and syntax one of R. M. Wilson's scraps of *The Lost Literature of Medieval England,* p. 99:

In clento cou bache   kenelm kynebearn
lith under [haȝe]   thorne hæuedes bereaved.

'In Clent by the cow-stream   Kenelm the king's child
lies under hawthorn,   robbed of his head.'

I think Tolkien put this in only because the model came from the depths of the Mark, indeed from Clent, five miles from his boyhood home in Rednal. Wilson's book came out in 1952, but the section on Kenelm had come out separately as an article in 1941.

20 If the War of the Ring had been World War II, 'then certainly the Ring would have been seized and used against Sauron; he would not have been annihilated but enslaved, and Barad-dûr would not have been destroyed but occupied. Saruman, failing to get possession of the Ring, would in the confusion and treacheries of the time have found in Mordor the missing links in his own researches into Ring-lore, and before long he would have made a Great Ring of his own with which to challenge the self-styled Ruler of Middle-earth.' One sees that the Ring = the A-bomb; Sauron = the Axis powers; the parties at the Council of Elrond = the Western Allies; Saruman = the U.S.S.R.; 'treacheries' and 'in Mordor' = the role of Anglo-American traitors and of German scientists in creating the Russian A-bomb. This is a proper allegory, exact in all parallels; but it is not *The Lord of the Rings.*

21 It is entirely appropriate that the Peter Jackson film of 2001 should have picked this sequence out and used it twice: once in the Mines of Moria, when Gandalf and Frodo are talking quietly, and again in the Gandalf voice-over at the end. The pronouns are significantly altered, however. First it is 'not for us to decide', then 'not for you to decide'. Both alterations make sense in their new contexts, but remove Tolkien's note of criticism.

22 See pp. 807, 835. 'Heathen' of course is a word used normally only by Christians and so out of place in Middle-earth. In Appendix (c) to his British Academy lecture Tolkien had remarked on the one place where the *Beowulf*-poet used this word of men, thinking it a mistake or an interpolation. By the 1950s he may have changed his mind, accepting stronger Christian and anti-heroic elements in *Beowulf, Maldon* and his own fiction.

23 The *TLS* reviewer Alfred Duggan was convinced of this; see p. 174 above. But compare Aragorn, p. 763: right does not give might, nor vice versa. The 'theory of courage' and Beorhtwold of course say unmistakably 'right is weak and might is wrong', though Tolkien did not believe that either.

24 Fair and uncommitted views of these concepts may be found in Herbert Butterfield's *The Whig Interpretation of History* (London: George Bell, 1931), and C. B. Cox's *The Free Spirit* (London: Oxford University Press, 1963). The former discusses Lord Acton (and his maxim) in some detail.

25 This comes in a reply to Mr David I. Masson's letter in the *TLS* (9 December 1955), remarking on several factual and thematic inaccuracies in the earlier review. The reviewer flatly denied them all. 'Hoity-toity', observed Tolkien. Further differences between good and evil characters are well set out by Brian Rosebury, in *Tolkien: A Critical Assessment,*

pp. 36–47. Good qualities include acceptance of diversity, moderation even in virtue, awareness of context and intellectual curiosity, this latter opposed in several ways to the lack of imagination and incessant self-regard picked out by Auden as the essential defining quality of the corrupted.

26 *The Tempest,* ed. Frank Kermode (Arden edition of the Works of Shakespeare, London: Methuen, 5th ed., 1954), p. liv.

Chapter 6

1 See *Biography,* pp. 35, 141, 168.

2 The quotations above are taken from reviews in the *Sunday Times* (30 October 1955) and *Daily Telegraph* (27 August 1954), from Mark Roberts's long account already cited in *Essays in Criticism* (1956), and from Edwin Muir's review in the *Observer* (22 August 1954).

3 C. N. Manlove, *Modern Fantasy,* p. 189.

4 *Works of Sir Thomas Malory,* ed. Vinaver, vol. III, p. 1259.

5 In *Letters,* p. 308, Tolkien said the phrase means 'O beautiful ones, parents of beautiful children'. This has a significance in context, for Fangorn's tragedy is to be childless; however, even untranslated it attains its main effect, of ceremoniousness.

6 I am thinking of Vera Lynn's famous rendering of 'We'll meet again, / Don't know where, don't know when, / But I know we'll meet again / Some sunny day'. No critic would ever argue that this is a great poem. However, in the context of wartime separations it may well have said something, very powerfully, for people ordinarily unaffected by poetry of any description.

7 There is a modern version of it in Joseph Jacobs's collection of *English Fairy Tales,* first published in London by David Nutt, 1890, but reprinted by the Bodley Head Press in 1968. Jacobs's source, however, goes back to 1814 and beyond. The fairy-tale makes it clear that Shakespeare had got the story right, and had not confused it, as modern editors usually assert, with 'Jack the Giant-killer'.

8 There is a confusion here in all indexes to *LOTR.* 'The Old Walking Song' — i.e. the one sung twice by Bilbo and once by Frodo — is at pp. 35, 75, and 965 (but not 1005). Though the song Frodo sings on p. 1005 is there *called* 'the old walking-song', it is in fact a variant of the verse indexed as 'A Walking Song', first seen on p. 76. Fluidity is, however, an element of all these verses. The elvish song on p. 1005 is a mixture of English and Sindarin variants from pp. 78 and 231, all three indexed as 'Elbereth . . . Elven hymns to'.

9 See *The Faerie Queene,* Book III canto III stanza 48, 'There shall a sparke of fire, which hath long-while / Bene in his ashes raked up and hid, / Be freshly kindled . . .' 'From the ashes a fire shall be woken,' says Bilbo.

10 The nature of elvish poetry is considered in much more detail by Patrick Wynne and Carl F. Hostetter in 'Three Elvish Verse Modes: *Ann-then-nath, Minlamad thent / estent*, and *Linnod'*, *Legendarium* pp. 113–39.

11 Tolkien's notes on this passage in *Road*, pp. 58–62, make it clear that Galadriel is making a wish for Frodo (one that comes true). Tolkien there refined his translation of the Quenya to 'May it be that' (thou shalt find Valinor) . . .

12 His poem 'The Nameless Land', printed in *Realities*, ed. G. S. Tancred, 1927, is, however, in a close imitation of the *Pearl* stanza-form.

13 There is an account of the finds, with photographs, in P. V. Glob, *The Bog People* (London: Faber and Faber, 1969).

14 Lewis's attention may have been drawn to Uhtred by M. D. Knowles, 'The Censured Opinions of Uhtred [sic] of Boldon', *Proceedings of the British Academy*, vol. 37 (1951), pp. 305–42.

15 The most convenient excerpt from this is in *Beowulf and its Analogues*, trans. G. Garmonsway and J. Simpson (London and New York: Dent and Dutton, 1968).

16 All these are asserted in *Byrhtferth's Manual*, ed. S. J. Crawford, Early English Text Society, Original Series 177 (London: Oxford U.P., 1929), pp. 82–5.

17 There is similarly no reference (or almost none) to any of these things in *Beowulf*. The person who steals the dragon's cup may have been a slave —the word is blurred in the manuscript. Two characters known from other sources to have had incestuous births pass without comment in *Beowulf*. These seem clear cases of the poet saying the best he could, or not saying the worst he could, of characters he knew had been pagan, slave-owning, ignorant of Christian sexual ethics. All this gave a lead to Tolkien.

18 Once again, a point much easier to check with the help of Richard Blackwelder's *Tolkien Thesaurus*.

19 There is an extensive 'reconstructed' account of this thesis in Carpenter, *Inklings,* Part One, section 3, especially pp. 42–5. See also Verlyn Flieger, *Splintered Light: Logos and Language in Tolkien's World* (1983; rev. edn. Kent, Ohio: Kent State U.P., 2002).

20 *The English and Scottish Popular Ballads,* ed. F. J. Child (5 vols., Boston: Houghton Mifflin, 1882–98), vol. II, p. 230, 'Sweet William's Ghost'.

21 Northrop Frye, *Anatomy of Criticism: four essays* (Princeton: Princeton U.P., 1957), p. 33. The material cited here is from pp. 33–43 of the first essay, but see also p. 117 (on C.S. Lewis and Charles Williams), p. 186 (on Gothic revivals), p. 187 (on 'middle' worlds); and further N. Frye, *The Secular Scripture: a study of the structure of romance* (Cambridge, Mass.: Harvard U.P., 1976), where some remarks on Tolkien are made.

22 See Saxo Grammaticus, *The Danish History, Books I–IX,* trans. O. Elton with intro. by F. York Powell (London: David Nutt, 1894), p. 38.

23 Tolkien's 'neutral' style is well analysed and defended by Brian Rosebury, *Tolkien: A Critical Assessment*, pp. 65–71.

Chapter 7

1 I am most grateful to Mr Noad for showing me the full text of his essay, which had to be cut down considerably in its published form for reasons of space.

2 Tolkien's war service has been extensively studied by Mr John Garth, with the assistance of documents only released to the public in 1998. It is to be hoped that his researches will soon be published, their provisional title being *Tolkien's War*. I am most grateful to Mr Garth for showing me an early draft, which amplifies or corrects the account given in Humphrey Carpenter's *Biography* in many places.

3 In the first and second editions I expanded 'the undertaking' with the words '[to write *The Silmarillion*]'. This was clearly wrong, for 'the Silmarillion', at least, already existed. Perhaps 'the undertaking' here should be seen as 'the task of putting in order some or all of the legends of the earlier ages, referred to in the Appendices' of *The Lord of the Rings*, which is what is written earlier in the letter. The problem was one of presentation, see again *Lost Tales 1*, pp. 2–4.

4 Dates of parts of the *Unfinished Tales* given here and subsequently are deductions from Christopher Tolkien's notes, *UT*, pp. 4–13.

5 This is the opinion, for instance, of Robert Foster in *The Complete Guide to Middle-Earth* (London: George Allen & Unwin, 2nd ed., 1978), who argues in the 'Introduction' that the human conflicts of *The Lord of the Rings* gain force from their relation to the greater ones of *The Silmarillion*.

6 In the first version of 'The Passing of the Grey Company' (*The Return of the King*, 1st edn., 1955, p. 53), Gimli learns that Aragorn has looked in the palantír, and expresses astonishment. '"You forget to whom you speak," said Aragorn sternly, and his eyes glinted. "What do you fear that I should say: that I had a rascal of a rebel dwarf here that I would gladly exchange for a serviceable orc?"' (In the second edition and subsequently this last sarcastic question is eliminated).

7 For Tolkien's last word on the subject, see note 14 to chapter 5.

8 I am thinking of Ursula LeGuin's *Earthsea* trilogy, see my article 'The Magic Art and the Evolution of Words' in *Mosaic*, vol. 10, no. 2 (1977), pp. 147–64.

9 I discuss the inconsistencies, and the consistencies, in '*Alias Oves Habeo*: the Elves as a Category Problem', in *The Shadow-Walkers*, see note 16 to ch. 2; with further reference to Tolkien in my 'Introduction' to the volume, 'A Revolution Reconsidered: Mythology and Mythography in the Nineteenth Century'.

10 See J. F. Campbell's *Popular Tales of the Western Highlands* (4 vols., Paisley and London: Alexander Gardner, 1890–3), vol. 2, p. 75. Tolkien refers to this collection in the notes to 'On Fairy-Stories' (*Reader*, pp. 44, 45, 85).

11 This quotation is from the legend of St Michael in *The Early South Eng-*

lish Legendary, ed. C. Horstmann, Early English Text Society, Original Series 87 (London: Trübner, 1887), lines 253–8.

12 To labour this point further: Gandalf is a Maia, was called by Tolkien 'an angel', yet is perceived by Men — as his name indicates — as some sort of 'elf'. Conversely an ignorant Man, looking at Galadriel (an elf), might well think she was an 'angel', or of the same order as the Maia Melian. Both ladies would be so superior to him as to make fine distinction impossible.

13 Tolkien kept changing his mind about this: the strong implication of *LOTR,* p. 369 (confirmed by *Road,* p. 60), is that Galadriel, as last survivor of the leaders of the Noldorian revolt, was banned from returning to Valimar. In *The Silmarillion,* pp. 83–4, Galadriel acquiesces in the revolt out of the motive (surely not entirely a good one) 'to rule a realm [in Middle-earth] at her own will'. There is an echo of this when Frodo offers her the Ring at *LOTR,* p. 356, and she sees herself as 'a Queen'. In his later years, however, after 1968, Tolkien suggested that she was not banned, but self-exiled, having refused pardon (*UT,* pp. 230–1). And in 'the last month of his life' he wrote a more complicated account (*UT,* pp. 231–2), exculpating her entirely. This, I feel, was another example of the 'soft-heartedness' discussed on pp. 154, 319.

14 By Paul H. Kocher, *A Reader's Guide to The Silmarillion* (London and New York: Thames and Hudson, 1980), p. 56.

15 For older theories, see Kaarle Krohn, *Kalevalastudien* (Helsinki: Finnish Academy of Sciences, 1924–5). The modern remark quoted is from *Finnish Folk Poetry, Epic: An Anthology in Finnish and English,* ed. and trans. Matti Kuusi, Keith Bosley and Michael Branch (Helsinki: Finnish Literature Society, 1977), p. 526. This book however gives an excellent introduction to the *sampo* concept.

16 'Having the same mother, having different mothers': the terms are taken from the Eddic poem *Hamðismál* (about the death of the king of the Goths).

17 *Kalevala: the land of the heroes,* trans. W. F. Kirby (London and New York: Dent and Dutton, 1907, repr. 1977), vol. 2, p. 124. This is the translation Tolkien used. He no doubt read on and may have relished the moral at the end of the *runo* warning men against sending children to be fostered by strangers.

Chapter 8

1 The circumstances of its composition are explained in *Bibliography,* pp. 200–201. It began as a brief illustration of a point to be made in the 'Preface' to a George Macdonald story, 'but the story grew and took on a life of its own, and the preface was abandoned'.

2 See David Doughan, 'In Search of the Bounce: Tolkien Seen through Smith', in *Leaves from the Tree: J.R.R. Tolkien's Shorter Fiction,* ed. Alex Lewis (London: Tolkien Society, 1991), pp. 17–22; and Verlyn Flieger, *A*

Question of Time: J.R.R. Tolkien's Road to Faërie (Kent, Ohio, and London: Kent State University Press, 1997), ch. 11, 'Pitfalls in *Faërie*'; also Flieger, 'Allegory versus Bounce' (see note 6 below).

3 Flieger, *A Question of Time,* p. 232.

4 Compare 'the skin o' my nuncle Tim' in Sam's 'Rhyme of the Troll', *LOTR,* p. 201. Many years before, Tolkien had noted 'naunt' for 'aunt' in *Sir Gawain*; and Haigh's Huddersfield glossary of 1928 (see p. 72 above) showed that saying 'aunt' in stead of 'nont' was considered affected by his older informants. As often, old English survived only as vulgar modern English.

5 It is interesting, with hindsight, to read Tolkien's letter of 27 June 1925, applying from Leeds for the Chair of Anglo-Saxon at Oxford (*Letters,* pp. 11–12). Tolkien was clearly advertising himself as someone who could draw students into traditionally difficult and unpopular subjects, encourage 'friendly rivalry and open debate' between the literature and the language specialists and cultivate 'the growing neighbourliness of linguistic and literary studies'. Any 'neighbourliness' there was — Tolkien no doubt exaggerated it for effect — soon stopped growing. This was unfortunate, to say the least, for both sides.

6 I discuss the mechanics of solving an allegory like *Smith* in *Author,* pp. 297–304, and further in my half of an exchange with Dr Flieger, 'Allegory versus Bounce: Tolkien's *Smith of Wootton Major,*' *Journal of the Fantastic in the Arts* 12, no. 2 (2001), 186–200 (191–200).

7 I discuss the importance to Tolkien of the difficult word 'lay' in *Author,* pp. 233–36, 293.

8 In 'The Source of "The Lay of Aotrou and Itroun"', in *Leaves from the Tree: J.R.R. Tolkien's Shorter Fiction,* ed. Alex Lewis (London: Tolkien Society, 1991), pp. 63–71, Jessica Yates discusses the poem's 'kernel' extensively. T. Keightley's *The Fairy Mythology* of 1878 is indeed a probable source for Tolkien, and for Wimberly.

9 This is 'The Hoard', which had begun in 1923 as 'Iumonna Gold Galdre Bewunden'; see note 15 to ch. 2. In the 1962 version the passing of the gold from elf to dwarf, in stanzas 1 to 2, could be seen as a part of the events of *The Silmarillion* ch. 22, the death of Elu Thingol and the fall of Doriath.

10 I am grateful to John D. Rateliff for telling me about the poem 'Firiel', published first on pp. 30–32 of the 1934 volume (no. 4) of *The Chronicle of the Convents of the Sacred Heart,* produced by the convent at Roehampton. Sister Joan Loveday, the convent's archivist, provided Mr Rateliff with a copy, which he very kindly passed to me. I should add that Mr Rateliff is of the opinion that few of the poems in *TB* are entirely new, though early versions may still be extant only in obscure periodicals or hidden under pseudonyms — as was the case with 'The Clerkes Compleint'; see 'Preface' to this volume.

11 The best account of this theory is in *Inklings,* pp. 42–45, but see also 'On Fairy-Stories' (*Reader,* pp. 68–75, 87–90).

12 *Early South English Legendary,* ed. Horstmann, 'Life of St. Brendan', lines 55–56.

Chapter 9

1 Sir George Webbe Dasent, *Popular Tales from the Norse* (Edinburgh: David Douglas, rev. ed. 1903), p. xx. Dasent's first edition came out in 1851.

2 The essay began as a lecture given to the University of St Andrews in March 1939, but was expanded for publication in 1947, and further revised later; see *Bibliography,* p. 301.

3 See John Butt and Kathleen Tillotson, *Dickens at Work* (London: Methuen paperback, 1968), p. 116.

4 The origin of both works in Tolkien's agreement with C. S. Lewis to write, respectively, a time-travel and a space-travel story is discussed by John D. Rateliff, '*The Lost Road, The Dark Tower,* and *The Notion Club Papers:* Tolkien and Lewis's Time Travel Triad', in *Legendarium,* pp. 199–218. The article is revealing also about the dates of composition, and about the two authors' mutual co-operation.

5 Anders Stenström points out, in 'A Mythology? For England?' in *Proceedings of the Tolkien Centenary Conference,* ed. Patricia Reynolds and Glen H. GoodKnight (Milton Keynes: Tolkien Society; Altadena, Calif.: Mythopoeic Press, 1995), pp. 310–14, that Tolkien does not seem actually to have used the phrase. The general intention, however, is clear.

6 See for instance R. M. Wilson, *The Lost Literature of Medieval England,* pp. 14–16.

7 It is impossible to even sketch a coverage of the — often highly derivative — Tolkien imitations. A mere glance round a bookshop will show titles like C. D. Simak, *The Fellowship of the Talisman* (1978), James Blaylock, *The Elfin Ship* (1982), David Eddings, *Guardians of the West: Book One of the Malloreon* (1987), R. A. Salvatore, *The Halfling's Gem* (1990). I would guess that at least fifty authors, many of them highly successful in their own right, show evident debt to Tolkien; and this is ignoring his deep influence on 'Dungeons and Dragons' motifs, and on electronic games. His example created a genre *almost* single-handed: I note some signs of a non-Tolkienian but analogous tradition in my introduction to William Morris, *The Wood Beyond the World* (London: Oxford University Press, World's Classics reprint, 1980), p. xvii.

8 In this discussion I use the Norse forms Sigurthr, Brynhildr, for characters in Old Norse texts; Sifrit, Prünhild, for the characters in the Middle High German *Nibelungenlied;* and the anglicised Sigurd, Brynhild, for 'composite' characters, characters outside any particular text or group of texts. The variety does help to explain why Tolkien thought it normal for his elvish names to have several different forms.

9 I am grateful to Johann Schimanski, of the Tolkien Society of Norway,

for inviting me to give a lecture including some of this material in 1987. His criticisms and those of others present, including Anders Stenström, editor of *Arda*, sharpened my thoughts considerably. The lecture appeared eventually in *Arda*, the journal of the Swedish Tolkien Society, vol. 7 (1987), pp. 18–39, under the title 'Long Evolution: "The History of Middle-earth" and its merits.'

10 A point made strongly by C. S. Lewis; see his essay 'It All Began with a Picture . . .' in *Of Other Worlds,* ed. Walter Hooper (New York: Harcourt, Brace, World, 1967).

11 See the references given in note 14 to chapter 5.

12 'And other' is a favourite carelessness: 'wizards and other powers', 'runic and other messages', 'Old Norse and other materials'. The distinction I make between the 'tough-minded' and the 'tender-minded' on p. 333 is relevant.

13 Calling the War of the Ring a 'largely racial war' seems to me an anachronism. It is of course very largely a war between species; and to people nowadays, acutely sensitive to racial politics, this may seem to be a metaphor for race. There is no sign, however, that Tolkien thought that way. The Corsairs of Umbar have the same racial origin as the Gondorians; *LOTR,* pp. 1022–23. When Tolkien encountered racial politics in person, he reacted angrily and contemptuously, regardless of cost; see *Letters,* pp. 37–38.

14 It is interesting (to philologists) to note that, just like 'addictive', the words 'racism' and 'genocide' remained missing from the *OED* as late as 1979. This is not to say that such things did not exist in the Victorian mind or in the nineteenth century. In the rural Worcestershire of Tolkien's youth, however, peaceful and racially entirely homogeneous, they would have taken a good deal of explaining, just as they would in the fictional Shire.

15 See Golding's essay 'Fable', in *The Hot Gates* (London: Faber and Faber, 1965), p. 87.

16 See for instance the speech of Egeus in Chaucer's 'Knight's Tale', lines 1984–90. The *topos* is also used by C. S. Lewis's character the Greek slave-philosopher Fox, in Lewis's 1956 novel *Till We Have Faces.*

17 See Swanwick, 'A Changeling Returns', in Karen Haber, ed., *Meditations on Middle-earth* (New York: Byron Press, 2001), pp. 33–46 (45). This volume contains valuable responses by, among other major contemporary writers of fantasy, George Martin, Poul Anderson, Terry Pratchett, and Ursula Le Guin.

18 For the quotation, see the last page of T. H. White, *The Book of Merlyn* (Austin: University of Texas Press, 1977).

Afterword

1 For thorough analyses of the two deficiencies mentioned, see respectively Darko Suvin, *Metamorphoses of Science Fiction* (New Haven and

London: Yale University Press, 1979), and C. S. Ferns, *Aldous Huxley: Novelist* (London: Athlone Press, 1980). Tolkien liked science fiction, and had some (not very obvious) similarities to Huxley.

2 See William James, *The Will to Believe and Other Essays* (New York: Longmans Green, 1896), pp. 65–66, and further *Pragmatism* (same imprint, 1907), pp. 11–14.

3 I am referring in the paragraph above to such works as Ruth S. Noel, *The Mythology of Middle-earth* (Boston: Houghton Mifflin, 1977), Timothy R. O'Neill, *The Individuated Hobbit: Jung, Tolkien and the Archetypes of Middle Earth* (Boston: Houghton Mifflin, 1979), Anne C. Petty, *One Ring to Bind Them All: Tolkien's Mythology* (University: University of Alabama Press, 1979), especially p. 103. But see also the books cited in note 28 to chapter 1. For a detailed critique of one particular work, see my review of Jane Chance Nitzsche, *Tolkien's Art: A Mythology for England* (London: Macmillan, 1979), in *Notes and Queries* N.S. vol. 27 (1980), pp. 570–72.

4 *Four Quartets,* 'East Coker', lines 174–81, quoted here from *The Complete Poems and Plays of T. S. Eliot* (London: Faber and Faber, 1969).

5 All of these have been discussed above, except 'worship'. If one re-reads the line from Milton's sonnet quoted on p. 221 above, one can see that Milton meant 'worship' to mean 'honour or revere as a supernatural being . . . or as a holy thing'. But that idolatrous sense vanishes if one gives 'worship' its older sense (derived from 'worth') of 'regard . . . with honour or respect'. Tolkien surely appreciated the way an insult to 'our fathers' could be read as a compliment.

6 Tolkien was perhaps amused by the proverb, 'Where there's a will there's a way'. It is not recorded till 1822, but would have sounded much the same in Old English. He made it into a line of alliterative poetry, accordingly, in *LOTR,* p. 787, 'Where will wants not, a way opens'. 'Where there's a whip there's a will', say the orcs, *LOTR,* p. 910. In the Old Norse *Hamðismál* there is a discouraging variant, *Illt er blauðom hal brautir kenna,* 'It's no good showing a coward the road', or as I would put it, 'Where there's no will there's no way'. This often seems more appropriate.

7 Two of these have been discussed above; for 'fallow', see *Memoriam Essays,* pp. 299–300; 'Quickbeam' is a dictionary joke. *Cwicbéam,* 'live-tree', is glossed in Anglo-Saxon dictionaries as 'poplar' or 'aspen', a decision Tolkien knew was wrong (a) because poplars were imports, like rabbits, (b) because in England 'quicken' or 'wicken' is still the common word for 'mountain-ash'. Quickbeam accordingly is a rowan-Ent (*LOTR,* p. 471); but he has become a 'quick-tree' in the modern sense, not the old one.

8 J. L. Lowes, *The Road to Xanadu: A Study in the Ways of the Imagination* (London: Constable, 1927), p. 44.

INDEX

Abel, 242
'abide,' 118–19
Acemannesceaster, 32
'Achilles and the Tortoise,' 337
'Across the Broad Ocean,' 360–61
Acton, Lord, 137
Adam, 107–8
Adam and Eve, 140–41, 236, 241, 242. *See also* Creation
'addictive,' 139–40, 148, 232, 285
adjectives, 71, 74, 107, 140, 220
Adventures of Tom Bombadil, The, 35, 36, 105–6, 227, 230, 281, 283, 317. *See also* Bombadil, Tom
ægishjálmr, 266
Ælfscýne, 58
Ælfwine, 122, 299–300, 301, 305–6, 307
Ælfwine Widlást, 300
Aeneas, 148, 279
Aeneid, 148, 228
Aerin, 265
Æsc, 305
'Agnes and the Merman,' 353
'Ainulindalë,' 236
Ainur, 236, 239
Aire, 65*n*
Airmanareiks, 17
'Akallabêth,' 287
Akeman Street, 32, 33, 36
Alaric, 150
Albanac, 97*n*

Alboin, 295–96, 297, 300, 301
Albuera, 82
'Alcestis,' 316
Alcuin, 199, 204, 206
'Aldarion and Erendis: The Mariner's Wife,' 244, 346
'Alf,' 277
Alfred, King, 29, 141–42, 152, 297, 330
Allan, Jim, 242*n*
allegories, 5, 39, 43–44, 46, 48, 76, 91, 99, 135, 167–73, 178, 191–92, 199, 202, 203, 243, 272, 274, 292, 347
alliteration, 20, 107, 125–26, 183, 192–93, 196, 216, 221, 224, 318
allure, 58–59
Alpharts Tod, 17
Alvíssmál, 75
Aman, 232, 249, 287, 288
ambiguities, 253–56
'American temperament,' roots of, 348
Amon Hen, 142, 143, 161, 162–63
anachronisms, 65–70, 71, 136
Anacreon, 325
analogies, 19–20, 34
analogues, 103, 170, 196–204
Anatomy of Criticism, The (Frye), 210–12
'ancestors,' 353
'Ancient Runes of the Finnish People, The,' 349–50

Ancrene Riwle, 348
Ancrene Wisse, 6, 7, 26, 39–40, 41–42, 44, 72*n*, 81, 294, 348
Andersen, Hans Christian, 238, 344
Andersson, Theodore, 310
Andromeda, 216
Anduin, 101
Andúril, 212–13
Andvari, 61
Angband, 234
angels, 151, 191, 238–40
Angles, 102
Anglican Church, 275
Anglo-Saxon Chronicle, 124
Anglo-Saxons, 14, 58, 115, 117, 125, 126, 130, 131, 172, 182, 183, 202, 208–9, 297, 333, 352
Angrod, 250
Animal Farm (Orwell), 329
'Annals of Aman,' 225
'Annals of Valinor,' 225
ann-thennath, 194–95
Annunciation, 201
Anórien, 170, 213
anthropology, 86, 197
anti-escapism, 327
anti-heroes, 212
anti-literary attitudes, 13, 177
antipathy, 1–5, 136
'apartheid,' 338
Apollinaris, Sidonius, 19
'applicability,' 169, 172, 173, 242, 331

117192